Rules for Predicate Logic

In using the rules **UI**, **EI**, and **UG**, let the expression (...w...) denote any sentence or sentence form which results from replacing all occurrences of *u* free in the sentence or sentence form (...u...) by occurrences of *w* free in (...w...), and let *u* and *w* be any variables or constants, unless otherwise specified. Let the same be true for rule **EG**, except that the expression (...w...) must denote a sentence form which results from replacing *one or more* (but not necessarily all) occurrences of *u* free in (...u...) by occurrences of some variable *w* free in (...w...).

Rule UI: $(u)(...u...)$ / ∴ (...w...)

[handwritten: Hol not required]
[handwritten: all variables firmed replaced free]

Rule EI: $(\exists u)(...u...)$ / ∴ (...w...)

Provided:

1. *w* is not a constant.
2. *w* does not occur free previously in the proof.

Rule UG: $(...u...)$ / ∴ $(w)(...w...)$

Provided:

1. *u* is not a constant.
2. *u* is not free in a line obtained by **EI**.
3. *u* is not free in an assumed premise within whose scope (...u...) occurs.
4. To each *w* free in (...w...) there corresponds a *u* free in (...u...).

Rule EG: $(...u...)$ / ∴ $(\exists w)(...w...)$

Provided:

1. To each *w* free in (...w...) there corresponds a *u* free in (...u...).

Rule QN:
1. $(u)(...u...)$ :: $\sim(\exists u)\sim(...u...)$
2. $(\exists u)(...u...)$ :: $\sim(u)\sim(...u...)$
3. $(u)\sim(...u...)$ :: $\sim(\exists u)(...u...)$
4. $(\exists u)\sim(...u...)$ :: $\sim(u)(...u...)$

Rule ID: $(...u...)$
$u = w$ / ∴ (...w...)

Logic and Philosophy

Logic and Philosophy

A Modern Introduction

Howard Kahane
University of Kansas

Wadsworth Publishing Company, Inc.,
Belmont, California

L. C. Cat. Card No.: 69–16015
Printed in the United States of America

2 3 4 5 6 7 8 9 10—74 73 72 71 70

Preface

Introductory logic texts tend to fall into two categories: "baby" texts, well within the grasp of average students but rather thin with respect to subject matter, and "high-powered" texts, containing an abundance of material that is too difficult for the average student. This book is offered as an alternative to both categories; it attempts to provide *clarity* and relative *ease of comprehension* (even for those who feel "symbol shy"), while at the same time providing full coverage of the basic materials that comprise the core of modern logic.

In addition to the standard materials of introductory logic texts, this book has some unusual features and an exceptionally broad *range* of subject matter:

Part One, which presents a standard version of sentential logic, is distinguished by a longer than usual account of some of the basics which average students so often fail to grasp (such as truth-functionality, the difference between constants and variables, etc.). It also contains a more adequate explanation and defense of the use of material implication than is usual in introductory texts, as well as a section on strategy rules for proof construction.

Part Two, on predicate logic, includes a *complete* set of quantifier rules as well as a uniquely detailed explanation as to why the quantifier rules must be as complicated as they are. In addition, a section is included on identity and on definite descriptions.

Part Three, which concerns Aristotelian logic, contains a chapter on definitions (brought up to date somewhat) and a chapter on fallacies in addition to the standard material on syllogisms, Venn diagrams, etc.

Part Four concerns inductive logic and the philosophy of science, treated under the three categories of induction, probability, and scientific method.

Greater emphasis is placed on purely *philosophical* problems than is usual in introductory logic texts.

Part Five deals with the *application* of modern symbolic logic to other areas of knowledge. Other logic texts either have no applications at all, or else present applications from science or mathematics. This text is unique in that it applies logic to traditional and modern problems within philosophy itself, such as the problems of dispositionals, counterfactuals, and the analytic-synthetic distinction.

Part Six concerns the nature of axiom systems. Properties of axiom systems, such as completeness and consistency, are discussed; and axiom systems for sentential and predicate logic are outlined and discussed. (However, no proofs are presented, and the systems are not developed in detail. Instead, emphasis is placed on the sort of thing that *nonlogicians* would want to know, such as the *general nature* of axiom systems.)

Finally, there are two appendices, one containing elementary material on the intuitive logic of sets and the other containing an alternative (and simpler) set of quantifier rules.

This book contains enough material to cover a two-semester course, with perhaps a bit left over; but the material is organized so as to allow the greatest possible flexibility in the choice of subject matter for a one-semester course (although Parts One and Two—on modern symbolic logic—are presupposed in much of the material in later chapters). It is expected that, on the average, it will take about one semester to cover Parts One and Two plus any one or two of the other four parts. Most of the material in Part Three on traditional Aristotelian logic can be grasped without any knowledge of modern sentential or predicate logic.

The text also contains several important pedagogical devices, including a glossary of key terms, a bibliography, and a number of example boxes placed at crucial points throughout the first half of the book. In addition, there are exercises on the material in the first three parts of the text, with the answers to even numbered exercises provided in a special section at the end of the book. (Additional exercises, with answers, are available in the companion study guide by Warner Morse.)

It is not an easy task to present fairly difficult material—especially material requiring special symbols—so that it may be grasped by average as well as bright students. In attempting to accomplish this task, *precision* (or is it *premature* precision?) occasionally has been sacrificed. An early example is the definition of atomic sentences, which is technically incorrect in a way that is not likely to bother beginning students. Another example is my failure to distinguish between object-language and meta-language variables in Parts One, Two, and Three (the distinction is finally introduced in Part Six). In addition, instead of employing a variety of illustrative sentences, which would have made more interesting reading, the same standard sentences (about the activities of Art, Betsy, Harry, Judith, etc.) are repeated over and over again. This repetition is used to help students to concentrate on *form*, which is the essence of deductive logic, rather than on distracting content. (The examples and exercises in the companion study guide have more varied and interesting content.)

I learned my logic from the late Hans Reichenbach, and my debt to him is obvious. I am also indebted to many other teachers, in particular to Nelson Goodman, although our differences of opinion on several subjects tend to cloud this fact. I must also mention my debt to Carl Hempel, since the viewpoint on philosophy of science expressed in this text more nearly resembles his than that of any other eminent philosopher.

In addition, I wish to thank the many students in my logic classes at Whitman College and the University of Kansas for their invaluable aid; my colleagues at the University of Kansas — especially Warner Morse, Richard Cole, and, above all, Arthur Skidmore — for their expert advice and assistance; my friend Alan Hausman, of Ohio State University, for more than I've heretofore owned up to; and my secretarial assistants, Mrs. Carol Kellogg and, especially, Mrs. Pamela Cobb, for their patience and perseverance.

The publisher's readers of the early drafts of my manuscript were Robert Barrett, of Washington University, Thomas Blakeley, of Boston College, Nino Cocchiarella, of Indiana University, Arthur Lord, of Centralia College, and Kenneth H. Small, of the University of Washington. Dr. Small deserves special mention and thanks for his detailed and very helpful review.

Finally, just in case they're listening somewhere, my thanks to Leon Satinoff, who first gave me the idea of writing a logic text, and to Edward Schouten Robinson.

Lawrence, Kansas   H. K.

Table of Contents

Chapter Twelve

Traditional Syllogistic Logic—II

Chapter Thirteen

Fallacies

Part Four

Induction and Science

Chapter Fourteen

Induction

Chapter Fifteen

Probability

Part Six

Axiom Systems

Chapter Twenty

Axiom Systems

Appendix A

Elementary Intuitive Logic of Sets

Appendix B

Alternative Set of Quantifier Rules

I am uneasy to think I approve of one object, and disapprove of another; call one thing beautiful, and another deform'd; decide concerning truth and falsehood, reason and folly, without knowing upon what principles I proceed.—David Hume, A Treatise of Human Nature

Part One Chapter One

1

Arguments

Logic attempts to distinguish between correct and incorrect arguments. In general, an **argument** consists of one or more sentences, called *premises*, which are offered in support of another sentence, called a *conclusion*.

2

Contexts of Discovery and Justification

When someone makes an assertion, two important questions can be raised. First, we can ask how the person came to think of the thing asserted; and, second, we can ask for reasons for accepting it. The first question is in the area, or context, of **discovery**; the second, the area, or context, of **justification**.

In general, logic is not concerned with the context of discovery. The mental processes used in thinking of hypotheses or conclusions are of interest to the psychologist, not the logician. Rather, the logician is interested in arguments and reasons which are, or might be, presented in support of hypotheses or conclusions. In other words, the logician is interested in the context of *justification*.

This difference between discovery and justification is illustrated by the difference between the sometimes agonizing thought processes necessary to "figure out" solutions to difficult problems and the arguments we then present in their defense. Often, the discovery process, the figuring out, is long and involved, while the argument presented to justify the conclusion arrived at by this long process is elegantly simple.

Again, a scientist may first think of a scientific theory in a dream. But the arguments for the correctness of his theory which he presents to his fellow scientists would not refer to the dream. The dream and its contents are part of the process of *discovering* the theory, not part of the process of *justifying* it.

3

Deductive and Inductive Arguments

It is convenient to divide arguments into two kinds, **deductive** and **inductive**. The fundamental property of a valid deductive argument is this: *If its premises are true then its conclusion must be true also*; or, to put it another way, if the premises of a valid deductive argument are true, then its conclusion *cannot be false*. The truth of its premises, so to speak, "guarantees" the truth of its conclusion.

The question naturally arises as to *why* the premises of a valid deductive argument, if true, guarantee the truth of its conclusion. Unfortunately, no easy answer can be given.* Perhaps the best answer we can give at this point is that, speaking metaphorically, the information contained in the conclusion of a valid deductive argument is already "contained in" its premises. We are not usually aware of this fact because it is contained in the premises implicitly, not explicitly, along with other information not contained in the conclusion.

---

* Indeed, we cannot give an answer acceptable even to a majority of philosophers. In philosophy, fundamental questions, such as this one, tend to be the most controversial. The general policy followed in the first three main parts of this text is to avoid taking sides in such controversies, whenever this can be done without seriously affecting the intent and validity of the material presented.

Examples:

We know that if the premises of the valid deductive argument

1. If Art went to the show last night,
    then Betsy went also.

2. Art went to the show last night.

/ ∴   3. Betsy went also.

are true, then the conclusion (sentence 3) must be true also. The truth of the premises of this argument guarantees the truth of its conclusion. Or consider the valid deductive argument:

1. All undergraduates are intelligent.

2. All freshmen are undergraduates.

/ ∴   3. All freshmen are intelligent.

According to its second premise, all freshmen fall into the class of under-graduates, all of whom according to its first premise, are intelligent. So there is a sense in which the two premises taken together contain the information stated in the conclusion that all freshmen are intelligent.

In contrast to deductive arguments, the truth of the premises of a valid* *inductive* argument provides good *but not conclusive* grounds for the acceptance of its conclusion. It is possible, and unfortunately all too common, for a valid inductive argument to have true premises and a false conclusion.

---

* Some logicians use the term "valid" to apply only to acceptable *deductive* arguments and use such terms as "correct", "strong", "acceptable", etc., to apply to acceptable inductive arguments.

Example:

The following valid inductive argument could have been constructed prior to the 1960 U. S. presidential election:

1. Up to now (1960), all U. S. presidents have been Protestant.

/ ∴   2. The next U. S. president will be Protestant.

This is a valid inductive argument in the sense that anyone who had no other pertinent information at that time would have been justified in accepting the conclusion on the strength of the true premise, although in fact the conclusion later turned out to be false.

Again speaking metaphorically, we cannot guarantee that a valid inductive argument with true premises will have a true conclusion because (unlike the case for deductive arguments) the conclusion of an inductive argument is *not* contained in its premises, either implicitly or explicitly.

Inductive arguments are considered in more detail in Part Four of this text, where the "logic" of scientific inference is discussed; the first three parts of this text deal exclusively with *deductive* logic.

4

Argument Forms   Consider the following argument:

1. All Abadabs are Bugaboos.

2. Charles is an Abadab.

/ ∴   3. Charles is a Bugaboo.

In this argument, if premises 1 and 2 both are true, then the conclusion must be true also. But are both premises true? We have no way of knowing, since, presumably, we don't know anything about Abadabs or Bugaboos and consequently don't know whether Charles is or is not an Abadab. But in spite of this, it is clear that *if* the premises are true (*if* all Abadabs are Bugaboos and Charles is an Abadab), *then* the conclusion must be true. We know this because of the *form* of the argument and not because of any knowledge of Abadabs or Bugaboos. So it is clear that what makes this argument a *valid* argument is its *form*. *Any* argument having the same form—that is, any argument of the form

1. All _____ are _ _ _ _ _ _ _.

2. _ _ _ _ _ _ _ _ _ _ is a _____.

/∴ 3. _ _ _ _ _ _ _ _ _ _ is a _ _ _ _ _ _.

where each pair of similar lines (solid lines, long-dotted lines, and short-dotted lines) are filled in with the same expression—is deductively valid. And, of course, there are many other valid argument forms.

Examples:

(Arguments (I), (II), and (III) all have the same form. Argument (IV), also a valid argument, has a different form.)

(I)   1. All humans are mortal.

        2. Socrates is human.

/∴   3. Socrates is mortal.

(II)   1. All Abadabs are Bugaboos.

        2. Art is an Abadab.

/∴   3. Art is a Bugaboo.

(III) 1. All communists are socialists.

2. Art is a communist.

/ ∴ 3. Art is a socialist.

(IV) 1. It will rain, or it will snow.

2. It is not the case that it will rain.

/ ∴ 3. It will snow.

5

*Sentences and
Propositions*

Logic is concerned primarily with **argument forms**, and only secondarily with arguments, for all arguments which have a valid argument form are valid, and all other arguments are invalid. Thus, the principal task of deductive logic is to provide a method for distinguishing valid deductive argument forms from invalid deductive argument forms.*

Consider the sentences "Snow is white", "Schnee ist weiss", and their equivalents in many other languages. Although they are different **sentences** (for example, the first has eleven letters, the second fourteen), they seem to have something in common, for they seem to "say the same thing, only in different words". Sentences of this kind are said to express the same **proposition**.

Throughout Parts One and Two of this book, we shall speak of *sentences* (having in mind declarative sentences) but not of propositions, because many philosophers deny that there are such things as propositions; and even those who think they exist differ as to their exact nature. However, the choice to speak of sentences, rather than propositions, in no way affects the basic material to be presented; a logic concerned with propositions would be just like the one developed in this book.

---

* Occasionally, in Parts One and Two, the word "deductive" will be omitted from phrases such as "valid deductive argument form", "invalid deductive argument", etc., when it is clear from the context that it is *deductive* validity-invalidity that is being discussed.

6

Truth and Validity

In Section 4, we mentioned valid and invalid *arguments* and *argument forms*. But it makes no sense to speak of valid or invalid *sentences*. Validity and invalidity are properties of arguments, inferences, and the like, and not of sentences. Sentences are either *true* or *false*.

It is important to realize that a valid deductive argument can have a false conclusion. This can happen if one or more of its premises are false. Similarly, an invalid argument can have a true conclusion. In fact, every combination of validity-invalidity and truth-falsehood can occur, except one: *a valid deductive argument with true premises cannot have a false conclusion.*

Examples:

Valid Arguments

(I)   *True premises and true conclusion:*

1.   All humans are mortal.

2.   Socrates is human.

/ ∴   3.   Socrates is mortal.

(II)   *True premises and false conclusion:*

(This cannot occur; an argument with true premises and a false conclusion must be invalid.)

(III)   *False premise(s) and true conclusion:*

1.   All stones are mortal.

2.   Socrates is a stone.

/ ∴   3.   Socrates is mortal.

(IV)   *False premise(s) and false conclusion:*

      1.   All dogs are cats.

      2.   Socrates is a dog.

/ ∴   3.   Socrates is a cat.

Invalid Arguments

(V)   *True premises and true conclusion:*

      1.   All humans are mortal.

      2.   Socrates is mortal.

/ ∴   3.   Socrates is human.

(Notice that (V) has a different form than the first four arguments.)

(VI)   *True premises and false conclusion:*

      1.   All humans are mortal.

      2.   Fido is mortal.

/ ∴   3.   Fido is human.

(The existence of an argument of this form with true premises and a false conclusion indicates that *all* arguments of this form are invalid, even those —such as (V) above—which have true conclusions. The fact that (V) has a true conclusion is an accident, a contingent fact, which logic does not guarantee. The premises of arguments having the same form as (V) do *not* provide good deductive grounds for their conclusions.)

(VII)   *False premise(s) and true conclusion:*

      1.   All humans are stones.

      2.   Socrates is a stone.

/ ∴   3.   Socrates is human.

(VIII)   *False premise(s) and false conclusion:*

1.   All <u>stones</u> are <u>mortal</u>.

2.   <u>Socrates</u> is <u>mortal</u>.

/ ∴   3.   <u>Socrates</u> is a <u>stone</u>.

(In this last example, premise 2 is true, premise 1 false. Thus, *taken as a unit*, the premises are false.)

7

Soundness,
Validity and
Truth

A valid argument, with true premises and, consequently, a true conclusion, is said to be a **sound argument**. In general, logic is not concerned with the soundness of arguments, because, with one exception, logic alone cannot determine whether the premises of an argument are true or false. (The one exception concerns premises which are *logically* true or false. See Chapter Nine, Section 1.)

Chapter Two

*Sentential
Logic—I*

1

*Atomic and
Compound
Sentences*

An **atomic** sentence is one which contains no other sentence as a part. All sentences formed by combining two or more smaller sentences are **compound**.

Examples:

Atomic Sentences

1. Betsy went to the show.

2. All humans are mortal.

3. Art went to the show.

4. Socrates is mortal.

Compound Sentences

1. Art went to the show and Betsy went to the show.

2. Either Art went to the show or Betsy went to the show.

3. Either all humans are mortal or else they're not.

4. If Betsy went to the show, then Art went also.

5. If all humans are mortal, then Socrates is mortal.

6. Betsy or Art went to the show.

   > (Sentence 6 may appear to be an atomic sentence, but it is compound, since it asserts that Betsy went to the show or Art went to the show.)

7. If Betsy went to the show, then either Art or Charles went also.

The logic to be dealt with in Chapters Two, Three, and Four, called **Sentential Logic**, or **Propositional Logic**, deals with the logical relationships holding *between* sentences, atomic or compound, without taking the interior structure of atomic sentences into account.

2

Use of New Symbols

We now introduce a few new symbols, in order to save time and effort and to increase our ability to handle complex arguments. Use of these symbols also helps to eliminate a great deal of the vagueness and ambiguity of many English words and sentences. The power of a symbolic notation to increase our ability to handle complex arguments is illustrated by the use of symbols in arithmetic. Imagine the difficulty of multiplying, say, eighty-six thousand three hundred seventy-seven by ninety-four without the use of the symbols 0, 1, 2, 3, etc.

3

Conjunction

The words used to connect sentences into compound sentences are called **sentence connectives.** The word "and" is frequently used in this way, as for example: "Art went to the show *and* Betsy went to the show". Compound sentences formed by this use of the word "and" are called

conjunctions, and the two sentences joined together by the "and" are called **conjuncts** of the conjunction.

Let's abbreviate the sentence "Art went to the show" by the capital letter *A*, the sentence "Betsy went to the show" by the capital letter *B*, and the connective "and" by the dot " · ". (The symbol & often is used instead of " · ".) Then the sentence "Art went to the show and Betsy went to the show" can be symbolized as *A* · *B*. Now consider all of the possible truth values* of the two conjuncts of this sentence. First, if both *A* and *B* are true (that is, if both Art and Betsy did go to the show), then it is obvious that the compound sentence *A* · *B* is true. Second, if *A* is true and *B* is false, then *A* · *B* is false. Third, if *A* is false and *B* true, then *A* · *B* is false. And finally, if both *A* and *B* are false, then *A* · *B* is false. There are no other possible combinations of truth values for the sentences *A* and *B*. So anyone who is given the actual truth values of *A* and *B* can "figure out" the truth value of the compound sentence *A* · *B*, because (as was just illustrated) the truth value of that compound sentence *depends on* (is a function of) the truth values of its component parts. The same is true with respect to *any* compound sentence formed from two shorter sentences by means of the sentence connective " · ". Therefore, it can be said that " · " is a *truth-functional sentence connective*, since the truth values of the compound sentences formed by its use are uniquely determined by the truth values of their two conjuncts.

The information about the compound sentence *A* · *B* contained in the above paragraph can be put into the form of a table, called a **truth table**, as follows:

	A	*B*	*A* · *B*
1.	True (**T**)	True (**T**)	True (**T**)
2.	True (**T**)	False (**F**)	False (**F**)
3.	False (**F**)	True (**T**)	False (**F**)
4.	False (**F**)	False (**F**)	False (**F**)

Line 1 of this truth table states that if *A* and *B* both are true, then *A* · *B* is true. Line 2 states that if *A* is true and *B* false, then *A* · *B* is false, and so on.

---

* The truth value of a true sentence is "true" and of a false sentence is "false".

Many English words other than "and" often can be symbolized by the dot, because at least part of their function in many sentences is the same as that of the word "and". For example, the word "but" often means "and on the contrary" or "and on the other hand". Thus, the word "but" in the compound sentence "Art is smart, *but* he's a poor athlete" serves to inform the reader that additional information is coming which is significantly different from that which preceded. Since in this case the information preceding the word "but" is favorable to Art, the use of that word prepares us for the fact that unfavorable information is to follow. When the word "but" is symbolized by the dot, the part of its meaning which signals a switch of this kind is lost. It is the **truth-functional** part of its meaning captured by the dot which is important for logic. Therefore, symbolization of the word "but" by the dot is acceptable for our purposes.

Many other English words and phrases often can be symbolized by the dot. Some examples are "however", "yet", "on the other hand", and "still".

4

Variables and Constants

The above truth table concerns the sentences A, B, and $A \cdot B$. But clearly, the information it contains about these sentences equally well applies to any two sentences connected by the dot. For example, we can construct a similar truth table for the sentences C ("Charles is a logician"), D ("Don is a mathematician"), and $C \cdot D$, as follows:

	C	D	$C \cdot D$
1.	T*	T	T
2.	T	F	F
3.	F	T	F
4.	F	F	F

Obviously, the truth table concerning *any* two sentences and their conjunction will be just like the two truth tables just presented. This

* T = "true"; F = "false".

fact can be expressed in the form of a general truth table in the following way:

	_____	_ _ _	_____ · _ _ _
1.	T	T	T
2.	T	F	F
3.	F	T	F
4.	F	F	F

In each use of this truth table, the blanks are to be filled in by *any* sentences, atomic or compound, provided only that whatever sentence is placed in the first solid line blank is also placed in the second, and whatever sentence is placed in the first dotted line blank also is placed in the second.

It is customary to use letters instead of solid and dotted lines. Thus, the above truth table can be written as follows:

	p	*q*	*p* · *q*
1.	T	T	T
2.	T	F	F
3.	F	T	F
4.	F	F	F

In effect, this truth table indicates that given any two sentences *p* and *q*:

1.   If *p* and *q* both are true, then their conjunction, *p* · *q*, is true;

2.   If *p* is true and *q* false, then their conjunction, *p* · *q*, is false;

3.   If *p* is false and *q* true, then their conjunction, *p* · *q*, is false;

4.   If *p* and *q* both are false, then their conjunction, *p* · *q*, is false.

Sentential Logic

Since this truth table specifies the truth value of any conjunction, given the truth values of its two conjuncts, it can be said to *define or specify the meaning of* the dot symbol.

It is important to understand that in the above truth tables, the small letters *p* and *q are not abbreviations for sentences.* Rather they serve as place holders. It is only when we replace them by capital letters (abbreviations for sentences) that we get expressions which are sentences. Place holders such as *p* and *q* are called *variables*, in this case **sentence variables** (because they are to be replaced by abbreviations for sentences).*

Except where otherwise specified, we shall conform to the convention that the small letters *p*, *q*, *r*, and so on, are to be used as sentence variables, and the capital letters *A*, *B*, *C*, and so on, as sentence abbreviations, referred to as **sentence constants**.

The difference between variables and constants is of fundamental importance, for all of the basic rules of sentential logic are written in terms of sentence variables, and the proper use of these rules cannot be grasped unless the difference between sentence variables and sentence constants is clearly understood.

5

Sentences and Sentence Forms

Expressions such as *p · q* containing only sentence variables and sentence connectives are called **sentence forms**. Of course, sentence forms are not sentences. But if we replace all of the variables in a sentence form by expressions (atomic or compound) which are sentences, then the resulting expression will be a sentence. For instance, if we replace the variables *p* and *q* in the sentence form *p · q* by the sentence constants *A* and *B* respectively, then the resulting expression, *A · B*, will be a sentence. The sentence *A · B* is said to be a *substitution instance* of the sentence form *p · q*.

All sentences are substitution instances of many sentence forms. For instance, the sentence *A · B*, which is a substitution instance of the sentence form *p · q*, also is a substitution instance of the sentence form *p*, because replacement of *p* (the one variable in the sentence form *p*) by the compound sentence *A · B* results in the sentence *A · B*.

---

* Actually, we will be using *p*, *q*, etc., both as place holders *and* as what are called "meta-linguistic variables". (This distinction is made clear in Part Six, where axiom systems and the distinction between object language and meta-language are discussed.)

Because sentence forms are not sentences, they are neither true nor false. But all of their substitution instances are sentences, and hence all of their substitution instances are either true or false.

This difference between sentences and sentence forms is of fundamental importance to logic, and anyone who fails to grasp it will have difficulty in understanding and using the rules and theorems to be presented in later chapters.

6

Negation

The word "not" (and its variants) may also be regarded as a truth functional sentence connective. (And then sentences such as "Art did not go to the show" must be regarded as compound sentences.) Abbreviating the sentence "Art went to the show" by *A*, and the word "not" by ~ (often called *tilde*), the statement "It is not the case that Art went to the show" can be symbolized as ~*A*. (Similarly, the equivalent sentence "Art did not go to the show", as well as many other variations, can be symbolized as ~*A* also.)

Now let's consider the possible truth values for compound sentences formed by use of the negation sign. Unlike the case for conjunctions, there are only two possibilities. Take the sentence *A*. Either *A* is true, in which case ~*A* is false, or *A* is false, in which case ~*A* is true. This information can be put into the form of a truth table, as follows:

A	~*A*
T	F
F	T

Of course, we can generalize again, because the truth table for *any* sentence and its negation will be just like the one for *A* and ~*A*. We can express this general fact by constructing a truth table using the variable *p*, as follows:

p	~*p*
T	F
F	T

Sentential Logic

This truth table asserts that given any sentence:

1. If that sentence is true, then its negation is false.

2. If that sentence is false, then its negation is true.

7

Parentheses and Brackets

Consider the mathematical expression "3 + 3 × 4 = 24". Is this expression true or false? The answer is that if the expression states that the sum of 3 plus 3 (which is 6) times 4 equals 24, then it is true. But if it states that 3 plus the product of 3 times 4 (that is, 3 plus 12) equals 24, then it is false. But as the expression stands, it is not clear which of these two things it states. As it stands, the expression is *ambiguous*. To remove this kind of ambiguity from mathematical expressions, it is customary to use parentheses and brackets. Thus, (3 + 3) × 4 = 24, while 3 + (3 × 4) = 15.

Similarly, parentheses, brackets, "[" and "]", and braces, "{" and "}", are used to remove ambiguity in logic. Consider once again the sentences "Art went to the show", *A*, and "Betsy went to the show", *B*. To deny *A* and assert *B*, we can write $\sim A \cdot B$. To deny *A and* deny *B*, we can write $\sim A \cdot \sim B$. And to deny the *combination* (the conjunction) $A \cdot B$, we can write $\sim (A \cdot B)$, using the parentheses to indicate that it is the *combination* or *conjunction* of *A* and *B* which is being denied. (Notice that to deny the *conjunction* $A \cdot B$ is neither to deny *A* nor to deny *B*.)

To summarize: The sentence $\sim A \cdot B$ asserts that Art did not go to the show, but Betsy did. The sentence $\sim A \cdot \sim B$ asserts that Art did not go and Betsy didn't either (that is, neither Art nor Betsy went). And the sentence $\sim (A \cdot B)$ asserts that it is false that *both* Art *and* Betsy went. (Notice that the sentences $\sim A \cdot \sim B$ and $\sim (A \cdot B)$ are not equivalent, as is proved by the fact that if Art went to the show but Betsy didn't, then the sentence $\sim A \cdot \sim B$ is false while the sentence $\sim (A \cdot B)$ is true.)

When symbolizing more complex sentences, we can use brackets as well as parentheses if we wish to do so. For instance, we can symbolize the sentence "It is not the case both that Art will go and that Betsy and Charles won't" either as $\sim (A \cdot \sim (B \cdot C))$, or as $\sim [A \cdot \sim (B \cdot C)]$. (Similarly, for the present we allow symbolizations of sentences such as "Art and Betsy went" either with or without parentheses, that is, either as $A \cdot B$ or as $(A \cdot B)$.)

8

Disjunction

Another frequently used sentence connective is the English word "or" (and its variants, particularly "either . . . or"). There are two different senses of this connective in common use. One, the **exclusive** sense, is illustrated by the sentence "Art took the makeup exam on Tuesday or on Wednesday". The implication of this sentence is that Art took the makeup exam on Tuesday or on Wednesday, *but not on both Tuesday and Wednesday*. The other sense of the term "or" is called its **inclusive** sense, or sometimes its *nonexclusive* sense. If a football coach exclaims, "We'll beat either Notre Dame or Army", his assertion is not false if the team wins *both* of these games. The coach means to say that either we'll beat Notre Dame, or we'll beat Army, *or we'll beat both Notre Dame and Army*.

In legal documents, this inclusive sense of the term "or" usually is expressed by the phrase "and/or". Thus a contract might state that "Repairs will be made by the lessor and/or his agent", meaning that repairs will be made by one or the other, or both.

Two sentences connected by the word "or" form a compound sentence called a **disjunction**, and the two sentences so connected are called *disjuncts* of the disjunction.

The symbol $\vee$, called *vee* (or *vel*), is introduced to symbolize the *inclusive* sense of the word "or", and like the dot, $\vee$ is a truth functional connective. Abbreviating the sentence "We'll beat Notre Dame" by the capital letter N, and the sentence "We'll beat Army" by the capital letter A, we can symbolize the sentence "We'll beat Notre Dame or Army" as $N \vee A$.

Now let's consider all of the possible combinations of truth values of N and A. First, if both N and A are true, then $N \vee A$ is true. Second, if N is true and A false, then $N \vee A$ is true. Third, if N is false and A true, then $N \vee A$ is true. Finally, if both N and A are false, then $N \vee A$ is false. The following truth table summarizes our findings:

Sentential Logic

N	A	N ∨ A
T	T	T
T	F	T
F	T	T
F	F	F

And once again, we can generalize. The truth table for *any* two sentences connected by ∨ will be the same as the one for *N* and *A*. Using the variables *p* and *q*, we indicate this in a truth table, as follows:

p	q	p ∨ q
T	T	T
T	F	T
F	T	T
F	F	F

This truth table indicates that given any two sentences *p* and *q*, their disjunction *p* ∨ *q* is false *only* when both *p* and *q* are false; otherwise it is true.

Examples:

English Sentence	Symbolization
1. Art or Betsy went to the show.	1. *A* ∨ *B*
2. It will rain tomorrow or it will snow.	2. *R* ∨ *S*
3. Art went to the show, or Betsy went, or Charles went.	3. *A* ∨ (*B* ∨ *C*)

Sentences in which ∨ occurs can contain other statement connectives also. For instance, if we want to deny the sentence "Art or Betsy went to the show" (that is, deny *A* ∨ *B*), then we can symbolize our denial as

$\sim(A \lor B)$. (In English, the denial of "Art or Betsy went to the show" can be made by asserting the sentence "*Neither* Art *nor* Betsy went to the show". In general, sentences of the form "Neither *p* nor *q*" are symbolized as $\sim(p \lor q)$, or as $\sim p \cdot \sim q$.)

Examples:

(Let A = "Art will go", B = "Betsy will go", C = "Charles will go", and D = "Don will go".)

	English Sentence		Symbolization
1.	Art will go or Betsy won't go.	1.	$A \lor \sim B$
2.	Either Art and Betsy will go, or Charles will go.	2.	$(A \cdot B) \lor C$
3.	Charles won't go, or Don or Art will.	3.	$\sim C \lor (D \lor A)$
4.	Art and Betsy will go, or neither Charles nor Don will go.	4.	$(A \cdot B) \lor \sim (C \lor D)$
5.	Art and Charles will go, and Don or Betsy will go also.	5.	$(A \cdot C) \cdot (D \lor B)$
6.	It is not the case that either Art and Betsy will go or Charles won't.	6.	$\sim [(A \cdot B) \lor \sim C]$

As previously indicated, a sentence whose major connective is an inclusive "or" asserts that at least one of its disjuncts is true, leaving open the question whether or not *both* disjuncts are true. But a sentence whose major connective is an *exclusive* "or" asserts that (1) at least one of its disjuncts is true (as do disjunctions formed by the inclusive ("or")); and (2) *at least one disjunct is false*. Thus, there is a sense in which the whole meaning of the inclusive "or" is only part of the meaning of the exclusive "or". So if we symbolize an exclusive use of the word "or" by $\lor$, we lose part of its meaning. Surprisingly, in most arguments in which the exclusive "or" is used, no harm is done if we symbolize the "or" by means of $\lor$. This is because the validity of such arguments depends on that part of the meaning of the exclusive ∨ which it shares with the inclusive "or", namely that part of its meaning which asserts that at least one disjunct is true.

But there are some arguments for which this is not the case. An example is the argument

1. Art took the makeup exam on Tuesday or on Wednesday (*T* or *W*).

2. Art took the makeup exam on Tuesday (*T*).

/ ∴ 3. Art did *not* take the makeup exam on Wednesday (∼ *W*).

If the inclusive "or" is used to symbolize the "or" in the first premise of this argument, then the resulting argument will be invalid, since it will state that

1. Art took the makeup exam on Tuesday, or Art took the makeup exam on Wednesday, or Art took the makeup exam on Tuesday and Wednesday.

2. Art took the makeup exam on Tuesday.

/ ∴ 3. Art did *not* take the makeup exam on Wednesday.

But the original argument is valid. Consequently, this cannot be what is meant by the original argument. The trouble is that the "or" in the first premise of the original argument is the *exclusive* "or", and this time the additional claim made by the exclusive "or" cannot be omitted. We must not only assert that Art took the makeup exam on at least one of the two days (stated in symbols as $T \lor W$), but also *deny* that he took the exam on both days (stated in symbols as $\sim(T \cdot W)$). Thus, we must symbolize the first premise as $(T \lor W) \cdot \sim(T \cdot W)$.

In general, the whole meaning of a sentence of the form $p \lor q$, in which the "or" is used in the exclusive sense, can be symbolized as $(p \lor q) \cdot \sim(p \cdot q)$.

9

Material
Implication

Consider the sentence "If Art goes to the show, then Betsy will go to the show". This compound sentence contains two atomic sentences, namely "Art goes to the show" and "Betsy goes to the show", joined together by the sentence connective "If _____ then _____". A compound sentence of this kind is called a **conditional**, or **hypothetical**, or **implication**. The sentence between the "if" and the "then" is called its **antecedent**, and the sentence after the "then" its **consequent**. Thus, the general form of a conditional sentence is "if (antecedent) then (consequent)".

In English, there are many other ways to assert a conditional sentence. For instance, the above conditional could be stated as "Assuming that Art goes, Betsy will go also", or as "Betsy will go, if Art does", etc.

Conditional sentences differ with respect to the kind of connection they express between antecedent and consequent. For example, the connection between antecedent and consequent in the sentence "If Art or Betsy will go, then Betsy or Art will go" is *logical*, while in the sentence "If Art goes, then Betsy will go" the connection is *factual*.

But perhaps the most important way in which conditionals differ is with respect to truth-functionality. Although a very few of the conditionals uttered in daily life are truth-functional, the vast majority are not.

Consider the conditional sentence "If Art went to the show, then Betsy went also", partially symbolized as (1): "If A then B", and suppose that Charles and Don wager as to the truth value of this sentence, Charles betting that it is true, Don that it is false. Clearly, if Art did go, but Betsy didn't, so that A is true and B false, then sentence (1) is false, and Don wins the bet. So the second line of the truth table for sentence (1) must contain an **F**.

But suppose neither Art nor Betsy went to the show, so that both A and B are false. Then it is not clear who should win the bet. Surely, Charles would be foolish to agree that sentence (1) is false, and hence agree that Don wins the bet. For he could argue that although Betsy didn't go, sentence (1) doesn't assert that she did go, but only that she did *if Art did*. Since Art didn't go, sentence (1) is not false.

On the other hand, it would be equally foolish of Don to agree that Charles wins the bet, that is, to agree that sentence (1) is true, and hence that Charles wins the bet. For he could argue that sentence (1) asserts that Betsy went *if Art went*, but asserts nothing about what happened to Betsy if Art didn't go. Since Art didn't go, we can't say sentence (1) is true.

It would seem, then, that in cases when both its antecedent and consequent are false, the truth value of the conditional sentence (1): "If A then B" is not determined by the truth values of its component sentences. Thus, sentence (1) contains a *non*-truth-functional use of the connective "If _____ then _ _ _ _ _ _". This causes little difficulty in ordinary betting situations (for example, Charles and Don could agree that if A turns out to be false, then the bet is off), but it won't do for logic. Logic requires a truth table for material implication in which all four lines contain either a **T** or an **F**. That is, logic requires a completely truth-functional definition for the sentence connective symbol ⊃.

The above example illustrates the difficulty which arises when both antecedent and consequent of a conditional are false. Thus, it illustrates the difficulty presented by the fourth line of the truth table for "if _____ then _ _ _ _ _ _." sentences. But the same sort of problem arises with respect to the third line, and even the first line, of the truth table for "if _____ then _ _ _ _ _ _ " sentences.

Consider the conditional sentence (2): "If Smith puts off his operation, then he'll be dead within six months", pronounced by a doctor about a particular cancer patient. Suppose Smith puts off the operation, but is killed crossing the street two weeks later, so that both the antecedent "Smith puts off the operation" and consequent "He'll be dead within six months" are true. (This is the case for line 1 of the truth table for sentence (2).) Surely, the doctor is *not* justified in claiming that sentence (2) is true just because both its antecedent and consequent are true, for the consequent is true *accidentally*, and not because the antecedent is true. The doctor meant to assert not simply that Smith would be dead within six months if he were not operated on, but rather that if not operated on *his cancerous condition would cause his death* (if nothing else did first). So we are not justified in placing a **T** on line 1 of the truth table for sentence (2). But we aren't justified in placing an **F** on line 1 either, for Smith *might* have died of cancer within six months if he had not been killed in an auto accident.

It seems then, that the use of "If _____ then _ _ _ _ _ _." in sentence (2): "If Smith puts off his operation, then he'll be dead within six months" is not truth-functional.

However, our main concern here is not how conditionals differ but rather how they are alike, for we want to utilize the meaning common to all uses of the connective "If _____ then _ _ _ _ _ _" as the *entire* meaning of the sentence connective $\supset$. And it turns out that every conditional sentence, truth-functional or not truth-functional, is such that *if its antecedent is true and its consequent false, then the whole conditional sentence is false*. Therefore, part of what we do in asserting a conditional sentence is to *deny* the conjunction of its antecedent with the negation of its consequent.

We use this partial meaning shared by all conditional sentences as the *total* meaning of **material implication**. Thus, a sentence having the form $p \supset q$ is taken to mean the same thing as, and hence to be equivalent to, a sentence having the form $\sim(p \cdot \sim q)$. Consequently, the truth table for a sentence having the form $p \supset q$ must be the same as the truth table for an analogous sentence having the form $\sim(p \cdot \sim q)$.

The general method for determining the truth values of compound sentences is presented in Chapter Three. Let's anticipate a bit here and informally derive the truth table for sentences having the form $\sim(p \cdot \sim q)$:

Consider the sentence "It is not the case both that Art went to the show and Betsy didn't", symbolized as $\sim(A \cdot \sim B)$. There are four possible combinations of truth values for A and B:

Case I: A is true and *B* is true (line 1 of the truth table for the sentence $\sim(A \cdot \sim B)$):
Since *B* is true, $\sim B$ is false. Hence $(A \cdot \sim B)$ is false, and $\sim(A \cdot \sim B)$ true. Therefore, line 1 of the truth table for $\sim(A \cdot \sim B)$ must contain a **T**.

Case II: A is true and *B* false (line 2 of the truth table for the sentence $\sim(A \cdot \sim B)$):
Since *B* is false, $\sim B$ is true. Hence $(A \cdot \sim B)$ is true, and $\sim(A \cdot \sim B)$ false. Therefore, line 2 of the truth table for $\sim(A \cdot \sim B)$ must contain an **F**.

Case III: A is false, *B* true (line 3 of the truth table):
Since *B* is true, $\sim B$ is false. Thus $(A \cdot \sim B)$ is false, and $\sim(A \cdot \sim B)$ true. Therefore, line 3 of the truth table for $\sim(A \cdot \sim B)$ must contain a **T**.

Case IV: *A* is false and *B* is false (line 4 of the truth table):

Since *A* is false, ($A \cdot \sim B$) is false. Hence, $\sim(A \cdot \sim B)$ is true. Therefore, line 4 of the truth table for $\sim(A \cdot \sim B)$ must contain a **T**.

Summing up, the truth table for $\sim(A \cdot \sim B)$, and therefore for $A \supset B$, is as follows:

A	*B*	$\sim(A \cdot \sim B)$	$A \supset B$
T	T	T	T
T	F	F	F
F	T	T	T
F	F	T	T

Once again, we can generalize, since the truth table for any two sentences connected by $\supset$ will be the same as the one for $A \supset B$. Using the variables *p* and *q*, we indicate this in a truth table, as follows:

p	*q*	$p \supset q$
T	T	T
T	F	F
F	T	T
F	F	T

We take this truth table to provide a definition, or specification of meaning, for the symbol $\supset$.*

When symbolizing conditional sentences of ordinary English, it must be remembered that most ordinary conditionals are *not* truth-functional. Thus, when they are symbolized by means of $\supset$, only part of their meaning is captured (namely the part they share with all conditionals), the other part being lost. In general, the part captured by material implication is all that is needed to solve problems containing implications.

---

* Another reason for defining $\supset$ as we have defined it is explained in Chapter Five, Section 7.

10

*Material
Equivalence*

Two sentences are said to be **materially equivalent** if they have the same truth value. We introduce the symbol ≡ to be used in symbolizing material equivalence. (The symbols "iff" (if and only if) and ↔ also are used.) Thus, to assert that Art's having gone to the show (*A*) is materially equivalent to Betsy's having gone to the show (*B*), we can write "*A* is materially equivalent to *B*", or simply $A \equiv B$. (This sentence can also be expressed in English as "Art went to the show if, and only if, Betsy went to the show".) Obviously, the sentence $A \equiv B$ is true if and only if *A* and *B* have the same truth value; and in general a sentence $p \equiv q$ is true if and only if *p* and *q* have the same truth value. Hence the truth table for material equivalence must be:

p	*q*	$p \equiv q$
T	T	T
T	F	F
F	T	F
F	F	T

We take this truth table to provide a definition, or specification of meaning, for the symbol ≡.

Material equivalences are themselves equivalent to two directional conditionals. (Hence the term "biconditional" used to apply to equivalences.) For instance, the material equivalence "Art went to the show if, and only if, Betsy went to the show", in symbols $A \equiv B$, is equivalent to the two-directional conditional "If Art went to the show, then Betsy went to the show, and if Betsy went to the show, then Art went to the show", in symbols $(A \supset B) \cdot (B \supset A)$. This can be verified by proving that the truth table for $A \equiv B$ is the same as the truth table for $(A \supset B) \cdot (B \supset A)$.

The same problem concerning truth-functionality which arises for implications arises also for equivalences.* In general, the question as to

---

* Indeed, it arises for disjunctions also. Consider the disjunction "Either we operate or the patient dies". In this case, the truth of the left disjunct "We operate" does not guarantee the truth of the whole compound sentence "Either we operate or the patient dies", even if the patient does not die, because it *may* be that the patient wouldn't have died even if we had *not* operated.

when equivalences can be symbolized by means of ≡ is answered in the same way that the similar question is answered concerning implications.

Exercise 2–1:

For each sentence on the left, determine the sentence form (or forms) on the right of which it is a substitution instance. (Remember that a sentence can be a substitution instance of many sentence forms.)

1.	A	a.	p
2.	$A \supset B$	b.	q
3.	$(A \lor B) \supset C$	c.	$\sim p$
4.	$(\sim A \lor B) \supset C$	d.	$p \supset q$
5.	$\sim (A \lor B) \supset C$	e.	$\sim p \supset q$
6.	$\sim (\sim A \lor B) \supset C$	f.	$\sim (p \supset q)$
7.	$\sim [(A \lor B) \supset C]$	g.	$\sim (\sim p \supset q)$
8.	$\sim [\sim (A \lor B) \supset C]$	h.	$(p \lor q) \supset r$
9.	$\sim [\sim (\sim A \lor B) \supset C]$	i.	$(p \lor q) \supset \sim r$
10.	$\sim [(\sim A \lor B) \supset C]$	j.	$(\sim p \lor q) \supset r$
		k.	$\sim (\sim p \lor q) \supset r$
		l.	$\sim (p \lor q) \supset r$
		m.	$\sim [\sim (\sim p \lor q) \supset r]$
		n.	$\sim [(p \lor q) \supset r]$
		o.	$\sim [\sim (p \lor q) \supset r]$

Chapter Three

1

*Truth Table
Analysis*

In Chapter Two, truth table definitions were introduced for several truth-functional sentence connectives. This basic content of Chapter Two can be summarized in two truth tables, as follows:

p	$\sim p$
T	F
F	T

p	q	$p \cdot q$	$p \vee q$	$p \supset q$	$p \equiv q$
T	T	T	T	T	T
T	F	F	T	F	F
F	T	F	T	T	F
F	F	F	F	T	T

We can determine the truth value of any compound sentence containing sentences connected by one of these truth-functional connectives, when provided with the truth values of the sentences so connected, simply by looking at the appropriate blank in the truth tables and noting whether there is a **T** or an **F** in that blank.

But obviously, this method can be used to determine the truth values of more complicated sentences also. Suppose Art and Betsy are running for class president, and consider the sentence "It's not the case either that Art and Betsy will run or that Betsy won't run", symbolized as $\sim[(A \cdot B) \lor \sim B]$. Assume further we are told that in fact Art and Betsy both will run, so that A and B both are true. Then we can "figure out" the truth value of $\sim[(A \cdot B) \lor \sim B]$ as follows: Since A and B both are true, $(A \cdot B)$ must be true, by line 1 of the truth table for " $\cdot$ ". And since B is true, $\sim B$ must be false, by line 1 of the truth table for " $\sim$ ". Hence, $[(A \cdot B) \lor \sim B]$ must be true, by line 2 of the truth table for " $\lor$ ". And finally, since $[(A \cdot B) \lor \sim B]$ is true, its negation $\sim[(A \cdot B) \lor \sim B]$ must be false, by line 1 of the truth table for " $\sim$ ".

The following diagram illustrates this process of truth table analysis as it was carried out on the sentence $\sim[(A \cdot B) \lor \sim B]$:

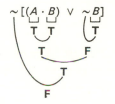

Notice that the process starts with the smallest units of the sentence and proceeds to larger and larger units, until the last loop determines the truth value of the sentence as a whole.

This method, sometimes called **truth table analysis**, sometimes **case analysis**, can be used to determine the truth value of any compound sentence containing more than one sentence connective from the truth values of its component sentences.

Examples:

(In these examples, assume A, B, and C are true, D, E, and F false.)

1.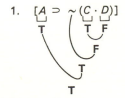

(Notice that the negation sign negates the whole compound sentence (C · D), and therefore is treated *after* the truth value of (C · D) is determined.)

2.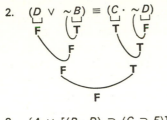

3.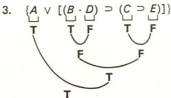

(Notice that the major connective in this sentence—that is, the connective which connects two component sentences to form sentence 3 as a whole—is ∨, and that therefore it is not really necessary to analyze the right hand disjunct, because the left hand disjunct—namely A—is true, and consequently the whole sentence is true.)

4.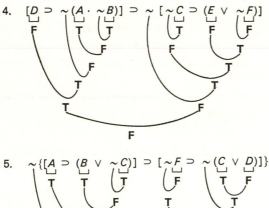

5.

Exercise 3–1:

If A and B are true, and C, D, and E false, what are the truth values of the following compound sentences?

1. $(A \lor D) \supset E$

2. $A \equiv (C \lor B)$

3. $B \supset (A \supset C)$

4. $\sim[(A \cdot \sim B) \supset (C \cdot \sim D)]$

5. $[(A \cdot B) \cdot C] \lor [(A \cdot C) \lor (A \cdot D)]$

6. $A \supset [(B \supset C) \supset (D \supset E)]$

7. $[(\sim A \cdot \sim B) \supset C] \lor (A \supset B)$

8. $[(A \supset \sim B) \lor (C \cdot \sim D)] \equiv [\sim(A \supset D) \lor (\sim C \lor E)]$

9. $[(E \lor \sim D) \cdot \sim A] \supset \{(\sim A \cdot \sim B) \cdot [(C \cdot D) \cdot E]\}$

10. $[A \supset (\sim A \lor A)] \cdot \sim[(\sim A \cdot A) \supset (A \cdot A)]$

2

Tautologies, Contradictions, and Contingent Sentences

A **tautologous sentence form** is one such that all of its substitution instances are true. An example is the sentence form $p \supset (q \supset p)$. This sentence form can be shown to be tautologous by an examination of *all* of its substitution instances, putting them into four categories as follows: first, substitution instances in which both p and q are replaced by true sentences (whether atomic or compound is not important); second, substitution instances in which p is replaced by a true sentence and q a false one; third, substitution instances in which p is replaced by a false sentence and q a true one; and finally, substitution instances in which both p and q are replaced by false sentences.

Let's begin by examining a substitution instance of the first kind, say the sentence $H \supset (K \supset H)$, where both H and K are true sentences. Its truth table analysis is as follows:

And of course, truth table analysis will yield a **T** for *every* substitution instance of $p \supset (q \supset p)$ in which both p and q are replaced by true sentences.

Now consider a substitution instance of the second kind, say $M \supset (N \supset M)$, in which p is replaced by the true sentence M, and q by the false sentence N. The truth table analysis for $M \supset (N \supset M)$ is:

And once again truth table analysis will yield a **T** for *every* substitution instance of $p \supset (q \supset p)$ in which p is replaced by a true sentence and q by a false one.

Next, consider a substitution instance of the third kind, say the sentence $C \supset (D \supset C)$, in which p is replaced by the false sentence C, and q by the true sentence D. The truth table analysis for $C \supset (D \supset C)$ (and all cases of the third kind) is:

Finally, consider a substitution instance of the fourth kind, say the sentence $F \supset (G \supset F)$, in which p is replaced by the false sentence F, and *q* by the false sentence *G*. The truth table analysis for this sentence (and for all substitution instances of the fourth kind) is:

So it turns out that *all substitution instances of p ⊃ (q ⊃ p) whatsoever are true sentences*, no matter what the truth values of their component sentences. It is the *form* or *structure* of these sentences (plus the meanings of their logical terms, such as ⊃), and not the truth values of their component sentences, which make them true. A sentence form all of whose substitution instances are true, is said to be a *tautologous sentence form*, or simply a *tautology*. (Informally, substitution instances of tautologous sentence forms also can be called *tautologies*, although some logicians reserve that word for sentence forms only.)

The above discussion of substitution instances of the sentence form *p ⊃ (q ⊃ p)* makes it obvious that the truth table for it is as follows:

p	*q*	*p ⊃ (q ⊃ p)*
T	T	T
T	F	T
F	T	T
F	F	T

And it also makes obvious the general method for determining the truth table for any given sentence form, and thus for all of its substitution instances.

Now consider a second sentence form, namely the form (*p* · ∼*p*). What is its truth table? First, unlike the case for the sentence form *p ⊃ (q ⊃ p)*, the truth table for *p* · ∼*p* has only two lines, instead of four, since *p* · ∼*p* has only one variable, namely *p*, instead of two.* And second, its truth

---

* In general the number of lines in the truth table of a given sentence form is equal to 2^n, where *n* is the number of variables in the sentence form. Thus a sentence form with one variable has $2^1 = 2$ lines in its truth table, one with two variables has $2^2 = 4$ lines, one with three variables has $2^3 = 8$ lines, and so on.

table has all **F**'s, instead of all **T**'s. This is proved by the following truth table analysis:

(The analysis below the sentence form $p \cdot \sim p$ is for the first case, in which p is replaced by a true sentence, and the analysis above $p \cdot \sim p$ is for the second case, in which p is replaced by a false sentence.)

Thus the truth table for $p \cdot \sim p$ is:

p	$p \cdot \sim p$
T	F
F	F

Since only **F**'s occur in its truth table, it follows that *all substitution instances of $p \cdot \sim p$ are false*, no matter what the truth values of the sentences which replace p. It is the *form*, or *structure*, of the substitution instances which makes them false, and not the truth values of their component sentences. A sentence form all of whose substitution instances are false is said to be a **contradictory sentence form**, or simply a **contradiction**. (Informally, substitution instances of contradictory sentence forms also can be referred to as *contradictions*, although some logicians reserve this term for sentence forms only.)

It is important to see that not all false sentences are contradictions. For instance, if Art goes to the show and Betsy does not, then the sentence "If Art goes then Betsy goes", in symbols $A \supset B$, is false. But it is not a contradiction, since it is *not* a substitution instance of a contradictory sentence form. Thus the notion of a contradictory sentence is different from that of a merely false sentence.

It is interesting to note that we cannot prove that a sentence is *not* contradictory by showing that it is a substitution instance of a noncontradictory sentence form. This is due to the fact that *all* sentences, even contradictory sentences, are substitution instances of *some* noncontradictory sentence form or other. For instance, $S \cdot \sim S$ is a substitution instance of the form p, as well as the form $p \cdot q$, and both of these sentence forms are noncontradictory.

Finally, consider a third sentence form, namely $(p \supset q) \supset q$. We can determine its truth table by means of the following analysis:

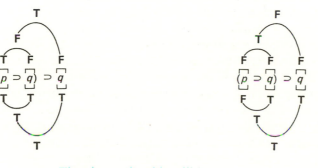

Thus its truth table will be:

p	q	$(p \supset q) \supset q$
T	T	T
T	F	T
F	T	T
F	F	F

Notice that there is at least one **T** and one **F** in this truth table. This means that we cannot determine the truth value of a substitution instance of this sentence form without knowing the truth value of its component sentences, since some substitution instances of $(p \supset q) \supset q$ are true and some false. A sentence form which has at least one **T** and one **F** in its truth table is said to be a **contingent sentence form**. Informally, substitution instances of contingent sentence forms which are *not* substitution instances of any tautologous or contradictory sentence forms can be referred to as *contingent sentences*.

Notice that we cannot say that all substitution instances of contingent sentence forms are contingent sentences, since *all* sentences are substitution instances of some contingent sentence form or other. For instance, all sentences are substitution instances of the sentence form *p*, which is a contingent sentence form.

(If a truth table analysis of a given sentence yields at least one **T** and one **F**, then it is not necessary to continue the analysis further in order to determine the nature of that sentence form, since it must be contingent. For example, if we start the truth table analysis of the sentence form $(p \supset q) \supset q$ with the first and last lines of its truth table, then it is not necessary to continue on to lines two and three, since one **T** and one **F** have already been obtained and the sentence form must be a contingent one.)

The division of sentences into tautologies, contradictions, and contingent sentences is of fundamental importance. In the first place, as will be indicated in Chapter Four, corresponding to every *valid deductive argument form* there is a *tautologous sentence form* whose antecedent is the set of premises of that argument form and whose consequent is the conclusion of that argument form, so that there is a basic relationship between tautologies and valid argument forms. And in the second place, the truth values of all tautologies and contradictions can be determined by means of logic alone, without appeal to experience, or any kind of empirical test, while this is not the case for contingent sentences. Thus the division into tautologies, contradictions, and contingent sentences is pertinent to basic philosophical questions about the ways in which knowledge can be acquired. (For instance, it is pertinent to the controversies concerning the analytic-synthetic and a priori-a posteriori distinctions to be discussed in Chapter Nineteen.)

Exercise 3–2:

Determine which of the following sentence forms are tautologous, which contradictory, and which contingent:

1. $p \lor (q \supset \sim p)$

2. $\sim [p \supset (p \lor \sim p)]$

3. $(p \lor q) \supset [q \lor (p \supset p)]$

4. $p \supset [q \supset (p \supset r)]$

5. $[(p \cdot q) \cdot r] \lor [(p \cdot r) \lor (p \cdot q)]$

6. $\{(r \supset s) \supset [p \cdot (r \lor s)]\} \equiv [p \supset (s \supset r)]$

7. $\{[p \cdot (q \lor r)] \supset p\} \equiv q$

8. $\sim [p \supset (\sim p \supset \sim q)] \cdot (\sim p \cdot q)$

9. $[\sim (\sim p \supset \sim q) \lor (\sim p \cdot \sim q)] \supset \sim (\sim p \cdot \sim q)$

10. $\{p \supset [(q \lor r) \lor (s \lor \sim q)]\} \lor \sim p$

3

*Symbolizing
Compound
Sentences*

Some English sentences are difficult to translate simply because they are long or complex.

Examples:

Let A = "Art goes (will go)", B = "Betsy goes (will go)", C = "Charles goes (will go)", and D = "Don goes (will go)".

English Sentence	Symbolic Translation
1. If Art and Betsy go, then neither Charles nor Don will go.	1. $(A \cdot B) \supset (\sim C \cdot \sim D)$ or $(A \cdot B) \supset \sim (C \lor D)$
2. Either Art and Betsy go, or neither Charles nor Don will go.	2. $(A \cdot B) \lor (\sim C \cdot \sim D)$ or $(A \cdot B) \lor \sim (C \lor D)$

3. Art and Betsy will go if and only if either Charles or Don won't go.

3. $(A \cdot B) \equiv (\sim C \lor \sim D)$

4. If it's not the case that both Art and Betsy go, then either Charles or Don will.

4. $\sim (A \cdot B) \supset (C \lor D)$

5. If Art goes, then Betsy will also if Charles doesn't.*

5. $A \supset (\sim C \supset B)$

6. Either Betsy will go if Art does, and Don will go if Charles does, or else Art will and Don won't go.

6. $[(A \supset B) \cdot (C \supset D)] \lor (A \cdot \sim D)$

In general, the grammatical structure of a sentence mirrors its logical structure, so that most English sentences can be correctly symbolized simply by following grammatical structure, replacing grammatical connectives such as "or", "if and only if", and "if-then", by their logical counterparts $\lor$, $\equiv$, and $\supset$. But there are exceptions. In some cases, grammatical structure does *not* mirror logical structure, and we cannot simply replace grammatical connectives by their logical counterparts.

An example of the latter is the sentence (I): "Bombing China is equivalent to an act of war against China". The temptation to symbolize the sentence as $C \equiv W$ (where C = "We bomb China" and W = "We commit an act of war against China"), replacing the grammatical phrase "is equivalent to" by its apparent logical counterpart $\equiv$. But that would be a mistake. Someone who asserts (I) does not mean to assert an *equivalence*. He does not mean to assert *both* that if we bomb China then we commit an act of war against China *and* that if we commit an act of war against China then we bomb China. What he means to say is simply that if we bomb China then we commit an act of war against China. So he means to assert a *conditional*, namely $C \supset W$.

To avoid mistakes of this kind due to overly mechanical translation, we have to pay close attention to the meanings that particular English

---

* (This might also be stated in English as "If Art goes, then Betsy will also *provided* Charles doesn't". Or the word "assuming" might be substituted for the word "provided". But all three sentences are correctly symbolized in the same way.)

sentences convey in given contexts, realizing that natural languages are quite flexible both in grammatical construction and in their use of grammatical connectives. The same expressions can mean quite different things in different contexts.

There are two English connectives which are especially troublesome, namely "only if" and "unless".

Consider the sentence "You will be allowed to play only if you clean your room first", spoken by a mother to her son. Symbolizing "you will be allowed to play" as P, and "you clean your room first" as C, that sentence becomes "P only if C". Clearly, in this case the mother is telling her son *at least* that if he does *not* clean up first, then he will *not* be allowed to play; that is $\sim C \supset \sim P$. In Chapter Four, it will be shown that $\sim C \supset \sim P$ is equivalent to $P \supset C$. So part of the meaning of "P only if C" is that $P \supset C$. But in certain contexts, the child can reasonably assume that his mother intends to imply that if he does clean up his room first, then he will be allowed to play; that is, she intends to imply $C \supset P$. So in this kind of case, the total meaning of "P only if C" is $(P \supset C) \cdot (C \supset P)$, or what amounts to the same thing, $P \equiv C$. This is a fairly common use of the connective "only if".

Now consider a second common use of "only if", as used in the sentence "You'll be able to run the four minute mile only if you practice hard" (symbolized as "M only if P"). A track coach might well make such a statement to his prize miler, even if he does not know, and does not mean to predict, that if the miler practices hard, then he *will* run the mile in under four minutes. The coach might intend to say simply that if the runner does *not* practice hard ($\sim P$), then he will *not* be able to run a four minute mile ($\sim M$). And then the core of the meaning of this use of "M only if P" will be $\sim P \supset \sim M$, or what amounts to the same thing, $M \supset P$. But the coach might *not* mean to say that if the runner practices hard (P), then he *will* be able to run the four minute mile (M). That is, the coach might *not* mean to assert that $P \supset M$. And if so, then in this case the total truth functional meaning of "M only if P" would be $M \supset P$. This is probably the most common use of the connective "only if".

There is no mechanical way to determine which of the two senses of "only if" is being used in a given case. We must determine what is intended in each case by an examination of the *context* of its use, plus our general knowledge of English usage.

The situation is similar with respect to the symbolization of sentences containing the connective "unless". Thus, in certain contexts, the sentence "You cannot play unless you clean up first" ($\sim P$ unless C), is correctly symbolized as $(P \supset C) \cdot (C \supset P)$, or what amounts to the same thing, as $P \equiv C$, while the sentence "You cannot run the four minute mile unless you practice hard" ($\sim M$ unless P), is correctly symbolized simply as $M \supset P$.

Exercise 3–3:

Symbolize the following sentences, letting G = "George runs (will run) for class president", H = "Harry runs (will run) for class president", and J = "Judith runs (will run) for class president":

1. If Harry runs for class president, then Judith won't run.

2. But if Harry doesn't run, then Judith will.

3. If Harry and Judith both run, then George won't run.

4. Harry will run only if Judith doesn't.

5. George will run unless Judith runs.

6. It won't happen that Harry and Judith both run.

7. If Judith runs, then either Harry won't run or George will.

8. Harry will run if, and only if, Judith runs.

9. Neither Judith nor George will run.

10. George will run, and if Judith runs then Harry will also.

Sentential Logic

11. On the assumption that Harry will run if George does, it follows that Judith won't run.

12. Supposing that George runs provided Judith does, it follows that Harry will if Judith won't run.

Chapter Four

*Sentential
Logic—III*

1

*Arguments and
Argument Forms*

As stated in Chapter One, an **argument** is a series of sentences (premises) plus another sentence (the conclusion), where the premises are presented in support of the conclusion. For example, the two sentences

1. If Art went to the show, then Betsy went also.

/ ∴   Either Art didn't go to the show or else Betsy did go.

comprise an argument. An **argument form** is a group of sentence forms such that all of its substitution instances are arguments. For example, all substitution instances of the form

1. $p \supset q$

2. $p \; / \therefore \; q$

are arguments, and hence that form is an argument form. (Of course in substituting into an argument form, every occurrence of a given sentence variable must be replaced by the same sentence wherever that variable occurs in the argument form.)

Examples:

The following arguments are substitution instances of the argument form
1. $p \supset q$
2. $p \mathbin{/} \therefore q$:

(I)   1. $p \supset q$

      2. $p \mathbin{/} \therefore q$

(II)   1. $A \supset B$

      2. $A \mathbin{/} \therefore B$

(III)*   1. $(A \lor B) \supset C$

        2. $(A \lor B) \mathbin{/} \therefore C$

(IV)   1. $\sim (A \cdot B) \supset (C \lor D)$

       2. $\sim (A \cdot B) \mathbin{/} \therefore (C \lor D)$

2

Valid Arguments and Argument Forms

A **valid argument form** is an argument form none of whose substitution instances have true premises and a false conclusion. All substitution instances of a valid argument form are *valid arguments*. These two facts are of crucial importance for logic and almost everything else to be said in this chapter depends on them.

There are several methods for determining the validity of argument forms. We present one of the fairly simple methods:

Since no substitution instance of a valid argument form can have true premises and a false conclusion, it follows that every line of the truth table for a *valid* argument form which contains **T**'s for all of its premises must also contain a **T** for its conclusion. It also follows that the truth table for an *invalid* argument form must have at least one line which contains **T**'s

---

* We obtain this argument as a substitution instance of the argument form in question by substituting $(A \lor B)$ for p in both premises, and C for q in premise 2 and in the conclusion.

for all of its premises, but an **F** for the conclusion. Hence, *truth table analysis* constitutes a simple method for determining the validity of argument forms in sentential logic.

Examples:

Consider the argument form:

(I) 1. $p \supset q$

2. $\sim q / \therefore \sim p$

The truth table analysis for (I) is as follows:

			First Premise	Second Premise	Conclusion
	p	q	$p \supset q$	$\sim q$	$\sim p$
1.	T	T	T	F	F
2.	T	F	F	T	F
3.	F	T	T	F	T
4.	F	F	T	T	T

Notice that there is a **T** for *both* premises only on line 4 of this truth table, and there also is a **T** for the conclusion on that line. Hence, there is no substitution instance of this argument form having all of its premises true and its conclusion false, since the only case in which all of the premises of an argument of this form are true also is a case in which its conclusion is true. Therefore this argument form, usually called **Modus Tollens (MT)**, is a *valid* argument form.

An example of a valid argument having this form is:

1. If Art went to the show then Betsy went also.

2. But Betsy didn't go.

/ ∴ 3. Art didn't go either.

Or, in symbols:

1. $A \supset B$

2. $\sim B$

/ ∴ 3. $\sim A$

Now consider the argument form:

(II) 1. $p \supset q$

2. $\sim p$ / ∴ $\sim q$

Its truth table analysis is as follows:

			First Premise	Second Premise	Conclusion
	p	q	$p \supset q$	$\sim p$	$\sim q$
1.	T	T	T	F	F
2.	T	F	F	F	T
3.	F	T	T	T	F
4.	F	F	T	T	T

Both premises yield a **T** on the third and fourth lines of this truth table. But although the conclusion yields a **T** on the fourth line, it yields an **F** on the third. Thus, the third line of this truth table indicates that it is possible for a substitution instance of the argument form in question to have true premises and a false conclusion, and therefore proves that the argument form is not deductively valid. An example of an invalid argument which has this form is the following:

1. If Art went to the show, then Betsy went also.

2. But Art didn't go.

/ ∴ 3. Betsy didn't go either.

Or, in symbols:

1. $A \supset B$

2. $\sim A$

/∴ 3. $\sim B$

Clearly, this argument is invalid; for instance, Betsy may have decided to go to the show alone.

3

Proofs Using Valid Argument Forms

In this section, we introduce a proof technique involving the use of valid argument forms. For this purpose, we require a list of valid argument forms such that all valid arguments can be obtained as substitution instances of one or a combination of the forms on the list.

A **proof of an argument** is a list of sentences all of which are either premises of the argument or else follow from previous sentences on the list by means of valid argument forms, where the last sentence on the list is the conclusion of the argument.

Example:

Let A = "Art goes", B = "Betsy goes", C = "Charles goes". Then the following constitutes a proof of the three-premise argument whose conclusion is line 5:

1. $A \supset B$ p

2. $B \supset C$ p

3. $\sim C$ p /∴ $\sim A$

(The notation *p* to the right of lines 1, 2, and 3, indicates that these three lines are premises.)

| 4. | ~B | 2, 3, **MT** |
| 5. | ~A | 1, 4, **MT** |

(The notation to the right of line 4 indicates that line 4 "follows" from lines 2 and 3 by means of the valid argument form Modus Tollens (**MT**), introduced in the last section, and similarly for the notation to the right of line 5.)

Since every line of this proof is either a premise or follows from a premise by means of one or more uses of a valid argument form, the argument as a whole is valid.

The number of valid argument forms is infinite. So clearly we can't prove and list *every* valid argument form. On the other hand we don't want to list only the minimum number of argument forms required for a complete sentential logic, for the paucity of argument forms in such a system would make proofs quite difficult to construct and much longer than is desirable. The usual procedure is to strike a happy medium, proving and listing about ten to twenty valid argument forms, including most of the commonly used forms, making sure that the system is *complete* (that is, making sure that every valid argument of sentential logic can be proved by means of the listed valid argument forms). We choose a list of eighteen valid argument forms (with variations), a list which breaks down into two classes, namely **implicational argument forms** and **equivalence argument forms**. (Actually, the system will not be complete until the rule of conditional proof is introduced later in the chapter.)

We list eight valid implicational argument forms. Strictly speaking, we should say that these valid implicational forms are *permissive rules of inference*, which permit the assertion of the conclusion of a substitution instance as a line in a proof whenever the premises of that substitution instance occur previously in that proof. Thus, in the last example (above), we are permitted by Modus Tollens to assert line 4, ~B, because ~B is the conclusion of a substitution instance of Modus Tollens, and both premises of that substitution instance occur on previous lines in the proof (namely on lines 1 and 3).

The following is the list of eight valid implicational argument forms (with variations) to be used in the construction of argument proofs:

Valid Implicational Argument Forms (Rules of Inference)

1. **Modus Ponens (MP):**
$p \supset q$
$p / \therefore q$

2. **Modus Tollens (MT):**
$p \supset q$
$\sim q / \therefore \sim p$

3. **Disjunctive Syllogism (DS):**
$p \vee q$
$\sim p / \therefore q$
$p \vee q$
$\sim q / \therefore p$

4. **Simplification (Simp):**
$p \cdot q / \therefore p$
$p \cdot q / \therefore q$

5. **Conjunction (Conj):**
p
$q / \therefore p \cdot q$

6. **Hypothetical Syllogism (HS):**
$p \supset q$
$q \supset r / \therefore p \supset r$

7. **Addition (Add):**
$p / \therefore p \vee q$

8. **Constructive Dilemma (CD):**
$p \supset q$
$r \supset s$
$p \vee r / \therefore q \vee s$

The proof that Modus Tollens is a valid argument form has already been given (p. 46). In the example below, another one of the eight implicational forms is proved valid. It is left to the reader to prove that the six other listed implicational forms are *valid*.

Example:

Hypothetical Syllogism (**HS**) has the form:

1. $p \supset q$

2. $q \supset r / \therefore p \supset r$

Its truth table analysis is as follows:

				First Premise	Second Premise	Conclusion
	p	q	r	$p \supset q$	$q \supset r$	$p \supset r$
1.	T	T	T	T	T	T
2.	T	T	F	T	F	F
3.	T	F	T	F	T	T
4.	T	F	F	F	T	F
5.	F	T	T	T	T	T
6.	F	T	F	T	F	T
7.	F	F	T	T	T	T
8.	F	F	F	T	T	T

This truth table shows that both premises are true in cases 1, 5, 7, and 8, and in each of these cases the conclusion is true also. Hence, an argument of this form cannot have true premises and a false conclusion, and so must be valid.

(Notice that the above truth table has eight lines instead of four. This results from the fact that there are *three* letters used in the argument form Hypothetical Syllogism, p, q, and r, and the number of lines in a truth table always equal 2^n, where n equals number of letters used.)

Implicational argument forms are *one directional*. For example, the argument form Simplification permits the inference from $A \cdot B$ to A, but *not* the reverse inference from A to $A \cdot B$. The sentence $A \cdot B$ *implies* the sentence A, but is *not equivalent* to it.

But now, consider the valid inference from A to $\sim \sim A$. In this case, we *can reverse* the process, that is, we *can* validly infer from $\sim \sim A$ to A. This reversibility is due to the fact that the sentence A not only *implies* the sentence $\sim \sim A$ but also is equivalent to it, and *equivalent* sentences imply each other.

And again we can generalize. Clearly, both of the following argument forms are valid:

1. $p / \therefore \sim \sim p$

2. $\sim \sim p / \therefore p$

Since these two argument forms are just the reverse of each other, we can simplify matters by combining them into one "two-directional" argument form. Let's introduce the symbol : : and use it to indicate that an argument form is two directional. Then we can combine the above two one-directional (implicational) forms into one two-directional (equivalence) form as follows:

$p :: \sim \sim p$

In effect, this equivalence argument form permits the inference from any substitution instance of p to the analogous substitution instance of $\sim \sim p$, *and* from any substitution instance of $\sim \sim p$ to the analogous substitution instance of p. Thus, it permits all of the inferences permitted by the *two* implicational argument forms $p /\therefore \sim \sim p$ and $\sim \sim p /\therefore p$ taken together.

There are an infinite number of valid equivalence argument forms. We permit the use of ten (with variations), listed here with their standard names:

Valid Equivalence Argument Forms

9. $p :: \sim \sim p$
    (Double Negation) (DN)

10. $\sim (p \cdot q) :: (\sim p \vee \sim q)$
    (De Morgan's Theorem) (DeM)
    $\sim (p \vee q) :: (\sim p \cdot \sim q)$
    (De Morgan's Theorem) (DeM)

11. $(p \vee q) :: (q \vee p)$
    (Commutation) (Comm)
    $(p \cdot q) :: (q \cdot p)$
    (Commutation) (Comm)

12. $[p \vee (q \vee r)] :: [(p \vee q) \vee r]$
    (Association) (Assoc)
    $[p \cdot (q \cdot r)] :: [(p \cdot q) \cdot r]$
    (Association) (Assoc)

13. $[p \cdot (q \vee r)] :: [(p \cdot q) \vee (p \cdot r)]$
    (Distribution) (Dist)
    $[p \vee (q \cdot r)] :: [(p \vee q) \cdot (p \vee r)]$
    (Distribution) (Dist)

14. $(p \supset q) :: (\sim q \supset \sim p)$
    (Contraposition) (Contra)

15. $(p \supset q) :: (\sim p \vee q)$
    (Implication) (Impl)

16. $[(p \cdot q) \supset r] :: [p \supset (q \supset r)]$
    (Exportation) (Exp)

17. $p :: (p \cdot p)$ (Tautology) (Taut)
    $p :: (p \lor p)$ (Tautology) (Taut)

18. $(p \equiv q) :: [(p \supset q) \cdot (q \supset p)]$
    (Equivalence) (Equiv)
    $(p \equiv q) :: [(p \cdot q) \lor (\sim p \cdot \sim q)]$
    (Equivalence) (Equiv)

When we use an equivalence argument form, we move from a given expression to one which is equivalent to it. Hence, we can use equivalence argument forms on parts of lines without fear of changing truth values, and hence without fear of inferring from true premises to a false conclusion.

For instance, we can use Double Negation to infer validly from $A \lor B$ to $\sim \sim A \lor B$, because A is equivalent to $\sim \sim A$ and hence $A \lor B$ is equivalent to $\sim \sim A \lor B$.

This constitutes an important difference between *equivalence* argument forms and *implicational* argument forms, since implicational argument forms must be used on whole lines only.

There are several ways to determine the validity of equivalence argument forms. One fairly intuitive way is to prove by truth table analysis that the sentence form to the left of the :: sign is equivalent to the sentence form to the right. For instance, the truth table analysis

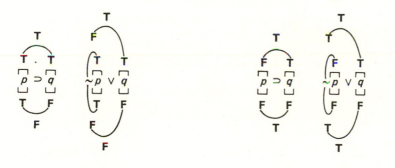

proves that the argument form **Implication (Impl)**

$(p \supset q) :: (\sim p \lor q)$

is a valid equivalence argument form, because it shows that the two sentences $p \supset q$ and $\sim p \vee q$ are equivalent.

Example:

The truth table analysis

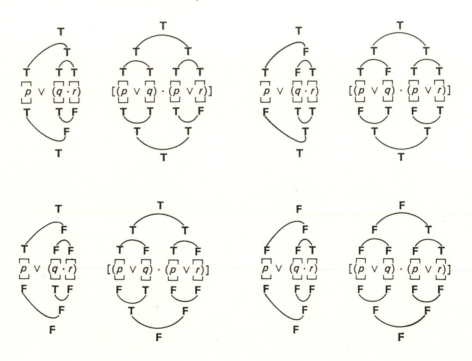

proves that the equivalence argument form Distribution, namely $[p \vee (q \cdot r)] :: [(p \vee q) \cdot (p \vee r)]$, is valid, because it shows that the sentence forms $p \vee (q \cdot r)$ and $(p \vee q) \cdot (p \vee r)$ are equivalent.

It is left to the reader to prove that the other listed equivalence forms are valid.*

4

Principles of Strategy

Books on chess and checkers often start out with a brief summary of the *rules of the game*, a list of rules indicating which kinds of moves are permitted. But the major part of a book of this kind discusses, not *permissive* rules, but rather what might be called *principles of strategy*. In most cases in actual games, the permissive rules allow more than one move. For instance, there are twenty permitted opening moves in a game of chess. But only a very few of these are likely to lead to winning positions. The major task of a good chess book is to enable the chess student to get the "feel" of good play, and to become familiar with principles of good strategy, that is, principles which *in general* lead to strong positions. For example, in chess, other things being equal, it is good strategy to develop a piece into the center of the board rather than to one side. (Of course, as every chess tyro soon learns, *sometimes* strict adherence to conventional strategy leads to disaster.)

The analogy between the game of chess and the "game" of logic problem-solving is very close. The eighteen valid argument forms (plus several rules to be added later) correspond to the rules of chess. They determine which steps (moves) are permitted in an argument or proof. But generally they permit many steps at any given point in a proof, only a very few of which are likely to lead to "winning the game", that is, deriving the conclusion of the argument. A good "logic player" is one who develops a "feel" for good play, perhaps by becoming familiar with a set of strategy principles. Of course principles useful to one person may not be useful to another, due to psychological differences between persons. The few hints given below have proved useful to many students; the reader must decide for himself which, if any, are useful to him.

(However, just as chess strategy principles are not part of the rules of chess, so logic strategy principles are not part of the rules of logic. In fact

---

* Instead of using valid equivalence *argument* forms, many logic texts introduce about ten tautological equivalence *sentence* forms, such as $p \equiv \sim \sim p$, $(p \supset q) \equiv (\sim p \lor q)$, etc., plus a rule of inference permitting inferences from substitution instances of one side of these equivalences to analogous substitution instances of the other side.

Proofs in such a system are almost identical with proofs in our system. In fact, the differences between the two systems are entirely theoretical.

logic strategy belongs not to the context of justification, but rather to the context of discovery, since it does not provide justifications for steps in proofs, but rather serves as a psychological aid in the *discovery* of proofs. The *justification* for the assertion of a line in a proof must always be a valid argument form or rule of inference.)

Consider the argument

1. $[A \lor (\sim B \supset C)] \supset [\sim D \lor (C \cdot E)]$

2. $\sim [\sim D \lor (C \cdot E)]$
     $/ \therefore \sim [A \lor (\sim B \supset C)]$

The beginner is likely to be overwhelmed by the large number of letters in this argument, or perhaps by the complexity of its premises, and thus be unable to discover a proof for it. But if he tries to "see" the premises and conclusion in terms of their major forms, he will discover that the proof is quite simple. Notice that the major connective of the premise on line 1 is an implication, and that that premise has the form $p \supset q$. Now notice that the major connective of line 2 is negation, and that line 2 has the form $\sim q$, since what is negated on line 2 is the consequent (q) of line 1. (So the first two lines of the proof have the forms $p \supset q$ and $\sim q$.) Clearly here is an opportunity to employ the argument form Modus Tollens, to obtain $\sim p$, which in this case is $\sim [A \lor (\sim B \supset C)]$, the desired conclusion. So we have "figured out" a simple proof:

1. $[A \lor (\sim B \supset C)] \supset [\sim D \lor (C \cdot E)]$ p

2. $\sim [\sim D \lor (C \cdot E)]$ $p / \therefore \sim [A \lor (\sim B \supset C)]$

3. $\sim [A \lor (\sim B \supset C)]$ 1, 2 **MT**

A simple proof indeed, once attention is paid to the general forms of the sentences which make up the proof.

Now consider another argument:

1. $\sim (A \lor B)$

2. $\sim A \supset C / \therefore C$

Notice first that the letter B does not occur in the conclusion and that it occurs in the premises only once. Obviously, the information its presence adds to premise 1 is not necessary in deriving the conclusion. A letter that occurs only once in the premises of an argument and not at all in the conclusion is excess baggage, to be gotten rid of, or (if possible) ignored. In this case, we can get rid of the superfluous letter B, thus separating the information it contains (which is not needed to derive the conclusion) from the other information contained in premise 1 (which *is* needed to derive the conclusion). We can do so by means of DeMorgan's Theorem, which should have suggested itself anyway because of the form of the first premise. So the start of our proof should be as follows:

1. $\sim(A \lor B)$ p

2. $\sim A \supset C$ $p / \therefore C$

3. $\sim A \cdot \sim B$ 1, **DeM**

The obvious next step is

4. $\sim A$ 3, **Simp**

thus getting rid of the unwanted letter B. And concluding with

5. C 2, 4 **MP**

Now consider another proof:

1. $C \supset A$ p

2. $M \supset B$ p

3. $B \supset C$ p

4. M $p / \therefore A$

Notice that the letter A, which occurs in the conclusion, is connected to the letter C in one of the premises, and C to B, and B to M. It is often useful to trace the connections between the letters occurring in an argument in this way, starting with the letter (or letters) which occur in the conclusion. And then, having done so, it is often good strategy to begin the proof with the letter (or letters) *most distant from* those in the conclusion, which in this case means beginning with the letter *M*. So in this case, it is good strategy to begin the proof by using lines 2 and 4, which contain the letter *M*, to obtain a new line in the proof, namely line:

5.   *B*   2, 4 **MP**

The proof then continues

6.   *C*   3, 5 **MP**

7.   *A*   1, 6 **MP**

This proof also illustrates the fact that usually it is not useful to use the same line in a proof over and over again. "Fresh information" (unused lines in a proof) usually is more useful. Thus, after line 6 has been written down, every premise has been used in the proof except premise 1. At this point, the information in premise 1 is untapped, unused, while the information on line 6 is fresh, in the sense that it is *psychologically* new information. This is a strong clue that it is time to use line 6, in conjunction with premise 1, as in fact it is used to obtain line 7.

Let's reexamine the proof considered on page 57. That proof went as follows:

1. $\sim(A \lor B)$

2. $\sim A \supset C$ / $\therefore$ *C*

3. $\sim A \cdot \sim B$ 1, **DeM**

4. $\sim A$ 3, **Simp**

5.   *C*   2, 4 **MP**

As stated before, the key to the proof is line 3, obtained by means of DeMorgan's Theorem. But line 4 is interesting also, since it illustrates the use of Simplification, and the power of breaking down large sentences into smaller ones. In general, a letter (or negated letter) alone on a line is very useful in obtaining a desired conclusion. And the most common method for obtaining a letter alone on a line is by means of Simplification.

Finally, in problem solving it is often good strategy to *work backward from the conclusion* as well as forward from the premises. If we work backward from the conclusion and find a sentence which appears derivable from the premises, then we have discovered an intermediate target to aim at, and have divided a relatively difficult task into two easier ones.

Consider the argument

1.	$A \supset B$	p
2.	$C \supset B$	$p \,/\therefore (A \lor C) \supset B$

We can work backward from the conclusion, as follows:

1.	$(A \lor C) \supset B$	p (the conclusion)
2.	$\sim(A \lor C) \lor B$	1, Impl
3.	$(\sim A \cdot \sim C) \lor B$	2, DeM
4.	$B \lor (\sim A \cdot \sim C)$	3, Comm
5.	$(B \lor \sim A) \cdot (B \lor \sim C)$	4, Dist

At this point, we have learned that the conclusion $(A \lor C) \supset B$ is equivalent to $(B \lor \sim A) \cdot (B \lor \sim C)$. So by working backward from the conclusion, we have learned that the problem can be solved by working *forward* from the premises toward the intermediate sentence $(B \lor \sim A) \cdot (B \lor \sim C)$. This turns out to be fairly easy to do, as the following illustrates:

1.	$A \supset B$	p
2.	$C \supset B$	$p \,/\therefore (A \lor C) \supset B$
3.	$\sim A \lor B$	1, Impl
4.	$B \lor \sim A$	3, Comm

5.	$\sim C \lor B$	2, **Impl**
6.	$B \lor \sim C$	5, **Comm**
7.	$(B \lor \sim A) \cdot (B \lor \sim C)$	4, 6 **Conj**

We are now ready to reverse the process of working backward from the conclusion, as follows:

8.	$B \lor (\sim A \cdot \sim C)$	7, **Dist**
9.	$(\sim A \cdot \sim C) \lor B$	8, **Comm**
10.	$\sim (A \lor C) \lor B$	9, **DeM**
11.	$(A \lor C) \supset B$	10, **Impl**

So by working backward from the conclusion as well as forward from the premises, we are able to construct proofs which might otherwise elude us.

It is important to realize that in informally working backward from the conclusion, we must use only the ten *equivalence* inference rules. We cannot use the eight implicational rules in this process because implicational rules are *one directional*, and hence in the construction of the actual proof, the process of working backward from the conclusion would not be reversible.

5

*Common Errors
in Problem
Solving*

There are several kinds of mistakes which beginners are likely to make in deriving proofs for arguments:

Using implicational forms on parts of lines

The valid implicational forms (Nos. 1 through 8) are to be used on *complete lines only*. For instance, we cannot go from

5.	$(A \cdot B) \supset C$	

to

6.	$(A \supset C)$	5, **Simp**

dropping the letter *B* by Simplification. The reason is that the form of this process, namely $(p \cdot q) \supset r / \therefore (p \supset r)$, is *not* the form of Simplification, and, in fact, is an invalid argument form. (An example of an invalid argument which has this form is the following: If George drives an automobile 70 miles per hour, and smashes into a reinforced concrete structure, then he will be killed. Therefore, if George drives an automobile 70 miles per hour, then he will be killed.)

Examples:

The *proper* use of implicational argument forms is illustrated by the following example, once again concerning Simplification:

1. $(A \vee \sim B) \cdot (C \vee \sim A)$ $p / \therefore (A \vee \sim B)$

2. $(A \vee \sim B)$ **1, Simp**

In this case, the " $\cdot$ " in line 1 is the *major connective*. Thus the *whole* of line 1 has the form $(p \cdot q)$ required for the use of the valid argument from Simplification.

Another example of the proper use of implicational forms is the following:

1. $A \supset B$ p

2. $B \supset C$ $p / \therefore A \supset C$

3. $A \supset C$ **1, 2 HS**

This is a correct use of the implicational form Hypothetical Syllogism (**HS**), because **HS** requires that one *whole line* in a proof have the form $(p \supset q)$, and another *whole line* have the form $(q \supset r)$, and this proof does have two such lines, namely line 1, which has the form $(p \supset q)$, and line 2, which has the form $(q \supset r)$. Therefore **HS** permits the assertion of line 3, since that *whole line* has the required form $(p \supset r)$.

However, bear in mind that although the ten equivalences (Nos. 9 through 18) *may* be used on whole lines, just as the implicational forms, they also may be used on parts of lines, as in the following example:

1. $\sim(A \cdot B) \supset C$ $/ \therefore (\sim A \lor \sim B) \supset C$

2. $(\sim A \lor \sim B) \supset C$ 1, **DeM**

The use of equivalence argument forms on parts of lines is justified because their use always leads from a given sentence to an *equivalent* sentence.

Reluctance to use Addition

Even after proving that Addition is a valid argument form, students are reluctant to use it, because they believe that somehow it is "cheating" to be able to "add" letters to a line simply at will. But a little thought about the matter should convince the student that no cheating is involved in the use of Addition. Consider the example:

Art will go. Therefore either Art will go
or Betsy will go.

symbolized as

1. A $/ \therefore A \lor B$

2. $A \lor B$ 1, **Add**

If we accept the sentence "Art will go", then we must also accept the sentence "Either Art will go or Betsy will go", since Art's going alone makes that sentence true, whether Betsy goes or not.

This is sometimes overlooked because increasing the number of letters in a sentence often *adds to* or *strengthens* an assertion (as, for example, when someone says "Art will go", and then amends that statement to say "Art will go *and* Betsy will go"). But when the extra letter is added by means of $\lor$, the assertion is *weakened*, not strengthened. In a sense, the sentence "Art will go" is stronger than the sentence "Art will go or Betsy will go", since from the latter we can infer neither that Art will go nor that

Betsy will go, but rather only the much weaker conclusion that one *or* the other (or both) will go.

The following extreme case nicely illustrates the weakening effect of the use of Addition:

1.	*A*	*p* / ∴ (*A* ∨ ~*A*)
2.	*A* ∨ ~*A*	1, **Add**

In this extreme case, the use of Addition leads to the *weakest possible* kind of assertion, namely a tautology, which has no factual content whatever.

Reluctance to use Distribution

In this case, the reluctance generally stems, not from doubts as to its validity, but rather from inability to spot places where its application will be useful. The following proof contains a typical useful application of Distribution:

1.	(*A* ∨ *B*) ⊃ *C*	*p* / ∴ *A* ⊃ *C*
2.	~(*A* ∨ *B*) ∨ *C*	1, **Impl**
3.	(~*A* · ~*B*) ∨ *C*	2, **DeM**
4.	*C* ∨ (~*A* · ~*B*)	3, **Comm**
5.	(*C* ∨ ~*A*) · (*C* ∨ ~*B*)	4, **Dist** (the crucial use of **Dist**)
6.	(*C* ∨ ~*A*)	5, **Simp**
7.	(~*A* ∨ *C*)	6, **Comm**
8.	(*A* ⊃ *C*)	7, **Impl**

Notice that the use of Distribution is crucial in the process of getting rid of the unwanted letter *B*, which occurs in the premise but not the conclusion. Notice also that it is the *second* of the two distributive equivalence forms which were employed, and that it was employed from *left to right* (that is, the move was from line 4, whose form $[p \lor (q \cdot r)]$ is the form of the *left* side of the second distributive equivalence form, to line 5, whose form $[(p \lor q) \cdot (p \lor r)]$, is the form of the *right* side of that form). This is the most common use of Distribution, because the line obtained in this way always has a " $\cdot$ " as its major connective, and thus has the form $(p \cdot q)$ necessary for the use of Simplification.

Trying to prove what cannot be proved

The number of mistakes of this kind is much too large to catalogue. We consider two such mistakes, committed perhaps because they are very similar to two valid procedures:

Consider the following four argument forms:

1. $(p \lor q) \supset r$
   $/ \therefore p \supset r$

2. $(p \cdot q) \supset r$
   $/ \therefore p \supset r$

3. $p \supset (q \lor r)$
   $/ \therefore p \supset r$

4. $p \supset (q \cdot r)$
   $/ \therefore p \supset r$

The first and fourth of these argument forms are valid. The second and third are *invalid*, as we can prove by truth table analysis.

The important point is not to waste time and effort trying to prove substitution instances of invalid forms. For example, in trying to prove that the argument

1. $(A \cdot B) \supset C$

2. $\sim(\sim B \lor D)$

3. $(C \cdot \sim D) \supset E$ $\qquad\qquad / \therefore A \supset E$

is valid, it is useless to try to derive the sentence $A \supset C$ from line 1 alone since the form of such an inference, namely the form $[(p \cdot q) \supset r]$, $/ \therefore (p \supset r)$ is invalid. The sentence $A \supset C$ *can* be derived in this proof, but *not* from line 1 alone.

Similarly, it is useless to try to derive the sentence $A \supset B$ from the sentence $A \supset (B \lor C)$, since the form of such an inference, namely the form $p \supset (q \lor r)$, $/\therefore (p \supset q)$, is invalid.

Failure to notice the scope of a negation sign

A mistake of this kind is usually merely an oversight; however, it is quite common. In particular, negation signs which negate a whole sentence, or a large unit in a sentence, are misconstrued as negating only one letter. Thus, in a sentence such as $\sim(A \lor B)$, the negation sign sometimes is misconstrued as negating merely the letter A, instead of the whole unit $(A \lor B)$. The remedy for this kind of error is care, plus the realization that a negation sign before a unit set off by parentheses (or brackets) negates that entire unit.

Exercise 4–1:

Using the 18 valid argument forms, prove that the following arguments are valid:

(A)   1. $A \cdot B$

2. $B \supset C$

$/\therefore$ 3. C

(B)   1. $A \supset B$

2. $C \supset A$

3. C

$/\therefore$ 4. B

(C)   1. $A \supset B$

2. $C \cdot A$

$/\therefore$ 3. $B \lor D$

(D)   1. $A \supset B$

2. $\sim(B \cdot C)$

$/\therefore$ 3. $A \supset \sim C$

(E)   1. $(F \supset G) \lor H$

2. $\sim G$

3. $\sim H$

$/\therefore$ 4. $\sim F$

(F)   1. $F \supset G$

2. $\sim(H \cdot G)$

3. H

$/\therefore$ 4. $\sim F$

(G) 1. $\sim(H \lor \sim K)$

2. $L \supset H$

/∴ 3. $L \supset M$

(H) 1. $M \equiv N$

/∴ 2. $\sim N \lor M$

(I) 1. $(A \cdot B) \lor (C \cdot D)$

2. $\sim A$

/∴ 3. C

(J) 1. $D \lor \sim A$

2. $\sim(A \cdot \sim B) \supset \sim C$

3. $\sim D$

/∴ 4. $\sim C$

(K) 1. $(A \cdot B) \supset C$

2. $A \cdot \sim C$

/∴ 3. $\sim B$

(L) 1. $\sim A$

2. $\sim B$

3. $(A \lor B) \equiv C$

/∴ 4. $\sim(C \cdot D)$

(M) 1. $S \lor (\sim R \cdot T)$

2. $R \supset \sim S$

/∴ 3. $\sim R$

(N) 1. $A \supset B$

2. $C \supset D$

3. $(B \lor D) \supset E$

4. $\sim E$

/∴ 5. $\sim(A \lor C)$

(O) 1. $R \supset (\sim A \cdot T)$

2. $B \lor \sim S$

3. $R \lor S$

/∴ 4. $A \supset B$

(P) 1. $A \supset (B \supset C)$

/∴ 2. $(\sim C \cdot D) \supset (B \supset \sim A)$

(Q) 1. $\sim(A \cdot B) \equiv \sim C$

2. $(D \lor E) \supset C$

/∴ 3. $E \supset A$

(R) 1. $D \supset B$

2. $D \supset (B \supset W)$

3. $B \supset (W \supset S)$

/∴ 4. $D \supset S$

(S) 1. $P \supset [(Q \cdot R) \lor S]$

2. $(Q \cdot R) \supset \sim P$

3. $T \supset \sim S$

/∴ 4. $P \supset \sim T$

(T) 1. $K \supset [(L \lor M) \supset R]$

2. $(R \lor S) \supset T$

/∴ 3. $K \supset (M \supset T)$

(U) 1. $(P \lor R) \cdot (P \lor Q)$

2. $(Q \cdot R) \supset (V \supset W)$

3. $\sim W$

4. $\sim [(P \supset S) \supset \sim (S \supset W)]$

/∴ 5. $V \supset S$

(V) 1. $A \supset B$

2. $C \supset D$

/∴ 3. $(A \lor C) \supset (B \lor D)$

(W) 1. $A \equiv B$

2. $\sim (A \cdot \sim R) \supset (A \cdot S)$

/∴ 3. $\sim (B \cdot S) \supset \sim (A \cdot R)$

(X) 1. $\sim [D \cdot \sim (E \lor B)]$

2. $\sim (E \lor F)$

3. $C \supset (E \lor A)$

/∴ 4. $\sim (\sim A \cdot \sim B) \lor \sim (C \lor D)$

Chapter Five

*Sentential
Logic—IV*

1

*Conditional
Proofs*

We now introduce an important new rule to be used in deductive proofs, the **rule of conditional proof**. Except for premises, every line in a given proof is a logical consequence of some previous line in that proof, and hence a logical consequence of one or more of the premises. We might keep track of the premises on which a given line depends, say by listing them to the left of each line, as in the following example:

1	1.	$A \supset B$	p
2	2.	$\sim B$	p
3	3.	$A \vee C$	p / $\therefore$ C
1, 2	4.	$\sim A$	1, 2 **MT**
1, 2, 3	5.	C	3, 4 **DS**

The numbers to the left of line 4 indicate that line 4 depends on the first two premises, and the numbers to the left of line 5 indicate that line 5, the conclusion, depends on all three premises (because it depends on premise 3 and line 4, and line 4 in turn depends on premises 1 and 2).

But we often reason to the conclusion of an argument by means of assumptions not stated as premises of that argument. Here is an example (much simpler than those we ordinarily deal with in daily life, although as a matter of fact it cannot be proved valid by means of the 18 valid argument forms presented in the last chapter):

1. $A \supset B$ $p / \therefore A \supset (A \cdot B)$

where A = "Art went to the show" and B = "Betsy went to the show". We can prove that this argument is valid by reasoning as follows: Assume that Art went to the show, and thus that A is true. Then B also is true, by Modus Ponens. Hence, if A is true, *then* $(A \cdot B)$ is true, i.e., $A \supset (A \cdot B)$ is true.

Now let's put this proof into symbols, keeping track of the premises (including our assumption) on which each line depends:

1	1.	$A \supset B$	$p / \therefore A \supset (A \cdot B)$
2	2.	A	**Assumed Premise** (or simply **AP**)
1, 2	3.	B	1, 2 **MP**
1, 2	4.	$(A \cdot B)$	2, 3 **Conj**

What we have proved so far is that *if A then* $(A \cdot B)$. So we are entitled to assert that

1	5.	$A \supset (A \cdot B)$	2, 4 **Conditional Proof** (or simply **CP**)

The important point to notice is that the conclusion, line 5, depends only on the *original premise*, and not on the assumed premise stated on line 2. This is true because line 5 does not *categorically* assert that $(A \cdot B)$ is the case, but only that $(A \cdot B)$ is the case *on the condition* that A is the case.

(The notation to the right of line 5 indicates that the technique used is that of conditional proof (**CP**) involving an *assumed premise* (an assumption not stated as a premise in the original problem), and lists the line of the assumed premise as well as the last line which depends on the assumed premise.)

Instead of keeping track of the premises to the left of a proof, we introduce a different (and very common) notation, which is illustrated by the same example, as follows:

1.	$A \supset B$		$p \ / \therefore \ A \supset (A \cdot B)$
→2.	A		**AP**
3.	B		1, 2 **MP**
4.	$(A \cdot B)$		2, 3 **Conj**
5.	$A \supset (A \cdot B)$		2, 4 **CP**

The arrow pointing at line 2 indicates that line 2 contains an assumed premise not given as part of the original problem. The line drawn down from line 2 to below line 4 indicates that lines 2, 3, and 4 *depend on* line 2 (in addition to the original premise). And the horizontal line drawn between lines 4 and 5 indicates that the lines to follow *do not* depend on line 2; that is, it indicates that the scope of the assumed premise ends with line 4.

Another way to consider conditional proofs is this. In a sense, *every* valid argument is conditional, since the truth of the conclusion is conditional upon the truth of the premises on which the conclusion depends. What is different about a so-called "conditional" proof is simply that some lines in a conditional proof depend on a line (the assumed premise) on which the conclusion does not depend, a line that was not given as a premise in the original problem. It is as though a line is introduced as a premise, a conclusion is drawn from it (in conjunction with the other premises), and then that premise is "discharged" as a premise, being retained rather as a *condition* on the acceptance of the conclusion, that is, retained as the antecedent of a new conditional conclusion.*

For instance, suppose we know (as in the above example) that if Art

---

* Obviously, once an assumed premise is discharged, we no longer can use it, or any line which depends on it, to derive additional lines. For instance, in the above example, we cannot assert as line 6 the sentence $\sim \sim (A \cdot B)$, following from line 4 by **DN**, since we have already discharged line 2 as a premise.

Sentential Logic

went to the show, then Betsy went also ($A \supset B$), and then are told that Art definitely did go (A). On the basis of this information we can conclude (validly) that Art and Betsy both went to the show ($A \cdot B$). But suppose we then are told that the information that Art went to the show is not reliable; perhaps he went, perhaps not. In that case, we no longer can conclude (validly) that Art and Betsy both went to the show. However, we can reason that since the assumption that Art went to the show (in conjunction with the premise that $A \supset B$) led to the conclusion that Art and Betsy both went to the show, it still is the case that *if* Art went to the show, *then* Art and Betsy both went. That is, it still is the case that $A \supset (A \cdot B)$. A proof of this kind is a *conditional proof*, because it involves temporary use of a premise which is later discharged *as a premise* but retained as the antecedent of a conditional conclusion.

In the above example, only one assumed premise was used. But *any number* of assumptions can be introduced into a proof, provided that every one is eventually discharged, so that the conclusion of the argument depends only on the given premises. And an assumption need not be the antecedent of the conclusion. *Any* assumption may be made, again provided only that it is eventually discharged. Of course it is good strategy to use certain assumed premises and not others, but the *rules of logic* permit the use of any assumed premise later discharged. The following is a typical example:

1.	$A \supset (B \supset C)$	p
2.	$B \supset (C \supset D)$	$p \mathbin{/} \therefore A \supset (\sim D \supset \sim B)$
→3.	A	AP
→4.	B	AP
5.	$B \supset C$	1, 3 MP
6.	C	4, 5 MP
7.	$C \supset D$	2, 4 MP
8.	D	6, 7 MP
9.	$B \supset D$	4, 8 CP
10.	$\sim D \supset \sim B$	9, Contr
11.	$A \supset (\sim D \supset \sim B)$	3, 10 CP

In this example, there are *two* assumed premises, *A* and *B*. One, *A*, is the antecedent of the conclusion, but the other obviously is not. And it is not the antecedent of the (complex) consequent either. Rather it is the antecedent of the *contrapositive** of the consequent. This illustrates two fine points of strategy: first, if the consequent of the conclusion is itself a conditional statement, then it may be useful to have more than one assumed premise; and second, it sometimes is useful to assume the antecedent of the *contrapositive* of a conditional rather than the antecedent of the conditional itself.

Examples:

The following proofs contain correct uses of the rule of conditional proof:

(I)
1.	$A \supset B$	p
2.	$C \vee \sim A$	$p / \therefore A \supset (B \cdot C)$
3.	A	AP
4.	B	1, 3 MP
5.	$\sim \sim A$	3, DN
6.	C	2, 5 DS
7.	$B \cdot C$	4, 6 Conj
8.	$A \supset (B \cdot C)$	3, 7 CP

(II)
1.	$(A \vee B) \supset (C \cdot D)$	p
2.	$(D \vee E) \supset F$	$p / \therefore A \supset F$
3.	A	AP
4.	$A \vee B$	3, Add
5.	$C \cdot D$	1, 4 MP
6.	D	5, Simp

* The *contrapositive* of a given sentence is the sentence obtained from the given sentence by means of contraposition.

Sentential Logic

	7.	$D \vee E$	6, **Add**
	8.	F	2, 7 **MP**
	9.	$A \supset F$	3, 8 **CP**
(III)	1.	$(Z \supset Y) \supset X$	p
	2.	$T \vee S$	p
	3.	$\sim (Z \cdot T)$	p
	4.	$\sim Y \supset \sim S$	p / $\therefore$ X
	5.	Z	**AP**
	6.	$\sim Z \vee \sim T$	3, **DeM**
	7.	$\sim \sim Z$	5, **DN**
	8.	$\sim T$	6, 7 **DS**
	9.	S	2, 8 **DS**
	10.	$S \supset Y$	4, **Contr**
	11.	Y	9, 10 **MP**
	12.	$Z \supset Y$	5, 11 **CP**
	13	X	1, 12 **MP**
(IV)	1.	$(M \vee N) \supset P$	p / $\therefore$ $[(P \vee Q) \supset R] \supset (M \supset R)$
	2.	$(P \vee Q) \supset R$	**AP**
	3.	M	**AP**
	4.	$M \vee N$	3, **Add**
	5.	P	1, 4 **MP**
	6.	$P \vee Q$	5, **Add**
	7.	R	2, 6 **MP**
	8.	$M \supset R$	3, 7 **CP**
	9.	$[(P \vee Q) \supset R] \supset (M \supset R)$	2, 8 **CP**

Using **CP**, prove that in Exercise 4-1 arguments P through T and V through X are valid. (Notice that the use of **CP** tends to make proofs shorter and easier.)

2

Indirect Proofs

We now introduce another powerful rule, permitting a kind of proof called an **indirect proof** (sometimes called a **reductio ad absurdum proof**).

If we derive a contradiction from a given set of premises, then we have proved that at least one of the premises in that set is false. This follows from the fact that we cannot derive false sentences from true ones, plus the fact that contradictions are false sentences. Now consider, say, a four premise argument, and assume we know that three of its four premises are true. Then if we derive a contradiction from that set of four premises, we have proved that the fourth premise in the set is false (since at least one member of the set is false, and we assume that the other three are true). But it follows then that we also have proved that the negation of the fourth premise is true (since the negation of a false sentence is true). We have here the main idea behind the *indirect*, or *reductio ad absurdum, proof*.

For instance, consider the argument

1. $A \supset B$

2. $B \supset C$

3. A $/ \therefore C$

If we add the negation of the conclusion, namely $\sim C$, to the above set of premises, to obtain the set of premises

1. $A \supset B$ *p*

2. $B \supset C$ *p*

3.	A	p
4.	$\sim C$	**AP**

then we can obtain a contradiction as follows:

5.	$\sim B$	2, 4 **MT**
6.	$\sim A$	1, 5 **MT**
7.	$A \cdot \sim A$	3, 5 **Conj**

Obviously, if premises 1, 2, and 3 are true, then the added premise 4, $\sim C$, is false. And if $\sim C$ is false, then C must be true. Hence, we have shown that the argument

1.	$A \supset B$	
2.	$B \supset C$	
3.	A	$/ \therefore C$

is valid, because we have shown that if its premises are true, then its conclusion, C, must be true.

The general method employed in an indirect proof, then, is to add the negation of the conclusion of an argument to its set of premises and derive a contradiction. The derivation of the contradiction proves that if the original premises are true, then the added premise must be false, and consequently proves that if the original premises are true then the *negation* of the added premise must be *true*. Since the negation of the added premise is the conclusion of the argument in question, derivation of the contradiction proves that if the original premises are true then the conclusion must be true, and hence proves that the argument is valid.

Another way to see that the rule of indirect proof is valid involves noticing that an indirect proof is just a special kind of conditional proof.*

---

* Since this is the case, it follows that we don't really need the rule of indirect proof, in that our system is complete without it. We include the rule anyway, because it helps to shorten many proofs and because it has been customary to do so throughout most of the long history of logic, as the name *reductio ad absurdum* suggests.

Consider the following proof:

1.	$A \lor B$	p
2.	$A \supset B$	$p \mathbin{/} \therefore B$
3.	$\sim B$	**AP**
4.	$\sim A$	2, 3 **MT**
5.	A	1, 3 **DS**
6.	$A \cdot \sim A$	4, 5 **Conj**

At this point, the rule of indirect proof permits the assertion of conclusion *B*:

7.	B	3, 6 **IP** (indirect proof)

Line 7 is permitted in an indirect proof because the premise assumed (in line 3) is the negation of the conclusion, *B*; and by means of that assumed premise (plus the original premises) a contradiction was derived.

Step 7 can be shown to be valid by making two things clear:

(1) A contradictory sentence implies any and every sentence. This is illustrated by the following argument:

1.	$A \cdot \sim A$	$p \mathbin{/} \therefore X$
2.	A	1, **Simp**
3.	$A \lor X$	2, **Add**
4.	$\sim A$	1, **Simp**
5.	X	3, 4 **DS**

Obviously, the conclusion *X* might have been *any* sentence whatever. Therefore, from the contradiction $A \cdot \sim A$, indeed from any contradiction, it is clear that *any* sentence whatever can be obtained.

Sentential Logic

(2) Once a contradiction is obtained, the desired conclusion can be obtained by a conditional proof.

Consider the indirect proof again, but this time without the last line:

1.	$A \lor B$	p
2.	$A \supset B$	$p / \therefore B$
→ 3.	$\sim B$	AP
4.	$\sim A$	2, 3 MT
5.	A	1, 3 DS
6.	$A \cdot \sim A$	4, 5 Conj

Suppose now that we treat the proof as an ordinary conditional proof. Then the conclusion B can be derived within the scope of the assumed premise:

7.	B	2, 5 MP

However, the proof is not complete at this point. We have not derived line 7 by means of the original premises alone, because line 7 lies within the scope of the assumed premise $\sim B$. What has been proved is that:

8.	$\sim B \supset B$	3, 7 CP

But from this point it is a simple matter to obtain B:

9.	$\sim \sim B \lor B$	8, Impl
10.	$B \lor B$	9, DN
11.	B	10, Taut

This example illustrates the fact that whenever the negation of the conclusion of an argument is taken as an assumed premise in a conditional proof and a contradiction is derived, then it must be possible to obtain the conclusion of the argument by means of the procedure just illustrated (so that the conclusion depends on the original premises, but not on the assumed premise). But since this *always* can be done, there is little point in *actually* doing so in every case. Instead, we permit the use of the rule of indirect proof, which we now see is simply a shortened form of conditional proof.

In general then, once a contradiction is obtained, the conclusion of an argument can be asserted. Here is another example of an indirect proof:

1.	$A \supset X$	p
2.	$(C \lor \sim X) \supset A$	p / $\therefore X$
3.	$\sim X$	AP (the negation of the conclusion)
4.	$\sim A$	1, 3 MT
5.	$\sim (C \lor \sim X)$	2, 4 MT
6.	$\sim C \cdot \sim \sim X$	5, DeM
7.	$\sim C \cdot X$	6, DN
8.	X	7, Simp
9.	$X \cdot \sim X$	3, 8 Conj
10.	X	3, 9 IP

Notice that the contradiction obtained is simply the conjunction of the assumed premise and the conclusion. This is perfectly permissible; the derivation of *any* explicit contradiction is all that is required. (An *explicit* contradiction is a contradiction having the form $p \cdot \sim p$.) Notice also that the proof does not stop with line 8. The proof must continue because line 8 depends on the assumed premise $\sim X$, so that all that has been proved up to that point is $\sim X \supset X$. But once the explicit contradiction is obtained, the rule of indirect proof permits the assertion of the conclusion *independently* of the assumed premise, since it is clear that the conclusion *could be* derived by means of an ordinary conditional proof.

Example:

Another example of an indirect proof is the following:

1.	$(A \lor B) \supset (C \cdot D)$	p
2.	$\sim(\sim A \lor \sim C)$	p
3.	$\sim(A \supset \sim D) \supset E$	p / $\therefore$ E
→ 4.	$\sim E$	AP (the negation of the conclusion)
5.	$\sim\sim(A \supset \sim D)$	3, 4 **MT**
6.	$(A \supset \sim D)$	5, **DN**
7.	$\sim\sim A \cdot \sim\sim C$	2, **DeM**
8.	$\sim\sim A$	7, **Simp**
9.	A	8, **DN**
10.	$A \lor B$	9, **Add**
11.	$C \cdot D$	1, 10 **MP**
12.	D	11, **Simp**
13.	$\sim D$	6, 9 **MP**
14.	$D \cdot \sim D$	12, 13 **Conj**
15.	E	4, 14 **IP**

Exercise 5–2:

Prove valid, first without using **IP** or **CP**, and then using **IP**, and compare the lengths of the corresponding proofs.

(A)				(B)		
	1.	$A \supset B$			1.	$H \supset (A \supset B)$
	2.	$C \supset A$			2.	$\sim C \supset (H \lor B)$
	3.	$C \lor (B \cdot D)$ / $\therefore$ B			3.	$H \supset A$ / $\therefore$ C $\lor$ B

(C)   1. $P \lor Q$

        2. $Q \supset (R \cdot S)$

        3. $(R \lor P) \supset T$ / $\therefore$ T

(E)   1. $A \supset \sim(B \lor C)$

        2. $\sim D \supset (\sim A \supset \sim E)$

        3. $\sim(\sim E \lor F)$

        4. $\sim F \supset (A \supset B)$ / $\therefore$ D

(D)   1. $(A \lor B) \supset (C \supset \sim D)$

        2. $(D \lor E) \supset (A \cdot C)$ / $\therefore$ $\sim D$

3

Proving
Argument Forms
Invalid

If an argument form is invalid, then it is not possible to construct a valid proof for it. But failure to construct a valid proof does not prove that an argument form is invalid. It may be that such a proof exists, but we were not ingenious enough to find it. Instead, we can prove an argument form invalid by presenting a substitution instance of that form which has true premises and a false conclusion. This follows from the fact that no substitution instance of a valid argument form can have true premises and a false conclusion.

Example:

Argument form

1. $p \supset q$

2. $q \supset r$ / $\therefore$ $r \supset p$

Substitution instance (where **T** is a true sentence, and **F** a false one)

1. F $\supset$ T

2. T $\supset$ T

      T

                                  F

                           / $\therefore$ T $\supset$ F

We have shown here that this substitution instance has true premises and a false conclusion, and hence constitutes an invalid argument. So it follows that the argument form of which it is a substitution instance also is invalid.

4

*Proving
Arguments
Invalid*

It might be thought that an invalid *argument* can be proved invalid by showing that it is a substitution instance of an invalid argument form, just as a valid argument can be proved valid by showing that it is a substitution instance of a valid argument form. But this is not the case, because *every* argument, valid or invalid, is a substitution instance of *some* invalid argument form or other.

Example:

The valid two-premise argument

1. $A \supset B$

2. A $/ \therefore B$

(in fact every two-premise argument) is a substitution instance of the invalid argument form

1. p

2. q $/ \therefore r$

Instead, arguments can be proved invalid by a slightly different method. Consider the invalid argument:

1. $A \supset B$

2. $B \supset C$ $/ \therefore C \supset A$

Its invalidity is not due to the fact that it is a substitution instance of an invalid argument form (since all arguments are), but rather to the fact that it is *not* a substitution instance of *any valid* argument form, for if it were a substitution instance of even one valid argument form, then it would be valid. Therefore, to prove that it is an invalid argument, we must prove that it is not a substitution instance of *any* valid argument form. We can do this by showing that it *is* a substitution instance of a particular invalid argument form, sometimes called its propositional form. The **propositional form** of an argument is the argument form obtained from that argument by replacing each capital letter (sentence constant) in the argument by a small letter (sentence variable), taking care to observe the usual rule that a given capital letter must be replaced by the same small letter throughout the substitution procedure.

Examples:

The propositional form of the argument

1. $A \supset B$

2. $B \supset C$ $/ \therefore C \supset A$

is

1. $p \supset q$

2. $q \supset r$ $/ \therefore r \supset p$

And the propositional form of the argument

1. $(M \cdot N) \supset P$

2. $\sim P$ $/ \therefore P \supset \sim Q$

is

1. $(p \cdot q) \supset r$

2. $\sim r$ $/ \therefore r \supset \sim s$

It can be proved that if the propositional form of a given argument is invalid, then *all* argument forms of which that argument is a substitution instance are invalid, and consequently, the argument itself is invalid. Therefore, to prove that an argument is invalid, prove that its propositional form is invalid. And to prove that its propositional form is invalid, prove that at least one of its substitution instances has true premises and a false conclusion.

Example:

The propositional form of the argument

1. *A* ⊃ *B*

2. *B*   / ∴ *A*

is

1. *p* ⊃ *q*

2. *q*   / ∴ *p*

Let **T** be a true sentence, and **F** a false one, and we can prove quite easily that the substitution instance

1. **F** ⊃ **T**

2. **T**   / ∴ **F**

of the above argument form has true premises and a false conclusion (by means of truth table analysis). Hence the original argument is invalid.

Of course in practice we can simplify this procedure considerably by omitting the middle step involving argument forms.

Example:

Using the simplified method for proving invalidity, we can prove the above argument invalid as follows:

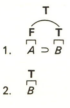

1. $A \supset B$

2. B $/ \therefore A$

This shows that the argument can have true premises and a false conclusion, and therefore demonstrates that it is invalid.

To put it another way, the above method for proving arguments invalid constitutes a method for showing that (whatever the actual truth values of the premises and conclusion of an argument) it *could have* true premises and a false conclusion.

It is interesting to notice what happens when we try to prove a *valid* argument invalid by this method. Consider the argument

1. $[(A \cdot B) \supset \sim C]$

2. C

3. A $/ \therefore \sim B$

In this example, we must assign a **T** to B, in order to falsify the conclusion, and a **T** to A, as well as to C, in order to render the second and third premises true. But notice that if we do so, then we falsify the first premise, as the following indicates:

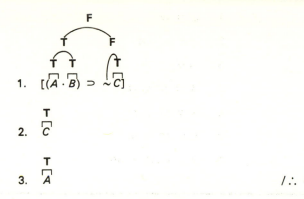

1. $[(A \cdot B) \supset \sim C]$

2. C

3. A

$/ \therefore \sim B$

So there is no way to falsify the conclusion and at the same time render *all* of the premises true. The argument is valid.*

Exercise 5–3:

Prove that the following arguments are invalid:

(A) 1. $A \supset B$

2. $(C \cdot B) \vee D$

$/ \therefore$ 3. A

(B) 1. $A \supset \sim B$

2. $(B \cdot C) \vee A$

$/ \therefore$ 3. $\sim B$

(C) 1. $P \supset Q$

2. $R \supset S$

3. $R \vee Q$

$/ \therefore$ 4. $P \vee S$

---

* Indeed, this method constitutes a mechanical procedure for determining *validity* (as well as invalidity) in propositional logic. For if we prove that there is no way to assign truth values so as to make the conclusion of an argument false and all of its premises true, then we have proved the argument is valid. Unfortunately, this truth table method of proving validity will not work in all cases in the *predicate logic* to be presented in the next chapter.

(D)   1. $A \supset (B \cdot C)$ (E)   1. $Q \supset W$

      2. $\sim D \lor \sim E$ 2. $\sim P \supset \sim W$

      3. $D \supset (A \lor F)$ 3. $\sim N$

      4. $F \supset (C \supset E)$ 4. $W \supset (P \lor Q)$

/∴   5. $F \lor \sim D$ 5. $R \supset (S \lor T)$

                                                            6. $S \supset (Q \lor N)$

                                                      /∴   7. $R \supset (\sim Q \supset W)$

5

Proving
Premises
Inconsistent

In general, logic alone cannot determine the truth values of premises. But if the premises of an argument (taken as a unit) are *contradictory*, that is, *inconsistent*, then at least one of them must be false, and this fact can be proved by logic alone. To prove that an argument has inconsistent (contradictory) premises, derive a contradiction from the premises by means of the eighteen valid argument forms (plus **CP** or **IP**).

Consider an argument whose premises are

   1. $A \supset B$ p

   2. $A \supset \sim B$ p

   3. A p

From these premises we can derive a contradiction, as follows:

   4. B 1, 3 **MP**

   5. $\sim B$ 2, 3 **MP**

   6. $B \cdot \sim B$ 4, 5 **Conj**

Since line 6 is a contradiction, it must be false. And if it is false, then at least one premise must be false, since line 6 follows validly from the premises. Thus, taken together, the premises form a false conjunction.

Sentential Logic

But that conjunction is not contingently false, since its falsehood was proved by logic alone. So it must be false because it is *contradictory*, that is, inconsistent.

We also can prove that a set of premises is inconsistent by truth table analysis. For instance, we can do so for the above argument, as follows:

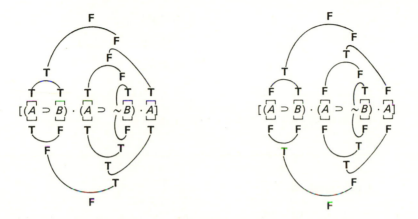

However, the method of truth table analysis often is quite tedious, and cannot be employed in the predicate logic to be introduced in the next chapter. So it is preferable to prove that the premises of an argument are inconsistent by deriving an explicit contradiction from them.

Examples:

(I)

1.	$P \supset Q$	p
2.	$P \cdot \sim Q$	p
3.	P	2, **Simp**
4.	Q	1, 3 **MP**
5.	$\sim Q$	2, **Simp**
6.	$Q \cdot \sim Q$	4, 5 **Conj**

(Therefore, the premises are inconsistent.)

(II)   1. $(A \lor B) \supset C$ p

        2. $B \cdot D$ p

        3. $\sim C$ p

        4. $\sim(A \lor B)$ 1, 3 **MT**

        5. $\sim A \cdot \sim B$ 4, **DeM**

        6. B 2, **Simp**

        7. $\sim B$ 5, **Simp**

        8. $B \cdot \sim B$ 6, 7 **Conj**

(Therefore, the premises are inconsistent.)

Exercise 5–4:

Prove that the following arguments all have inconsistent premises:

(A)   1. $A \cdot \sim B$

       2. $B \supset A$

       3. $A \supset B \ / \therefore B$

(B)   1. $\sim A \lor B$

       2. $\sim B \lor \sim A$

       3. $A \ / \therefore B$

(C)   1. $A \supset (B \lor C)$

       2. $\sim(\sim A \lor C)$

       3. $\sim B \ / \therefore C$

(D)   1. $A \supset (C \supset B)$

       2. $(B \cdot C) \lor A$

       3. $C \lor (B \cdot A)$

       4. $B \supset \sim C$

       5. $D \lor B$

       6. $B \cdot \sim A \ / \therefore B \lor (A \supset D)$

(E)   1. $A \supset (B \supset C)$

       2. $\sim[\sim C \lor (A \lor \sim D)]$

       3. $\sim\{\sim A \lor [C \supset (B \cdot D)]\}$

           $/ \therefore (A \lor C) \supset D$

6

Proving Premises Consistent

An *argument form* has *consistent premises* (that is, noncontradictory premises) if at least one of its substitution instances has all true premises. Consequently, to prove that an argument form has consistent premises, find and present one such substitution instance.

Example:

Suppose the premises of an argument form are:

1. $p \supset q$ p
2. $p \supset \sim q$ p

Then we can prove that these premises are consistent by presenting the following substitution instance, where **F** is a false sentence:

Since both premises of this substitution instance are true, its premises, as well as the premises of the argument form of which it is a substitution instance, are consistent.

To prove that an *argument* has consistent premises, we need only show that its *propositional form* has consistent premises.

Example:

Consider the premises of the following argument:

1. $A \supset B$

2. $A \supset \sim B$ $/ \therefore \sim A$

The propositional form of this argument is:

1. $p \supset q$

2. $p \supset \sim q$ $/ \therefore \sim p$

But we already know that there is a substitution instance of this form with true premises, namely

1. $F \supset F$

2. $F \supset \sim F$ $/ \therefore \sim F$

where F is some false sentence. Consequently, the premises of the original argument are consistent.

Of course, in practice we can simplify this procedure by omitting the step involving argument forms.

Example:

Using the simplified method, we can prove that the premises

1. $A \supset B$

2. $A \supset \sim B$

of an argument are consistent as follows:

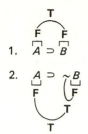

1. $A \supset B$

2. $A \supset \sim B$

Exercise 5–5:

Prove that the following sets of premises are consistent:

(A)
1. $B \supset A$
2. $C \supset B$
3. $\sim C \cdot A$

(B)
1. $A \cdot \sim B$
2. $B \lor \sim C$
3. $\sim (\sim C \cdot B)$

(C)
1. $(A \lor B) \supset \sim C$
2. $C \supset A$
3. $D \supset C$

(D)
1. $A \supset (B \cdot \sim C)$
2. $D \supset E$
3. $\sim (\sim D \lor F)$
4. $D \supset (A \lor C)$
5. $C \supset (\sim F \supset \sim C)$

(E)
1. $P \supset (\sim D \supset Q)$
2. $\sim [(Q \lor \sim R) \cdot (\sim P \lor D)]$
3. $\sim P \lor [\sim D \supset (Q \supset R)]$

7

**Material
Implication and
Valid Argument
Forms**

Recall that in the discussion of material implication in Chapter Two, it was pointed out that most implications used in daily life are not truth-functional. Nevertheless, we introduced the truth-functional implication, *material implication*, and gave reasons for defining it as we did.

Now we are able to provide another, perhaps even stronger, reason for translating implications by means of material implication, and for using the particular truth table definition of material implication given in Chapter Two. The reason is that we want intuitively valid arguments and argument forms to remain valid when translated into our notation, and we want intuitively invalid arguments and argument forms to remain invalid. If we use any other truth table definition for implication, then we will be unable to attain this goal.

To illustrate this fact, we shall consider the following four argument forms:

(I)   1.   If p then q*

      2. p $/ \therefore \sim q$

(II)   1.   If p then q

      2. p $/ \therefore q$

(III)   1.   If p then q

      2. $\sim p$ $/ \therefore \sim q$

(IV)   1.   If p then q

      2. $\sim p$ $/ \therefore q$

The first of these argument forms is obviously invalid. Symbolizing its first premise by means of material implication (defined as in Chapter Two), we can prove that argument form (I) is invalid by truth table analysis, as follows:

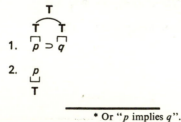

---

* Or "p implies q".

Notice however, that this truth table proof makes use of the fact that there is a **T** on *line 1* of the truth table for material implication. If there were an **F**, then we could not prove that (I) is invalid. On the contrary, we could prove it valid as follows:

		First Premise	Second Premise	Conclusion
p	*q*	*p ⊃ q*	*p*	*~ q*
T	T	F	T	F
T	F	F	T	T
F	T	T	F	F
F	F	T	F	T

(This truth table would prove that (I) is valid, because it would indicate that none of its substitution instances can have true premises and a false conclusion, since it would indicate that *both* premises of such a substitution instance can never be true simultaneously.)

So we cannot place an **F** on line 1 of the truth table for material implication. Instead, we must place a **T** on that line, in order to preserve the invalidity of certain intuitively invalid argument forms.

Now consider argument form (II) above. This argument form, Modus Ponens, obviously is valid. Indeed, if we allow symbolization of its first premise by means of material implication, then we have already proved that it is valid by truth table analysis. Of course, the truth table proof made use of the fact that there is an **F** on *line 2* of the truth table given for material implication. If there were a **T**, then we could not prove Modus Ponens valid. Indeed, we could prove it *invalid* by truth table analysis, as follows:

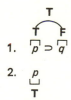

1.

2.

$/ \therefore \overline{q}$ **F**

So it is clear that we cannot allow a **T** on line 2 of the truth table for material implication. Instead, we must place an **F** on that line, in order to preserve the validity of certain valid argument forms (such as Modus Ponens).

Next, consider argument form (III) above. This form obviously is not valid. In fact, its invalidity has been so infamous in the history of philosophy that reasoning which has this form has acquired a special title of its own, namely "fallacy of denying the antecedent". Symbolizing the first premise of (III) by means of material implication, defined as in Chapter Two, we can prove that (III) is invalid by means of truth table analysis, as follows:

1. $p \supset q$

2. $\sim p$

$/\therefore \sim q$

But again, this truth table proof makes use of the particular truth table given for material implication, in this case making use of the fact that there is a **T** on *line 3* of that truth table. If there were an **F**, then we could not prove that (III) is invalid. On the contrary, we could prove it valid, as follows:

p	q	First Premise $p \supset q$	Second Premise $\sim p$	Conclusion $\sim q$
T	T	T	F	F
T	F	F	F	T
F	T	F	T	F
F	F	T	T	T

(This truth table would prove the argument form in question valid, because it would indicate that none of its substitution instances could have true premises and a false conclusion.)

So it is clear that we cannot allow an **F** on line 3 of the truth table for material implication. Instead, we must place a **T** on that line, in order to preserve the invalidity of certain intuitively invalid argument forms.

Sentential Logic

Finally, consider argument form (IV) above. Clearly, this form also is not valid. Symbolizing the first premise of (IV) by means of material implication defined as in Chapter Two, we can prove that (IV) is invalid by truth table analysis, as follows:

1. $\overset{\displaystyle T}{\overset{\displaystyle \overset{F\qquad F}{\frown}}{\overline{p} \supset \overline{q}}}$

2. $\underset{\displaystyle T}{\overset{\displaystyle \sim p}{\underset{F}{\sqcup}}}$

$/ \therefore \overset{\displaystyle F}{\overline{q}}$

But, as before, this truth table analysis makes use of the particular truth table given for material implication, in this case making use of the fact that the *fourth line* of that truth table contains a T. If there were an F on that line, then we could not prove (IV) invalid. On the contrary, we could prove it valid, as follows:

		First Premise	Second Premise	Conclusion
p	q	$p \supset q$	$\sim p$	q
T	T	T	F	T
T	F	F	F	F
F	T	T	T	T
F	F	F	T	F

It follows that we cannot allow an F on line 4 of the truth table for material implication. We must place a T on that line in order to preserve the invalidity of certain intuitively invalid argument forms.

The general conclusion to be drawn from the four examples above is that we must use material implication, defined as it was in Chapter Two, to assure that our translations of certain valid arguments and argument forms will be valid, and to assure that our translations of certain invalid arguments and argument forms will be invalid.

Part Two Chapter Six

Predicate Logic Predicate Logic—I

The propositional logic presented in the first five chapters deals with the internal structure of compound sentences, but *not* with the internal structure of atomic sentences. We now develop a logical system, called **predicate logic**, **functional logic**, or **quantifier logic**, which deals with the interior structure of atomic as well as compound sentences.

Predicate logic provides a method for proving the validity of many valid arguments which are invalid when symbolized in the notation of sentential logic. For example, the standard syllogism

1. All humans are mortal.

2. All Greeks are human.   / ∴ All Greeks are mortal.

must be symbolized in sentential logic in some way such as

1. *A*

2. *B*   / ∴ *C*

Symbolized in this way, the argument clearly is invalid. But certainly there is some wider sense of validity according to which this syllogism is valid, and this wider sense is captured by predicate logic.

1

Individuals and Properties

Consider the sentence "Art is happy". This sentence asserts that some particular object or entity, Art, has a certain property, namely the property of being happy. If we let the capital letter *H* denote the property of being happy, and let the small letter *a* name the individual, Art, we can symbolize this sentence as *Ha*. Similarly, the sentence "Betsy is happy" can be symbolized as *Hb*, the sentence "Art is friendly" as *Fa*, and the sentence "Betsy is friendly" as *Fb*. The sentences *Fa*, *Fb*, *Ha*, and *Hb* are alike in that they have the same general structure. In each of these sentences a *property* is ascribed to some *individual entity*. This is one of the basic patterns of atomic sentences.

Another basic pattern is illustrated by the sentence "Art is taller than Betsy". This sentence asserts that there is a particular property (_____ being taller than _ _ _ _ _ _) which holds *between* two individual objects, namely between Art and Betsy. If we let *a* denote Art, *b* Betsy, and *T* the property of one thing being taller than another, we can symbolize the sentence "Art is taller than Betsy" as *Tab*. Similarly, we can symbolize the sentence "Betsy is taller than Art" as *Tba*. And if we let *F* denote the property of being a friend of (_____ is a friend of _ _ _ _ _ _), then we can symbolize the sentence "Art is a friend of Betsy" as *Fab*, and so on.

Properties such as *taller than* and *is a friend of*, which hold between two or more entities, are called **relational properties**. The particular properties in question are *two place* relational properties, since they hold between two entities. But we can also have three, four, etc., place properties. For instance the property of being between two other objects (_____ is between _ _ _ _ _ _ and ....) is a *three place* relational property.

In some respects, the above analysis of the structure of atomic sentences is very much like those given in traditional grammar texts. For instance, a traditional grammar text would analyze the sentence "Art is human" as containing a *subject*, "Art", and a *predicate*, "is human". (Indeed, the term "predicate" is often used by logicians instead of the term "property". Hence the name "predicate logic".) However, traditional grammars generally analyze *all* atomic sentences into this subject-predicate form. For instance, they construe the sentence "Art is taller than Betsy" as ascribing a predicate, being taller than Betsy, to a subject, Art. This is quite different from our analysis, for our analysis construes the sentence "Art is taller than Betsy" as concerning *two* subjects (or two individual objects or entities), namely Art and Betsy, and construes that sentence as stating that a relational predicate (or property) holds *between* them. Of course we also can construe the sentence "Art is taller than Betsy" as ascribing the nonrelational property of being-taller-than-Betsy to Art, in which case that sentence will be symbolized as Ta, but to do so is to mask part of the structure of that sentence.

We shall now be more specific about the two notational conventions introduced above. First, *capital letters* will be used to denote properties, whether relational or nonrelational. And second, *small letters* (up to and including the letter t) will be used to denote individual objects, things, entities, etc., that is, any things that can have properties ascribed to them about which we wish to speak. (The one exception is properties themselves. For the time being we rule out sentences which ascribe properties to properties themselves.)

These two new notational conventions are to be used in addition to those previously introduced. We still allow the use of capital letters as sentence abbreviations, and the use of the small letters from p through z as sentence variables, just as in propositional logic.

Capital letters used to denote properties are called **property constants**, and small letters (up to and including t) used to denote things, objects, individual entities, etc., are called **individual constants**. (We reserve the small letters u through z for use as **individual variables**, replaceable by individual constants. Their use is explained on p. 99.)

Examples:

Let H denote the property of honesty, B the property of beauty, a Art, and b Betsy. Then the following expressions are sentences:

1. Ha (Art is honest.)

2. Bb (Betsy is beautiful.)

3. $Ha \cdot Bb$ (Art is honest and Betsy is beautiful.)

4. $Ha \lor Bb$ (Art is honest or Betsy is beautiful.)

5. $Ha \supset Bb$ (If Art is honest then Betsy is beautiful.)

6. $\sim (Hb \cdot \sim Bb)$ (It is not the case that Betsy is both honest and not beautiful.)

7. $Bb \supset \sim (Ha \cdot Hb)$ (If Betsy is beautiful then it is not the case that both Art and Betsy are honest.)

In developing a predicate logic, we are not abandoning the propositional logic previously developed, but rather including it within predicate logic. Hence we can have mixed sentences. An example is the sentence "Art will go to the show and Betsy is beautiful" symbolized as $A \cdot Bb$. Of course we also can symbolize that sentence so as to reveal the structure of the two atomic sentences "Art will go to the show" and "Betsy is beautiful", as $Sa \cdot Bb$. And we also can symbolize it as $Sa \cdot B$. This illustrates the fact, pointed out before, that letters can serve more than one function. For instance, the letter B in this example serves in one place as a sentence constant and in another as a property constant. This ambiguity is harmless because it is clear in every case which function a letter is serving. A property constant always occurs with some letter next to it, while a sentence constant never does.

The expression formed by combining a property constant and an individual constant is a sentence. The sentence Ha referred to above is an example. It has a truth value, namely the value **T** if Art is indeed honest, and **F** if he is not. But what about the expression formed by combining a property constant with an *individual variable*, say the form Hx? In the first place, this form is not a sentence, since x is a variable. (Writing Hx is like writing $H\_\_$, where the solid line serves as a place holder, to be filled in by an individual constant.) So the form Hx is neither true nor false. But in the second place, since we can obtain a sentence from Hx by replacing the variable x with a small letter denoting some object or entity, Hx is a *sentence form*. For instance, the substitution instance Ha, obtained from the sentence form Hx by replacing x with a, is a sentence.

Examples:

The following are examples of sentence forms and some of their substitution instances which are sentences:

Sentence Form	Sentence
1. *Hy*	1. *Hb*
2. *Bx* ⊃ *Hy*	2. *Bb* ⊃ *Ha*
3. (*Hx* · *Bx*) ⊃ *Hy*	3. (*Hb* · *Bb*) ⊃ *Ha*

Of course each of the above sentence forms has many other substitution instances which are sentences. For instance, the second sentence form, *Bx* ⊃ *Hy*, also has the following substitution instances which are sentences: *Bb* ⊃ *Hb*, *Ba* ⊃ *Hb*, *Ba* ⊃ *Ha*, and *Ba* ⊃ *Hc*.

2

Quantifiers

In sentential logic, to obtain a sentence from a sentence form, we have to replace all of the sentence variables in the sentence form by sentence constants. Thus from the sentence form *p* ⊃ *q* we obtain the sentence *A* ⊃ *B*, as well as many others. In predicate logic this also can be done, as was explained above. Thus from the sentence form *Hx* we obtain the sentence *Hb*. However, it is a fact of fundamental importance (both for logic and for philosophy in general) that in predicate logic a sentence can be obtained from a sentence form *without* replacing its individual variables by individual constants. For example, we can obtain a sentence from the sentence form *Hx* without specifying some particular entity which has the property *H*, by specifying instead *how many* entities we want to assert have that property. This idea is familiar from its use in ordinary English. For instance, in English we can form a sentence by ascribing the property of honesty to a particular man. The sentence "Art is honest" is an example. But we can also form a sentence by saying *how many* men are honest. The sentences "All men are honest" and "Some men are honest" are examples.

In predicate logic there are three principal degrees of "how many" which can be expressed, namely *all*, *some*, and *none*.* By "some" is meant "at least one", and any amount between none and all is considered to be some. Thus the sentences "Almost all men are honest", "Some men are honest", "At least one man is honest", etc., all are symbolized in the same way.

Now let's introduce two new symbols, called **quantifiers**, used in stating how many. The first is the **universal quantifier**, used to assert that *all* entities have some property or properties. The symbols (x), (y), etc., that is, individual variables placed between parentheses, are used for this purpose. Thus to symbolize the sentence "Everything moves", start with the sentence form Mx and prefix the universal quantifier (x), to obtain the sentence $(x)(Mx)$, read as "For all x, x moves", or "For all x, Mx" or "Given any x, Mx", etc.

Just how many x's constitute all depends on how many things we want our language to be able to deal with. For instance, in some systems for arithmetic, we want the individual constants to denote numbers, so that in such a system the number of x's will be infinite. The **domain of discourse** for a system for arithmetic would be (so to speak) the "world of numbers". Usually, the domain of discourse is not explicitly specified, but is assumed implicitly to be "everything", or perhaps all concrete (as opposed to abstract) things.

The notation of predicate logic can be used to symbolize sentences which are more complex than the ones so far considered. For example, the sentence "All humans are mortal", of syllogistic fame, can be symbolized as $(x)(Hx \supset Mx)$ (where H = "human", and M = "mortal"). This sentence can be read "For all x, if x is human, then x is mortal", or "Given any x, if x is human then x is mortal", which is roughly what the sentence "All humans are mortal" asserts. Notice that "All humans are mortal" is *not* symbolized as $(x)(Hx \cdot Mx)$, for that says that given any x, it is *both* human *and* mortal, or, what amounts to the same thing, that all things are both human and mortal, and this is not what the sentence "All humans are mortal" means.

---

* Of course, there are variations on these three, for instance, "not all", "all _____ are not _ _ _ _ _ _", etc.

Examples:

The following are examples of English sentences and their correct symbolization in the predicate notation (using obvious abbreviations):

English Sentence	Symbolization
1. (All)* sugar tastes sweet.	1. $(x)(Sx \supset Tx)$
2. If something is a piece of sugar, then it tastes sweet.	2. $(x)(Sx \supset Tx)$
3. Everything is either sweet or bitter.	3. $(x)(Sx \vee Bx)$
4. Either everything is sweet or else everything is bitter.	4. $(x)Sx \vee (x)Bx$

(Notice that 3 and 4 are *not* equivalent.)

5. Not everything is movable.	5. $\sim(x)Mx$
6. Nothing is movable.	6. $(x) \sim Mx$
7. Everything is immovable.	7. $(x) \sim Mx$

(Notice that 6 and 7 *are* equivalent.)

8. All tall humans are friendly.	8. $(x)[(Tx \cdot Hx) \supset Fx]$
9. If all tall humans are friendly, then so is John.	9. $(x)[(Tx \cdot Hx) \supset Fx] \supset Fj$
10. If all humans are mortal, then so are all dogs.	10. $(x)(Hx \supset Mx) \supset (x)(Dx \supset Mx)$
11. All humans are either friendly or liars.	11. $(x)[Hx \supset (Fx \vee Lx)]$
12. It is not the case that all humans are either friendly or liars.	12. $\sim\{(x)[Hx \supset (Fx \vee Lx)]\}$

* In English, the quantifiers "all" and "some" often are omitted when context makes it clear what is being asserted.

Of course, there is nothing sacred about the variable x. For instance, the sentence "Sugar tastes sweet" can be symbolized as $(y)(Sy \supset Ty)$ or $(z)(Sz \supset Tz)$, just as well as $(x)(Sx \supset Tx)$. All three of these sentences say the same thing. (In math we can write $(y + z) = (z + y)$ just as well as $(x + y) = (y + x)$; both of these formulas say the same thing.)

In sentential logic, parentheses are used to remove ambiguity. For instance, the parentheses in the sentence $\sim(A \cdot B)$ indicate that the negation sign negates the whole compound sentence, and not just the atomic sentence A. The parentheses indicate the *scope* of the negation sign, that is, how much of the sentence the negation sign negates.

In predicate logic parentheses serve a similar function. For instance, in the symbolization $(x)(Hx \supset Mx)$, the second set of parentheses indicates that the *scope* of the (x) quantifier is the entire remaining part of the sentence, namely $(Hx \supset Mx)$. Similarly, the scope of the (x) quantifier in the sentence $(x)[(Hx \cdot Fx) \supset Mx]$ is indicated by the set of square brackets, and is the remaining portion of the sentence.

In general then, the *scope* of a quantifier is the extent of a formula *bound* by that quantifier, and is indicated by parentheses (or brackets). However, to simplify matters, we permit parentheses to be omitted if the scope of a quantifier only extends over the next minimal sentence form or atomic sentence. For example, the sentence "Everything is heavy" can be symbolized as $(x)(Hx)$, or as $(x)Hx$ (omitting the second set of parentheses).

The linguistic form $(x)Hx$ is a sentence, but the form Ky is not. What about the form $(x)Hx \supset Ky$? The answer is that it is *not* a sentence, because it contains an individual variable which is not quantified, namely the variable y. Unquantified variables are said to be **free variables**. Quantified variables, such as x in the above example, are said to be **bound variables**. If a linguistic form contains one or more free variables, then it is not a sentence.

The form $(x)Hx \supset Kx$ also is not a sentence, since the second x in this expression is free. If we want both x variables to be bound, we must write the expression as $(x)(Hx \supset Kx)$.

Finally, it should be noted that merely being within the scope of *any* quantifier is not sufficient to make a variable a *bound* variable. To be bound in this sense, a variable must be within the scope of a quantifier using the same letter. Thus the y in $(x)(Fy \supset Gx)$ is not bound, although it is within the scope of the (x) quantifier.

We now introduce a second kind of quantifier, the **existential quantifier**, used to assert that *some* entities, or at least one entity, etc., have a given property. The symbol "$(\exists x)$" is used for this purpose. Thus to symbolize the sentence "Something is heavy", or the sentence "At least one thing is heavy", etc., start with the sentence form Hx and prefix an existential quantifier to it. The result is the sentence $(\exists x)Hx$, read "There is an x such that x is heavy", or "For some x, x is heavy", etc.

In the above explanation of quantified sentences, we construed quantifiers as stating *how many*. But there is another, and perhaps more revealing, way to construe sentences symbolized by means of quantifiers—namely as condensed versions of much longer sentences of a certain kind.

Imagine a limited universe containing, say, only four individual entities. What would quantified sentences assert in such a universe? For instance, what would the sentence $(x)Fx$ assert? The answer is that it would assert that *Fa and Fb and Fc and Fd*. In other words, it would assert that $(Fa \cdot Fb) \cdot (Fc \cdot Fd)$. Thus in this limited universe, the symbolization $(x)Fx$ would be shorthand for the expression $(Fa \cdot Fb) \cdot (Fc \cdot Fd)$, called the **expansion** of $(x)Fx$ with respect to that limited universe.

But of course our logic is applicable to the real universe, which contains many more than four individual entities. Can we construe quantified sentences in a universally applicable logic as a shorthand way of writing very long conjunctions? The answer is that we *could* construe them in this way *if* (1) there were only a finite number of entities in the real universe, and (2) we had a name in our language for every entity. But unfortunately, we do not have a name for every entity in the real universe of discourse, and the number of entities we want to talk about is not finite. For instance, in arithmetic, we want to be able to assert the sentence "Every even number is divisible by 2", i.e., assert that 2 is divisible by 2, *and* 4 is divisible by 2, *and* 6 is divisible by 2, etc. But since the number of numbers is infinite, we cannot actually write down a conjunction equivalent to the sentence "Every even number is divisible by 2". Instead we must use a universal quantifier to symbolize that sentence. (For instance, using obvious abbreviations, we can symbolize it as $(x)[(Nx \cdot Ex) \supset Dx]$.) And so we cannot say that a universally quantified sentence is *equivalent* to any very long conjunction which we might construct.

Nevertheless, it is intuitively helpful to think of sentences such as $(x)Fx$, $(x)(Hx \supset Mx)$, etc., as shorthand for very long conjunctions.

Now consider a sentence containing an *existential* quantifier, say the sentence $(\exists x)Fx$. In a limited universe containing only four objects, this sentence would assert *not* that *Fa and Fb and Fc and Fd* (since that is what is asserted by $(x)Fx$, but rather that *Fa or Fb or Fc or Fd*. So its expansion in this limited universe would be $[(Fa \lor Fb) \lor (Fc \lor Fd)]$.

Examples:

The following are expansions in a language containing four individual constants:

Quantified Symbolization	Expansion
1. $(\exists x)(Fx \cdot Gx)$	1. $[(Fa \cdot Ga) \lor (Fb \cdot Gb)]$ $\lor [(Fc \cdot Gc) \lor (Fd \cdot Gd)]$
2. $(\exists x)[Fx \lor (Gx \cdot Hx)]$	2. $\{[Fa \lor (Ga \cdot Ha)]$ $\lor [Fb \lor (Gb \cdot Hb)]\}$ $\lor \{[Fc \lor (Gc \cdot Hc)]$ $\lor [Fd \lor (Gd \cdot Hd)]\}$
3. $\sim(\exists x)Fx$	3. $\sim[(Fa \lor Fb) \lor (Fc \lor Fd)]$

or, applying De Morgan's law,

$$[(\sim Fa \cdot \sim Fb) \cdot (\sim Fc \cdot \sim Fd)]$$

4. $(x)[(Fx \cdot Gx) \supset \sim Hx]$	4. $\{[(Fa \cdot Ga) \supset \sim Ha] \cdot [(Fb \cdot Gb) \supset \sim Hb]\} \cdot \{[(Fc \cdot Gc) \supset \sim Hc] \cdot [(Fd \cdot Gd) \supset \sim Hd]\}$

One of the common errors in symbolizing concerns sentences of the form "Some _____ are _____", for example, the sentence "Some humans are mortal". The correct symbolization for this sentence is $(\exists x)(Hx \cdot Mx)$, because the sentence asserts that there is something, x, which is both human and mortal. The temptation is to symbolize that sentence as $(\exists x)(Hx \supset Mx)$, by analogy with the symbolization of the sentence "All humans are mortal", which is correctly symbolized as $(x)(Hx \supset Mx)$. But in this case the similarity of structure of the two

English sentences is misleading. (Sentences having the same form as $(\exists x)(Hx \supset Mx)$ are rarely spoken in everyday life.)

To see the difference between the sentence $(\exists x)(Hx \cdot Mx)$ and the sentence $(\exists x)(Hx \supset Mx)$, examine their expansions, namely $[(Ha \cdot Ma) \lor (Hb \cdot Mb)] \lor \ldots$ and $[(Ha \supset Ma) \lor (Hb \supset Mb)] \lor \ldots$ (The dots are used in the sense of "and so on", or "etc.", since we cannot in fact completely write down an infinitely long conjunction or disjunction.) The expansion $[(Ha \cdot Ma) \lor (Hb \cdot Mb)] \lor \ldots$ is true because there are some things which are both human and mortal, but the expansion $[(Ha \supset Ma) \lor (Hb \supset Mb)] \lor \ldots$ would be true even if there were no humans at all, mortal or immortal. The reason it would be true is this: Suppose "a" denotes some piece of chalk. Then the disjunct $Ha \supset Ma$ is true, since its antecedent Ha is false. Therefore, since one of its disjuncts is true, the whole long disjunction $[(Ha \supset Ma) \lor (Hb \supset Mb)] \lor \ldots$ is true. Its truth, so to speak, has nothing to do with the mortality of human beings; it would be true even if there were no human beings in the entire universe. But the expansion $[(Ha \cdot Ma) \lor (Hb \cdot Mb)] \lor \ldots$ would *not* be true if there were no human beings, since if that were the case, then all of its disjuncts would be false. (For instance, if there were no human beings in the universe, then $Ha \cdot Ma$ and $Hb \cdot Mb$ and $Hc \cdot Mc$, and indeed *every* disjunct of the infinitely long disjunction in question would be false, and so the infinitely long disjunction itself would be false.)

Examples:

The following examples of symbolizations of English sentences illustrate the correct use of the existential quantifier:

Sentences	Symbolizations
1. Some things are human, and some are mortal.	1. $(\exists x)Hx \cdot (\exists x)Mx$
2. Some mortal humans are tall.	2. $(\exists x)[(Hx \cdot Mx) \cdot Tx]$
3. Some things are both human and mortal.	3. $(\exists x)(Hx \cdot Mx)$
4. It is not the case that some things are human.	4. $\sim (\exists x)Hx$
5. Some things are not human.	5. $(\exists x) \sim Hx$

Predicate Logic

(Notice that sentences 4 and 5 are *not* equivalent.)

6. If some humans are mortal, then Art is mortal.

6. $(\exists x)(Hx \cdot Mx) \supset Ma$

7. There is something such that if it is placed in water, then it will dissolve.

7. $(\exists x)(Px \supset Dx)$

(Sentence 7 is an example of the kind of sentence which is rarely uttered in everyday life.)

Sentences can occur with mixed quantifiers. An example is the sentence "There is something larger than everything", symbolized as $(\exists x)(y)Lxy$, and read "There is some x such that for all y, x is larger than y". (Of course, this sentence is false, since there is nothing larger than itself. But it is meaningful, and so we want to have a way to symbolize it.)

Notice that this example utilizes a **relational property** or **relational predicate**, specifically a *two place* relational property, since it holds between two entities.

We can also have sentences with two or more quantifiers of the same kind. An example is the sentence "Everyone loves everyone", symbolized as $(x)(y)[(Px \cdot Py) \supset Lxy]$, and read "For all x, and for all y, if x is a person and y is a person, then x loves y", or "Given any x and any y, if both x and y are persons, then x loves y", etc.

And we can have sentences with *three place*, or *four place*, etc., relational predicates. An example is the sentence "Art is sitting *between* Betsy and Judith", symbolized as *Babj*.

Examples:

The following are several other examples of sentences with multiple quantifiers:

Sentences	Symbolizations
1. Everyone loves someone (or other).	1. $(x)[Px \supset (\exists y)(Py \cdot Lxy)]$
2. Someone loves someone (or other).	2. $(\exists x)[Px \cdot (\exists y)(Py \cdot Lxy)]$

3. Someone loves everyone.

4. No one loves everyone.

5. No one loves anyone.

6. If someone is shy, then someone loves someone (or other).

3. $(\exists x)[Px \cdot (y)(Py \supset Lxy)]$

4. $\sim(\exists x)[Px \cdot (y)(Py \supset Lxy)]$, or
$(x)[Px \supset (\exists y)(Py \cdot \sim Lxy)]$

5. $\sim(\exists x)[Px \cdot (\exists y)(Py \cdot Lxy)]$, or
$(x)[Px \supset \sim(\exists y)(Py \cdot Lxy)]$

6. $(\exists x)(Px \cdot Sx) \supset (\exists y)[Py \cdot (\exists z)(Pz \cdot Lyz)]$

3

Proving Arguments Valid in Predicate Logic

The proof technique of propositional logic, involving the eighteen valid argument forms plus **CP** and **IP**, is incorporated into predicate logic intact. For example, the following proof can occur within predicate logic:

1. $Fa \supset Ga$ p

2. Fa $p\ /\therefore\ Ga$

3. Ga 1, 2 **MP**

Notice that in the use of Modus Ponens in this proof the expressions Fa and Ga are *treated as units*, just as we treated the capital letters, A, B, etc. in propositional logic. Thus, we consider the expression on line 1 to be a substitution instance of the sentence from $p \supset q$, where the unit Fa is substituted for p and the unit Ga is substituted for q.

The following is another example of a proof in predicate logic employing the proof apparatus of propositional logic:

1. $(x) \sim (\overset{p}{\overbrace{Fx}} \cdot \overset{q}{\overbrace{Gx}})$ $p\ /\therefore\ (x)(\sim Fx \lor \sim Gx)$

2. $(x)(\sim \overset{p}{\overbrace{Fx}} \lor \sim \overset{q}{\overbrace{Gx}})$ 1, **DeM**

In this case, the application of De Morgan's Theorem to line 1 does *not* involve the whole of line 1. This is permissible because, as stated in Chapter Four, the eleven *equivalence* forms among the eighteen valid argument forms can be employed on parts as well as wholes of sentences and sentence forms.

But the eight *implicational forms* cannot be employed on parts of sentences. Their use is restricted to whole sentences, as in the previous example containing a valid use of Modus Ponens. Thus, the following proof is *not* permitted in predicate logic:

1. $(x)(Fx \supset Gx)$ p

2. Fx $p \; / \therefore Gx$

3. Gx 1, 2 **MP**

because the whole of line 1 has the form $(x)(p \supset q)$, and not the form $(p \supset q)$ necessary for the application of Modus Ponens.

Inference rules

We introduce five valid argument forms (**inference rules**) to be used in predicate logic proofs in addition to the valid argument forms of propositional logic. The first four of these rules concern the dropping and adding of quantifiers.

Universal Instantiation (UI): Consider the argument

1. $(x)(Fx \supset Gx)$ p

2. Fa $p \; / \therefore Ga$

Suppose $Fx = $ "x is friendly" and $Gx = $ "x is gentle". Then line 1 asserts that for all x, if x is friendly, then x is gentle, or that everything that is friendly is gentle. Surely it follows from this that if a particular x, say the person a, is friendly, then he's also gentle, because whatever is true of *everything* must be true of any *particular* thing. Hence it is legitimate to write as the next line in the proof

3. $Fa \supset Ga$ 1, **UI** (Universal Instantiation)

Then we can assert the conclusion

4.   *Ga*   2, 3 **MP**

   We call the rule of inference which permits the leap from line 1 to line 3
Universal Instantiation, because it yields an *instance* (*Fa* ⊃ *Ga*) of the
universal generalization (*x*)(*Fx* ⊃ *Gx*).
   It is important to note that a universal quantifier must quantify a *whole
line* in a proof in order to be dropped by **UI**. Thus **UI** cannot be applied
to the line

1.   (*x*)*Fx* ⊃ (∃*y*)*Gy*

   to obtain

2.   *Fa* ⊃ (∃*y*)*Gy*

because the (*x*) quantifier in line 1 does not quantify the whole of that line.
   Similarly, **UI** cannot be applied to the line

1.   ∼(*x*)(*Fx* ⊃ *Gx*)

   to obtain

2.   ∼(*Fa* ⊃ *Ga*)

The (*x*) quantifier in line 2 does not quantify the whole of that line, since
it does not quantify the negation sign.
   Perhaps a better intuitive understanding of the nature and general
validity of **UI** can be obtained by again thinking of symbolizations containing quantifiers as a kind of shorthand for expanded expressions. Take
the quantified expression (*x*)(*Fx* ⊃ *Gx*). Its expansion is [(*Fa* ⊃ *Ga*)
· (*Fb* ⊃ *Gb*)] · . . . If we take this *expansion* as a premise, rather than the
expression itself, then we can infer to *Fa* ⊃ *Ga* by Simplification (plus
Association), without the need to appeal to a new inference rule at all.
Uses of rule **UI**, which permit passage from (*x*)(*Fx* ⊃ *Gx*) to *Fa* ⊃ *Ga*,

are like uses of Simplification, which permit passage from $[(Fa \supset Ga) \cdot (Fb \supset Gb)] \cdot \ldots$ to $Fa \supset Ga$.

Examples:

The following are examples of correct uses of **UI**:

(I)
	1.	$(x)[(Fx \cdot Gx) \supset Hx]$	p
	2.	$(Fy \cdot Gy) \supset Hy$	1, **UI**
	3.	$(Fa \cdot Ga) \supset Ha$	1, **UI**
	4.	$(Fx \cdot Gx) \supset Hx$	1, **UI**

(II)
	1.	$(x)(y)[(Fx \cdot Gy) \supset Hxy]$	p
	2.	$(y)[(Fx \cdot Gy) \supset Hxy]$	1, **UI**
	3.	$(Fx \cdot Gz) \supset Hxz$	2, **UI**
	4.	$(Fx \cdot Gx) \supset Hxx$	2, **UI**
	5.	$(Fx \cdot Gy) \supset Hxy$	2, **UI**

(III)
	1.	$(x)[(Fx \cdot Gx) \supset Hax]$	p
	2.	$(Fx \cdot Gx) \supset Hax$	1, **UI**
	3.	$(Fy \cdot Gy) \supset Hay$	1, **UI**
	4.	$(Fa \cdot Ga) \supset Haa$	1, **UI**

Universal Generalization (UG): Now consider the proof:

1.	$(x)(Fx \supset Gx)$	p
2.	$(x)(Gx \supset Hx)$	p / $\therefore$ $(x)(Fx \supset Hx)$
3.	$Fy \supset Gy$	1, **UI**
4.	$Gy \supset Hy$	2, **UI**
5.	$Fy \supset Hy$	3, 4 **HS**

The derivation of line 5 illustrates the main reason for introducing the four quantifier rules, namely to provide a way to use the eight implicational forms of propositional logic in predicate logic proofs. If we were not allowed to drop quantifiers, the eight implicational forms could not be used on lines containing quantified sentences, because they must be used on whole sentences or sentence forms only.

6.	$(x)(Fx \supset Hx)$	5, **UG** (Universal Generalization)

We introduce the rule called **Universal Generalization (UG)** in order to permit valid steps like the one from line 5 to line 6. Subject to certain restrictions to be discussed later, rule **UG** permits the addition of any universal quantifiers *which quantify whole sentences*.

In the example just given, the addition of the universal quantifier clearly is legitimate, since the validity of all previous steps did not require that the letter y be used. *Any* letter could have been used, or *every* letter, taken one at a time. Hence, the step to $(x)(Fx \supset Hx)$ is legitimate.

This use of **UG** should be familiar to students of geometry. In geometry, a proof that a given triangle has a particular property is considered to be proof that *all* triangles have that property, provided that the given triangle is *arbitrarily selected*. Similarly, **UG** is a valid step (with the exceptions to be noted below) provided that it is applied in cases where the actual letters employed (in the above example the letter y) are arbitrarily selected, and any other letters could have been selected with the same result.

Examples:

The following proof contains correct uses of **UG**:

1.	$(x)(y)(Fxy \supset Gyx)$	p
2.	$(y)(Fxy \supset Gyx)$	1, **UI**
3.	$(Fxy \supset Gyx)$	2, **UI**
4.	$(x)(Fxy \supset Gyx)$	3, **UG**
5.	$(z)(Fxz \supset Gzx)$	3, **UG**
6.	$(z)(Fzy \supset Gyz)$	3, **UG**

7.	$(x)(z)(Fzx \supset Gxz)$	6, **UG**
8.	$(y)(x)(Fxy \supset Gyx)$	4, **UG**

Existential Instantiation (EI): Next, consider the proof

1.	$(x)(Hx \supset Kx)$	p
2.	$(\exists x)Hx$	p / $\therefore$ $(\exists x)Kx$
3.	Hy	2, **EI** (Existential Instantiation)

In this proof, line 3 follows from line 2 by the inference rule called **Existential Instantiation (EI)**.

Technically, we should not permit this step from line 2 to line 3, because y is a variable. Instead, we should introduce a new set of terms, construed not as *variables*, but rather as *unknowns*, or *ambiguous names*. The difference between a variable and an unknown is illustrated by an example from algebra. In the algebraic theorem

$$(x)(y)[(x + y) = (y + x)]$$

x and y function as variables, since the theorem is true of all numbers. (The expansion of this theorem is $[(1 + 1 = 1 + 1) \cdot (1 + 2 = 2 + 1)]$ $\cdot [(2 + 1 = 1 + 2) \cdot (1 + 3 = 3 + 1)] \cdot \ldots$ running through all combinations of two numbers.) But in the algebraic problem

1.	$x + 1 = 3$
2.	$x = 2$

the x on line 1 functions not as a variable but as an *unknown value*, to be discovered, as it is on line 2, where it turns out to be the number two. So also, in the step from

2.	$(\exists x)Hx$

to

3.	Hy

the letter y serves not as a variable but as an *unknown*, in the sense that if $(\exists x)Hx$ is *true*, then there is *some* value of x (exactly which one being unknown), which has the property H. In line 3 we call that unknown value y.

This use of the term y also is familiar from its use in the law. For example, if it is not known who has committed a particular crime, although it is known that *someone* (at least one person) committed it, that person may be referred to as "John Doe". We could adopt the John Doe notation if we wanted to, so that from line 2

2. $(\exists x)Hx$

we would go to

3. Hjd

But it turns out that it is not necessary to do so. So for the sake of simplicity, we permit the letters x, y, z, etc., to serve not only as variables, but also as unknowns, or as ambiguous names (such as "John Doe"), just as is done in algebra.

Existential Generalization (**EG**): So far, the proof in question reads as follows:

1.	$(x)(Hx \supset Kx)$	p
2.	$(\exists x)Hx$	p / $\therefore$ $(\exists x)Kx$
3.	Hy	2, **EI**

Continuing,

4.	$Hy \supset Ky$	1, **UI***
5.	Ky	3, 4 **MP**
6.	$(\exists x)Kx$	5, **EG** (Existential Generalization)

The step from line 5 to line 6 is justified by the inference rule **Existential Generalization** (**EG**). The step obviously is valid, since if some John Doe or other has the property K, then there is something that has that property.

Subject to certain restrictions to be discussed later, we are permitted to drop and add existential quantifiers at will by means of the rules **EI** and

---

* Just as in line 3, the letter y serves as an unknown, or ambiguous name, and not as a variable, even though we informally refer to it as a variable.

EG respectively, *provided they are dropped from or added to whole lines of proofs.*

Examples:

The following proofs contain examples of correct uses of **EI** and **EG**:

(I)
1.	$(\exists x)(\exists y)(Fx \cdot Gxy)$		p
2.	$(\exists y)(Fx \cdot Gxy)$		1, **EI**
3.	$(\exists y)(Fz \cdot Gzy)$		1, **EI**
4.	$(Fz \cdot Gzy)$		3, **EI**
5.	$(Fx \cdot Gxy)$		2, **EI**
6.	$(\exists z)(Fz \cdot Gzy)$		5, **EG** (or 4, **EG**)
7.	$(\exists x)(Fx \cdot Gxy)$		5, **EG** (or 4, **EG**)
8.	$(\exists y)(\exists x)(Fx \cdot Gxy)$		7, **EG**
9.	$(\exists z)(\exists x)(Fx \cdot Gxz)$		7, **EG**
10.	$(\exists x)(\exists z)(Fz \cdot Gzx)$		6, **EG**

(II)
1.	$(\exists x)[Fx \cdot (y)Gxy]$		p
2.	$Fx \cdot (y)Gxy$		1, **EI**
3.	$Fz \cdot (y)Gzy$		1, **EI**
4.	$(y)Gxy$		2, **Simp**
5.	Gxy		4, **UI**
6.	$(\exists y)Gxy$		5, **EG**
7.	$(\exists x)(\exists y)Gxy$		6, **EG**
8.	$(\exists z)(\exists y)Gzy$		6, **EG**
9.	Fz		3, **Simp**
10.	$Fz \cdot (\exists z)(\exists y)Gzy$		8, 9 **Conj**
11.	$(\exists x)[Fx \cdot (\exists z)(\exists y)Gzy]$		10, **EG**

Chapter Seven

Predicate Logic—II

1

Rationale behind the Precise Formulation of the Quantifier Rules

While the general idea behind the use of the four quantifier rules is quite simple (as well as quite intuitive), their *precise formulation* turns out to be one of the most complex (as well as nonintuitive) parts of predicate logic. Consequently, we present a brief discussion of the major considerations which must be taken into account in such a precise formulation, before presenting the rules themselves in their precise form.

Consider the following use of **EI**:

(I) 1. $(\exists x)Hx$ *p*

  2.   *Ha*   1, **EI** (invalid)

Step 2 clearly is invalid. Although it follows from 1 that *some entity or other* has the property *H*, it surely does not follow that whatever is named by the individual constant *a* is that entity. For instance, if H is the property of being heavy, and a names some light object, say a certain piece of chalk, then 1 is true, since there surely is *some* entity which is heavy, but 2 is false, since the piece of chalk in question is *not* heavy. In general then, we must forbid steps such as the one from 1 to 2, by requiring that *no individual constant occur on a line in a proof as a result of an application of EI.*

Now consider the proof

(II)	1.	$(\exists x)Fx$		p
	2.	$(\exists x)Gx$		$p\ /\therefore\ (\exists x)(Fx \cdot Gx)$
	3.	Fx		1, **EI**
	4.	Gx		2, **EI** (invalid)
	5.	$Fx \cdot Gx$		3, 4 **Conj**
	6.	$(\exists x)(Fx \cdot Gx)$		5, **EG**

Suppose Fx = "x is a fox" and Gx = "x is a goose". Then premise 1 asserts that something is a fox, which is true, and 2 that something is a goose, which also is true. But the conclusion 6 asserts that something is *both* a fox *and* a goose, which obviously is false. The trouble occurs at line 4, which results from line 2 by **EI**. Although line 2 justifies the assertion that *some x or other* is a goose, it does *not* justify the assertion that *the x which is a fox is a goose*. But use of the same free variable on line 4 which already occurred free on line 3 permits derivation of this unwarranted conclusion. Consequently, we must forbid uses of **EI** of this kind by requiring that *each variable introduced free into a proof by EI not occur free previously in the proof.* (Of course, we could have used some variable *other* than x on line 4. For instance, we could have used the variable y, to obtain Gy on that line, since y does not occur free previously in the proof.)

Now consider the use of **UG** in the following proof:

(III)	1.	Fa		p
	2.	$(x)Fx$		1, **UG** (invalid)

Suppose Fa = "Art is friendly". Then the use of **UG** which yields line 2 consists in passing from the assertion that one particular entity (Art) is friendly, to the assertion that everything is friendly. Surely it is incorrect to conclude that because *one particular* entity has a certain property, *every* entity does. Consequently, we must restrict the use of **UG** by *forbidding universal generalization on a constant.*

Consider another invalid use of **UG**:

(IV)
1. $(\exists x)Fx$ $p / \therefore (x)Fx$
2. Fy 1, **EI**
3. $(x)Fx$ 2, **UG** (invalid)

Assuming again that Fx = "x is friendly", sentence 1 asserts that *something* is friendly, while 3 asserts the falsehood that *everything* is friendly. The trouble here is that the y on line 2 resulted from an application of **EI** to line 1, so that in generalizing on y to obtain line 3 we generalized on a variable obtained by **EI**. Surely it is incorrect to assert that because *some* entity has a certain property, *every* entity does. Consequently, we must forbid uses of **UG** (such as the one on line 3 of this proof) which permit the passage from "some" to "all". We can do this by *forbidding the use of* **UG** *on a variable resulting from a use of* **EI**.

A slightly different, but still invalid, use of **UG** is contained in the following proof:

(V)
1. $(x)(\exists y)Lyx$ $p / \therefore (\exists y)(x)Lyx$
2. $(\exists y)Lyx$ 1, **UI**
3. Lyx 2, **EI**
4. $(x)Lyx$ 3, **UG** (invalid)
5. $(\exists y)(x)Lyx$ 4, **EG**

Suppose Lyx = "y is larger than x", and the universe of discourse has been restricted to numbers only. Then premise 1 asserts the arithmetic truth that given any number x, there is some number y which is larger than x. That is, 1 asserts that there is some number larger than any given number.* So the premise of this argument is true. But its conclusion, line 5, is false, since it asserts that there is some number y which is larger than all numbers. This must be false, since no number is larger than itself. So in going from 1 to 5 we have passed from a true premise to a false conclusion.

It is rather difficult to see what went wrong in this proof, and in particular what is wrong with the use of **UG** used to obtain line 4. After all, the x free on line 3, to which **UG** was applied, does not result from an application of **EI**, as in the previous invalid proof. Rather it results from an application of **UI** to line 1, so that we seem to be simply dropping and then adding the same universal quantifier. This *seems* as harmless as the similar process in the proof

1.	$(x)Fx$	p
2.	Fx	1, **UI**
3.	$(x)Fx$	2, **UG**

But the use of **UG** in Proof (V) is not harmless by any means. The mere fact that x is free on line 3 of Proof (V), *a line obtained by EI*, is sufficient to make the application of **UG** to x invalid. It is as though (to use a metaphor) the "taint" of **EI** placed on the y variable in line 3 "rubbed off" the y variable on to the other variable, x, free on that line. In general, we must forbid uses of **UG** such as the one on line 4 of this proof. And we can do so by *forbidding universal generalization on a variable free in a line obtained by EI*, whether that variable became free by means of **EI** or not. (Notice that by forbidding such applications of **UG** we eliminate not only the invalid use of **UG** in Proof (V), but also the invalid use of **UG** in Proof (IV).)

This restriction on **UG** represents the very first clear-cut case of a non-intuitive element in our presentation of either the sentential or the predicate logic, for this restriction is neither intuitive nor counter-intuitive. Its justification is that without it, or some similar restriction, we would be able

---

* This assertion is a truth of arithmetic because the series of numbers has no end. We know intuitively that this must be true, because we know that we can always add one to any number, no matter how large, to obtain a larger number, then add one more to obtain an even larger number, and so on, indefinitely.

to go from true premises to false conclusions, while with it we cannot do so.

Next consider the following proof:

(VI)

1. Fy AP /∴ $(z)[Fz \supset (x)Fx]$
2. $(x)Fx$ 1, **UG** (invalid)
3. $Fy \supset (x)Fx$ 1, 2 **CP**
4. $(z)[Fz \supset (x)Fx]$ 3, **UG**

Suppose $Fy =$ "y is friendly". Then the conclusion, which depends on no premises whatever, asserts that if anything is friendly, then everything is friendly, an obviously false statement. We can guard against this kind of invalid use of **UG** by *forbidding universal generalization on a variable free in an assumed premise, where the universal generalization occurs within the scope of the assumed premise.* This restriction rules out the use of **UG** on line 2 of the above proof, because it occurs within the scope of the assumed premise 1. But it does not rule out the valid use of **UG** which yields line 4, because line 4 is outside the scope of the assumed premise 1.

To some extent, this restriction on **UG** is nonintuitive, just like the previous one. It, too, is justified by the fact that without it we could go from true premises to false conclusions.

One might naïvely characterize a particular application of **EI** or **UI** as a process in which a quantifier is dropped and all of the variables thus freed are replaced by a particular variable. Thus, in the following use of **EI**,

1. $(\exists x)(Fx \cdot Gx)$ p
2. $(Fy \cdot Gy)$ 1, **EI**

the quantifier $(\exists x)$ is dropped, and each x thus freed is replaced by a free y. (Of course we could just as well have replaced each x by itself.) The important point is that there is a *one-to-one correspondence* between the x's freed by dropping the $(\exists x)$ quantifier and the free y's which replaced

         Predicate Logic

them. That is, to each x freed by dropping the $(\exists x)$ quantifier in line 1, there corresponds a y free in line 2; *and* to each y free in line 2, there corresponds an x in line 1 which is freed by dropping the $(\exists x)$ quantifier.

The question naturally arises as to whether all valid uses of **UI**, **EI**, **UG**, and **EG**, are required to have one-to-one correspondences of this kind. Surprisingly, it turns out that there are two cases in which this one-to-one correspondence cannot be required, if our logic is to be complete.

The first case concerns **UI**. Consider the argument

(VII)	1.	$(\exists y)(x)Lyx$	p / $\therefore$ $(\exists x)Lxx$
	2.	$(x)Lyx$	1, **EI**
	3.	Lyy	2, **UI** (valid)
	4.	$(\exists x)Lxx$	3, **EG**

Suppose the domain of discourse is limited to human beings only, and suppose $Lyx = $ "y loves x". Then the premise of this argument asserts that there is someone who loves everyone, while its conclusion asserts that there is someone who loves himself. Now it may be that this premise is true, and it may be that it is false. But *if* it is true, *then* surely the conclusion is true also, for if it is true that someone loves everyone then it follows that that person loves himself, since everyone includes himself. So we must have a way to infer from the premise of this argument to its conclusion, and the most intuitive way is to permit inferences like the one on line 3. Notice that there is *not* a one-to-one correspondence between free y variables on line 3 and bound x variables on line 2. Since we must allow the step from line 2 to line 3, it follows that *we cannot require a one-to-one correspondence between x and y variables in the application of UI.*

The other case in which we cannot require a one-to-one correspondence concerns **EG**. Consider the argument:

(VIII)	1.	$(x)Fxx$	p / $\therefore$ $(x)(\exists y)Fxy$
	2.	Fxx	1, **UI**
	3.	$(\exists y)Fxy$	2, **EG** (valid)
	4.	$(x)(\exists y)Fxy$	3, **UG**

Suppose $Fxx =$ "x is identical with x". Then premise 1 asserts that everything is identical with itself, which is true, and the conclusion asserts that given any x, there is something (y) identical with x, which is true also, since the y in question for any particular x is itself. Clearly, if 1 is true, and it is, then 4 is true also. We must permit a step such as the one from 2 to 3 in order to enable us to draw the conclusion on line 4. So in general, *we cannot require a one-to-one correspondence between x and y variables in the application of EG*.

The primary aim in the use of **UI** and **EI** is to drop a quantifier and *free* the variables which it bound. Consequently, we must forbid uses of **UI** and **EI**, in which the variable which is supposed to be freed ends up bound. The following is an example involving **UI**:

(IX) 1. $(x)(\exists y)Lyx$ p

      2. $(\exists y)Lyy$ 1, **UI** (invalid)

Suppose $Lyx =$ "y is larger than x", and x and y range over numbers only. Then 1 asserts the true statement that given any number x, there is some number larger than x, while 2 asserts the falsehood that there is some number larger than itself. The trouble is that the x variable in 1, which the application of **UI** is supposed to free, is replaced in 2 by a *bound y* variable.

Similarly, the use of **EI** in the following proof is invalid:

(X) 1. $(\exists x)(y) \sim Dxy$ p

      2. $(y) \sim Dyy$ 1, **EI** (invalid)

Suppose $Dxy =$ "x dislikes y", and let's restrict the domain of discourse to human beings. Then 1 asserts that there is someone who doesn't dislike anyone, which is true (surely there is a newborn baby somewhere who doesn't dislike anyone), while 2 asserts that no one dislikes himself, which (unfortunately) is false.

In general, we can block invalid uses of **UI** and **EI** of this kind by requiring that *when a quantifier is dropped, all the variables thus freed be replaced by free variables* (or, in the case of **UI**, by free variables *or constants*).

A restriction similar to the one just placed on **UI** and **EI** must be placed on **EG** and **UG**. For instance, when we add an existential quantifier, we want to quantify occurrences of one variable only, and not two. Consider the following use of **EG**:

(XI) 1. $(\exists x)(\exists y)Fxy$ p

2. $(\exists y)Fxy$ 1, **EI**

3. Fxy 2, **EI**

4. $(\exists x)Fxx$ 3, **EG** (invalid)

This time, suppose $Fxy = $ "x is the father of y" and the domain of discourse is restricted to human beings. Then 1 asserts (truly) that someone is the father of someone (or other), while 4 asserts (falsely) that someone is the father of himself. The trouble is that in generalizing on the y variable in 3 we quantified occurrences of not one, but two of the free variables which occur in 3.

Similarly, when we add a *universal quantifier*, we want to quantify occurrences of one variable only, and not two. The unhappy consequence of capturing occurrences of *two* variables is illustrated by the following argument:

(XII)

1. Fx AP

2. $Fx \lor \sim Hy$ 1, **Add**

3. $\sim Hy \lor Fx$ 2, **Comm**

4. $Hy \supset Fx$ 3, **Impl**

5. $(x)(Hx \supset Fx)$ 4, **UG** (invalid)

6. $Fx \supset (x)(Hx \supset Fx)$ 1, 5 **CP**

7. $(y)[Fy \supset (x)(Hx \supset Fx)]$ 6, **UG**

Suppose $Fx = $ "x is friendly" and $Hx = $ "x is human". Then the conclusion, which depends on no premises whatever, asserts that if anything is friendly, then all humans are friendly, an obviously false statement.

Hence the argument must be invalid. The trouble is that in generalizing on the y variable on line 4, we quantified occurrences of not one, but two of the free variables which occur on that line.

In general, we can block this kind of invalid use of **EG** and **UG** by requiring that *in each use of* **EG** *or* **UG**, *the occurrences of only one variable in the original formula be bound by the newly introduced quantifier in the resulting formula.*

We stated previously that when applying **UI** we cannot require a one-to-one correspondence between bound x variables in the original formula and free y variables in the resulting formula, because this would block perfectly valid inferences, such as the one in proof (VII) from $(x)Lyx$ to Lyy. But we can, and must, require that *if one occurrence of some bound variable "x" is freed by* **UI** *and replaced by a free "y" variable, then all "x" variables freed by this application of* **UI** *must be replaced by free occurrences of the "y" variable.* This restriction on **UI** blocks the following invalid use of **UI**:

(XIII) 1. $(x)(Ox \lor Ex)$ p

        2. $(Ox \lor Ey)$ 1, **UI** (invalid)

        3. $(y)(Ox \lor Ey)$ 2, **UG**

        4. $(x)(y)(Ox \lor Ey)$ 3, **UG**

Suppose $Ox =$ "x is odd" and $Ex =$ "x is even", and the domain of discourse is restricted to positive whole numbers. Then 1 asserts (truly) that every number x is either odd or even, while 4 asserts (falsely) that given *any* two numbers, x and y, either x is odd or y is even. (That sentence 4 is false can be seen by considering the substitution instance of 4 obtained by replacing x by *2* and y by *1*, since this substitution instance of 4 asserts that either *2* is odd or *1* is even.)

The question as to whether a similar restriction must be placed on **EI** depends on how the restrictions on **UG** have been worded. Consider the following example:

(XIV) 1. $(\exists x)(Fx \lor Gx)$ p

        2. $Fx \lor Gy$ 1, **EI** (?)

Should we allow the step from 1 to 2 by **EI**, even though only one of the x variables freed by dropping the existential quantifier from sentence 1 is replaced by a y variable? The answer is that it depends on how we have restricted **UG**. The essential thing is to forbid passage from 1 to

3.　　$(x)(Fx \lor Gy)$　　　　　　　　　　　2, **UG**

It turns out that we can block this inference either by putting a restriction on **UG**, forbidding the inference from 2 to 3, or on **EI**, forbidding the inference from 1 to 2. Most sets of quantifier rules place the restriction on **EI**. However, it happens that the set of rules to be presented in the next section places appropriate restrictions on both **EI** and **UG** (because to do otherwise would make the statement of the rules slightly more complicated).

On p. 121 above, it was shown that we must permit uses of **UI** such as the one from $(x)Lyx$ to Lyy. But what about similar uses of **EI**, such as the one inferring from $(\exists x)Fxy$ to Fyy? Should we allow these also? The answer is "no", because all such uses of **EI** are invalid. But it turns out that all cases in which such inferences might arise are forbidden by the restriction (already mentioned) that a free variable introduced into a proof by **EI** must not occur free previously in the proof. The following argument contains an example:

(XV)　1.　　$(\exists y)(\exists x)Fxy$　　　　　　　　　　p

　　　2.　　　　$(\exists x)Fxy$　　　　　　　　　　1, **EI**

　　　3.　　　　　Fyy　　　　　　　　　　2, **EI** (invalid)

It was also shown on p. 121 that we must permit uses of **EG** like the one from Fxx to $(\exists y)Fxy$. But what about similar uses of **UG**, such as the one inferring from Fxx to $(y)Fxy$? Should we allow these inferences also? Again the answer is "no", because all such inferences are invalid. In general, we must require that *in the use of UG, if a free "x" in the original formula is replaced by a "y" which becomes bound in the resulting formula, then all free occurrences of "x" in the original formula must be replaced by bound "y" variables in the resulting formula.*

The above constitutes a catalogue of the kinds of inferences we must forbid (as well as two kinds we must permit). It is suggested that before going on to the precise formulation of the quantifier rules the reader go over the fifteen proofs presented as examples to become clear as to exactly which kinds of inferences we want to permit, and which kinds we must forbid.

2

Precise Formulation of the Quantifier Rules

In order to state the precise version of the quantifier rules economically, we need a way to refer to a great many expressions at once. For example, we want our precise statement of rule **UI** somehow to refer to, and permit, all of the following inferences:

(I) 1. $(x)Fx$

/∴ 2. Fy

(II) 1. $(x)Fx$

/∴ 2. Fx

(III) 1. $(z)(Fz \supset Gz)$

/∴ 2. $(Fy \supset Gy)$

(IV) 1. $(x)(Fx \supset Gx)$

/∴ 2. $(Fx \supset Gx)$

(V) 1. $(x)(y)Fxy$

/∴ 2. $(y)Fxy$

(VI) 1. $(y)(z)Fyz$

/∴ 2. $(z)Fxz$

(VII) 1. $(x)[Fx \supset (\exists y)Gy]$

/∴ 2. $Fx \supset (\exists y)Gy$

(VIII) 1. $(x)Fxy$

/∴ 2. Fyy

(IX) 1. $(x)[(Fx \cdot Gx) \supset (\exists x)Hx]$

/∴ 2. $[(Fy \cdot Gy) \supset (\exists x)Hx]$

In each of these examples, line 1 consists of a universal quantifier plus a formula quantified by it. Suppose we refer to the variables so quantified as u.* Then we can say that in each of the above examples, sentence 1 has the form

$(u)(\ldots u \ldots)$

* Technically, this use of the letter u violates a convention set down earlier, since u is not being used here as the same kind of variable as, say, x and y. (The same is true of the use of w on the next few pages.)

and we can use this scheme to represent any expression in which the initial quantifier, whether (x), (y), or (z), etc., quantifies the whole remainder of the expression.

In each of the above examples, line 2 is obtained from line 1 by dropping the initial universal quantifier and replacing all of the occurrences of the variable bound only by that quantifier either by occurrences of itself or by occurrences of some other variable. For example, in (III), the (z) quantifier was dropped and each z variable bound in 1 was replaced by a y variable free in 2, and in (IV), the (x) quantifier was dropped, and each x variable bound in 1 was replaced by itself in 2. In general, we can say that in each of the above uses of **UI** we move from an expression of the form

$$(u)(\ldots u \ldots)$$

to an expression of the form

$$(\ldots w \ldots)$$

where u and w are variables, and the expression $(\ldots w \ldots)$ resulted from replacing all occurrences of u free in $(\ldots u \ldots)$ by occurrences of w free in $(\ldots w \ldots)$.

There are two things to notice. First, the phrase "occurrence of u free in $(\ldots u \ldots)$" refers to occurrences of u which, although bound in the *entire* expression $(u)(\ldots u \ldots)$, are *free* once the (u) quantifier is dropped, and thus are not bound by a quantifier which occurs within the expression $(\ldots u \ldots)$ itself. For example, the inference in (IX), above, can be said to have the form

1. $(u)(\ldots u \ldots)$

/∴   2. $(\ldots w \ldots)$

where we let (u) be (x), $(\ldots u \ldots)$ be $[(Fx \cdot Gx) \supset (\exists x)Hx]$, and $(\ldots w \ldots)$ be $[(Fy \cdot Gy) \supset (\exists x)Hx]$. In this inference, when the universal quantifier (x) is dropped, the first two x variables in $[(Fx \cdot Gx) \supset (\exists x)Hx]$ become free, but the third x does not, because it still is bound by an existential quantifier, namely $(\exists x)$. So we require that the first two variables be replaced by variables *free* in (...w...), but do *not* require that the third x variable be free in (...w...), because that x is bound in (...u...), and so can remain bound in (...w...).

The second thing to notice is that we must replace all occurrences of u free in (...u...) by *free* occurrences of w in (...w...). This is to take account of the discussions of invalid inferences contained on pp. 122—124 above.

The schematic notation just introduced also is used in the formulation of **EI**, **UG**, and (with a slight modification) **EG**. For instance, we shall characterize **UG** as a process in which we move from an expression (...u...) to an expression (w)(...w...), by replacing all free occurrences of u in (...u...) by occurrences of w free in (...w...). (Of course, such occurrences of w will be bound in the whole expression (w)(...w...). The point is that they not be bound by a w quantifier occurring within (...w...).)

We now are ready to state our precise version of the quantifier rules:

In using the rules **UI**, **EI**, and **UG**, let the expression (...w...) denote any sentence or sentence form which results from replacing all occurrences of u free in the sentence or sentence form (...u...) by occurrences of w free in (...w...), and let u and w be any variables or constants,* unless otherwise specified. Let the same be true for rule **EG**, except that the expression (...w...) denotes a sentence form which results from replacing *one or more* (but not necessarily all) occurrences of u free in (...u...) by occurrences of some variable w free in (...w...).

Rule UI: (u)(...u...) / ∴ (...w...)

(The precise statement as to how (...w...) results from (...u...) eliminates the invalid uses of **UI** discussed on p. 124, while not eliminating any of the valid uses of **UI** discussed on p. 121.

Rule EI: $(\exists u)$(...u...) / ∴ (...w...)

Provided: 1. w is not a constant.

2. w does not occur free previously in the proof.

---

* Of course u cannot be a constant in the cases of UI and EI, and w cannot be a constant in the cases of EG and UG.

(The first proviso eliminates the invalid uses of **EI** discussed on pp. 116–117 and the second those discussed on p. 117. In addition, the requirements discussed on pp. 120—121, 122, and 124—125 also are satisfied by this formulation of rule **EI**.)

Rule UG: $(\dots u \dots) / \therefore (w)(\dots w \dots)$

Provided: 1. u is not a constant.

        2. u is not free in a line obtained by **EI**.

        3. u is not free in an assumed premise within whose scope $(\dots u \dots)$ occurs.

        4. To each w free in $(\dots w \dots)$ there corresponds a u free in $(\dots u \dots)$.

(The first proviso eliminates the invalid uses of **UG** discussed on pp. 117—118, the second those discussed on pp. 118–119, the third those discussed on p. 120, and the fourth those discussed on pp. 123—124. In addition, the restriction on **UG** discussed on p. 125 also is satisfied by this formulation of rule **UG**.)

And finally,

Rule EG: $(\dots u \dots) / \therefore (\exists w)(\dots w \dots)$

Provided: 1. To each w free in $(\dots w \dots)$ there corresponds a u free in $(\dots u \dots)$.

(The proviso eliminates the invalid uses of **EG** discussed on p. 123. Notice that the special formulation given for rule **EG** as to how $(\dots w \dots)$ is to result from $(\dots u \dots)$ permits the valid use of **EG**, discussed on pp. 121–122, which would be eliminated if we used the same formulation as for **UI**, **EI**, and **UG**.)

One final point. With one exception, the rules as stated can handle expressions containing vacuous quantifications such as $(x)(x)Fx$, $(x)(y)Fy$, etc. It is not absolutely necessary that we consider such expressions to be meaningful sentences; a complete system for logic can be constructed without them. But it is useful to allow such sentences, and customary to do so. The one case of this kind not handled by the quantifier rules presented here concerns rule **EG**. As we have stated it, rule **EG** forbids inferences such as the one from $(x)Fx$ to $(\exists y)(x)Fx$. But we can easily extend the rules to include such cases if we wish, by adding the condition that vacuous quantifiers can be added at any time.

Since the four quantifier rules (precisely stated) are quite complex and not entirely intuitive, a fair amount of study and practice are required to master them. The following examples are included as an aid in their mastery.

Examples:

The following proofs contain examples of both valid and invalid uses of the four quantifier rules.

(I)
1. $(\exists x)(\exists y)(Fx \supset Gy)$ p

2. $(\exists y)(Fx \supset Gy)$ 1, **EI**

3. $Fx \supset Gy$ 2, **EI**

4. $Fx \supset Gx$ 2, **EI** (invalid, because x occurs free previously in the proof, namely on line 2.)

5. $Fa \supset Gy$ 2, **EI** (invalid, because a is a constant.)

6. $(\exists x)Fx \supset Gy$ 3, **EG** (invalid, because $(\exists x)$ does not quantify the whole of 6.)

7. $(\exists x)(Fx \supset Gy)$ 3, **EG**

8. $(z)(\exists x)(Fx \supset Gz)$ 7, **UG** (invalid, because y was introduced into the proof free by **EI**.)

(II)
1. $(\exists x)(y)[Fxy \supset (\exists z)(Gxz \supset Hy)]$ p

2. $(y)[Fxy \supset (\exists z)(Gxz \supset Hy)]$ 1, **EI**

3. $(y)[Fzy \supset (\exists z)(Gzz \supset Hy)]$ 1, **EI** (invalid, because every x free in $(y)[Fxy \supset (\exists z)(Gxz \supset Hy)]$ is not replaced by a z free in line 3.)

4.	$Fxx \supset (\exists z)(Gxz \supset Hx)$	2, **UI**
5.	$Fxx \supset (Gxz \supset Hx)$	4, **EI** (invalid, because $(\exists z)$ does not quantify the whole of line 4.)
→6.	Fxx	**AP**
7.	$(\exists z)(Gxz \supset Hx)$	4, 6 **MP**
8.	$Gxu \supset Hx$	7, **EI**
9.	$(\exists y)(Gyu \supset Hx)$	8, **EG** (valid)
10.	$(\exists z)(\exists y)(Gyz \supset Hz)$	9, **EG** (invalid, because to each z free in $(\exists y)(Gyz \supset Hz)$ there does *not* correspond an x free in $(\exists y)(Gyu \supset H)$.)
11.	$(\exists y)(Gyu \supset Hy)$	8, **EG**
12.	$(\exists z)(\exists y)(Gyz \supset Hy)$	11, **EG**
13.	$Fxx \supset (\exists z)(\exists y)(Gyz \supset Hy)$	6, 12 **CP**
14.	$(x)[Fxx \supset (\exists z)(\exists y)(Gyz \supset Hy)]$	13, **EG** (invalid, because x was introduced into the proof free by **EI**.)
15.	$(\exists x)[Fxx \supset (\exists z)(\exists y)(Gyz \supset Hy)]$	13, **UG**

Perhaps the task of mastering the four quantifier rules can be lightened a bit by concentration on their *nonintuitive* elements.

Take rule **UG**. This rule contains four restrictions, and hence appears quite formidable at first glance. But in actual applications of **UG**, even beginners are unlikely to violate the first or fourth restrictions. For instance, even beginners would not be tempted to violate the first restriction on **UG** and infer from Fa to $(x)Fx$. So beginners should concentrate on the second and third restrictions. In particular, they should be on the lookout for invalid inferences such as the one from 3 to 4 in the proof

1.	$(x)(\exists y)(Fx \cdot Gyx)$	p
2.	$(\exists y)(Fx \cdot Gyx)$	1, **UI**
3.	$Fx \cdot Gyx$	2, **EI**
4.	$(x)(Fx \cdot Gyx)$	3, **UG** (invalid)

which violates the second restriction on **UG**. Similarly, they should look out for invalid inferences like the one from 1 to 2 in the proof

1.	$Fy \supset (x)Gx$	AP
2.	$(z)[Fz \supset (x)Gx]$	1, **UG** (invalid)

which violates the third restriction on **UG**.

Now consider rule **UI**. Since there are no restrictions placed on this rule, about the only thing to bear in mind in its use is that rule **UI** *permits* inferences such as the one from 2 to 3 in the proof

1.	$(\exists x)(y)(Fxy \supset Gx)$	p
2.	$(y)(Fxy \supset Gx)$	1, **EI**
3.	$Fxx \supset Gx$	2, **UI** (valid)

Next, consider rule **EI**. Although it contains two restrictions, few will be tempted to violate the first one, and infer, say, from $(\exists x)Fx$ to Fa. And once the need for the second restriction has been pointed out, few will be tempted to violate it, and infer, say, from 2 to 4 in the proof

1.	$(\exists x)Fx$	p
2.	$(\exists x)Gx$	p
3.	Fx	1, **EI**
4.	Gx	2, **EI** (invalid)

So there should be no great difficulty in mastering rule **EI**.

Finally, consider rule **EG**. This rule contains one restriction, but even beginners are unlikely to violate it. Instead, the problem with **EG** is that it *permits* inferences which seem at best nonintuitive. For instance, it permits the inference from 2 to 3 in the proof

1.	$(x)(Fx \supset Ga)$	p
2.	$Fa \supset Ga$	1, **UI**
3.	$(\exists x)(Fa \supset Gx)$	2, **EG** (valid)

This inference is valid because the instructions for the application of rule **EG** specify that in using **EG**, the expression (...*w*...) results from the replacement of *one or more* (but not necessarily all) occurrences of *u* free in (...*u*...) by occurrences of some variable *w* free in (...*w*...).

To sum up, in using the four quantifier rules, students should pay special attention to the second and third restrictions on **UG**, the second restriction on **EI**, and the fact that certain somewhat nonintuitive inferences are permitted by **UI** and **EG**. And, of course, it must be remembered that these rules are to be applied to whole lines of proofs only. Inferences such as the one from 1 to 2 in the proof

1.	~ (*x*)*Fx*	*p*
2.	~ *Fx*	1, **UI** (invalid)

are *never* valid.

Exercise 7–1:

Indicate which of the inferences in the following proofs are invalid, and state *why* they are invalid.

(A)	1.	(∃*x*)(*y*)(*Fxy*)	*p*
	2.	(*y*)(*Fxy*)	1, **EI**
	3.	(*Fxx*)	2, **UI**
	4.	(∃*x*)(*Fxx*)	3, **EG**
(B)	1.	(∃*x*)*Fx*	*p*
	2.	(∃*x*)*Gx*	*p*
	3.	*Fy*	1, **EI**
	4.	*Gy*	2, **EI**

	5.	$Fy \cdot Gy$	4, **Conj**
	6.	$(\exists y)(Fy \cdot Gx)$	5, **EG**
	7.	$(\exists z)(\exists y)(Fy \cdot Gz)$	6, **EG**
(C)	1.	$(x)(\exists y)(Fx \supset Gy)$	p
	2.	$(\exists y)(Fx \supset Gy)$	1, **UI**
	3.	$(Fx \supset Gy)$	2, **EI**
	4.	$(x)(Fx \supset Gy)$	3, **UG**
	5.	$(\exists y)(x)(Fx \supset Gy)$	4, **EG**
(D)	1.	$(x)(\exists y)(Fx \supset Gy)$	p
	2.	Fx	**AP**
	3.	$(\exists y)(Fy \supset Gy)$	1, **UI**
	4.	$Fy \supset Gy$	3, **EI**
	5.	Gy	2, 4 **MP**
	6.	$(\exists w)(Fw \supset Gy)$	4, **EG**
	7.	$Fw \supset Gy$	6, **EI**
	8.	$(\exists w)(Fw \supset Gw)$	7, **EG**
	9.	$(\exists w)[(Fw \supset Gw) \cdot Gy]$	5, 8 **Conj**
	10.	$Fx \supset (\exists w)[(Fw \supset Gw) \cdot Gy]$	2, 9 **CP**
	11.	$(x)\{Fx \supset (\exists w)[(Fw \supset Gw) \cdot Gy]\}$	10, **UG**
(E)	1.	$(x)(y)[(z)Fzx \supset (Gy \cdot Hd)]$	p
	2.	$(y)[(z)Fza \supset (Gy \cdot Hd)]$	1, **UI**
	3.	$(z)Fza \supset (Ga \cdot Hd)$	2, **UI**
	4.	$Fba \supset (Ga \cdot Hd)$	3, **UI**
	5.	$(\exists y)[Fby \supset (Gy \cdot Hd)]$	4, **EG**

→ 6.	*Fby*	**AP**
7.	*Gy · Hd*	5, 6 **MP**
8.	*Hd*	7, **Simp**
9.	*(∃x)Hx*	8, **EG**
10.	*Gy*	7, **Simp**
11.	*(x)Gx*	10, **UG**
12.	*Fby ⊃ (x)Gx*	6, 11 **CP**
13.	*(y)Fby ⊃ (x)Gx*	12, **UG**

3

Rule QN

We now add four related equivalence rules (applying the name **QN** for **Quantifier Negation** indiscriminately to all of them), which are very useful in constructing proofs in predicate logic:

1. $(u)(\ldots u \ldots) :: \sim(\exists u)\sim(\ldots u \ldots)$

2. $(\exists u)(\ldots u \ldots) :: \sim(u)\sim(\ldots u \ldots)$

3. $(u)\sim(\ldots u \ldots) :: \sim(\exists u)(\ldots u \ldots)$

4. $(\exists u)\sim(\ldots u \ldots) :: \sim(u)(\ldots u \ldots)$

where the expression $(\ldots u \ldots)$ is some sentence or sentence form, generally (but not necessarily) containing at least one occurrence of u free in $(\ldots u \ldots)$.*

Rule **QN** permits the assertion of one side of these equivalence argument forms once the other side has been obtained in a proof.

---

* Our predicate logic system is complete without Rule **QN**, but custom and utility dictate its inclusion.

Example:

The following proof illustrates the correct use (as well as usefulness) of rule **QN**:

1. $(\exists x)(Fx \cdot Gx) \supset (x) \sim (Hx \supset Kx)$ p

2. $(\exists x)(Hx \supset Kx)$ p / $\therefore$ $(x)(Fx \supset \sim Gx)$

3. $(\exists x)(Fx \cdot Gx) \supset \sim (\exists x)(Hx \supset Kx)$ 1, **QN**

4. $\sim \sim (\exists x)(Hx \supset Kx)$ 2, **DN**

5. $\sim (\exists x)(Fx \cdot Gx)$ 3, 4 **MT**

6. $(x) \sim (Fx \cdot Gx)$ 5, **QN**

7. $(x)(\sim Fx \vee \sim Gx)$ 6, **DeM**

8. $(x)(Fx \supset \sim Gx)$ 7, **Impl**

Notice that rule **QN** may be applied on parts of lines, unlike the four rules for dropping and adding quantifiers. The derivation of line 3 in the above proof is an example.

It is fairly easy to provide an intuitive justification for rule **QN**. Take its first formulation, namely

$$(u)(\ldots u \ldots) :: \sim (\exists u) \sim (\ldots u \ldots)$$

Clearly, all substitution instances of the left hand side of this expression are equivalent to the analogous substitution instances of its right hand side. An example is the left hand substitution instance "Everything is movable" (in symbols $(x)Mx$), which is equivalent to the analogous right hand substitution instance, "It is not the case that something is not movable" (in symbols $\sim (\exists x) \sim Mx$).

In like manner, it is fairly easy to become convinced that all four versions of rule **QN** are intuitively acceptable.

In addition, we can provide proofs for the four versions of rule **QN**, in that we can prove that corresponding equivalences are what are called "theorems of logic", discussed further in Chapter Nine. For instance, we can prove that the sentence $(\exists x)Fx \equiv \sim(x)\sim Fx$, the equivalence corresponding to a substitution instance of the **QN** form $(\exists u)(\ldots u \ldots)$ $:: \sim(u)\sim(\ldots u \ldots)$, is a theorem of logic.

Exercise 7–2:

Prove valid:

(A) 1. $(x)(Fx \supset Kx)$

　　 2. $(x)\sim(\sim Rx \cdot Kx)$
　　　　 $/ \therefore (x)(\sim Rx \supset \sim Fx)$

(B) 1. $(x)(Kx \supset \sim Lx)$

　　 2. $(\exists x)(Mx \cdot Lx)$
　　　　 $/ \therefore (\exists x)(Mx \cdot \sim Kx)$

(C) 1. $(x)(Sx \supset \sim Px)$
　　　　 $/ \therefore \sim(\exists x)(Sx \cdot Px)$

(D) 1. $(x)(Gx \supset Hx)$

　　 2. $(\exists x)(Ix \cdot \sim Hx)$

　　 3. $(x)(\sim Fx \vee Gx)$
　　　　 $/ \therefore (\exists x)(Ix \cdot \sim Fx)$

(E) 1. $(x)[(Ax \cdot Bx) \supset Cx]$

　　 2. $Aa \cdot Ba$

　　 3. $\sim Cb / \therefore \sim(Ab \cdot Bb)$

(F) 1. $\sim(\exists x)Fx / \therefore Fa \supset Ga$

(G) 1. $(x)[(Bx \cdot Ax) \supset Dx]$

　　 2. $(\exists x)(Qx \cdot Ax)$

　　 3. $(x)(\sim Bx \supset \sim Qx)$
　　　　 $/ \therefore (\exists x)(Dx \cdot Qx)$

(H) 1. $(x)[(Rx \vee Qx) \supset Sx]$

　　 2. $(\exists y)(\sim Qy \vee \sim Ry)$

　　 3. $(\exists z)\sim(Pz \vee \sim Qz)$
　　　　 $/ \therefore (\exists w)Sw$

(I) 1. $(\exists x)[Fx \cdot (y)(Gy \supset Hxy)]$
　　　　 $/ \therefore (\exists x)[Fx \cdot (Ga \supset Hxa)]$

(J) 1. $(x)[Px \supset (Ax \vee Bx)]$

　　 2. $(x)[(Bx \vee Cx) \supset Qx]$
　　　　 $/ \therefore (x)[(Px \cdot \sim Ax) \supset Qx]$

(K)   1. $(\exists x)[Ax \cdot (y)(Qy \supset Lxy)]$

       2. $(x)[Ax \supset (y)(Iy \supset \sim Lxy)]$
/ ∴ $(x)(Qx \supset \sim Ix)$

(L)   1. $(x)(Ax \supset Hx)$

       2. $(\exists x)Ax \supset \sim (\exists y)Gy$
/ ∴ $(x)[(\exists y)Ay \supset \sim Gx]$

(M)   1. $\sim (\exists x)(Axa \cdot \sim Bxb)$

       2. $\sim (\exists x)(Cxc \cdot Cbx)$

       3. $(x)(Bex \supset Cxf)$
/ ∴ $\sim (Aea \cdot Cfc)$

(N)   1. $(x)[Px \supset (Qx \lor Rx)]$

       2. $(x)[(Sx \cdot Px) \supset \sim Qx]$
/ ∴ $(x)(Sx \supset Px)$
$\supset (x)(Sx \supset Rx)$

(O)   1. $(x)[(Fx \lor Gx) \supset (Hx \cdot Kx)]$

       2. $(x)\{(Hx \lor Lx)$
$\supset [(Hx \cdot Nx) \supset Px]\}$
/ ∴ $(x)[Fx \supset (Nx \supset Px)]$

(P)   1. $(x)[Ax \supset (Bx \supset \sim Cx)]$

       2. $\sim (\exists x)(Cx \cdot Dx) \supset (x)(Dx \supset Ex)$
/ ∴ $\sim (\exists x)[Dx \cdot (\sim Ax \lor \sim Bx)]$
$\supset (x)(Dx \supset Ex)$

(Q)   1. $(x)(Ex \lor Gx)$

       2. $(x)(y)[(\sim Lx \lor Mx) \supset Nyx]$
/ ∴ $(x)[\sim (\exists y)(Gy \lor Lx)$
$\supset (\exists z)(Ez \cdot Nzx)]$

(R)   1. $(x)[(\exists y)(Ay \cdot Bxy) \supset Cx]$

       2. $(\exists y)\{Dy \cdot (\exists x)[(Ex \cdot Fx) \cdot Byx]\}$

       3. $(x)(Fx \supset Ax)$ / ∴ $(\exists x)(Cx \cdot Dx)$

(S)   1. $(x)(Ax \supset Bx)$ / ∴ $(x)[(\exists y)$
$(Ay \cdot Cxy) \supset (\exists z)(Bz \cdot Cxz)]$

(T)   1. $(\exists x)Fx \supset (x)[Px \supset (\exists y)Qxy]$

       2. $(x)(y)(Qxy \supset Gx)$
/ ∴ $(x)[(Fx \cdot Px) \supset (\exists y)Gy]$

Chapter Eight

1

*Proving
Invalidity*

In Chapter Five it was stated that we can prove that an argument is invalid in sentential logic by proving that there is a substitution instance of the propositional form of that argument having true premises and a false conclusion.

This method works for *some* arguments expressed in the predicate logic notation. For instance, it works for arguments which do not contain any quantified expressions, such as the invalid argument:

1. $Fa \supset Ga$

2. Fa $/ \therefore \sim Ga$

But it does not work for *most* arguments expressed in the predicate logic notation. For instance, it does not work for the invalid argument:

1. $(x)(\exists y)Gyx$ $/ \therefore (\exists y)(x)Gyx$

We now introduce two methods for proving the invalidity of arguments of this kind.

The first method makes use of the fact that logic must hold in universes other than the *actual* universe. It must hold in *all possible* universes and, in particular, in universes containing very few entities.

Consider the invalid argument

1. $(\exists x)(Fx \cdot Gx)$

2. $(\exists x)(Gx \cdot Hx)$

/ ∴   3. $(\exists x)(Fx \cdot Hx)$

and assume a universe of discourse containing exactly two individuals, *a* and *b*. In this two-individual universe, the above argument is equivalent to the expansion

1. $(Fa \cdot Ga) \lor (Fb \cdot Gb)$

2. $(Ga \cdot Ha) \lor (Gb \cdot Hb)$

/ ∴   3. $(Fa \cdot Ha) \lor (Fb \cdot Hb)$

To prove that this is an invalid argument, we assign truth values to the units in this expansion, to prove that the premises can be true while the conclusion is false:

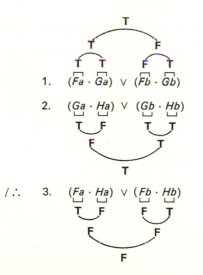

This proves that in a universe of discourse containing exactly two entities, *a* and *b*, the premises $(\exists x)(Fx \cdot Gx)$ and $(\exists x)(Gx \cdot Hx)$ both could be true while the conclusion $(\exists x)(Fx \cdot Hx)$ is false. Therefore, the argument is invalid.

So the first method for proving invalidity involves replacing quantified sentences by equivalent sentences (for a limited universe of discourse) which contain no quantifiers, and then employing the truth-functional method of propositional logic.

Examples:

The following are proofs of invalidity using the limited universe method:

Argument

1. $(x)(Ax \supset Bx)$

2. $(x)(Ax \supset \sim Cx)$

/∴ 3. $(x)(Bx \supset \sim Cx)$

Proof of Invalidity

Assume a universe with exactly one entity, *a*. In this universe, the above argument is equivalent to the expansion

1. $Aa \supset Ba$

2. $Aa \supset \sim Ca$

/∴ 3. $Ba \supset \sim Ca$

which is proved invalid by assigning truth values, as follows:

1. $\overset{\displaystyle T}{\overset{\displaystyle \frown}{\underset{\displaystyle Aa \supset Ba}{\overset{F \quad\ T}{}}}}$

2.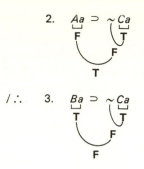

$$Aa \supset \sim Ca$$

/∴ 3. $Ba \supset \sim Ca$

Argument

1. $(x)(\exists y)Gyx$

/∴ 2. $(\exists y)(x)Gyx$

Proof of Invalidity

Assume a universe of discourse containing exactly two individuals, a and b. In this universe, the argument in question is equivalent to the expansion

1. $(Gaa \lor Gba) \cdot (Gab \lor Gbb)$

/∴ 2. $(Gaa \cdot Gab) \lor (Gba \cdot Gbb)$

which is proved invalid by assigning truth values as follows:

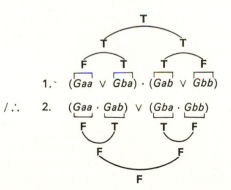

1. $(Gaa \lor Gba) \cdot (Gab \lor Gbb)$

/∴ 2. $(Gaa \cdot Gab) \lor (Gba \cdot Gbb)$

However, we must remember that the expansion of an argument for a one-individual or two-individual universe of discourse may be valid even though the expansion for a larger universe of discourse is invalid. For instance, the expansion of the argument

1. $(\exists x)(Fx \cdot Gx)$

2. $(\exists x)(Fx \cdot Hx)$ $/ \therefore (\exists x)(Gx \cdot Hx)$

for a one-individual universe of discourse, namely

1. $Fa \cdot Ga$

2. $Fa \cdot Ha$ $/ \therefore Ga \cdot Ha$

is valid, but its expansion in a two-individual universe of discourse is invalid, as previously demonstrated.

Another way to prove the invalidity of an argument in predicate logic is to find an obviously invalid argument in the *real* universe of discourse which has the *same form* as the given argument. Consider the argument

1. $(x)(Ax \supset Bx)$

2. $(x)(Cx \supset Bx)$ $/ \therefore (x)(Ax \supset Cx)$

We can prove that this argument is invalid by constructing an argument of the same form which we already know is invalid. For instance, if $Hx = $ "x is human", $Mx = $ "x is mortal", and $Dx = $ "x is a dog", then we already know that the argument

1. $(x)(Hx \supset Mx)$

2. $(x)(Dx \supset Mx)$ $/ \therefore (x)(Hx \supset Dx)$

is invalid (since we know that all humans are mortal and all dogs are mortal but all humans are *not* dogs). Hence our original argument must also be invalid, since it has the same form.

This method also can be employed with respect to a limited domain within the real universe of discourse. For example, if we restrict the universe of discourse to numbers, we can show that the above argument is invalid by finding an invalid argument in mathematics having the same form. An example would be the argument

1.　$(x)(Fx \supset Gx)$

2.　$(x)(Hx \supset Gx)$　　　　　　　　　　$/ \therefore (x)(Fx \supset Hx)$

where Fx = "x is greater than five", Gx = "x is greater than zero", and Hx = "x is greater than ten". Another way to write this argument would be

1.　$(x)[(x > 5) \supset (x > 0)]$

2.　$(x)[(x > 10) \supset (x > 0)]$　　　　$/ \therefore (x)[(x > 5) \supset (x > 10)]$

Since it is true that all numbers greater than five also are greater than zero, and all numbers greater than ten are greater than zero, but false that all numbers greater than five also are greater than ten, it follows that this argument is invalid, and hence that the original argument, having the same form, also is invalid.

Example:

We can prove the argument

1.　$(\exists x)(Fx \cdot Gx)$

2.　$(\exists x)(Gx \cdot Hx)$　　　　　　　　$/ \therefore (\exists x)(Fx \cdot Hx)$

invalid by constructing the following invalid mathematical argument having the same form:

1.　$(\exists x)[(x \text{ is odd}) \cdot (x > 10)]$

2.　$(\exists x)[(x > 10) \cdot (x \text{ is even})]$

$/ \therefore$　3.　$(\exists x)[(x \text{ is odd}) \cdot (x \text{ is even})]$

Clearly, premise 1 is true (e.g., the number eleven is odd and greater than ten), and premise 2 is true (e.g., the number twelve is even and greater than ten), while the conclusion is false (since there is no number which is both odd and even).

Exercise 8–1:

Prove that the following arguments are *in*valid.

(A) 1. $(\exists x)(Ax \cdot \sim Bx)$

     2. $(\exists x)(Ax \cdot \sim Cx)$

     3. $(\exists x)(\sim Bx \cdot Dx)$

/∴ 4. $(\exists x)[Ax \cdot (\sim Bx \cdot Dx)]$

(B) 1. $(x)(Fx \supset Gx)$

     2. $(x)(\sim Fx \supset Ex)$

/∴ 3. $(x)(\sim Gx \supset \sim Ex)$

(C) 1. $(\exists x)(Px \cdot \sim Qx)$

     2. $(x)(Rx \supset Px)$

/∴ 3. $(\exists x)(Rx \cdot \sim Qx)$

(D) 1. $(x)[(Px \cdot Qx) \supset Rx]$

     2. $(\exists x)(Qx \cdot \sim Rx)$

     3. $(\exists x)(Px \cdot \sim Rx)$

/∴ 4. $(\exists x)(\sim Px \cdot \sim Qx)$

(E) 1. $(x)(Px \supset Qx)$

     2. $(x)(Qx \supset Rx)$

/∴ 3. $(\exists x)(Px \cdot Rx)$

(F) 1. $(x)[Mx \supset (Nx \supset Px)]$

     2. $(x)(\sim Qx \supset \sim Px)$

/∴ 3. $(x)[\sim Qx \supset (Mx \lor Nx)]$

(G) 1. $(\exists x)(Ax \cdot Bx)$

     2. $(x)(\sim Bx \lor \sim Cx)$

/∴ 3. $(x)(\sim Ax \lor \sim Cx)$

(H) 1. $(\exists x)(Ax \lor \sim Bx)$

     2. $(x)[(Ax \cdot \sim Bx) \supset Cx]$

/∴ 3. $(\exists x)Cx$

(I) 1. $(x)(\exists y)Fxy$

     2. $(\exists x)(\exists y) \sim Fxy$

/∴ 3. $(\exists x)(y)Fxy$

(J) 1. $(x)[Fx \supset (\exists y)Gxy]$

     2. $(\exists x)Fx$

     3. $(\exists x)(\exists y)Gxy$

/∴ 4. $(x)(\exists y)Gxy$

2

Consistency and
Inconsistency of
Premises

Just as in propositional logic, so also in predicate logic, the whole method for proving the consistency of premises is *part* of the method for proving the invalidity of an argument with those premises.

Example:

We can prove that the argument

1.　$(x)(Fx \supset Gx)$

2.　$(x)(Gx \supset Hx)$

3.　$(\exists x)Fx$　　　　　　　　　　　　　$/ \therefore (\exists x)Hx$

has consistent premises by finding an argument having the same form which contains all true premises. (The truth value of the conclusion is irrelevant to the consistency of the premise.) For instance, if the universe of discourse is restricted to numbers, then the argument

1.　$(x)[(x > 10) \supset (x > 5)]$

2.　$(x)[(x > 5) \supset (x > 0)]$

3.　$(\exists x)(x > 10)$　　　　　　　　　$/ \therefore (\exists x)(x > 0)$

which has the same form as the original argument, contains only true premises, and hence the premises of the original argument must be consistent.

The method used to prove that the premises of an argument in predicate logic are *in*consistent is the same as the method in sentential logic, namely the derivation of a contradiction by means of valid inference forms.

Example:

The argument whose premises are

1. $(x)(Fx \supset Gx)$ p
2. $(x)(Fx \supset \sim Gx)$ p
3. $(\exists x)Fx$ p

is proved inconsistent by deriving an explicit contradiction, as follows:

4. Fx 3, **EI**
5. $Fx \supset Gx$ 1, **UI**
6. $Fx \supset \sim Gx$ 2, **UI**
7. Gx 4, 5 **MP**
8. $\sim Gx$ 4, 6 **MP**
9. $Gx \cdot \sim Gx$ 7, 8 **Conj**

Incidentally, this proves that whatever the conclusion of this argument happens to be, the argument is valid, since from a contradiction *any and all* conclusions validly follow.

3

Difficult Symbolizations

A good deal of care is needed in the symbolization of sentences containing words or phrases such as "only", "none but", and "unless".

Consider the sentence (I): "Only men are strong". Restricting the universe of discourse to human beings, we can symbolize (I) correctly as $(x)(Sx \supset Mx)$.

However, there is a great temptation to symbolize (I) incorrectly as $(x)(Mx \supset Sx)$, thus interpreting it to mean that all men are strong. But to say that *only* men are strong is not to say that *all* men are strong. Suppose it is true that some men are strong and some not, but no women (or children) are strong. Then the sentence "All men are strong" is false (since some men are not strong) while the sentence "Only men are strong" is true. Hence, the symbolization $(x)(Mx \supset Sx)$ cannot be a correct symbolization of (I).

Another way to look at the problem is this. To say that only men are strong is to say that anyone who is not a man is not strong, or what amounts to the same thing, that all nonmen are nonstrong. Since the sentence "All nonmen are nonstrong" is correctly symbolized as $(x)(\sim Mx \supset \sim Sx)$, the equivalent sentence (I): "Only men are strong" also is correctly symbolized in this way. And since $(x)(\sim Mx \supset \sim Sx)$ is equivalent to $(x)(Sx \supset Mx)$, it follows that sentence (I) is correctly symbolized as $(x)(Sx \supset Mx)$.

Sentences containing the phrase "none but" are handled in a similar fashion. For instance, the sentence (II): "None but men are strong" is correctly symbolized as $(x)(Sx \supset Mx)$. (Thus sentences (I) and (II) are equivalent.)

The phrase "none but" in a sentence of this kind means roughly the same thing as the phrase "none except". For instance, the sentence "None but the ignorant are happy" means the same thing as the sentence "None, except the ignorant, are happy". Therefore both of these sentences are to be symbolized in the same way, as $(x)(Hx \supset Ix)$.

English usage also permits the word "unless" to be used in place of the words "only", "none but", or "none except". For instance, instead of saying (I): "Only men are strong" or (II): "None but men are strong", we can say (III): "No one is strong unless he is a man". All of these sentences say roughly the same thing, and hence for our purposes can be symbolized in the same way.

There are several fairly complex sentence patterns involving quantifiers which occur quite frequently in normal English usage. (Of course, each one has a great many variations.) Some of these are "All _____ who _____ are _____" (example: "All men who are intelligent are honest"); "All _____ and _____ are _____" (example: "All men and women are honest"); "All _____ are _____ and _____" (example: "All men are intelligent and honest"); "All

_____ are _ _ _ _ _ _ or ...." (example: "All men are intelligent or honest"); "Not all _____ are _ _ _ _ _ _" (example: "Not all men are honest"); "No _____ who _ _ _ _ _ _ are ...." (example: "No men who are intelligent are honest"); and so on.

While most of these are easily symbolized, two or three are tricky. For instance, the sentence (IV): "All women *and* children are exempt from the draft" is correctly symbolized as $(x)[(Wx \lor Cx) \supset Ex]$, but *not* as $(x)[(Wx \cdot Cx) \supset Ex]$, for the latter asserts that all things which are *both* women *and* children are exempt, while the implication of (IV) is that all things that are *either* women *or* children are exempt.

In this case, the "and" in the antecedent of (IV) misleads us into using the symbol " $\cdot$ " instead of $\lor$. However, there *is* a fairly straightforward symbolization of (IV) containing the symbol " $\cdot$ ", namely $(x)(Wx \supset Ex) \cdot (x)(Cx \supset Ex)$. To say that all women are exempt from the draft and all children are exempt from the draft is to say that all women and children are exempt from the draft. And, indeed, $(x)(Wx \supset Ex) \cdot (x)(Cx \supset Ex)$ and $(x)[(Wx \lor Cx) \supset Ex]$ are equivalent.

Examples:

The following are examples of English sentences with correct symbolizations (using obvious abbreviations):

1. All men who attend college are well educated.
   $(x)[(Mx \cdot Cx) \supset Ex]$

2. All men and women are adults.
   $(x)[(Mx \lor Wx) \supset Ax]$

3. All men are intelligent *and* handsome.
   $(x)[Mx \supset (Ix \cdot Hx)]$

4. All women are intelligent *or* beautiful.
   $(x)[Wx \supset (Ix \lor Bx)]$

5. Not all men are handsome.
   $\sim (x)(Mx \supset Hx)$ or
   $(\exists x)(Mx \cdot \sim Hx)$

6. No men are handsome.
$(x)(Mx \supset \sim Hx)$ or
$\sim(\exists x)(Mx \cdot Hx)$

7. No men who attend college are ignorant.
$(x)[(Mx \cdot Ax) \supset \sim Ix]$ or
$\sim(\exists x)[(Mx \cdot Ax) \cdot Ix]$

8. There are no ignorant men who have attended college.

(Sentence 8 is equivalent to 7 and hence is symbolized in the same way as 7.)

The above examples concern symbolizations containing only one quantifier. Those containing two or more quantifiers often are much more difficult.

Consider the sentence (V): "If someone is too noisy then everyone in the room will be annoyed". Restricting the universe of discourse to human beings, we can partially symbolize (V) as

If $(\exists x)(Nx)$ then $(y)(Ry \supset Ay)$

and then complete the symbolization as

$(\exists x)(Nx) \supset (y)(Ry \supset Ay)$

But the sentence (VI): "If someone is too noisy, then everyone in the room will be annoyed with him", which seems very much like sentence (V), must be symbolized somewhat differently. We cannot partially symbolize (VI) as

If $(\exists x)(Nx)$ then $(y)(Ry \supset Ayx)$

and then complete the symbolization as

$(\exists x)(Nx) \supset (y)(Ry \supset Ayx)$

because the last x variable in this expression is a *free variable*, so that this expression is not a sentence.

And we cannot rectify this error simply by extending the scope of the existential quantifier. That is, we cannot correctly symbolize sentence (VI) as

(VII) $(\exists x)[Nx \supset (y)(Ry \supset Ayx)]$

Although (VII) *is* a sentence, it is not equivalent to sentence (VI). Sentence (VII) asserts that there is at least one person such that if that person is too noisy then everyone in the room will be annoyed with him. This would be true if everyone became annoyed when one person, say Smith, was too noisy, but not when some other person, say Jones, was too noisy. But the implication of sentence (VI) is that if *anyone* is too noisy then everyone will be annoyed at that person. So (VI) cannot be correctly symbolized by (VII). Instead, we can symbolize sentence (VI) as

$(x)[Nx \supset (y)(Ry \supset Ayx)]$

using a *universal x* quantifier.

The misleading English word in this case is the word "someone", which sometimes functions as an existential quantifier and sometimes as a universal quantifier. The words "something", "somewhere", "sometime", etc., also are misleading in the same way. Hence it is wise to pay close attention to the meaning of a sentence in which any of these terms occur before deciding whether its correct symbolization requires an existential or a universal quantifier.

Perhaps one final comment is in order on the use of terms like "someone", for it still may seem strange that sentence (V) is correctly symbolized as $(\exists x)(Nx) \supset (y)(Ry \supset Ay)$, using an existential quantifier whose scope is restricted to the antecedent of the symbolization, while sentence (VI) is correctly symbolized as $(x)[Nx \supset (y)(Ry \supset Ayx)]$, using a universal quantifier whose scope is the whole of the symbolization. But perhaps this nonintuitiveness can be dispelled to some extent by pointing out that the symbolization $(\exists x)(Nx) \supset (y)(Ry \supset Ay)$ is *equivalent* to the symbolization $(x)[Nx \supset (y)(Ry \supset Ay)]$. In other words, there is a sense in which the term "something" functions as a universal quantifier in (V) just as it does in (VI). (The significance of all of this material will become clearer after logical truths are discussed in Chapter Nine.)

Now consider the sentence (VIII): "If someone is too noisy, then if everyone in the room is annoyed, someone will complain". We can partially symbolize this sentence as

If $(\exists x)(Nx)$ then   [if $(y)(Ry \supset Ay)$ then $(\exists z)(Cz)$]

and complete the symbolization as

$(\exists x)(Nx) \supset [(y)(Ry \supset Ay) \supset (\exists z)(Cz)]$

But, again, the sentence (IX): "If someone is too noisy, then if all of the people in the room are annoyed, they all will dislike him", which seems very much like sentence (VIII), must be symbolized somewhat differently. We cannot partially symbolize it as

If $(\exists x)(Nx)$ then   [if $(y)(Ry \supset Ay)$ then (Dyx)]

and complete the symbolization as

$(\exists x)(Nx) \supset [(y)(Ry \supset Ay) \supset (Dyx)]$

because the last x and y variables in this symbolization are *free variables*, so that this expression is not a sentence. Instead, the correct symbolization of (IX), analogously to the correct symbolization of (VI), is

$(x)\{Nx \supset (y)[(Ry \supset Ay) \supset (Ry \supset Dyx)]\}$

Examples:

The following are examples of English sentences with correct symbolizations.

1. Everyone loves someone (or other).
   $(x)[Px \supset (\exists y)(Py \cdot Lxy)]$
   $(Px = "x$ is a person")

2. Everyone loves everyone.
   $(x)[Px \supset (y)(Py \supset Lxy)]$ or
   $\sim (\exists x)[Px \cdot (\exists y)(Py \cdot \sim Lxy)]$

3. Someone loves everyone.
$(\exists x)[Px \cdot (y)(Py \supset Lxy)]$ or
$(\exists x)[Px \cdot \sim(\exists y)(Py \cdot \sim Lxy)]$

4. Someone loves someone (or other).
$(\exists x)[Px \cdot (\exists y)(Py \cdot Lxy)]$

5. No one loves everyone.
$(x)[Px \supset (\exists y)(Py \cdot \sim Lxy)]$ or
$\sim(\exists x)[Px \cdot (y)(Py \supset Lxy)]$

6. No one loves anyone.
$(x)[Px \supset \sim(\exists y)(Py \cdot Lxy)]$ or
$\sim(\exists x)[Px \cdot (\exists y)(Py \cdot Lxy)]$

7. Not everyone loves everyone.
$\sim(x)[Px \supset (y)(Py \supset Lxy)]$ or
$(\exists x)[Px \cdot (\exists y)(Py \cdot \sim Lxy)]$

8. Not everyone loves someone (or other).
$\sim(x)[Px \supset (\exists y)(Py \cdot Lxy)]$ or
$(\exists x)[Px \cdot (y)(Py \supset \sim Lxy)]$

(For examples 9–13, assume the universe of discourse to be restricted to numbers only.)

9. There is some number larger than any number.
$(\exists x)(y)Lxy$

10. There is some number larger than some number (or other).
$(\exists x)(\exists y)Lxy$

11. All numbers are larger than some number (or other).
$(x)(\exists y)Lxy$

12. There is no number larger than all numbers.
$\sim(\exists x)(y)Lxy$ or $(x)(\exists y)\sim Lxy$

13. Not all numbers are larger than some number (or other).
$\sim(x)(\exists y)Lxy$ or $(\exists x)(y)\sim Lxy$

14. All barbers who don't shave themselves are shaved by someone who is a barber.
$(x)[(Bx \cdot \sim Sxx) \supset (\exists y)(By \cdot Syx)]$
or $\sim(\exists x)[(Bx \cdot \sim Sxx) \cdot (y)(By \supset \sim Syx)]$

15. All barbers who don't shave themselves are not shaved by any barbers.
$(x)[(Bx \cdot \sim Sxx) \supset \sim(\exists y) (By \cdot Syx)]$ or $\sim(\exists x)[(Bx \cdot \sim Sxx) \cdot (\exists y)(By \cdot Syx)]$

16. If someone is a barber who does not shave himself, then he is shaved by someone who is a barber.

(Sentence 16 is equivalent to 14.)

17. If someone is a barber who does not shave himself, then he is not shaved by anyone who is a barber.

(Sentence 17 is equivalent to 15.)

18. If someone is a barber who does not shave himself, then someone does not get shaved by any barber.
$(\exists x)(Bx \cdot \sim Sxx) \supset (\exists y)[Py \cdot (z)$
$(Bz \supset \sim Szy)]$
$(Py = ``y \text{ is a person}".)$

19. If there is anyone who does not shave himself, then if no one is shaved by any barber, he (who does not shave himself) will not be shaved by any barber.
$(x)\{(Px \cdot \sim Sxx) \supset \{(y)$
$[Py \supset \sim (\exists z)(Bz \cdot Szy)]$
$\supset \sim (\exists v)(Bv \cdot Svx)\}\}$

20. If there is someone who does not shave himself, then if no barber shaves anyone, there is someone who is not shaved by anyone.
$(\exists x)(Px \cdot \sim Sxx) \supset \{(y)[By \supset (z)$
$(Pz \supset \sim Syz)] \supset (\exists u)[Pu \cdot (w)$
$(Pw \supset \sim Swu)]\}$

Exercise 8–2:

Symbolize the following sentences (using the indicated predicate letters), so as to reveal as much of the internal structure of each sentence as possible.

1. Women are fickle. ($Wx = ``x \text{ is a woman}"$; $Fx = ``x \text{ is fickle}"$)

2. A barking dog never bites. ($Bx = ``x \text{ barks}"$; $Dx = ``x \text{ is a dog}"$; $Nx = ``x \text{ never bites}"$)

3. There are large dogs. ($Dx = ``x \text{ is a dog}"$; $Lx = ``x \text{ is large}"$)

4. Not all women are fickle. ($Wx = ``x \text{ is a woman}"$; $Fx = ``x \text{ is fickle}"$)

5. Some barking dogs are annoying. ($Dx = ``x \text{ is a dog}"$; $Bx = ``x \text{ barks}"$; $Ax = ``x \text{ is annoying}"$)

6. Nothing logical is difficult. ($Lx = ``x \text{ is logical}"$; $Dx = ``x \text{ is difficult}"$)

7. Some coeds are both beautiful and intelligent. ($Cx = ``x \text{ is a coed}"$; $Bx = ``x \text{ is beautiful}"$; $Ix = ``x \text{ is intelligent}"$)

8. Only the rich deserve the fair. ($Rx = ``x \text{ is rich}"$; $Fx = ``x \text{ is fair}"$; $Dxy = ``x \text{ deserves } y"$)

9. None but the rich deserve the fair. ($Rx = ``x \text{ is rich}"$; $Fx = ``x \text{ is fair}"$; $Dxy = ``x \text{ deserves } y"$)

10. No one deserves the fair unless he is rich. ($Rx = ``x \text{ is rich}"$; $Fx = ``x \text{ is fair}"$; $Dxy = ``x \text{ deserves } y"$)

11. Seniors and football players are excused. (Sx = "x is a senior"; Fx = "x is a football player"; Ex = "x is excused")

12. But junior women are not excused. (Jx = "x is a junior"; Wx = "x is a woman"; Ex = "x is excused")

13. Some people are happy only when drunk. (Px = "x is a person"; Hx = "x is happy"; Dx = "x is drunk")

14. Among dogs, mongrels, and only mongrels, are intelligent. (Dx = "x is a dog"; Ix = "x is intelligent"; Mx = "x is a mongrel")

15. Art won't get an A unless he studies with Judith. (a = "Art"; j = "Judith"; Ax = "x gets an A"; Sxy = "x studies with y")

16. Anyone who consults a psychiatrist ought to have his head examined. (Px = "x is a person"; Cxy = "x consults y"; Sx = "x is a psychiatrist"; Ex = "x ought to have his head examined")

17. No one learns anything unless he teaches it to himself. (Px = "x is a person"; Lxy = "x learns y"; $Txyz$ = "x teaches y to z")

18. Everyone owes something to someone. (Px = "x is a person"; $Oxyz$ = "x owes y to z")

19. Someone owes something to someone. (Px = "x is a person"; $Oxyz$ = "x owes y to z")

20. Someone owes something to everyone. (Px = "x is a person"; $Oxyz$ = "x owes y to z")

21. Someone owes everything to someone. (Px = "x is a person"; $Oxyz$ = "x owes y to z")

22. Everyone owes something to everyone. (Px = "x is a person"; $Oxyz$ = "x owes y to z")

23. If any sophomore fails, then he deserves to fail. (Sx = "x is a sophomore"; Fx = "x fails"; Dx = "x deserves to fail")

24. If any senior fails, then some junior ought to tutor him. (Sx = "x is a senior"; Fx = "x fails"; Jx = "x is a junior"; Txy = "x ought to tutor y")

25. If any sophomore fails, then every sophomore will fail. (Sx = "x is a sophomore"; Fx = "x fails")

26. If every senior fails, then if some seniors are intelligent, some seniors ought to be ashamed of themselves. (Sx = "x is a senior"; Fx = "x fails"; Ix = "x is intelligent"; Ox = "x ought to be ashamed of himself")

27. If any seniors fail, then if they are intelligent, some intelligent junior ought to tutor them. (Sx = "x is a senior"; Fx = "x fails"; Ix = "x is intelligent"; Jx = "x is a junior"; Oxy = "x ought to tutor y")

28. God only helps those who help themselves. (g = "God"; Hxy = "x helps y"; Px = "x is a person")

29. Only someone who hasn't sinned is permitted to cast stones at those who have. (Px = "x is a person"; Sx = "x has sinned"; Cxy = "x is permitted to cast stones at y")

30. Someone who sometimes sins against some people *always* sins against God. (*Px* = "*x* is a person"; *Sxyz* = "*x* sins against *y* at *z*"; *Tx* = "*x* is a time"; *g* = "God")

31. You can fool some of the people all of the time, and all of the people some of the time, but you can't fool all of the people all of the time. (*Px* = "*x* is a person"; *Tx* = "*x* is a time"; *Fxy* = "*x* can be fooled at *y*").

Chapter Nine

*Predicate
Logic—IV*

1

*Theorems of
Logic*

A **theorem of logic** is a sentence or sentence form obtainable as the conclusion of a valid deductive proof in which there are no given premises. In effect, then, a theorem of logic is an expression derivable without the use of *contingent* (factual) sentences as premises.* It is something that can be proved by *logic* alone.

All of the tautologies of sentential logic are theorems of logic by this definition, because they can be proved without the use of contingent premises. But they also can be proved by means of *truth table analysis*. In this respect, they differ from most of the theorems of predicate logic, for we can prove by truth table analysis only those theorems of predicate logic which are substitution

---

* We assume here that we do not permit sentence *forms* as *premises*, although they are permitted as what we have called *assumed* premises.

instances of tautologous sentence forms of sentential logic. (An example would be the sentence $(x)Fx \lor \sim(x)Fx$, which is a theorem of predicate logic and is provable by means of truth table analysis.)

But the other theorems of predicate logic must be (and can be) proved by means of the standard predicate logic proof method. Since they can*not* be proved by truth table analysis, they are *not* tautologies, at least not in the sense in which we are using that term.*

The class of theorems of logic can be divided into those which are *sentence forms*, and hence are neither true nor false, and those which are *sentences*, and hence are true. Indeed, we might call the latter **logical truths**, or **truths of logic**. Logical truths are especially important because they are truths provable (and hence knowable) without the aid of *contingent* information. They are, so to speak, truths knowable by means of logic alone. (This fact is of great importance for the problems discussed in Chapter Nineteen.)

Analogous to logical *truths* are logical *falsehoods*. We can say that a **logical falsehood** is a false sentence which can be *proved* false without the aid of *contingent* information, that is, proved false by logic alone. (The fact that there are logical falsehoods also is of importance to the problems discussed in Chapter Nineteen.)

Clearly, if no premises are used in proving that an expression is a theorem of logic, then either **CP** or **IP** must be employed; otherwise there would be no justification possible for the first line of the proof.

The following is a typical proof of a theorem of predicate logic employing **CP**:

To prove: $(\exists x)(Fx \cdot Gx) \supset [(\exists x)Fx \cdot (\exists x)Gx]$

1.	$(\exists x)(Fx \cdot Gx)$	**AP**
2.	$Fx \cdot Gx$	1, **EI**
3.	Fx	2, **Simp**
4.	$(\exists x)Fx$	3, **EG**
5.	Gx	2, **Simp**

---

* But the word "tautology" is sometimes used in other ways. For instance, some philosophers use it as a synonym for "theorem of logic".

6.	$(\exists x)Gx$	5, **EG**
7.	$(\exists x)Fx \cdot (\exists x)Gx$	4, 6 **Conj**
8.	$(\exists x)(Fx \cdot Gx) \supset [(\exists x)Fx \cdot (\exists x)Gx]$	1, 7 **CP**

In this proof, the antecedent of the theorem to be proved (the conclusion of the proof) is employed as the assumed premise of the conditional proof. However, sometimes it is easier to assume the negation of the consequent of the desired conclusion, derive the negation of the antecedent, and then obtain the conclusion by contraposition. This strategy is illustrated by the following proof:

To prove: $[(\exists x)Fx \lor (\exists x)Gx] \supset (\exists x)(Fx \lor Gx)$

1.	$\sim (\exists x)(Fx \lor Gx)$	**AP** (the negation of the consequent)
2.	$(x) \sim (Fx \lor Gx)$	1, **QN**
3.	$\sim (Fx \lor Gx)$	2, **UI**
4.	$\sim Fx \cdot \sim Gx$	3, **DeM**
5.	$\sim Fx$	4, **Simp**
6.	$(x) \sim Fx$	5, **UG**
7.	$\sim Gx$	4, **Simp**
8.	$(x) \sim Gx$	7, **UG**
9.	$\sim (\exists x)Fx$	6, **QN**
10.	$\sim (\exists x)Gx$	8, **QN**
11.	$\sim (\exists x)Fx \cdot \sim (\exists x)Gx$	9, 10 **Conj**
12.	$\sim [(\exists x)Fx \lor (\exists x)Gx]$	11, **DeM** (the negation of the antecedent)
13.	$\sim (\exists x)(Fx \lor Gx) \supset \sim [(\exists x)Fx \lor (\exists x)Gx]$	1, 12 **CP**
14.	$[(\exists x)Fx \lor (\exists x)Gx] \supset (\exists x)(Fx \lor Gx)$	13, **Contra**

Many theorems of logic are equivalences. In general, the easiest way to prove a theorem of logic which is an equivalence is to prove the two conditionals which together imply the equivalence, and then join the two conclusions by the rule of conjunction. The following proof is an illustration:

To prove: $(\exists x)(Fx \supset Ga) \equiv [(x)Fx \supset Ga]$

First prove that

$(\exists x)(Fx \supset Ga) \supset [(x)Fx \supset Ga]$

1.	$(\exists x)(Fx \supset Ga)$	**AP**
2.	$(x)Fx$	**AP**
3.	$Fx \supset Ga$	1, **EI**
4.	Fx	2, **UI**
5.	Ga	3, 4 **MP**
6.	$(x)Fx \supset Ga$	2, 5 **CP**
7.	$(\exists x)(Fx \supset Ga) \supset [(x)Fx \supset Ga]$	1, 6 **CP**

Then prove that

$[(x)Fx \supset Ga] \supset (\exists x)(Fx \supset Ga)$

8.	$\sim (\exists x)(Fx \supset Ga)$	**AP**
9.	$(x) \sim (Fx \supset Ga)$	8, **QN**
10.	$\sim (Fy \supset Ga)$	9, **UI**
11.	$\sim (\sim Fy \vee Ga)$	10, **Impl**
12.	$Fy \cdot \sim Ga$	11, **DeM, DN***

---

* Once a reasonable amount of manipulative ability has been acquired, easy steps, such as **DN**, can occasionally be combined with other steps, provided the skipped steps are cited to the right of the next line, as in line 12 of this proof.

13.	Fy	12, **Simp**
14.	$(x)Fx$	13, **UG**
15.	$\sim Ga$	12, **Simp**
16.	$(x)Fx \cdot \sim Ga$	14, 15 **Conj**
17.	$\sim [\sim (x)Fx \vee Ga]$	16, **DN, DeM**
18.	$\sim [(x)Fx \supset Ga]$	17, **Impl**
19.	$\sim (\exists x)(Fx \supset Ga) \supset \ \sim [(x)Fx \supset Ga]$	8, 18 **CP**
20.	$[(x)Fx \supset Ga] \supset (\exists x)(Fx \supset Ga)$	19, **Contra**

And finally, combine the two semiconclusions:

21.	$\{(\exists x)(Fx \supset Ga) \supset [(x)Fx \supset Ga]\}$ $\cdot \{[(x)Fx \supset Ga] \supset (\exists x)(Fx \supset Ga)\}$	7, 20 **Conj**
22.	$(\exists x)(Fx \supset Ga) \equiv [(x)(Fx \supset Ga)]$	21, **Equiv**

Notice that there are *three* assumed premises in this proof, and that the second assumed premise lies wholly within the scope of the first. (Incidentally, this theorem of logic illustrates the subtlety and nonintuitive character of many of the theorems of predicate logic.)

A fairly common proof procedure involves using **UG** as the final step in a proof:

To prove: $(x)[(y)Fy \supset Fx]$

1.	$(y)Fy$	**AP**
2.	Fx	1, **UI**
3.	$(y)Fy \supset Fx$	1, 2 **CP**
4.	$(x)[(y)Fy \supset Fx]$	3, **UG**

Now let's illustrate the use of the rule of *Indirect Proof* in proving theorems of logic:*

* The theorem proved is a substitution instance of the second version of rule **QN**, listed on p.135, and if made more general would constitute a proof of that rule.

Predicate Logic

To prove: $(\exists x)Fx \equiv \sim(x)\sim Fx$

First, we prove by **CP** that

$\sim(x)\sim Fx \supset (\exists x)Fx$

1.	Fx	**AP**
2.	$(\exists x)Fx$	1, **EG**
3.	$Fx \supset (\exists x)Fx$	1, 2 **CP**
4.	$\sim(\exists x)Fx$	**AP**
5.	$\sim Fx$	3, 4 **MT**
6.	$(x)\sim Fx$	5, **UG**
7.	$\sim(\exists x)Fx \supset (x)\sim Fx$	4, 6 **CP**
8.	$\sim(x)\sim Fx \supset (\exists x)Fx$	7, **Contr, DN**

A very ingenious proof indeed. Now we prove by **IP** that

$(\exists x)Fx \supset \sim(x)\sim Fx$

9.	$\sim[(\exists x)Fx \supset \sim(x)\sim Fx]$	**AP**
10.	$\sim[\sim(\exists x)Fx \lor \sim(x)\sim Fx]$	9, **Impl**
11.	$(\exists x)Fx \cdot (x)\sim Fx$	10, **DeM, DN**
12.	$(\exists x)Fx$	11, **Simp**
13.	Fy	12, **EI**
14.	$(x)\sim Fx$	11, **Simp**
15.	$\sim Fy$	14, **UI**
16.	$Fy \cdot \sim Fy$	13, 15 **Conj**
17.	$(\exists x)Fx \supset \sim(x)\sim Fx$	9, 16 **IP**

Finally, we combine the two semiconclusions:

18. $[(\exists x)Fx \supset \sim(x)\sim Fx]$
    $\cdot [\sim(x)\sim Fx \supset (\exists x)Fx]$ 8, 17 **Conj**

19. $(\exists x)Fx \equiv \sim(x)\sim Fx$ 18, **Equiv**

Exercise 9–1:

Prove that the following are theorems of logic: (These theorems are very important, since each one is a substitution instance of what might be called a *theorem schema*, and the proofs of the theorem schemas exactly parallel the proofs of their substitution instances. For example, the first theorem, $(x)(y)Fxy \equiv (y)(x)Fxy$, is a substitution instance of the general schema $(u)(w)(\ldots u, w \ldots) \equiv (w)(u)(\ldots u, w \ldots)$, and the proof of the schema exactly parallels the proof of its substitution instance.)

1. $(x)(y)Fxy \equiv (y)(x)Fxy$

2. $(x)Gy \equiv Gy$

3. $(\exists x)Gy \equiv Gy$

4. $(\exists x)(y)Fxy \supset (y)(\exists x)Fxy$
   (but *not* vice versa)

5. $(x)(Fx \cdot Gx) \equiv [(x)Fx \cdot (x)Gx]$

6. $[(x)Fx \lor (x)Gx] \supset (x)(Fx \lor Gx)$
   (but *not* vice versa)

7. $(x)(Fx \supset Gx) \supset [(\exists x)Fx \supset (\exists x)Gx]$
   (but *not* vice versa)

8. $(\exists x)(Fx \cdot Gx) \supset [(\exists x)Fx \cdot (\exists x)Gx]$
   (but *not* vice versa)

9. $(\exists x)(Fx \lor Gx) \equiv [(\exists x)Fx \lor (\exists x)Gx]$

In the following theorems, the letter P denotes any sentence, or sentence form, which does *not* contain a free occurrence of the variable x. Thus in line 10, P might be Fa, Fy, $(y)(Fy \supset Gy)$, etc.

10. $[(x)Fx \cdot P] \equiv (x)(Fx \cdot P)$

11. $(x)(Fx \lor P) \equiv [(x)Fx \lor P]$

12. $(x)(P \supset Fx) \equiv [P \supset (x)Fx]$

13. $(x)(Fx \supset P) \equiv [(\exists x)Fx \supset P]$

14. $(\exists x)(P \cdot Fx) \equiv [P \cdot (\exists x)Fx]$

15. $(\exists x)(P \lor Fx) \equiv [P \lor (\exists x)Fx]$

16. $(\exists x)(Fx \supset P) \equiv [(x)Fx \supset P]$

17. $(\exists x)(P \supset Fx) \equiv [P \supset (\exists x)Fx]$

2

Identity

The word "is", and its derivatives, are ambiguous. Consider the following sentences:

John is tall.

Mark Twain is Samuel Clemens.

In the first sentence, the word "is" indicates that the property of being tall is a property of John. (This sometimes is called the *predicating function* of the word "is".) But in the second sentence, no property is predicated of Mark Twain. In this sentence, the word "is" indicates an *identity* between the person who is Mark Twain and the person who is Samuel Clemens. It would be correct to symbolize the first sentence as *Tj*, but *in*correct to symbolize the second sentence as *Ct* (where $t =$ "Mark Twain", and $C =$ "Samuel Clemens"). We introduce a new symbol, namely $=$, to indicate identity. And then, using this new symbol, we can symbolize the sentence

Mark Twain is Samuel Clemens.

as

$t = c$

3

Proofs Involving Identity

Consider the following argument:

1. *Wtf*   (Mark Twain wrote Huck Finn.)

2. $t = c$ (Mark Twain is Samuel Clemens.)

/ ∴   3. *Wcf*   (Samuel Clemens wrote Huck Finn.)

Clearly, this argument is valid. But so far, our system provides no justification for step 3. We now introduce such a justification, namely the **rule of identity**, which states, in effect, that we may substitute identicals for identicals. The rule can be schematized as follows:

1. $(\ldots u \ldots)$

2. $u = w$ / ∴ $(\ldots w \ldots)$

where u and w are any individual constants or individual variables, and where $(\ldots w \ldots)$ results from $(\ldots u \ldots)$ by the replacement of one or more free occurrences of u by free occurrences of w.*

Examples:

The following examples illustrate the use of the identity sign and also the rule of identity in proofs.

(I)   1. $(x)(Fx \supset Gx)$ p

     2. $\sim Ga$ p

     3. $a = b$ p / ∴ $\sim Fb$

---

* To make the system complete we must add a rule permitting the assertion of a premise such as $(x)(x = x)$ at any time in a proof.

	4.	$Fa \supset Ga$	1, **UI**
	5.	$\sim Fa$	2, 4 **MT**
	6.	$\sim Fb$	3, 5 **Ident** (rule of identity)
(II)	1.	$(x)[(x = b) \supset Fx]$	p
	2.	$a = b$	$p \, / \therefore Fa$
	3.	$(a = b) \supset Fa$	1, **UI**
	4.	Fa	2, 3 **MP**

It is customary to symbolize expressions such as $\sim(a = b)$ as $a \neq b$. Using this symbolization, we can obtain the following proof:

(III)	1.	$(x)[(x \neq b) \supset Fx]$	p
	2.	$a \neq b$	$p \, / \therefore Fa$
	3.	$(a \neq b) \supset Fa$	1, **UI**
	4.	Fa	2, 3 **MP**

4

Symbolizing "At Least", "Exactly", "At Most", etc.

Once the identity sign is added to predicate logic, we can symbolize sentences stating quantities other than all, some (at least one), none, and their variations.

At least

We already know how to symbolize sentences containing the expression "at least one", namely by means of the existential quantifier. Thus the sentence "There is at least one student" can be symbolized as $(\exists x)Sx$.

But suppose we want to symbolize the sentence

There are at least *two* students.

We cannot do so simply by using two quantifiers. That is, we cannot symbolize that sentence as $(\exists x)(\exists y)(Sx \cdot Sy)$, because the x and y referred to might be the same entity. However, using the identity sign, we can correctly symbolize it as $(\exists x)(\exists y)[(Sx \cdot Sy) \cdot (x \neq y)]$. This expression says that there is an x which is a student, and a y which is a student, *and x is not identical with y*.

Similarly, we can symbolize the sentence

There are at least three students.

as

$$(\exists x)(\exists y)(\exists z)\{[(Sx \cdot Sy) \cdot Sz] \cdot \{[(x \neq y) \cdot (x \neq z)] \cdot (y \neq z)\}\}$$

And in the same way, we can handle the phrases "at least four", "at least five", and so on.

Exactly

Now consider the sentence

There is *exactly one* student.

In the first place, if there is *exactly one* student, then there is *at least one*. So *part* of the meaning of "exactly one" is captured by the phrase "at least one", and hence part of the meaning of the sentence "There is exactly one student" can be symbolized as $(\exists x)Sx$. But this sentence states not only that there is at least one student, but also that there is *at most one* student, since it asserts that there is *exactly one*. The problem is to symbolize not only "there is at least one student", but also "there is at most one student", and the solution is provided by the use of the identity symbol, as follows:

$$(\exists x)\{Sx \cdot (y)[Sy \supset (x = y)]\}$$

This asserts that there is at least one student, x, and given any allegedly *other* student, y, y is not *really* other than x, but rather is *identical with x*. That is, it asserts that there is *at least* one student, and *at most* one student.

Similarly, we can symbolize the sentence

There are exactly two students.

as

$$(\exists x)(\exists y)\{[(Sx \cdot Sy) \cdot (x \neq y) \cdot (z)\{Sz \supset [(z = x) \lor (z = y)]\}\}$$

And obviously, the same method can be applied in symbolizing the phrases "exactly three", "exactly four", etc.

At most

Once "at least" and "exactly" have been conquered, the rest is clear sailing. For example, the sentence

There is at most one student.

can be symbolized as

$$(x)\{Sx \supset (y)[Sy \supset (x = y)]\}$$

The reason for the universal quantifier is that this sentence asserts *not that there are any students*, but rather that *there is not more than one* student. It would be true if there were no students at all, as well as if there were exactly one.

Similarly, we can symbolize the sentence

There are at most *two* students.

as

$$(x)(y)\{[(Sx \cdot Sy) \cdot (x \neq y)] \supset (z)\{Sz \supset [(z = x) \lor (z = y)]\}\}$$

And in the same way we can handle sentences containing the phrases "at most three", "at most four", etc.

Other uses of identity

Use of the identity sign also provides a method for symbolizing many other kinds of sentences.

Consider the sentence

All races of human beings are cross fertile.

We cannot symbolize this sentence as $(x)(y)[(Rx \cdot Ry) \supset Cxy]$ (where $Rx = $ "x is a race of human beings" and $Cxy = $ "x is cross fertile with y"), because this symbolization implies that all races are cross fertile with themselves, which is not what is intended by the original sentence. However, using the identity sign, we can correctly symbolize that sentence as

$(x)(y)\{[(Rx \cdot Ry) \cdot (x \neq y)] \supset Cxy\}$

Examples:

Some other examples of the use of the identity sign in symbolizations are (restricting the universe of discourse to human beings):

1. Everyone loves exactly one person.
$(x)(\exists y)\{Lxy \cdot (z)[Lxz \supset (z = y)]\}$

2. Everyone loves exactly one *other* person.
$(x)(\exists y)\{[(x \neq y) \cdot Lxy]$
$\cdot (z)[Lxz \supset (z = y)]\}$

3. Everyone loves only himself (interpreted to mean that everyone loves himself and no one else).
$(x)\{Lxx \cdot (y)[(y \neq x) \supset \sim Lxy]\}$

4. At most, everyone loves only himself.
$(x)(y)[Lxy \supset (x = y)]$

5. Someone loves someone.
$(\exists x)(\exists y)Lxy$

6. Someone loves someone else.
$(\exists x)(\exists y)[Lxy \cdot (x \neq y)]$

7. Some people love only other people.
$(\exists x)(y)[Lxy \supset (x \neq y)]$

8. Some people love no one else.
$(\exists x)(y)[(x \neq y) \supset \sim Lxy]$

9. Only Art loves Betsy (interpreted to imply that Art does love Betsy).
$Lab \cdot (x)[Lxb \supset (x = a)]$

Predicate Logic

5

Definite Descriptions

We can refer to a person or entity by *name*, for example, "Samuel Clemens", "Mt. Everest", or by *description*, for example, "the author of Huck Finn", "the tallest mountain in the world". A description of this kind generally is called a **definite description**, because it picks out, or describes, *one definite entity*. The problem is to symbolize sentences containing definite descriptions using the apparatus of predicate logic (including =).

To say that, "The president of the United States is overworked", is to say that the one and only man who is president of the United States is overworked, since it would be inappropriate to talk about *the* president of the United States if there were more than one such person. Therefore, this sentence can be symbolized by first symbolizing "There is exactly one president of the United States", and then symbolizing the sentence that he is overworked. So the sentence "The president of the United States is overworked" is symbolized as

$$(\exists x)\{\{Px \cdot (y)[Py \supset (x = y)]\} \cdot Ox\}$$

The first conjunct in this symbolization asserts that some (at least one) entity is president of the United States, the second that at most one is, and the third that that entity is overworked.

Examples:

The following are examples of symbolizations of English sentences containing definite descriptions (again restricting the universe of discourse to human beings):

1. Everyone admires the most intelligent person in the world.
$(\exists x)\{(y)[(x \neq y) \supset Ixy] \cdot (z)Azx\}$
(where Ixy = "x is more intelligent than y" and Axy = "x admires y")

2. The most intelligent person in the world is also the most admired.
$(\exists x)(\exists y)\{\{(z)[(x \neq z) \supset Ixz] \cdot (w) [(y \neq w) \supset Ayw]\} \cdot (x = y)\}$
(where Axy = "x is more admired than y")

3. The most intelligent person in the world admires only intelligent people.
$(\exists x)\{(y)[(y \neq x) \supset Ixy] \cdot (z)$
$(Axz \supset Iz)\}$

4. The person most admired by Art is also admired by Betsy.
$(\exists x)\{(y)[(x \neq y) \supset Aaxy] \cdot Abx\}$
(where $Axyz = $ "x admires y more than z" and $Axy = $ "x admires y")

5. Art's father admires him.
$(\exists x)\{\{Fxa \cdot (y)[Fya \supset (x = y)]\}$
$\cdot Axa\}$

6. Art's father admires the most intelligent person in the world.
$(\exists x)\{(y)[(x \neq y) \supset Ixy] \cdot (\exists z)$
$\{Fza \cdot (w) [Fwa \supset (w = z)] \cdot Azx\}\}$

7. Every man admires the most beautiful woman.
$(\exists x)\{Wx \cdot (y)\{[Wy \cdot (y \neq x)] \supset Bxy\}$
$\cdot (z)(Mz \supset Azx)\}$
(where $Bxy = $ "x is more beautiful than y" and $Mx = $ "x is a Man")

But the same caution is necessary in symbolizing sentences containing phrases like "The tallest man in the world", "The chairman", etc., as is necessary in symbolizing other complicated sentences.

For one thing, sentences of this kind frequently are *ambiguous*, and hence before symbolizing them we must get clear as to which meaning we intend our symbolization to capture. A famous example concerns the sentence "The present king of France is *not* bald", which can mean either that there is one and only one present king of France and he is not bald, or that it is not the case that there is one (and only one) present king of France (bald or otherwise).

If the former is intended, then the sentence in question is correctly symbolized as

$(\exists x)\{\{Px \cdot (y)[Py \supset (x = y)]\} \cdot \sim Bx\}$
(where $Px = $ "x is, at present, king of France" and $Bx = $ "x is bald")

If the latter is intended, then it is correctly symbolized as

$\sim\{(\exists x)Px \cdot (y)[Py \supset (x = y)]\}$

or perhaps as

$\sim (\exists x)\{\{Px \cdot (y)[Py \supset (x = y)]\} \cdot Bx\}$

Caution also is necessary because phrases which usually function as definite descriptions occasionally do not. An example is the sentence,

Predicate Logic

"The next person who moves will get shot", snarled by a gunman during a holdup. Clearly, the gunman does not intend to assert that there is one and only one person who will get shot if he moves. It is more likely that he intends to say that *anyone* who moves will get shot. So his threat is correctly symbolized as

$$(x)[(Px \cdot Mx) \supset Sx]$$

Another example is furnished by the sentence "The female of the species is vain", which means something like "All females are vain" or "Most females are vain", but surely does *not* say anything about *the* one and only female.

Exercise 9–2:

Symbolize the following sentences, using the indicated letters.

1. Every student is more intelligent than some student (or other). ($Sx =$ "x is a student"; $Ixy =$ "x is more intelligent than y")

2. Some student is more intelligent than every other student. ($Sx =$ "x is a student"; $Ixy =$ "x is more intelligent than y")

3. Not every student is more intelligent than all other students. ($Sx =$ "x is a student"; $Ixy =$ "x is more intelligent than y")

4. Judith is the most intelligent student of all. ($Sx =$ "x is a student"; $j =$ "Judith"; $Ixy =$ "x is more intelligent than y")

5. Harry is more intelligent than any other student, except Judith. ($h =$ "Harry"; $Sx =$ "x is a student"; $Ixy =$ "x is more intelligent than y"; $j =$ "Judith")

6. Of all the intelligent students, Judith is the most beautiful. ($j =$ "Judith"; $Ix =$ "x is intelligent"; $Sx =$ "x is a student"; $Bxy =$ "x is more beautiful than y")

7. The two California senators like each other. ($Cx =$ "x is a California senator"; $Lxy =$ "x likes y")

8. The two California senators represent California in the U. S. Senate. ($Cx =$ "x is a California senator"; $Rxyz =$ "x represents y in z"; $c =$ "California"; $s =$ "the U. S. Senate")

9. If Harry isn't the most intelligent student, then there is only one student who is more intelligent than he is. ($h =$ "Harry"; $Sx =$ "x is a student"; $Ixy =$ "x is more intelligent than y")

10. The most intelligent student in the U. S. will receive the "most intelligent student" award from the president of the U. S. (Sx = "x is a U. S. student"; Ixy = "x is more intelligent than y"; $Rxyz$ = "x will receive y from z"; n = "the president of the U. S."; m = "the most intelligent student award")

We now can handle arguments containing sentences with definite descriptions. An example is the following argument:

The person who hired Art hires only college graduates.
Therefore, Art is a college graduate.

This argument can be symbolized and proved valid as follows:

1.	$(\exists x)\{\{(Px \cdot Hxa) \cdot (y)[(Py \cdot Hya) \supset (x = y)]\} \cdot (z)(Hxz \supset Cz)\}$	$/ \therefore Ca$
2.	$\{(Px \cdot Hxa) \cdot (y)[(Py \cdot Hya) \supset (x = y)]\} \cdot (z)(Hxz \supset Cz)$	1, **EI**
3.	$Px \cdot Hxa$	2, **Simp**
4.	Hxa	3, **Simp**
5.	$(z)(Hxz \supset Cz)$	2, **Simp**
6.	$Hxa \supset Ca$	5, **UI**
7.	Ca	4, 6 **MP**

Exercise 9–3:

Prove valid:

(A) 1. $Fa \cdot (x)[Fx \supset (x = a)]$
    2. $(\exists x)(Fx \cdot Gx) / \therefore Ga$

(B) 1. $(x)(Px \supset Qx)$
    2. $(x)(Qx \supset Rx)$
    3. $Pa \cdot \sim Rb / \therefore \sim (a = b)$

(C) 1. $(\exists x)\{\{Px \cdot (y)[Py \supset (y = x)]\} \cdot Qx\}$

2. $\sim Qa \: / \therefore \: \sim Pa$

(D) 1. $(x)(y)\{[Pxy \cdot (x \neq y)] \supset Qxy\}$

2. $(\exists x)(y)[(x \neq y) \supset Pxy] \: / \therefore \: (\exists x)(y)[(x \neq y) \supset Qxy]$

(E) 1. $(\exists x)\{Px \cdot \{(y)[Py \supset (y = x)] \cdot Qx\}\}$

2. $(\exists x) \sim (\sim Px \: \vee \: \sim Ex)$

(F) 1. $(\exists x)(y)\{[\sim Fxy \supset (x = y)] \cdot Gx\} \: / \therefore \: (x)\{\sim Gx \supset (\exists y)[\sim (y = x) \cdot Fyx]\}$

6

Properties of Relations

There are several interesting properties which relational properties themselves may possess.

Symmetry

Two-place relations (relations of the general form *Fxy*) all are either **symmetrical, asymmetrical**, or **nonsymmetrical**. A **symmetrical relation** is one such that if one thing bears that relation to a second, then the second must* bear it to the first. That is, a relation designated by *Fxy* is a symmetrical relation *iff*† it must be the case that

$(x)(y)(Fxy \supset Fyx)$

An example of a symmetrical relation is the property "_____ is married to _____", since given any *x* and *y*, if *x* is married to *y*, then *y* must be married to *x*.

An **asymmetrical relation** is just the opposite of a symmetrical relation. Thus an asymmetrical relation is one such that if one thing bears that relation to a second, then the second thing *cannot* bear it to the first. That is, a relation designated by *Fxy* is asymmetrical *iff* it must be the case that

$(x)(y)(Fxy \supset \sim Fyx)$

---

* The sense of "must" involved here, indeed even the use of that term in characterizing relations of this kind, is in dispute. The same is true for the use of the related term "cannot", to be used roughly as the negation of the term "must".

† That is, "if and only if".

An example is the relation "_____ is the father of _ _ _ _ _", since given any x and y, if x is the father of y, then it must be false that y is the father of x.

All relations which are neither symmetrical nor asymmetrical are **nonsymmetrical**. For example, the relation "_____ loves _ _ _ _ _" is nonsymmetrical, since loving someone entails neither being loved by that person nor not being loved by that person.

Transitivity

A **transitive relation** is one such that if one thing bears that relation to a second, and the second to a third, then the first must bear it to the third. That is, a relation designated by Fxy is transitive *iff* it must be the case that

$$(x)(y)(z)[(Fxy \cdot Fyz) \supset Fxz]$$

An example is the relation "_____ is taller than _ _ _ _ _", since if a given person is taller than a second, and the second is taller than a third, then the first must be taller than the third.

It is interesting to note that the statement of a property of a relation often is required in order to present a valid proof for an otherwise invalid argument. For instance, the argument

1. Tab (Art is taller than Betsy.)

2. Tbc (Betsy is taller than Charles.)

/ ∴ 3. Tac (Art is taller than Charles.)

is invalid *as it stands*, but can be made valid by the introduction of a premise concerning the transitivity of the relation "taller than", as follows:

1. Tab p

2. Tbc p

3. $(x)(y)(z)[(Txy \cdot Tyz) \supset Txz]$ p / ∴ Tac

4. $(y)(z)[(Tay \cdot Tyz) \supset Taz]$ 3, **UI**

5.	$(z)[(Tab \cdot Tbz) \supset Taz]$	4, **UI**
6.	$(Tab \cdot Tbc) \supset Tac$	5, **UI**
7.	$(Tab \cdot Tbc)$	1, 2 **Conj**
8.	Tac	6, 7 **MP**

An **intransitive relation** is one such that if one thing bears that relation to a second, and the second to a third, then the first *cannot* bear it to the third. That is, a relation designated by *Fxy* is intransitive *iff* it must be the case that

$$(x)(y)(z)[(Fxy \cdot Fyz) \supset \sim Fxz]$$

An example of an intransitive relation is the property "_____ is the father of _ _ _ _ _ _", since if one person is the father of a second, and the second of a third, then the first cannot be the father of the third (since he is the *grandfather* of the third).

All relations which are neither transitive nor intransitive are **nontransitive**. For example, the relation "_____ loves _ _ _ _ _ _" is nontransitive, since if one person loves a second, and the second loves a third, it follows neither that the first person loves the third nor that the first person doesn't love the third.

Reflexivity

The situation with respect to reflexivity is more complex.

A **totally reflexive** relation is one such that everything must bear that relation to itself. That is, a relation designated by *Fxy* is totally reflexive *iff* it must be the case that

$$(x)Fxx$$

An example is the relation "_____ is identical with _ _ _ _ _ _", since everything must be identical with itself.

Almost all interesting relations are *not* totally reflexive. There is no name in common use for relations which are not totally reflexive, but we can say that a relation designated by *Fxy* is not totally reflexive *iff* it is not necessarily the case that

$(x)Fxx$

An example would be the relation "_____ loves _____" (restricting the domain of discourse to human beings), since it is not necessarily true that all human beings love themselves.

A **reflexive relation** (which may or may not be totally reflexive) is one such that everything which bears that relation to anything must bear it to itself. That is, a relation designated by *Fxy* is reflexive *iff* it must be the case that

$(x)(y)[Fxy \supset (Fxx \cdot Fyy)]$

An example is the relation "_____ belongs to the same political party as _____", since if a given entity, say Art, belongs to the same political party as anyone else, say Betsy, then Art must belong to the same political party as himself, and so must Betsy.

Notice that "_____ belongs to the same political party as _____" is *not* totally reflexive, since *everything* does *not* belong to the same political party as itself. For example, a piece of chalk doesn't belong to any political party at all. But all totally reflexive relations *are* reflexive.

An **irreflexive relation** is one such that nothing can bear it to itself. That is, a relation designated by *Fxy* is irreflexive *iff* it must be the case that

$(x) \sim Fxx$

An example is the relation "_____ is taller than _____", since nothing can be taller than itself.

Finally, all relations which are neither reflexive nor irreflexive are **nonreflexive**. For example, the relation "_____ loves _____" is nonreflexive because (1) it is not reflexive (a person can love someone else, but not love himself), and (2) it is not irreflexive (a person can love someone else *and* also love himself).

Exercise 9–4:

(A) Determine the status of the following relations with respect to symmetry, transitivity, and reflexivity:

1. _____ loves _ _ _ _ _ _.

2. _____ is the father of _ _ _ _ _ _.

3. _____ is ≥ _ _ _ _ _ _.
(concerning numbers only)

4. _____ is north of _ _ _ _ _ _.

5. _____ is at least one year younger than _ _ _ _ _ _.

6. _____ is identical with _ _ _ _ _ _.

7. _____ is the brother of _ _ _ _ _ _.

8. _____ sees _ _ _ _ _ _.

9. _____ is president of _ _ _ _ _ _.

(B) Prove that all relations that are asymmetrical are irreflexive.

7

Higher Order Logics

The predicate logic system developed so far expressly forbids sentences which ascribe properties to properties themselves, and restricts quantification to *individual* variables. A predicate logic restricted in this way is said to be a **first order predicate logic**. We now will consider the bare bones of a higher order predicate logic.

Just as we can have individual variables, so we can have **property variables**. Let us use the capital letters *F*, *G*, *H*, and *K* as property variables, for the time being forbidding their use as property constants. The expression *Fa* will then be a sentence *form*, and not a sentence. But obviously, we can obtain a sentence from this expression by replacing the property variables *F* by a property constant. Thus, we can obtain the sentence *Sa* (where *Sx* = "*x* is smart") from the sentence form *Fa*. (Hence *Sa* is a *substitution instance* of *Fa*.)

But we also can obtain a sentence from the sentence form *Fa* by *quantifying* the property variable *F*. Thus we can obtain the sentences (*F*)(*Fa*), read "Art has every property", or "Given any property, *F*, Art has *F*", and (∃*F*)(*Fa*), read "Art has some property (or other)", or "There is some property *F* such that Art has *F*".

We also can have sentences which quantify both property variables and individual variables. An example would be the sentence "Everything has some property (or other)", symbolized as (*x*)(∃*F*)*Fx*.

Examples:

Some other examples of symbolizations containing quantified property variables are:

1. (*x*)(*F*)*Fx*   (Everything has every property.)

2. (∃*x*)(*F*)*Fx*   (Something has every property.)

3. (∃*x*)(∃*F*)*Fx*   (Something has some property [or other].)

4. (*F*)(∃*x*)*Fx*   (Every property belongs to something [or other].)

5. (∃*F*)(*x*)*Fx*   (Some property belongs to everything.)

6. ~(∃*x*)(*F*)*Fx*   (Nothing has all properties.)

7. . $(F)\{Fa \supset \sim(\exists x)[(Px \cdot Fx)$ (No one else has any property which
   $\cdot (x \neq a)]\}$ Art has.)

8. $(\exists F)\{Fa \cdot (y)\{[Py \cdot (y \neq a)]$ (Art has some property no one else
   $\supset \sim Fy\}\}$ has.)

Now that we have introduced property variables and the quantification of property variables, we can give a more precise definition of the identity symbol, for we can say that the expression $x = y$ means the same thing as $(F)(Fx \equiv Fy)$.* It follows then that $(x)(y)[(x = y) \equiv (F)(Fx \equiv Fy)]$, from which we can prove that the identity relation is transitive, symmetrical, and reflexive.

Higher order properties

So far, we have considered only properties of *individuals*. But *properties* themselves can have properties. For instance, *honesty* is a *rare* property, while (unfortunately) dishonesty is quite common. Similarly, courage is an honorable property, cowardice dishonorable.

Let's use the symbols A_1, B_1, C_1, etc., to refer to properties of properties. Then we can symbolize the sentence "Honesty is a rare property" as $R_1 H$, and the sentence "Courage is a useful property" as $U_1 C$. Similarly, we can symbolize the sentence "We all have useful properties" as $(x)[Px \supset (\exists F)(Fx \cdot U_1 F)]$, and so on.

Examples:

Some other examples of symbolizations containing properties of properties are:

1. $(F)U_1 F$ (All properties are useful.)

2. $(\exists F)(U_1 F \cdot R_1 F)$ (Some useful properties are rare.)

---

*Some would argue that $x = y$ means the same thing as "*It is necessary that* $(F)(Fx \equiv Fy)$".

3. $(\exists F)(G_1F \cdot Fa)$ (Art has some good properties
                                                      [qualities].)

4. $(\exists F)[(G_1F \cdot Fa) \cdot Fb]$ (Art and Betsy share some good
                                                      qualities.)

5. $(F)[(Fb \cdot G_1F) \supset Fa]$ (Art has all of Betsy's good qualities.)

6. $(x)\{(\exists F)\{Fx \cdot (G)[Gx \supset (F = G)]\}$ (Nothing which has only one property
    $\supset \sim(\exists H)(Hx \cdot G_1H)\}$ has any good properties.)

Unfortunately, higher order logics involving properties of properties have encountered important difficulties, which have as yet not been satisfactorily worked out. These problems are briefly discussed in Chapter Eighteen.

8

*Limitations of
Predicate Logic*

At the beginning of the discussion concerning predicate logic, it was pointed out that some valid arguments are invalid when symbolized in the notation of *sentential logic*. We then proceeded to develop *predicate logic*, which provides a method for symbolizing and proving those arguments valid.

But the question naturally arises as to whether there are other arguments which, although invalid using the notation and proof technique of predicate logic, are valid in some wider (perhaps ideal) deductive system. The answer is that there seem to be such valid arguments.

Consider the argument

1. Art believes that he'll go either to the
    show or to the concert (but not to both).

2. Art believes that he won't go to the show.

/ ∴ 3. Art believes that he'll go to the concert.

Clearly, this argument is valid in some sense or other. But there is no way to symbolize it in the standard predicate logic notation so that we can *prove* it is valid. For instance, if we symbolize the argument as

1. *Baf*

2. *Bag*

/ ∴ 3. *Bah*

where B = "believes that", f = "he'll go either to the show or the concert", g = "he won't go to the show", and h = "he'll go to the concert", then clearly we cannot prove that it is valid.

This is an example of an argument involving what are sometimes called *indirect contexts*. In this case, the clue that we are dealing with indirect contexts is the phrase "believes that". Other phrases of this kind are "knows that", "is looking for", "prays to", "is necessary that", etc.

In general, the logic of indirect contexts has not been worked out, at least not to the satisfaction of most philosophers. The whole area is one of extreme disagreement, and the predicate logic presented in this, and most other, textbooks is not able to deal adequately with it.

There are other kinds of cases where it is claimed that the predicate logic presented here is inadequate. We present two which are the center of interesting disputes.

The first is illustrated by the argument:

1. Art sang the Hamilton school song beautifully.

/ ∴ 2. Art sang the Hamilton school song.

Again, the argument is valid, and again it is claimed that we cannot *prove* that it is valid using the notation and proof technique of predicate logic.

But in this case, there is some question as to whether the claim of unprovability is correct. The argument in question looks very much like the argument considered earlier about Art being taller than Betsy. In that case, we found that there was, so to speak, a "missing premise", namely the premise that "taller than" is a transitive relation, something which everyone knows (in some sense or other). Similarly, we might say that *as it stands*, the argument we are dealing with here is invalid, but can be made valid by supplying a "missing premise", which everyone knows, namely the premise that if someone sang a particular song beautifully, then he sang that song. Once we add that "missing premise", the argument turns out to be provable quite easily in predicate logic.

Another dispute involves what we might call "semantically valid arguments".

Suppose for the moment that the term "bachelor" means exactly the same thing as "unmarried adult male". Then it is clear that the argument

1.   All bachelors are handsome.

/ ∴   2.   All unmarried adult males are handsome.

is valid in some sense or other. But again, it appears to be invalid in the predicate logic system developed in this text.

This time, there are no less than three lines of defense for predicate logic advocates. One is to suggest that we introduce a rule permitting the substitution of terms *synonymous* with any terms occurring in an argument as stated. This defense does require the admission that predicate logic *as normally formulated* is in need of at least a minor emendation.

Another way to defend predicate logic is to claim that we have here another case involving a "missing premise"; this time the premise that all bachelors are unmarried adult males.

And a third way is to *deny that the argument in question is valid*, on the grounds that *truly synonymous* expressions do not exist, at least not in natural languages. (This kind of argument is related to question about the so-called "analytic-synthetic" distinction, discussed in Chapter Nineteen.)

But it would be inappropriate to take sides in these disputes here.

Part Three Chapter Ten

Traditional Logic Definitions

The sentential and predicate logic systems discussed in the first nine chapters of this book were first developed in the late nineteenth and early twentieth century. But, they did not arise in a vacuum. Logic texts and systems have existed for over two thousand years, since the first system was developed by Aristotle. It has become customary to apply the term "symbolic" to systems like sentential and predicate logic, and the terms "traditional", "Aristotelian", and "syllogistic" to the earlier systems.*

In Part Three of this text, we present a fairly brief version of the material contained in traditional logic texts of recent times. (For instance, we include Venn diagrams, which are a product of the nineteenth century.)

---

* Traditional logic also employs special symbols, but the term "symbolic logic" is not used to refer to traditional logical systems.

1

Introduction

A **definition** is an explanation of the meaning of a word (or phrase). In this sense, definitions are about *words*, and not about the things words are used to talk about. For instance, the dictionary definition

Automobile: A self-propelled vehicle
suitable for use on a street or roadway

does not say anything about automobiles, but rather explains the meaning of the *word* "automobile". To be precise, then, we should place the term "automobile" and the phrase used to define it in quotes, to indicate that we are *speaking about* or *mentioning* words, and not *using* them. Thus, we should write the above definition as follows:

"Automobile" means the same as "self-propelled vehicle
suitable for use on a street or roadway".

We introduce the symbol $=df$ to abbreviate the phrase "means the same as". Thus the above definition can be written "automobile" $=df$ "self-propelled vehicle suitable for use on a street or roadway".

2

Lexical and Stipulative Definitions

There are many different kinds of definitions. Two important kinds are *lexical* and *stipulative*.

A **lexical definition** is one which attempts to *report usage*. Thus, all good dictionary definitions are lexical, since they tell how the words of a particular language actually are used by the speakers of that language.

Sometimes it is quite difficult to provide good lexical definitions. One reason for this is that words often are *ambiguous*, that is, have more than one meaning. An example is the word "mouth", which sometimes is used to refer to a portion of the human anatomy, and sometimes to the place where a river enters a larger body of water.

Often it is difficult to keep the different meanings of a term separate. For instance, one dictionary distinguishes 31 different meanings for the word "good". Clearly, some of these meanings must differ from others in very subtle ways, which easily could be confused. (This is the chief psychological reason for the ease with which the so-called "fallacy of equivocation" is committed. See p. 247 for a discussion of this fallacy.)

Another reason for the difficulty in providing good lexical definitions is that it often is quite difficult to find a set of properties such that all and only those things denoted by the term to be defined have that set of properties. Indeed, there may be no such set of properties. Take the word "automobile". Is there some set of properties such that all objects having that set are automobiles while no objects lacking them are automobiles? It is not clear that there is. But even if there is such a set of properties, *finding* it may be quite difficult indeed. Clearly, the definition cited above does not list such a set, since motorcycles, motor-scooters, go-carts, even tractors and tanks have the properties of being self-propelled and suitable for use on streets or roadways.

Finally, a major reason for the difficulty in providing good lexical definitions of words is that most words in natural languages are *vague*, that is, do not have a precise meaning. Is a three-wheeled motor vehicle an automobile? Is a station wagon? A bus? A truck? How small can an automobile be before it becomes a *toy* automobile? Ordinary usage does not provide answers to questions of this kind; the word "automobile" is vague. Another example is the word "tall". At what height does an adult male human being cease being short and become tall? Ordinary usage does not provide a precise answer to this question.

Notice that vagueness is not a matter of not fully understanding the meaning of a term. Even someone who *completely understands* the meanings of the terms "automobile" and "tall" cannot answer the questions raised above. And the reason is that there *is no* answer, since usage provides none.

Notice also that vagueness is not always a bad quality. Often, terms are vague because they are more useful that way. For instance, the word "tall" is useful precisely because it is vague, since "tall" is a term we often use when we don't choose to state the exact height of something precisely. If we always had to be absolutely precise in what we say, most of us would have to remain silent most of the time.

A **stipulative definition** is one which, instead of reporting actual usage, *specifies* or *stipulates* the meaning of a word or phrase. For instance, a state legislature may stipulate that for purposes of a particular statute the term "automobile" shall mean "self-propelled vehicle having more than three wheels whose primary purpose is to convey human beings from place to place". Or a college catalogue may define the term "college" as meaning "four-year accredited institution of higher learning".

Stipulative definitions can be divided into two main kinds, namely those which introduce brand new terms and those which stipulate new meanings for old terms ("reforming" definitions). For instance, we could stipulate that the brand-new term "multimarried" means "person married more than twice", and the brand-new term "auncle" means "aunt or uncle". Or we might stipulate that the old term "valid argument" means "argument for which there is a proof in sentential logic".

Stipulative definitions which specify new meanings for old terms also can be broken down into two kinds, namely those which *add to the meaning* of an old term, by reducing its vagueness, and those which *change the meaning* of an old term in areas in which they are already clear. For instance, we reduce the vagueness of the already existing term "sky-scraper" by defining it to mean "building over 500 feet tall". And we change the meaning of an old term in an area in which it is already clear when we define the term "democracy" to mean "dictatorship of the proletariat".

Reforming definitions play a particularly important role in the law and in science. In the law they are important because the answer to the question whether a statute applies in a particular case often hinges on the meaning of a term which is vague in everyday use. For example, if a particular statute levying a tax on automobiles failed to provide a stipulative definition of the term "automobile", there would be no way to know whether to levy the tax on motorcycles, motor-scooters, three-wheeled vehicles, taxis, station wagons, etc.

But it is not possible to remove the vagueness of a term completely. *Borderline* cases always can arise. For instance, in several states there has been litigation as to whether certain vehicles, such as go-carts, are automobiles under the statutory definitions. Or suppose a definition of "automobile" expressly excludes motorcycles from that category. Problems still might arise as to when something ceases to be a motorcycle and becomes an automobile. For given something that is clearly a motorcycle, we can continually modify it in relevant ways until finally, no matter how precisely we define terms, it will not be clear whether the modified vehicle is a motorcycle or an automobile.

Reforming definitions also are very important in science. In classifying plants and animals, scientists may take a term with an established meaning, and give it a different and (for their purposes) more useful meaning. For example, they have redefined the term "fish" so as to exclude whales, porpoises, etc., which they have classified as mammals along with many land animals which (superficially) they do not resemble. They have done so because they find it useful to have a classification in terms of such things as ancestry, and because whales and porpoises are structurally more similar to other mammals than to other sea animals.

Reforming definitions in science often are called *theoretical definitions*, because they draw on scientific theory. Thus the definition of "Morning Star" as "Venus when seen in the morning eastern sky" draws on the astronomical theory that causally relates the Morning Star with the planet Venus.

There is a tendency for all or most scientific hypotheses or theories to become embedded in definitions. For example, at one time it was not known that copper conducts electricity, so that at that time conductivity was not a defining characteristic of copper. But when it became well known that copper does conduct electricity, the *meaning* of the term "copper" began to change, so that now a metal that does not conduct electricity would not be called "copper" by a scientist.

3

Intensional, Extensional, and Ostensive Definitions

An **extensional definition** of a term is simply a list of *all* the things to which the term applies. For instance, the term "Scandinavian country" can be defined extensionally as meaning "Sweden or Norway or Denmark or Iceland". In most cases, it is very hard, if not impossible, to furnish an extensional definition of a term. For example, it would be impossible to define the term "human being" extensionally, since to do so we would have to list the name of every human being who ever has lived, or will live.

An **intensional definition** of a term lists a set of properties such that the term applies to all things having that set of properties, and to nothing else. For instance, the definition "male human being over 21 years of age who is as yet unmarried" might be given as an intensional definition of the term "bachelor", since it lists a set of properties something must possess to be a bachelor.

Notice that intensional definitions need not, and usually do not, list *all* of the properties common to everything named by the term defined. For instance, it may well be the case that all bachelors weigh more than 50 pounds, but if so this is an accidental fact, and not a defining property of bachelorhood. Even if there happens to be no bachelor who weighs less than 50 pounds, there *could be* one, in the sense that *if* something *were* to be male, human, over 21, and as yet unmarried, then that thing *would be* a bachelor according to our definition, even though that thing weighed less than 50 pounds.

An extensional definition is said to provide the *extensional meaning*, or the *extension*, of a term, and an intensional definition the *intensional meaning*, or the *intension*, of a term. It is important to notice that terms can have different intensional meanings and yet have the same extensional meaning. For example, the phrases "Most populous city in the U. S." and "City in which the U. N. Building is located" have different intensional meanings, but the same extensional meaning, since it just happens that New York is both the most populous city in the U. S. *and* the city in which the U. N. Building is located.

Finally, an **ostensive definition** of a term is one which indicates the meaning of that term by providing a *sample* of the things denoted. For instance, we can define "automobile" as "anything like Chevrolets, Fords, Volkswagens, Cadillacs, Plymouths, etc.". Or we can define "automobile" by *pointing to examples* of automobiles.

Good ostensive definitions often also indicate things *not* denoted by the term being defined. For example, in defining "automobile" by pointing to typical examples of automobiles, we might also point out that motorcycles, motor-scooters, etc., are *not* automobiles.

Obviously, ostensive definitions are risky, in a way that extensional definitions are not. An extensional definition gives the *complete* extension of a term, and thus leaves little margin for error, while an ostensive definition furnishes only *part* of the extension of a term. Suppose we define "ball" ostensively by pointing to several typical examples, which just happen to be red. Then a child might easily get the idea that "ball" denotes the color red. Or suppose we define "university" ostensively by reference to Harvard, Penn, U.C.L.A., Kansas, Oxford, etc. Then someone might conclude that Swarthmore, Oberlin, Reed, Whitman, etc., are universities, although in fact they are colleges, and not universities.

One way to reduce the possibility of error when presenting ostensive definitions is by careful selection of examples, both positive and negative. If we suspect that a child may interpret the term "ball" as a color term, then we include balls of several different colors in our ostensive sample. In the university example, we might include several colleges, say Wellesley, Goucher, and Smith, as examples of nonuniversities. But we can *never* preclude the possibility of error. For instance, one might conclude that Wellesley, Goucher, and Smith are not universities because they are *women*'s institutions, and thus be misled as to the meaning of the term "university".

4

Criteria for
Good
Definitions

The history of philosophy is full of suggestions as to the correct rules or criteria for good definitions. Criteria for good lexical definitions are the easiest to provide. Indeed, it may be that we need only require that a lexical definition correctly report the usage it claims to report.

Similarly, criteria for good *extensional* stipulative definitions present no problems.

But there is a great deal of controversy concerning criteria for good *intensional* stipulative definitions. We restrict the discussion to several of the standard criteria of this kind. The first four are traditional criteria of an informal nature, the remainder are those which all good definitions in formal systems (of the type discussed in Chapter Twenty) must satisfy.

A good definition must not be too wide or too narrow. A definition is *too wide* if it applies to things we don't want the term in question to apply to. For example, "wheeled self-propelled vehicle" is not a good definition of the term "automobile", because it also applies to airplanes, trains, motorcycles, etc.

A definition is *too narrow* if it does not apply to all of the things that we want the term in question to apply to. For instance, "wheeled vehicle propelled by an internal combustion engine and primarily intended for land travel" does not properly define the term "automobile", because it does not apply to automobiles powered by steam or electricity.

A good definition ought to avoid unnecessarily vague, ambiguous, obscure, or metaphorical language. Consider the expression "a certain type of self-propelled land vehicle" as a definition of the term "automobile". Clearly, an automobile *is* a certain type of self-propelled land vehicle. But *which* type? The definition does not say, and to that extent is unnecessarily vague. Or consider the expression "ship of the desert" as a definition of the term "camel". While this metaphorical description does indicate the main use to which camels are put in dry areas, it hardly is an adequate definition of the term "camel".

A good definition must not be circular. One standard way to state this criterion is to state that a definition is circular if it uses either the very word being defined or a grammatical variation of that word. Thus, the expression "one who engages in gardening" would constitute a circular definition of the term "gardener".

Unfortunately, this standard version of the circularity criterion is not satisfactory. For one thing, in certain contexts it is perfectly proper, even desirable, to define a word by means of a grammatical variation of itself. For instance, the definition of "gardener" as "one who engages in gardening" is perfectly acceptable, *provided* a noncircular definition of "gardening" is furnished.*

We can salvage the circularity criterion by rephrasing it to state that a good definition must not be *viciously* circular. Consider a definition of "teacher" as "one who engages in teaching", and a definition of "teaching" as "that activity engaged in by a teacher". Taken alone, these definitions are not viciously circular, but taken together, they are. In effect, they tell us that the word "teacher" means the same as "one who engages in that which is engaged in by a teacher", so that someone who does not already know the meaning of the word "teacher" still would not know to which things that term applies.

A good definition of a term states the essential properties of the things named by that term. There is a great deal of controversy concerning this "essential property criterion", primarily because it makes use of the distinction between *essential* and *accidental* properties which many philosophers reject.

---

* Another reason that this standard version of the circularity criterion is not satisfactory is that circular definitions of the kind called "recursive definitions" are perfectly acceptable. An example of a recursive definition is the definition of "WFF" given on page 362, Chapter Twenty. Since this definition employs the very term "WFF" which it defines, it is circular according to the above criterion.

But whether in the final analysis one accepts or rejects this distinction, there is a certain amount of plausibility in it. Take the term "bachelor". As stated before, it may well be that all bachelors have the property of weighing more than 50 pounds, as well as of being unmarried. But we would not refuse to call someone a bachelor *simply* because he weighed less than 50 pounds. We would be inclined to say that if it is a fact that all bachelors weigh more than 50 pounds, then it is an *accidental*, or *contingent*, fact. On the other hand, being unmarried is an *essential* property of being a bachelor. In other words, it is not just an accidental, or contingent, fact that all bachelors are unmarried; unmarriedness is an essential property of bachelorhood. The essential property criterion requires that a good definition list all of the essential properties which something must have to be the kind of thing named by the term being defined.

One of the important disputes over this criterion concerns the question as to whether *definitions themselves* determine which attributes are essential and which accidental or whether the very nature of the world does so. Put in other terms, the question is whether the defining attributes can be selected arbitrarily or whether the world itself "naturally" divides into kinds of things, each kind having its own "essences" or essential properties, so that a good definition merely states the essences of the various natural kinds. (The latter position is often called the doctrine of "natural kinds".)

If one accepts the view that definitions themselves arbitrarily determine which properties are essential, then the essential property requirement will, in general, be fulfilled automatically, and the criterion itself will be trivial. But if one accepts the doctrine of natural kinds, then the criterion will be of great importance.

The essential property criterion has been criticized on the grounds that it applies only to terms which serve as *names*. For instance, it is hard to see what is named by the logical connectives "or" and "and", and hard to imagine what it would mean to speak of "the essential properties" of "or-ness" and "and-ness".

The essential property criterion also has been objected to on the grounds that it is not appropriate for definitions of *relational* properties or *functions*. Terms for relational properties usually are best defined by means of what are called *contextual definitions*, that is, by definitions which define a term in the kind of context in which it occurs, not in isolation. The notion of essential properties seems out of place with respect to such definitions.

Consider the following contextual definition of "average density" which might be introduced into a scientific theory:

$$\text{average density of } x =_{df} \frac{\text{mass of } x \text{ (in grams)}}{\text{volume of } x \text{ (in cc.)}}$$

It is hard to see what could be meant by speaking of accidental or essential properties in a case such as this one, yet this is perhaps the most common type of definition both in science and in mathematics. So it can be argued that the essential property criterion does not apply to definitions in science and mathematics. If correct, this charge constitutes an important objection to that criterion.

Finally, the criterion has been criticized on the grounds that there is no satisfactory way to determine in many (or perhaps most) cases whether a given property is essential or accidental. Suppose we were to find something which in all other respects seemed to be copper, but which failed to conduct electricity. Would that thing merit the title "copper"? The answer is not clearcut. And even in cases where a clearcut answer is possible, it may change from time to time. (Several hundred years ago conductivity surely would have been considered an accidental property of copper, if a property at all.) Consequently, many philosophers have become convinced that at best it is *definitions themselves* which determine which properties are essential and which accidental and not the nature of the world, or any essences possessed by all of the things named by a term. That is, they have become convinced that all that the doctrine of essential attributes amounts to is that a property is an essential property if it is listed in a definition. Thus, if we choose to define "copper" in a certain way, then conductivity will be an essential property of copper. But if we choose to define "copper" in another way, then conductivity will not be an essential property of copper.

We now turn to the criteria for good definitions in formal systems.

A defined term must be eliminable from a system into which it is introduced. A term is said to be *eliminable* from a system if every sentence in the system in which it occurs can be replaced by an equivalent sentence in which that term does not occur. Suppose we construct a formal system suitable for use in Anthropology, in which the terms "male" and "married" are primitive terms (i.e., terms not defined in the system). Then we can introduce the term "bachelor" into the system as a defined term, letting it mean the same as "not-married male". Clearly, the term "bachelor" so defined is eliminable in the sense just stated. For instance, if the sentence "All bachelors are handsome" is a sentence in the system, then it can be replaced by the equivalent sentence "All not-married males are handsome", a sentence which does not contain the defined term "bachelor". Similarly, the term "bachelor" will be eliminable from all other sentences of the system.

A good definition must not permit the proof of something which cannot be proved without it. (This is often called the "nonconstructibility" criterion.) A famous example of the violation of this criterion concerns the so-called "pseudo-operator", symbolized by ∗. Suppose that in a system for arithmetic we stipulate that $[(x * y) = z] = df[(x < z) \& (y < z)]$.* Then using the other (valid) principles of arithmetic, we can construct the following proof:

1. $1 * 2 = 3$ (because $(1 < 3) \cdot (2 < 3)$)

2. $1 * 2 = 4$ (because $(1 < 4) \cdot (2 < 4)$)

/∴   3. $3 = 4$

which contradicts the truth of arithmetic that $3 \neq 4$, and obviously cannot be proved in an arithmetic system without the pseudo-operator definition. This proves that the pseudo-operator definition violates the criterion of nonconstructibility, and must be rejected.

Finally, *a good definition makes clear the form of the contexts in which the term defined is to be used.* (While it is not necessary to consider this criterion separately, pedagogically it is very useful to do so.) Consider the word "father". There are two different ways in which this term can be used, namely as a one-place and as a two-place property term. For example, in the sentence "John is a father" it functions as a one-place property term, while in the sentence "John is the father of Harry" it

* $x * y$ is read as "x star y".

functions as a two-place property term. Consequently, we must provide two separate definitions for the term "father", indicating the kind of contexts (i.e., one place or two place) in which it can occur. For instance, we could stipulate that "x is a father" $=df$ "x is male, and x is a parent of some y or other" (using obvious abbreviations: $Fx =df Mx \cdot (\exists y)Pxy$), and "$x$ is the father of y" $=df$ "x is male, and x is a parent of y" (in symbols—$Fxy =df Mx \cdot Pxy$).

Chapter Eleven

*Traditional
Syllogistic
Logic—I*

1

Introduction

Traditional syllogistic logic is primarily concerned with *categorical propositions*. **Categorical propositions** assert or deny relationships between classes. For instance, the sentence "All humans are mortal" is a categorical proposition, and asserts (roughly) that all members of the class of humans are members of the class of mortals.

The term "humans" is said to be the *subject* or *subject term*, and the term "mortal" the *predicate*, or *predicate term*, of the categorical proposition "All humans are mortal". Similarly, all categorical propositions contain a subject and a predicate, as well as some form of the verb "to be" ("is", "are", etc.) relating the subject and predicate.

2

*Four Kinds of
Categorical
Propositions*

There are four general kinds of categorical proposiitons: (1) **universal affirmative** propositions, having the general form "All *S* are *P*" (where *S* denotes some subject class and *P* some predicate class); (2) **universal negative** propositions, having the general form "No *S* are *P*"; (3) **particular affirmative** propositions, having the general form "Some *S* are *P*"; and (4) **particular negative** propositions, having the general form "Some *S* are not *P*".

It is customary to use the capital letter *A* in symbolizing universal affirmative propositions. Thus, the universal affirmative "All humans are mortal" is symbolized as *HAM* (where *H* = "human" and *M* = "mortal"). Similarly, it is customary to use *E* for universal negatives, *I* for particular affirmatives, and *O* for particular negatives. Thus, the universal negative "No humans are mortal" is symbolized as *HEM*, the particular affirmative "Some humans are mortal" as *HIM*, and the particular negative "Some humans are not mortal" as *HOM*. It also is customary to refer to universal affirmative propositions as *A* propositions, universal negative propositions as *E* propositions, and so on.

Notice that *A*, *E*, *I*, and *O*, propositions differ with respect to two kinds of properties; namely, (1) *quality* (being either affirmative or negative), and (2) *quantity* (being either universal or particular). For example, the *I* proposition "Some humans are mortal" is *affirmative* (quality), because it *affirms* that some humans are mortal, and *particular* (quantity), because it affirms that *some* (not all) humans are mortal. On the other hand, the *E* proposition "No humans are mortal" is *negative* (quality), because it *denies* that humans are mortal, and *universal* (quantity), because it denies of *all* humans that they are mortal.

3

*Relation of
Traditional
Logic to
Predicate Logic*

The relationship between traditional syllogistic logic with its four kinds of categorical propositions and the predicate logic discussed in Part Two of this book is quite close. For instance, assuming for the moment that the propositions to be dealt with are not required to have what is called "existential import" (to be discussed in Section 4), the proposition "All humans are mortal", symbolized as HAM in syllogistic logic, is roughly equivalent to the expression $(x)(Hx \supset Mx)$ of predicate logic. Similarly, the syllogistic logic expression HEM is roughly equivalent to the expression $(x)(Hx \supset \sim Mx)$, HIM to $(\exists x)(Hx \cdot Mx)$, and HOM to $(\exists x)(Hx \cdot \sim Mx)$.

Examples:

The following are examples of an A, E, I, and O sentence respectively, followed by symbolizations in syllogistic and predicate logic (again assuming that propositions are not required to have existential import):

1. "All scientists are philosophers".

    Syllogistic symbolization: SAP
    Predicate logic symbolization: $(x)(Sx \supset Px)$

2. "No scientists are philosophers".

    Syllogistic symbolization: SEP
    Predicate logic symbolization: $(x)(Sx \supset \sim Px)$

3. "Some scientists are philosophers".

    Syllogistic symbolization: SIP
    Predicate logic symbolization: $(\exists x)(Sx \cdot Px)$

4. "Some scientists are not philosophers".

    Syllogistic symbolization: SOP
    Predicate logic symbolization: $(\exists x)(Sx \cdot \sim Px)$

4

*Existential
Import*

At least in recent times it has been fairly well understood that if we want to retain many of the interesting features of traditional logic (and have that logic be *valid*), then we must make some sort of blanket restriction concerning what is called **existential import**. This blanket restriction roughly amounts to a decision to deal with only those categorical propositions whose terms all refer to nonempty classes.*

The adoption of such a restriction greatly reduces the number of propositions with which we are permitted to deal. For instance, assuming that there are no martians, its adoption precludes consideration of the proposition "All martians are intelligent", since the term "martians" will refer to an empty class.

5

Syllogistic Logic (Assuming Existential Import)

Let's assume for the moment that we have made the restriction concerning existential import. In other words, let's assume that we are dealing only with categorical propositions whose terms designate nonempty classes, and let's outline a part of the traditional logic which is valid on that assumption.

Analysis of the square of opposition

One of the most interesting features of traditional logic is the *square of opposition* (see page 202).

The square of opposition graphically illustrates several important features of traditional logic:

(1) *Corresponding* A *and* O *propositions are contradictories.* In general, **contradictory propositions** are such that *both cannot be true, and both cannot be false.* (So one must be true, the other false). For instance, the *A* proposition "All humans are mortal" is true, while its contradictory "Some humans are not mortal", an *O* proposition, is false.

(2) *Corresponding* E *and* I *propositions also are contradictory propositions.* Hence, both cannot be true, and both cannot be false. For example, the *I* proposition "Some humans are mortal" is true, and its contradictory "No humans are mortal", an *E* proposition, is false.

(3) *Corresponding* A *and* E *propositions are said to be contraries.* In general, **contrary propositions** are such that *both cannot be true*, but both

---

* Indeed, we must require that the *negations* of these classes also be nonempty. For instance, if *S* and *P* are the subject and predicate terms respectively of a proposition, then we must require not only that *S* and *P* have members, but also that non-*S* and non-*P* have members.

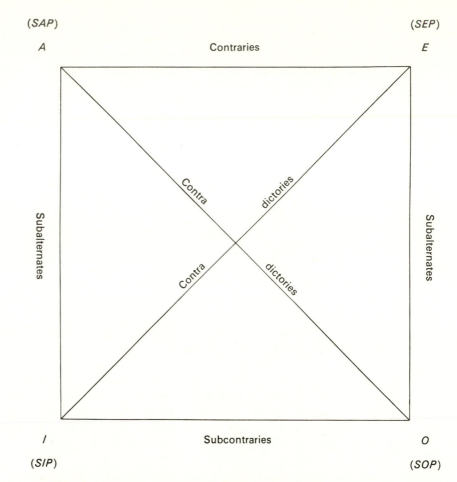

(SAP) A Contraries E (SEP)

Subalternates

Contra dictories

Contra dictories

Subalternates

I Subcontraries O

(SIP) (SOP)

can be false. For instance, the *A* proposition "All scientists are philosophers" is false, and its contrary "No scientists are philosophers", an *E* proposition, also is false (since some scientists are philosophers and some aren't). This is an example of contraries both of which are false. An example of contraries one of which is true, one false, would be the pair of propositions "All humans are mortal", a true *A* proposition, and "No humans are mortal", a false *E* proposition. But we cannot give an example of contrary propositions both of which are true, because this case cannot occur.

(4) *Corresponding* I *and* O *propositions are said to be subcontraries.* In general, **subcontrary propositions** are such that *both* cannot be false, but both can be true. For instance, the *I* proposition "Some scientists are philosophers" is true, and its subcontrary "Some scientists are not philosophers", an *O* proposition, also is true. An example of subcontrary propositions, one of which is true, one false, would be the pair of propositions "Some humans are mortal", a true *I* proposition, and "Some humans are not mortal", a false *O* proposition. But we cannot give an example of subcontraries both of which are false, because this case cannot occur.*

(5) *Corresponding* A *and* I *propositions are subalternates.* In general, **subalternate propositions** are such that *if the universal member of the pair* (for instance, an *A* proposition) *is true, then so is the particular member of the pair* (for instance, an *I* proposition). The propositions "All humans are mortal", a true *A* proposition, and "Some humans are mortal", a true *I* proposition, are subalternates.

Notice that if a particular *A* proposition is *false*, nothing can be inferred as to the truth value of its subalternate; it may be true or it may be false. For instance, the false *A* proposition "All scientists are philosophers" has as its subalternate the *true I* proposition "Some scientists are philosophers", while the false *A* proposition "All humans are immortal" has as its subalternate the *false I* proposition "Some humans are immortal". Notice also that subalternation, conceived as a rule of inference, is *one directional*; we can infer from the truth of an *A* proposition to the truth of its corresponding *I* proposition, but we cannot infer from the truth of an *I* proposition to the truth of its corresponding *A* proposition.

(6) Finally, *corresponding* E *and* O *propositions also are subalternates.* Hence, we can infer from the truth of an *E* proposition to the truth of its subalternate, the corresponding *O* proposition. For example, we can infer from the truth of the *E* proposition "No humans are immortal" to the truth of its subalternate "Some humans are not immortal". But again, we cannot infer from the *falsehood* of an *E* proposition to the falsehood of its corresponding *O* proposition.

---

* Some logic texts define subcontraries as pairs of particular propositions which differ only in quality. Similarly, they define contraries as pairs of universal propositions which differ only in quality. So long as we make a blanket assumption of existential import, it doesn't matter which definitions of these concepts we adopt. But it *does* make a difference if existential import is not assumed. See pp. 208-209.

Examples:

(I) On the assumption that the *A* proposition "All college students are intelligent", in symbols *CAI*, is true (whether in fact it is or not), we can infer that

1. *CII* is true (by subalternation),

2. *COI* is false (because *CAI* and *COI* are contradictories),

        and

3. *CEI* is false (because *CAI* and *CEI* are contraries).

(II) On the assumption that the *I* proposition "Some college students cheat on exams", in symbols *CIX*, is false, we can infer that

1. *CEX* is true (because *CIX* and *CEX* are contradictories),

2. *COX* is true (because *CIX* and *COX* are subcontraries),

        and

3. *CAX* is false (because *CEX* and *CAX* are contraries).

(III) On the assumption that the *E* proposition "No college students cheat on exams", in symbols *CEX*, is true, we can infer that

1. *CIX* is false (because *CEX* and *CIX* are contradictories),

2. *CAX* is false (because *CEX* and *CAX* are contraries,

        and

3. *COX* is true (by subalternation).

(IV) On the assumption that the *O* proposition "Some college students do not cheat on exams", in symbols *COX*, is true, we can infer only that *CAX* is false.

Other inference rules of traditional logic

(1) *Conversion.* A proposition is **converted** by replacing its subject term with its predicate term and its predicate term with its subject term. For instance, *SAP* converts to *PAS*, *SEP* converts to *PES*, *SOP* to *POS*, etc. But conversion is a *valid* process *only* if used on *E* or *I* propositions. We can validly infer from *SEP* to *PES*, and from *SIP* to *PIS*, but *not* from *SAP* to *PAS*, and *not* from *SOP* to *POS*. For example, we can validly infer from "No scientists are philosophers" to "No philosophers are scientists", but not from "All scientists are philosophers" to "All philosophers are scientists".

(2) *Conversion by Limitation.* On the assumption that all classes referred to have members (an assumption we have been making so far), we can validly infer from an *A* proposition to a particular related *I* proposition by the process called **conversion by limitation**. For instance, we can infer by conversion by limitation from the *A* proposition "All humans are mortal", in symbols *HAM*, to the *I* proposition, "Some mortals are human", in symbols *MIH*.

(3) *Obversion.* To **obvert** a proposition, change its quality (from affirmative to negative or from negative to affirmative), and replace its predicate with the negation or *complement* of the predicate. Using the bar symbol "–" placed over a term to symbolize the complement (negation) of that term (so that the complement of the term *P* is symbolized as $\bar{P}$), we can obvert, say the *E* proposition *SEP* ("No scientists are philosophers") by first changing the quality of that proposition from negative to affirmative, obtaining the proposition *SAP*, and then replacing the predicate with its complement, obtaining the proposition $SA\bar{P}$ ("All scientists are non-philosophers"). Thus, *SEP* obverts to $SA\bar{P}$. Similarly, *SAP* obverts to $SE\bar{P}$, *SIP* obverts to $SO\bar{P}$, and *SOP* obverts to $SI\bar{P}$. Obversion *always* is valid.

(4) *Contraposition.* To obtain the **contrapositive** of a proposition, replace its subject with the complement of its predicate and replace its

predicate with the complement of its subject. Thus, the contrapositive of SAP is $\bar{P}A\bar{S}$, and the contrapositive of SOP is $\bar{P}O\bar{S}$. Contraposition is valid for A and O propositions, but not for E and I propositions. Hence, we can validly infer from, say, SAP to $\bar{P}A\bar{S}$, and from $\bar{P}O\bar{S}$ to SOP, but not from SEP to $\bar{P}E\bar{S}$, and not from SIP to $\bar{P}I\bar{S}$.

(5) *Contraposition by Limitation.* Finally, again assuming that all classes referred to have members, we can validly infer from a given E proposition to a particular related O proposition by the process called **contraposition by limitation**. For instance, we can validly infer from the E proposition "No humans are immortal", in symbols HEI, to the O proposition "Some mortals (nonimmortals) are not nonhuman", in symbols $\bar{I}O\bar{H}$, by contraposition by limitation.

Contraposition by limitation obviously is valid, since it is simply the *combination* of subalternation (of an E proposition) and contraposition (of the resulting O proposition).

Notice that conversion, obversion, and contraposition are, in effect, *equivalence inference rules.* For instance, we can infer from SAP to $\bar{P}A\bar{S}$ by contraposition *and* also from $\bar{P}A\bar{S}$ to SAP. (Hence, to mix the notations of traditional and predicate logics for a moment, we can say that a sentence such as $SAP \equiv \bar{P}A\bar{S}$ is a logical truth of traditional syllogistic logic.) But conversion by limitation and contraposition by limitation are *not* equivalence rules. Rather they are *implicational inference rules.* For instance, we can infer from SAP to PIS by conversion by limitation, but *not* from PIS to SAP. (Hence, again mixing notations, we can say that a sentence such as $SAP \supset PIS$ is a logical truth of traditional logic, but *not* a sentence such as $SAP \equiv PIS$.)

Examples:

On the assumption that the A proposition "All college students are intelligent", in symbols CAI, is true, we can infer that

1. $CE\bar{I}$ is true (by obversion),

2. $\bar{I}A\bar{C}$ is true (by contraposition),

3. $\bar{I}EC$ is true (by obversion of $\bar{I}A\bar{C}$),

4. *IIC* is true (by conversion by limitation),

5. *CII* is true (by conversion of *IIC*),

6. *IOC̄* is true (by obversion of *IIC*),

7. *CŌĪ* is true (by contraposition of *IOC̄*).

Making use of the processes illustrated by the square of opposition, we also can infer from the truth of *CAI* that

8. *COI* is false (because *CAI* and *COI* are contradictories),

9. *ĪOC̄* is false (by contraposition of *COI*),

10. *CIĪ* is false (by obversion of *COI*),

11. *ĪIC* is false (by obversion of *ĪOC̄*),

12. *IEC* is false (because *IIC* and *IEC* are contradictories),

13. *CEI* is false (by conversion of *IEC*),

14. *CAĪ* is false (by obversion of *CEI*),

15. *IAC̄* is false (by contraposition of *CAĪ*).

6

Syllogistic Logic (Not Assuming Existential Import)

The logic developed in Section 5, above, rests on a *blanket* assumption of existential import. But no such blanket assumption is made in everyday life. For instance, someone uttering the proposition "Let him who is without sin cast the first stone" does not necessarily assume that there are any men free from sin. Similarly, a scientist who says "All objects cooled down to absolute zero will conduct electricity" does not intend to imply that anything ever will be cooled down to absolute zero.

The question naturally arises as to how much of the traditional logic just described is *invalid* if we do *not* make a blanket assumption of existential import, thus allowing that logic to deal with sentences about empty classes. The answer is this:

Subalternation is invalid. For instance, if there are no martians, then the *A* proposition, "All martians are immortal", in symbols *MAI*, is true (for if *A* propositions have no existential import, then *MAI* is equivalent to $(x)(Mx \supset Ix)$), while its subalternate "Some martians are immortal", in symbols *MII*, is false (for *MII* is equivalent to $(\exists x)(Mx \cdot Ix)$). So we cannot allow the inference by subalternation from an *A* to an *I* proposition. The same is true of subalternation going from an *E* to an *O* proposition.

Conversion by limitation and contraposition by limitation both are invalid. For instance, if there are no martians, then the *A* proposition "All martians are immortal", in symbols *MAI*, is true, while the *I* proposition obtained from it by conversion by limitation, namely the proposition "Some immortals are martians", in symbols *IIM*, is false.

A *and* E *propositions are not contraries.* We said before that two propositions are contraries if both cannot be true, but both can be false, and that *A* and *E* propositions are contraries. However, if we allow the use of empty classes, then both of two corresponding *A* and *E* propositions can be true, and hence, *A* and *E* propositions will not be contraries. For instance, if there are no martians, then the *A* proposition "All martians are immortal" (*MAI*) and the *E* proposition "No martians are immortal" (*MEI*) both are true. Hence, they are not contraries, at least not in the traditional sense. (However, if we define contraries as pairs of universal propositions which differ only in quality, then corresponding *A* and *E* propositions, such as *MAI* and *MEI* will be contraries, even allowing empty classes. But on this definition it will be possible to have contraries both of which are true [for instance *MAI* and *MEI*].)

I *and* O *propositions are not subcontraries.* We said before that two propositions are subcontraries if both cannot be false, but both can be true, and that *I* and *O* propositions are subcontraries. However, if we allow the use of empty classes, then both of two corresponding *I* and *O* propositions can be false, and hence, *I* and *O* propositions will not be subcontraries. For example, if there are no martians, then the *I* proposition "Some martians are immortal" (*MII*) and the *O* proposition "Some martians are not immortal" (*MOI*) both are false. Hence, they are not subcontraries in the traditional sense. (However, if we define subcontraries as pairs of particular propositions which differ only in quality, then *I* and *O* propositions still will be subcontraries even allowing empty classes. But it will be possible to have subcontraries both of which are false [for instance *MII* and *MOI*].)

To sum up, if we allow the subject or predicate terms of propositions to refer to empty classes, then subalternation, conversion by limitation, and contraposition by limitation all are invalid, *A* and *E* propositions are not contraries, and *I* and *O* propositions are not subcontraries.

What remains are the *diagonals* of the square of opposition (since *A* and *O*, as well as *E* and *I*, propositions are still contradictories), conversion (of *E* or *I* propositions), obversion, and contraposition (of *A* and *O* propositions).

Exercise 11–1:

(A) If it is false that all existentialists are theists, then what can be said about the truth value of the following?

1. *EET*
2. *TEE*
3. $\overline{T}IE$

4. $\overline{T}A\overline{E}$
5. *EOT*
6. *TIE*

(B) If it is false that any existentialists are theists, then what can be said about the truth values of the above six propositions?

(C) If *SAP* is true, what can be inferred about the truth values of the following:

1. $\overline{P}IS$
2. $SE\overline{P}$
3. $\overline{P}E\overline{S}$
4. $SI\overline{P}$
5. $\overline{P}ES$

6. $\overline{S}AP$
7. $\overline{P}O\overline{S}$
8. $\overline{S}OP$
9. $\overline{P}A\overline{S}$

(D)   If $\overline{SE\overline{P}}$ is false, what can be inferred about the truth values of the nine propositions in question (C)?

(E)   Suppose you know that the classes S, P, $\overline{S}$, and $\overline{P}$ all are nonempty (i.e., have members). And suppose you know that "No S are non-P". What else can you infer? (Justify your answers.)

7

*More on
Existential
Import*

In contrast to traditional logic, no blanket assumption of existential import is, or need be, made for sentences using the predicate logic notation. However, some of these sentences are false if (and indeed because) their predicates refer to empty classes. For instance, the sentence "Some martians are immortal", symbolized as $(\exists x)(Mx \cdot Ix)$, is false if there are no martians (because then all of its substitution instances—$Ma \cdot Ia$, $Mb \cdot Ib$, etc.—are false). So sentences of this kind do have what is perhaps a weaker kind of existential import.

On the other hand, some sentences symbolized in the predicate logic notation are *true* if (and indeed because) certain of their predicates refer to empty classes. For example, the sentence "All martians are immortal", symbolized as $(x)(Mx \supset Ix)$, and thus construed to assert that *if* a given thing is a martian, *then* it is immortal, is true if there are no martians (because then all of its substitution instances—$Ma \supset Ia$, $Mb \supset Ib$, etc.—are true, by virtue of their false antecedents). So sentences such as $(x)(Mx \supset Ix)$ *do not* have this weaker kind of existential import.

Notice, however, that we cannot determine whether an expression symbolized in the notation of predicate logic has this weaker kind of existential import merely by noting which kind of quantifier is employed in its symbolization. In particular, we cannot assume that all expressions containing (only) an existential quantifier *do* have existential import,* or that those containing (only) a universal quantifier *do not*. For one thing,

---

* Hence, the name "existential quantifiers" is misleading. Perhaps better names for the quantifiers would be "all quantifiers" and "some quantifiers". Indeed, in one logic text they are referred to as "all operators" and "some operators", which may well be even more apt.

the expression $(x)Fx$ *does* have this kind of existential import, since it is false if nothing has the property F. And for another, we can always replace a universal quantifier by an existential quantifier, and vice versa, by means of rule **QN**. For instance, we can replace the universal quantifier in the expression $(x)(Fx \supset Gx)$, which *does not* have existential import, to obtain the expression $\sim(\exists x) \sim (Fx \supset Gx)$, which also does not have existential import.

The restriction to propositions referring to nonempty classes placed on traditional logic constitutes a serious *limitation* on that logic. For one thing, a system having such a restriction cannot be used to reason about nonexistent entities or classes, a severe limitation indeed considering the importance of reasoning about entities we are trying to *prevent* from coming into existence (such as World War III).* For another, such a system provides no way to deny that a particular class has members, for a blanket requirement that all classes referred to have members rules out perfectly legitimate sentences such as "There are no unicorns".

Consequently, the fact that in predicate logic we are *not* restricted to sentences referring to nonempty classes makes that logic much more useful (as well as "logically neater") than a traditional system weighted down with such a restriction. And yet we gain this added usefulness without any great sacrifice, in particular without sacrificing the ability to build the weaker kind of existential import into any sentence we want to have it. For instance, if we want to symbolize the sentence "All martians are immortal" so that it will be false if there are no immortal martians, then we can do so by symbolizing it as $(x)(Mx \supset Ix) \cdot (\exists x)(Mx \cdot Ix)$.

8

Continuation of Traditional Syllogistic Logic

In this section, let's continue to permit the subject and predicate terms of propositions to refer to empty classes as well as to classes that have members, so that *SAP* will be roughly equivalent to $(x)(Sx \supset Px)$, *SEP* to $(x)(Sx \supset \sim Px)$, *SIP* to $(\exists x)(Sx \cdot Px)$, and *SOP* to $(\exists x)(Sx \cdot \sim Px)$. In other words, let's continue to do without any blanket assumption of existential import.

---

* Indeed the situation is even worse (in some ways), for since we cannot know for *sure* whether our attempts to prevent World War III will be successful or not, we cannot even know for sure whether sentences such as "All battles of World War III will be battles won by the U. S." can be considered at all in traditional logic.

Alternate terminology

Let's represent the null class, that is, the empty class, the class having no members, by O. Then $S = O$ will symbolize "The class S is empty", and $S \neq O$ will symbolize "The class S is not empty" (i.e., the class S has members). Let SP designate the class of things (if any) that are members of both classes S and P. And let $S\bar{P}$ designate the class of things (if any) that are members of both classes S and $\bar{P}$ (the complement of the class P). We now are ready to introduce another and quite revealing method for symbolizing categorical propositions:

(1) Consider the A proposition "All martians are pink", in symbols MAP. This proposition asserts that anything that is a martian also is pink. So it *denies* that anything is both a martian and *nonpink*. Thus, it denies that the class of things which are both martians and nonpink has any members. Hence, it can be correctly symbolized as $M\bar{P} = O$, which asserts that the class of things that are both martians and nonpink is empty.

(2) Now consider the E proposition "No martians are pink", in symbols MEP. This proposition denies that anything is both a martian and pink. So it *asserts* that the class of things which are both martians and pink is empty. Hence, it can be correctly symbolized as $MP = O$.

(3) Next, consider the I proposition "Some martians are pink", in symbols MIP. This proposition asserts that there are some things which are both martians and pink and thus that the class of things which are both martians and pink is not empty. Hence, it can be symbolized as $MP \neq O$.

(4) Finally, consider the O proposition "Some martians are not pink", in symbols MOP. This proposition asserts that there are some things which are both martians and *not* pink. That is, it asserts that the class of things which are both martians and *nonpink* is not empty. So it can be correctly symbolized as $M\bar{P} \neq O$.

To sum up: in general, letting S and P represent the subject and predicate terms respectively of categorical propositions, we can symbolize A propositions as SAP, or as $S\bar{P} = O$, E propositions as SEP, or as

Traditional Logic

$SP = O$, I propositions as SIP, or as $SP \neq O$, and O propositions as SOP, or as $S\bar{P} \neq O$.

Notice that this new way to symbolize categorical propositions clearly reveals that corresponding A and O propositions, and corresponding E and I propositions, are *contradictories*. (For instance, the E proposition $SP = O$ clearly contradicts the I proposition $SP \neq O$.) Notice also that this notation clearly reveals that A and E propositions do not assert the existence of anything (which is another way of saying that they *lack* the weaker kind of existential import), while I and O propositions do assert the existence of things, namely members of particular classes (which is another way of saying that they *possess* the weaker kind of existential import).

Exercise 11–2:

Symbolize the following propositions, using both of the notations introduced in Chapter Eleven.

EXAMPLE: All scientists are philosophers.
    a. SAP
    b. $S\bar{P} = O$

1. Some scientists are impractical.
    (S = "scientist"; P = "practical")

2. No philosophers are millionaires.
    (P = "philosopher";
    M = "millionaire")

3. All nonmathematicians are spendthrifts.
    (M = "mathematician";
    S = "spendthrift")

4. Some mathematicians are not practical. (M = "mathematician";
    P = "practical")

5. No nonscientists are nonmathematicians. (S = "scientist";
    M = "mathematician")

6. All philosophers are non-Republicans.
    (P = "philosopher";
    R = "Republican")

7. Some existentialists believe in God.
    (E = "existentialist"; B = "believer in God")

8. Some lawyers are drunks who have managed to pass a bar exam.
    (L = "lawyers"; D = "drunks who have managed to pass a bar exam")

9. Philosophers who reject useless pleasures are strangers to that which makes life worthwhile.
    (P = "philosophers who reject useless pleasures"; S = "strangers to that which makes life worthwhile")

Diagramming categorical propositions

It is both useful and informative to picture categorical propositions by means of *Venn Diagrams*.

First, let's represent the classes *S* and *P* by overlapping circles, as follows:

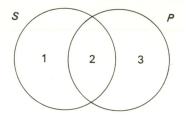

In this diagram, area 1 represents the class of things which are *S* but not *P* (that is, the class $S\bar{P}$), area 2 the class of things which are both *S* and *P* (that is, the class SP), and area 3 the class of things which are *P* but not *S* (that is, the class $\bar{S}P$).

Now consider the *A* proposition $S\bar{P} = O$, which asserts that the class $S\bar{P}$ is empty. We can diagram $S\bar{P} = O$ by *shading out the $S\bar{P}$ area*, that is, by shading out area 1 (to indicate that the class $S\bar{P}$ is empty), as follows:

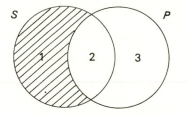

Next, consider the *E* proposition $SP = O$, which asserts that the class SP is empty. We can diagram $SP = O$ by *shading out the SP area*, that is, by shading out area 2 (to indicate that the class SP is empty), as follows:

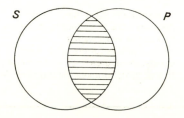

Now, consider the *I* proposition $SP \neq O$, which asserts that the class *SP* is *not* empty, but has at least one member. We can diagram $SP \neq O$ by *placing a letter* (say *X*) *in the SP area*, in other words, in area 2 (to indicate that the class *SP* is *not* empty), as follows:

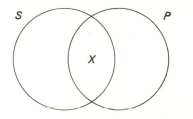

Finally, consider the *O* proposition $S\bar{P} \neq O$, which asserts that the class $S\bar{P}$ is not empty, but has at least one member. We can diagram $S\bar{P} \neq O$ by placing a letter *X* in the $S\bar{P}$ area, area 1 (to indicate that the class $S\bar{P}$ is not empty), as follows:

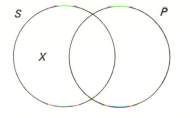

Chapter Twelve

*Traditional
Syllogistic
Logic—II*

1

Syllogisms

A **syllogism** is an argument containing three categorical propositions, namely two premises and a conclusion. One of the earliest syllogisms is the following:

1. All humans are mortal.

2. All Greeks are humans.

/∴ 3. All Greeks are mortal.

which can be symbolized as follows:

1. *MAP*

2. *SAM*

/∴ 3. *SAP*

The term *P*, the predicate of the conclusion, is said to be the **major term** of the syllogism, the term *S*, the subject of the conclusion, is said to be the **minor term**, and the term M, which occurs once in each premise, but not in the conclusion, is said to be the **middle term**. Every syllogism has exactly three terms, each one repeated twice.

The **mood** of a syllogism is determined by the kind of propositions it contains. For instance, the above syllogism contains three A propositions, and so its mood is AAA. Similarly, the mood for the syllogism

1. All mathematicians are philosophers.

2. Some scientists are mathematicians.

/∴ 3. Some scientists are philosophers.

which is symbolized as

1. *MAP*

2. *SIM*

/∴ 3. *SIP*

is AII.

The **figure** of a syllogism is determined by the positions of its major, minor, and middle terms in its premises. There are four figures, namely:

1. *M__P*
   S__M
/∴ *S__P*

3. *M__P*
   M__S
/∴ *S__P*

2. *P__M*
   S__M
/∴ *S__P*

4. *P__M*
   M__S
/∴ *S__P*

Notice that the order of premises is important in determining the figure of a syllogism. The rule is that the predicate of the conclusion, the major term, must occur in the first premise.

The **form** of a syllogism is simply the combination of mood plus figure. For instance, the two syllogisms discussed above have the forms *AAA*-I and *AII*-I respectively, and the syllogism

	1.	*MAP*
	2.	*MES*
/∴	3.	*SEP*

has form *AEE*-III. (This syllogism happens to be invalid, but invalid syllogisms are still syllogisms.)

Examples:

Some other examples of syllogisms and their forms are:

	1.	*IAO*-III		4.	*AIE*-I
		MIP			*MAP*
		MAS			*SIM*
/∴		*SOP*	/∴		*SEP*
	2.	*AEE*-IV		5.	*EEE*-III
		PAM			*MEP*
		MES			*MES*
/∴		*SEP*	/∴		*SEP*
	3.	*EOO*-II		6.	*EIO*-I
		PEM			*MEP*
		SOM			*SIM*
/∴		*SOP*	/∴		*SOP*

Traditional Logic

2

*Proving
Validity-
Invalidity of
Syllogisms*

If a syllogism having a given form is a *valid* syllogism, then all syllogisms having that form are valid, and if a syllogism having a given form is *invalid*, then all syllogisms having that form are invalid.*

Using Venn Diagrams to Prove Validity-Invalidity

Perhaps the simplest way to determine the validity-invalidity of syllogisms and of what we might call "syllogism forms" is by means of *Venn Diagrams.*

To diagram a syllogism, three overlapping circles are required, one for each term. In overlapping the three circles, seven areas are formed (plus an eighth outside the circle, representing the class $\overline{S}\,\overline{M}\overline{P}$):

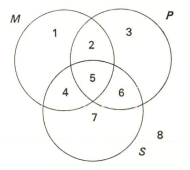

Area 1 represents the class $M\overline{P}\overline{S}$, 2 the class $MP\overline{S}$, 3 the class $\overline{M}P\overline{S}$, 4 the class $M\overline{P}S$, and so on. The *pair* of areas 1 and 4, taken together, represent the class $M\overline{P}$; the pair 3 and 6, the class $\overline{M}P$; the pair 6 and 7, the class $\overline{M}S$; and so on. (We need *two* areas to represent these classes because in drawing a third overlapping circle we divide each of the areas $M\overline{P}$, $\overline{M}P$,

---

* Except for the cases considered in Section 6 of this chapter.
In the Middle Ages, students determined the validity of a syllogistic form by reciting a chant containing a name for each of the valid moods in each figure. For instance, the name "bArbArA" occurs in the chant for the first figure, indicating that the form AAA-I is valid.

$\overline{M}S$, etc., in half.) If we write in class names, instead of numbers, then the three-circle diagram looks like this:

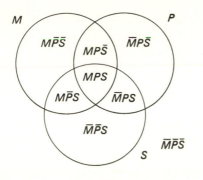

Consider the syllogism

1.   *MAP*

2.   *SAM*

—————————

/ ∴   3.   *SAP*

alternately symbolized as

1. $M\overline{P} = O$

2. $S\overline{M} = O$

—————————

/ ∴   3. $S\overline{P} = O$

To diagram its first premise, *MAP*, we shade out the two $M\overline{P}$ areas, namely 1 and 4:

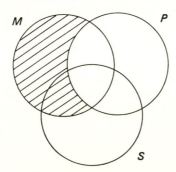

And to diagram its second premise, SAM, we shade out the two $S\overline{M}$ areas, namely 6 and 7:

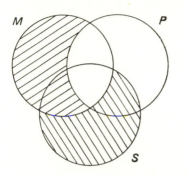

If we then were to diagram its conclusion, SAP, we would shade out the two $S\overline{P}$ areas, 4 and 7. But in diagramming the two premises of this argument, we have already shaded out 4 and 7, and hence *we have already diagrammed its conclusion*. This indicates (speaking metaphorically) that the information contained in the conclusion already is contained in the premises. Hence, the syllogism, and any syllogism having the form AAA-I, is valid, since it cannot have true premises and a false conclusion.

Now consider the syllogism

1. *MAP*

2. *SEM*

/∴ 3. *SEP*

alternately symbolized as

1. $M\overline{P} = O$

2. $SM = O$

/∴ 3. $SP = O$

To diagram its first premise, we shade out 1 and 4, and to diagram its second premise, we shade out 4 and 5, to get:

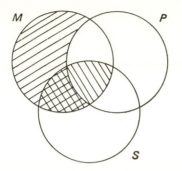

But to diagram its *conclusion*, we would have to shade out 5 and 6. It happens that we have shaded out 5, but we have *not* shaded out 6. So in diagramming the premises of this syllogism, we have *not* also diagrammed its conclusion. Hence, it is *possible* for its premises to be true and its conclusion false. The syllogism in question is invalid.

Examples:

(I) We can diagram the premises of the syllogism

1.   All philosophers are martians.

2.   No martians are stupid.

/∴ 3.   No philosophers are stupid.

in symbols

1.   *PAM*

2.   *MES*

/∴ 3.   *PES*

or

1. $P\bar{M} = O$

2. $MS = O$

/ ∴   3. $PS = O$

as follows:

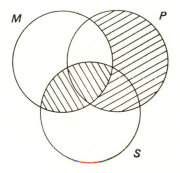

This proves that the syllogism is valid since in diagramming its premises we have shaded out areas 5 and 6 and, hence, also diagrammed its conclusion.

(II) We can diagram the premises of the syllogism

1.   No politicians are honest.

2.   Some Americans are politicians.

/ ∴   3.   Some Americans are not honest.

in symbols

1.   *PEH*

2.   *AIP*

/ ∴   3.   *AOH*

or

	1.	$PH = O$
	2.	$AP \neq O$
/∴	3.	$A\overline{H} \neq O$

as follows:

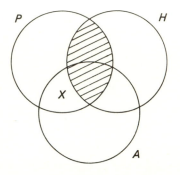

Although in diagramming the premises of this syllogism we have not quite diagrammed its conclusion (as will become evident in the next few paragraphs), we still have proved that this syllogism is valid. The reason for this is that the conclusion, $A\overline{H} \neq O$, asserts that 4 and 7 *both* are not empty (that is, it asserts that either 4 or 7 has something in it), and in diagramming the premises we have placed an X in 4. So the premises of this argument already contain the information which is contained in the conclusion.

(III) We can diagram the premises of the syllogism

	1.	No doctors are cigarette smokers.
	2.	Some doctors are philosophers.
/∴	3.	Some philosophers are cigarette smokers.

in symbols

1.   *DEC*

2.   *DIP*

/ ∴   3.   *PIC*

        or

1.   *DC = O*

2.   *DP ≠ O*

/ ∴   3.   *PC ≠ O*

as follows:

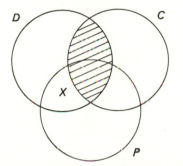

This proves that the syllogism is not valid, because in diagramming its premises we did *not* place an *X* either in 5 or in 6, which (roughly) is what would be required to diagram its conclusion.

In diagramming the premises of a syllogism, sometimes an *X* can be placed in either one of two areas. This is the case with respect to the syllogism

1.   *MAP*

2.   *SIP*

/ ∴   3.   *SIM*

alternately symbolized as

1. $M\bar{P} = O$

2. $SP \neq O$

/∴ 3. $SM \neq O$

We diagram the first premise as follows:

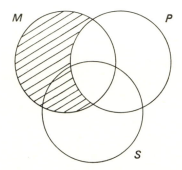

But in diagramming the second premise, the question arises as to whether to place an X in area 5 or in 6. The answer is that we should not place an X in either area, since the premises assert only that one or the other (or perhaps both) of the classes represented by these has members, without indicating definitely either that the class SMP (5) has members or that the class $S\overline{M}P$ (6) has members. To indicate that the premises merely tell us that either SMP or $S\overline{M}P$ has members, without telling us which one, we can place an X *on the line* between 5 and 6. And then, the diagram will look like this:

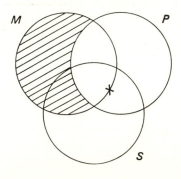

Is this syllogism valid? If it were, then in diagramming its premises, we would have placed an *X* either in 4 or in 5. Now clearly no *X* has been placed in 4, for that area is shaded out. And no *X* has been placed in 5 either, for the *X* was placed *on the line* between 5 and 6. So we cannot guarantee the truth of the conclusion *SIM*, on the basis of the evidence afforded by its premises, and hence the syllogism is *invalid*. (This is the *only* even mildly difficult kind of case which can arise in proving validity-invalidity by means of Venn Diagrams, so it is worthwhile to expend a little extra effort in order to understand it.*)

Five rules for determining validity-invalidity of syllogisms

An alternative (and much older) method for determining the validity-invalidity of syllogisms and syllogism forms is by means of rules stating properties which all valid syllogisms must possess.

But before introducing a set of five rules of this kind, we must discuss the concept of **distribution**. In traditional logic texts, it is usually stated that a term in a proposition is **distributed** if (roughly) it says something about *all* members of the class designated by that term. For instance, the *A* proposition "All scientists are mathematicians" is said to distribute its subject term, since it says something about *all* scientists (namely that they are mathematicians), but *not* its predicate term, because it does not say something about *all* mathematicians. (It surely does not say, or imply, that all mathematicians are scientists.)

Traditional logic texts work out the distribution properties of all four kinds of categorical propositions. Letting *S* stand for subject terms and *P* for predicate terms, we can summarize the findings of the traditional logician, as follows:

Table of Distribution

1. *A* propositions distribute *S*.

2. *E* propositions distribute *S* and *P*.

3. *I* propositions distribute neither *S* nor *P*.

4. *O* propositions distribute *P*.

---

* However, although the *theory* may be difficult to understand, cases of this kind present no problem *in practice*, since all syllogisms diagrammed by placing an *X* on a line are invalid. (Similarly, all syllogisms diagrammed by *doubly shading out an area* are invalid.)

Most students readily accept the results summarized in the first three lines of this table. But they find the idea expressed on the fourth line that *O* propositions distribute their predicate terms rather counterintuitive. And yet there is a certain plausibility to this idea. For instance, it seems plausible to say that the *O* proposition "Some scientists are not philosophers" distributes its predicate term, because it says of *all* philosophers that they are not some scientists (i.e., that they are excluded from part of the class of scientists). In any event, we must say that *O* propositions distribute their predicates, or the five rules about to be presented will not function properly.*

We now are ready to state a set of five rules for determining the validity of syllogisms:†

All valid syllogisms must have:

1. A middle term which is distributed at least once;

2. No term distributed in the conclusion which is not distributed in a premise;

3. At least one affirmative (nonnegative) premise;

4. A negative conclusion if and only if one of its premises is negative; and

5. At least one particular premise if the conclusion is particular.

Any syllogism which does not have all five of these properties is invalid. (The fifth rule is required only if we allow propositions to refer to empty classes.)‡

---

* Unfortunately, the traditional characterization of the concept of distribution is not satisfactory even with respect to *A*, *E*, and *I* propositions. Take the *A* proposition "All bachelors are unmarried adult males" (let's assume that "bachelor" *means* "unmarried adult male"). Clearly, if this proposition "refers to" all bachelors, thus distributing its subject term, then it also "refers to" all unmarried adult males, thus distributing its predicate terms. Hence, the traditional account of distribution is inadequate. It so happens that there are ways of getting around this difficulty, but they require decisions on philosophical problems beyond the scope of this text, and hence are omitted.

† (There are alternative sets.)

‡ A sixth rule, requiring that there be exactly three terms in a valid syllogism, often is added to these five. But this rule is unnecessary, since an argument which does not have exactly three terms, each one repeated twice, is not a syllogism according to the generally accepted definition of that term.

Traditional Logic

Examples:

(I) The syllogism

1.   Some mathematicians are scientists. (*MIS*)

2.   All philosophers are mathematicians. (*PAM*)

/ ∴   3.   Some scientists are philosophers. (*SIP*)

violates the rule requiring that the middle term be distributed at least once, and hence is invalid.

(II) The syllogism

1.   All mathematicians are scientists. (*MAS*)

2.   All philosophers are mathematicians. (*PAM*)

/ ∴   3.   All scientists are philosophers. (*SAP*)

violates the rule requiring that no term be distributed in the conclusion which is not distributed in a premise, and hence is invalid.

(III) The syllogism

1.   Some scientists are not mathematicians. (*SOM*)

2.   No mathematicians are philosophers. (*MEP*)

/ ∴   3.   Some scientists are not philosophers. (*SOP*)

violates the rule requiring at least one affirmative premise, and hence is invalid.

(IV) The syllogism

1. Some scientists are not mathematicians. (*SOM*)

2. All mathematicians are philosophers. (*MAP*)

/ ∴ 3. Some scientists are philosophers. (*SIP*)

violates the rule requiring that the conclusion be negative, if a premise is negative, and hence is invalid. (This rule also requires that a premise be negative if the conclusion is negative.)

(V) And the syllogism

1. No scientists are mathematicians. (*SEM*)

2. All mathematicians are philosophers. (*MAP*)

/ ∴ 3. Some scientists are not philosophers. (*SOP*)

violates the rule requiring that at least one premise be particular, if the conclusion is particular, and hence is invalid.

Exercise 12–1:

Put the following arguments into standard syllogistic form, and test for validity, using either the five rules of valid syllogism, or Venn Diagrams.

(A) 1. *HER*

2. *NIH̄*

/ ∴ 3. *NOR̄*

(B) 1. *BOM̄*

2. *BER̄*

/ ∴ 3. *RIM*

(C) 1. *PIN̄*

     2. *NAR̄*

/∴ 3. *RIP̄*

(D) 1. *PAN̄*

     2. *NAḠ*

/∴ 3. *GEP̄*

(E) 1. *S̄AP*

     2. *P̄EM*

/∴ 3. *S̄EM̄*

(F) 1. *HAP*

     2. *T̄EP*

/∴ 3. *HET̄*

(G) 1. *HIḠ*

     2. *NIH*

/∴ 3. *NIG*

(H) 1. *HOT̄*

     2. *TEM̄*

/∴ 3. *HOM̄*

(I) 1. *M̄AP*

     2. *S̄AM*

/∴ 3. *SAP̄*

3

Enthymemes

In arguments in daily life, we often omit premises which we feel confident everyone knows. For instance, someone might argue that Texas is larger than France, and hence, that some state in the United States is larger than France, omitting as understood the fact that Texas is a state in the United States.

Sometimes it is not a premise, but the *conclusion* of an argument which is omitted as obvious. And sometimes a premise *and* the conclusion are omitted. An example would be a mother who says, "Now son, it's eight o'clock, and all little boys have to go to bed at eight o'clock", thus omitting the premise that the son is a little boy, as well as the conclusion that the son has to go to bed.

Arguments which omit premises (or the conclusion) as "understood" are said to be **enthymemic arguments**, or simply **enthymemes.**

Strangely, there are cases of clearly valid enthymemic arguments for which it may be quite difficult to supply the missing premise or premises.

Indeed, often it is not realized that a premise has been omitted. The example given in Chapter Nine,

1.   Art is taller than Betsy.

2.   Betsy is taller than Charles.

/ ∴   3.   Art is taller than Charles.

while not a syllogism, illustrates this point. In the first place, although obviously valid in some sense, few realize that it is *invalid as it stands*, and fewer still would be able to supply the missing premise concerning the transitivity of the property designated by the term "_____ is taller than _ _ _ _ _ _".

Obviously, there is no point in declaring an argument in everyday life invalid when the addition of premises accepted by all concerned will render the argument valid. Life is short and we have neither the time nor the inclination to be precise and complete about everything.

On the other hand, what *seems* obvious often turns out to be incorrect when someone finally takes the trouble to spell it out in all of its details. This is particularly true in philosophy. So there is something to be said for the complete spelling out which *logic* and a precise logical notation make possible.

4

Sorites

Consider the argument

1.   *MAP*

2.   *SAM*

3.   *RAS*

/ ∴   4.   *RAP*

As it stands, it cannot count as a valid syllogism, since it contains four terms and three premises, and hence is not even a syllogism, much less a valid one. But clearly, it constitutes a valid argument of some sort or other. In order to bring it into the syllogistic framework, we can consider it to be an *enthymemic version* of a chain of two valid syllogisms. For instance, we can take the first two propositions as the premises of the valid syllogism:

1. MAP

2. SAM
_____

/ ∴ 3. SAP

and then use the conclusion *SAP* and the third proposition *RAS* as premises of the valid syllogism:

3. SAP

4. RAS
_____

/ ∴ 5. RAP

Let us refer to any argument of the kind just considered which can be treated as a chain of enthymemic syllogisms as a **sorites.***
An example of a sorites with more than three premises is

1. MAP

2. SAM

3. RIS

4. NEP
_____

/ ∴ 5. RON

This sorites breaks down into the following chain of valid syllogisms:

NEP	MEN	SEN
MAP	SAM	RIS
/ ∴ MEN	/ ∴ SEN	/ ∴ RON

* Originally, the term "sorites" referred only to a special kind of enthymemic syllogism chain. But in recent years it has come to refer indiscriminately to all kinds.

Since all three of these syllogisms are valid (which it is left to the reader to prove), the sorites as a whole is valid.

Exercise 12–2:

Translate the following sorites into standard form and determine whether they are valid or invalid.

(A)
1. Women are fickle.
2. No one is disliked who is good at logic.
3. Fickle people are disliked.
/∴ 4. No women are good at logic.

(B)
1. No skiers are nonathletic.
2. Some nutritionists are skiers.
3. Athletes are not brawny.
/∴ 4. Some nutritionists are nonbrawny.

(C)
1. Barbers are extroverts.
2. No good barbers are nonbarbers.
3. Some good barbers are highstrung.
/∴ 4. Some highstrung people are not extroverts.

(D)
1. No scientists are nonmathematicians.
2. Geologists are friendly.
3. No mathematicians are friendly.
/∴ 4. No geologists are scientists.

(E)
1. Occasionally, one finds a genius in graduate school.
2. No one can be admitted who isn't a college graduate.
3. People in graduate school are not college graduates.
/∴ 4. Some geniuses cannot be admitted to graduate school.

5

Syllogistics Extended

Many ingenious ways to extend the scope of syllogistic logic have been invented. Indeed, there seems to be no reason why syllogistic logic cannot be made as wide in scope as predicate logic. We now consider some of the simpler and more obvious ways of extending syllogistic logic:

(1) Many arguments containing four, five, and even six terms can be reduced to three terms, and thus into syllogistic form, by substituting synonyms, or by eliminating negation signs. For instance, we eliminate a negation sign, and reduce the number of terms in the nonsyllogistic argument*

1. All scientists are philosophers. (*SAP*)

2. No mathematicians are nonscientists. (*MES̄*)

/ ∴ 3. All mathematicians are philosophers. (*MAP*)

from four to three, by using *obversion* to replace its second premise with the equivalent proposition

2. All mathematicians are scientists. (*MAS*)

thus obtaining the valid syllogism

1. All scientists are philosophers. (*SAP*)

2. All mathematicians are scientists. (*MAS*)

/ ∴ 3. All mathematicians are philosophers. (*MAP*)

Similarly, we can reduce the number of terms in the nonsyllogistic argument

1. Some enclosed figures are squares. (*FIS*)

2. All triangles are enclosed figures. (*TAF*)

/∴ 3. Some three-sided enclosed figures are squares. (*EIS*)

---

* Sometimes it is said that an argument of this kind *is* a syllogism, but not a *standard form* syllogism, thus considering any set of three categorical propositions to constitute a syllogism, no matter how many terms it contains.

from four to three by replacing the phrase "three-sided enclosed figures" with its synonym "triangles", thus obtaining the syllogism

1. Some enclosed figures are squares. (*FIS*)

2. All triangles are enclosed figures. (*TAF*)

/∴ 3. Some triangles are squares. (*TIS*)

Of course, this syllogism is *invalid*, but it is a syllogism.

(2) We can translate many arguments into syllogistic form simply by making minor grammatical changes which do not essentially change the meanings of the propositions involved. For instance, we can translate the argument

1. All boy scouts do good deeds.

2. Some girl scouts do good deeds.

/∴ 3. Some girl scouts are not boy scouts.

into syllogistic form by replacing its first and second premises by the equivalent propositions "All boy scouts are doers of good deeds" and "Some girl scouts are doers of good deeds" respectively, thus obtaining the syllogism

1. All boy scouts are doers of good deeds. (*BAD*)

2. Some girl scouts are doers of good deeds. (*GID*)

/∴ 3. Some girl scouts are not boy scouts. (*GOB*)

Of course, this syllogism also is invalid.

(3) Many arguments are not in syllogistic form because they contain propositions which are not *categorical* propositions. Hence, they can be translated into syllogistic form by translating the propositions they con-

tain into categorical propositions. Sometimes, this can be accomplished by a simple change in word order. For instance, the proposition "Gamblers are all broke" may be translated into categorical form as "All gamblers are broke".

Sometimes, simply adding a suppressed quantifier will suffice to translate a proposition into categorical form. Thus, an argument containing the proposition "Women are fickle" may be translated into categorical form as "All women are fickle". And, clearly, "Every man is mortal" can be translated into the categorical proposition "All men are mortal".

(4) All *categorical* propositions say something about *classes*. Thus, technically, no *singular* proposition is a categorical proposition. Hence no syllogism can contain a singular proposition. (A *singular proposition* is a proposition one of whose terms refers to an *individual entity* rather than a class. Thus, "Socrates is mortal", "Art is tall", "This man is short", etc., all are singular propositions.)

But there are several standard ways to translate singular propositions into categorical propositions. One is simply to replace the singular term in such a proposition by a class term naming a class which can contain only one member (namely the individual referred to by the singular term). Thus, "Art is tall" can be translated into "All members of the class whose sole member is Art are tall". (We can also translate "Art is tall" into "All things identical with Art are tall", since only one thing, Art, is identical with Art.)

Using a method of this kind, we can translate the famous argument

1.   All men are mortal.

2.   Socrates is a man.

/ ∴   3.   Socrates is mortal.

into syllogistic form as follows:

1.   All men are mortal. (*HAM*)

2.   All members of the class whose sole
     member is Socrates are men. (*SAH*)

/∴   3.   All members of the class whose sole
     member is Socrates are mortal. (*SAM*)

Indeed, it has become customary to treat singular propositions as categorical propositions, considering *affirmative* singular propositions, such as "Socrates *is* a man" as *A* propositions, and *negative* singular propositions, such as "Socrates is *not* mortal" as *E* propositions, without bothering to translate as we have done above. Thus the argument

1. All men are mortal. (*HAM*)

2. Socrates is a man. (*SAH*)

/∴ 3. Socrates is mortal. (*SAM*)

is customarily treated as a syllogism, and indeed, a valid one.

(5) Sometimes a more radical translation procedure is required in order to translate propositions into categorical form, a procedure which involves the introduction of new classes. Take the proposition "We always have death and taxes". We can translate this sentence into categorical form by using the class of *times* (suggested by the temporal term "always"), to obtain the categorical proposition "All times are times in which we have death and taxes". (Notice that the subject class in this case is the class of times, and the predicate class is a *subclass* of the class of times, namely the class of times at which we have death and taxes.)

But, as usual, care must be used in translating. For instance, we don't want to translate the invalid argument

1. Every time Art gets an A on a logic exam he is happy.

2. Art always gets A's on logic exams.

/∴ 3. Art always is happy.

as

1. All times at which Art gets A's on logic exams are times at which Art is happy. (*LAH*)

2. All times are times at which Art gets A's on logic exams. (*TAL*)

/ ∴ 3. All times are times at which Art is happy. (*TAH*)

since the latter is a *valid* argument, and we don't want to translate invalid arguments into valid ones. The mistake was to translate the second premise, "Art always gets A's on logic exams", so as to have Art taking exams at *all* times. Clearly, what we mean when we say "Art always gets A's on logic exams" is more accurately rendered as "All times *at which Art takes exams* are times at which he gets A's". And if we correctly symbolize this premise, then the resulting argument will not even be a syllogism, much less a valid one.

Exercise 12–3:

Translate each of the following arguments into standard form, and test for validity, using either the five rules of valid syllogism or Venn Diagrams:

1. All logic classes are extremely interesting. So some classes which are harder than average are extremely interesting, since some logic classes are harder than average.

2. No logic classes are dreadfully boring, because no classes taught by philosophy teachers are boring, and all logic classes are taught by philosophy teachers.

3. All classes which are either interesting or difficult are uncrowded, due to the fact that all uncrowded classes are unexciting, and all interesting or difficult ones are exciting.

4. Only the rich deserve the fair. So it follows that some handsome men aren't nonrich, since some who deserve the fair aren't nonhandsome.

5. Because Harry enjoys himself only when he has lots of money and because Harry always enjoys going out with Judith, it follows that Harry only goes out with Judith when he has lots of money.

6

Technical Restrictions and Limitations

In Chapter Nine, we pointed out that there are intuitively valid arguments which are not provable using the machinery of predicate logic. One of the examples given there was the valid argument

1. Art believes that he'll go either to the show or to the concert (but not to both).

2. Art believes that he won't go to the show.

/∴ 3. Art believes that he'll go to the concert.

Unfortunately there also are valid arguments which are not provable using the machinery of traditional logic, even as we have extended it in Section 5 above. A famous example of an argument of this kind is the following:

1. All horses are animals.

/∴ 2. All heads of horses are heads of animals.

(Incidentally, this argument *is* provable in predicate logic.)

In recent years, much work has been done in an effort to extend the scope of syllogistic logic to make it equal to that of predicate logic. There seems to be no reason why this effort should not succeed, but so far, it has not.

In addition to being less complete than predicate logic, traditional syllogistic logic has other difficulties. In particular, it breaks down when applied to certain odd kinds of arguments. A typical example is the following:

1. All scientists are mathematicians.

2. Some brilliant scientists are not mathematicians.

/∴ 3. No scientists are brilliant scientists.

in symbols

1.   *SAM*

2.   *BOM*
   _____
/∴   3.   *SEB*

According to the five rules for valid syllogisms, this syllogism is invalid, since it contains a term which is distributed in its conclusion but not in a premise (namely the term *B*). And according to the Venn Diagram technique, the syllogism is invalid:

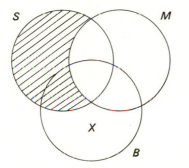

Nevertheless, this argument is valid, because *its premises are contradictory*. We can prove it is valid, using predicate logic machinery, as follows:

1. $(x)(Sx \supset Mx)$ *p*

2. $(\exists x)[(Bx \cdot Sx) \cdot \sim Mx]$ *p* /∴ $(x)[Sx \supset \sim(Sx \cdot Bx)]$

3. $(Bx \cdot Sx) \cdot \sim Mx$ 2, **EI**

4. $\sim Mx$ 3, **Simp**

5. $Bx \cdot Sx$ 3, **Simp**

6. Sx 5, **Simp**

7. $Sx \supset Mx$ 1, **UI**

8.	Mx	6, 7 **MP**
9.	$Mx \lor (x)[Sx \supset \sim(Sx \cdot Bx)]$	8, **Add**
10.	$(x)[Sx \supset \sim(Sx \cdot Bx)]$	4, 9 **DS**

(Notice that 4 and 8 explicitly contradict each other, so that *any* conclusion whatsoever could have been derived.)

Another typical argument which is not handled correctly either by the five rules of valid syllogisms or by Venn Diagrams is the following:

1. All philosophers are tall-or-nontall.

2. All philosophers are short-or-nonshort.

/∴ 3. Some tall-or-nontall things are short-or-nonshort.

in symbols

1.	PAT
2.	PAS
/∴ 3.	TIS

Again, using either Venn Diagrams or the five rules of valid syllogism, we arrive at the incorrect conclusion that this syllogism is invalid. Nevertheless, the argument is valid, this time because *its conclusion is logically true.* We can prove it is valid, using predicate logic machinery, as follows:

1.	$(x)[Px \supset (Tx \lor \sim Tx)]$	p
2.	$(x)[Px \supset (Sx \lor \sim Sx)]$	p /∴ $(\exists x)[(Tx \lor \sim Tx) \cdot (Sx \lor \sim Sx)]$
3.	$\sim Tx$	**AP**
4.	$\sim Tx \lor \sim Tx$	3, **Add**
5.	$\sim Tx$	4, **Taut**
6.	$\sim Tx \supset \sim Tx$	3, 5 **CP**

7.	$Tx \lor \sim Tx$	6, **Impl, DN**
→ 8.	$\sim Sx$	**AP**
9.	$\sim Sx \lor \sim Sx$	8, **Add**
10.	$\sim Sx$	9, **Taut**
11.	$\sim Sx \supset \sim Sx$	8, 10 **CP**
12.	$Sx \lor \sim Sx$	11, **Impl, DN**
13.	$(Tx \lor \sim Tx) \cdot (Sx \lor \sim Sx)$	7, 12 **Conj**
14.	$(\exists x)[(Tx \lor \sim Tx) \cdot (Sx \lor \sim Sx)]$	13, **EG**

(Notice that the two given premises were not used in deriving the conclusion. We didn't have to use them because the conclusion (being logically true) follows from the null set of premises.)

Obviously, something must be done to remedy the defects in syllogistic logic illustrated by these two examples. Two remedies come to mind. One is to say simply that *as syllogistic arguments* they are invalid, although they are valid in some *wider* system not yet worked out. This would be like the situation with respect to the argument on page 182 concerning Art's beliefs about his going to the show, for we concluded that this argument is invalid when formulated in the notation of predicate logic, even though it must be valid in some wider system.

Another way to combat these defects is to require both that the premises of a syllogism, taken together, be consistent (i.e., noncontradictory), and that its conclusion not be logically true.

But neither of these remedies is entirely satisfactory, and more work needs to be done on these problems before the traditional syllogistic logic will be entirely acceptable.

Chapter Thirteen

Fallacies

We commit a *fallacy* when we reason or draw conclusions incorrectly. Certain fallacious forms of reasoning have become quite well known and are discussed frequently in the literature. However, there is no standard, or indeed adequate, *classification* of fallacies. The account presented here generally follows the traditional one, but some changes have been made. To start with, let's divide fallacies into three kinds: **formal**, **informal**, and **inductive**.

1

Formal Fallacies

The term **formal fallacy** is generally applied to invalid argument forms which *resemble* valid argument forms of some specific deductive system. They are fallacies of *structure*, or *form*, as opposed to *content*. Our account is restricted to three kinds of formal fallacies, two of which are discussed quite frequently in the literature.

Any syllogism which violates one or

more of the five rules of valid syllogism commits a fallacy. For instance, an invalid syllogism which violates the rule requiring the middle term to be distributed at least once is said to commit the **fallacy of the undistributed middle**. An example is the syllogism

1. All humans are mortal.

2. Some mortals are not warmblooded.

/ ∴ 3. Some humans are not warmblooded.

which fails to distribute the middle term "mortal".*

Several fallacies resembling the valid argument forms of sentential logic have been given names and are quite famous. Two of these are the **fallacy of affirming the consequent** and the **fallacy of denying the antecedent**.

The fallacy of affirming the consequent has the general form

1. If p then q

2. q

/ ∴ 3. p

and is committed by the argument

1. If Art went to the show, then Betsy went to the show.

2. Betsy went to the show.

/ ∴ 3. Art went to the show.

The fallacy of denying the antecedent has the general form

1. If p then q

2. Not p

/∴ 3. Not q

---

* Other examples of syllogistic fallacies of this kind were discussed in Chapter Twelve, Section 2, where we presented five rules of valid syllogism.

and is committed by the argument

1. If Art went, then Betsy went.

2. It's not the case that Art went.

/∴ 3. It's not the case that Betsy went.

These two fallacies closely resemble the *valid* argument forms Modus Ponens and Modus Tollens. Indeed, Modus Ponens often is described as the process of *asserting the antecedent*, and Modus Tollens as the process of *denying the consequent*.

Another interesting formal fallacy, indeed one generally not catalogued, might be called the **fallacy of incorrect generalization**.

There are at least two famous (and disputed) examples of this fallacy in the philosophical literature. The first* (paraphrased) is as follows:

1. Rational nature exists as an end in itself.

    a. A man necessarily conceives of his own existence in this way, which makes it a subjective principle of action.

    b. But on the same rational grounds used by a man to establish his own existence as an end in itself, *every* rational being so conceives his own existence, which makes it an objective principle of action.

2. And therefore, the practical imperative will be: Everyone ought always to treat all rational beings as ends, and never solely as means.

The relevant fallacy here consists in inferring from the fact that each person conceives of his *own* existence in a certain way to the conclusion that everyone conceives of *everyone's* existence in that way. The only *valid* inference which can be drawn from the fact that *each person* conceives of *his own* existence in a particular way is that *everyone* conceives of *his own* existence in that way.

---

* From Immanuel Kant's *Foundation of the Metaphysics of Morals*.

The second example* (also paraphrased) is as follows:

1. Each person's happiness is a good to that person.

/ ∴ 2. The general happiness is a good to all persons.

In this argument we are asked to generalize from the fact that a's happiness is a good to a, in symbols Gaa, and b's happiness is a good to b, in symbols Gbb, and so on, to the conclusion that everyone's happiness is a good to everyone, in symbols $(x)(y)Gxy$.† But all that we are entitled to conclude is that given any person, *his own* happiness is a good to *that person*, or in symbols $(x)Gxx$. That is, from $Gaa \cdot Gbb \cdot \ldots$ we are entitled to conclude $(x)Gxx$. If we conclude $(x)(y)Gxy$, then we commit the fallacy of incorrect generalization.

2

*Informal
Fallacies*

In general, **informal fallacies** are fallacies of *content* rather than structure or form. We shall consider several which are much discussed in the literature.

The fallacy of equivocation

This fallacy is committed when one or more terms in an argument are used *ambiguously*.

Fallacies of equivocation can be divided into many different kinds. Perhaps the most frequently discussed is the **fallacy of four terms** (the name stemming from the fact that no *valid syllogism* has more than three terms). A famous example of this fallacy is the argument:

1. The end of a thing is its perfection.

2. Death is the end of life.

/ ∴ 3. Death is the perfection of life.

---

* From John Stuart Mill's *Utilitarianism*.

† Restricting the domain of discourse to human beings.

Anyone who considers this argument to be *sound* (that is, to be valid and have true premises) is likely to be treating the term "end" ambiguously, equating it with "goal" in the first premise, and with "final event" in the second premise. But when the term "end" is treated in this ambiguous way, the argument in question commits the fallacy of four terms, and hence is invalid. We can see this by substituting the terms "goal" and "final event" for the term "end", in the first and second premise respectively, to obtain the obviously invalid argument:

1. The goal of a thing is its perfection.

2. Death is the final event of life.

/ ∴ 3. Death is the perfection of life.

Of course the original argument can be made *valid* by having the term "end" mean the same thing in both premises. For instance, if we let "end" mean "final event" in both premises of the argument in question, we get the valid argument

1. The final event of a thing is its perfection.

2. Death is the final event of life.

/∴ 3. Death is the perfection of life.

But no one would be persuaded by this argument to accept its conclusion, since its first premise is so obviously false.

There are many other kinds of fallacies of equivocation. One of them involves the ambiguity of certain forms of the verb "to be", which was discussed in Chapter Nine. If we interpret a given form of the verb "to be" in more than one way, we run the risk of committing this fallacy. An example is furnished by the argument

1. Knowledge is power.

2. Ignorant men often have power.

/∴ 3. Ignorant men often have knowledge.

If we take the term "is" occurring in the first premise to be the "is" of identity (by analogy with "Mark Twain *is* Samuel Clemens"), then the argument is valid, but unsound, since its first premise ("Knowledge = power") is false. But if we take the term "is" to be used in some other, perhaps metaphoric, sense, then the argument is *in*valid (although both of its premises are true). The confusion is due to our tendency to construe the term "is" as signifying identity when *symbolizing* the argument and when testing its *validity*, while construing the term "is" metaphorically when thinking about the *truth* of the argument's first premise.

Another kind of fallacy of equivocation concerns the so-called "use-mention" distinction. We commit this fallacy when we confuse words with what they refer to. Some philosophers claim that the alleged difficulties with the identity substitution principle (discussed in Chapter Seventeen) arise because of a confusion of this kind.

The fallacy of composition

This fallacy is committed when we reason that some property possessed by every member of a class (or every part of a whole) also is possessed by that class (or that whole). For instance, we commit this fallacy when we reason from the shortness of each chapter in a book to the shortness of the book as a whole, or when we reason from the high quality of each component of a phonograph to the high quality of the phonograph as a whole. (A phonograph with high quality parts may itself be of poor quality because its parts are mismatched.)

It is important to notice that the fallacy of composition does not consist merely in *believing*, say, that every part of a whole has a particular property and also *believing* that the whole has that property. For instance, there is no error in believing that all the chapters of a particular book are short and also believing that the book as a whole is short. The fallacy consists in believing that *because* all the chapters of the book are short *it follows* that the book is short.

The fallacy of division

The fallacy of division is just the opposite of the fallacy of composition. We commit the fallacy of division when we infer that some property of a class (or whole) is a property of each of its members (or parts). For instance, we commit this fallacy when we infer from the great length of a book to the great length of each of its chapters, or from the difficulty of an exam to the difficulty of each of its questions. (An exam may be difficult even though none of its questions is difficult, provided there are too many questions or too little time to answer them.)*

It has been argued that the fallacies of composition and division are merely two members of the almost unlimited class of cases of reasoning from false premises, there being no special reason for singling them out. Take the inference from "Each chapter (part) of this book is short" to "The book as a whole is short". It is plausible to suppose that anyone who actually makes an inference of this kind must have an *implicit premise* in mind, perhaps the premise "Any property of all parts of a thing is a property of the whole of that thing".

Construed in this way, the argument, including the implicit premise, is just another common variety of reasoning validly but from false premises, and hence reasoning *unsoundly*.

The fallacy of amphiboly

This fallacy concerns ambiguity of *grammatical construction*, rather than of words or phrases. Fortune tellers, prophets, etc., frequently employ amphibolous sentences in order to make it more likely that their predictions will be accepted as correct.

One of the most famous examples of this sort of hedging, delivered by an ancient oracle to Pyrrhus, was the prediction "Pyrrhus the Romans shall, I say, subdue".

A modern counterpart concerning World War II is furnished by the fortune teller who predicted "Germany the Allies shall destroy", a pronouncement carefully constructed so that no matter which side won, the fortune teller appeared to have seen correctly into the future.

Argumentum ad hominem (argument to the man)

Often called the *genetic fallacy*, this fallacy consists in an attack on the man argued against, rather than on his arguments. The person who answers an argument of a Communist by saying that since it was uttered by a

---

* Some philosophers would argue that where *classes* are concerned, the fallacy of *equivocation* is committed, in addition to the fallacy of division. For instance, they would argue that classes are not large in the same sense that, say, human beings are large. Similar remarks apply to the fallacy of composition.

Traditional Logic

Communist it must be incorrect commits this fallacy, because he fails to address himself to the specific argument presented by the Communist.

But ad hominem arguments are not always fallacious. For instance, a lawyer who attacks the testimony of a witness by questioning his moral character argues ad hominem, but does not commit a fallacy.

The question as to when an ad hominem argument is fallacious, and when not, is quite complex. In general, it can be said that such an argument is *not* fallacious when the man argued against is or claims to be an *expert* on the question at issue. Courtroom witnesses, doctors, auto mechanics, lawyers, etc., often present arguments against which we, as nonexperts, may be unable to argue directly. In such cases, information about the *character* of an expert may well be an important kind of evidence in deciding whether to accept or reject his opinion.

But in these cases, we certainly do not prove by ad hominem arguments that the expert testimony or advice is incorrect. At best, ad hominem arguments only provide grounds for *cancelling* or *disregarding* the testimony or advice of the expert. They do *not* provide good grounds for assuming that his opinion is incorrect. For instance, if a doctor who advises operating on a particular patient turns out to be a charlatan, it is rash to conclude that no operation is necessary.

The tu quoque (*you too*) *fallacy*

This fallacy is a kind of argument ad hominem and is committed when someone argues that his opponent holds (or held) the view he now attacks, or engages in (or engaged in) the kind of activity he now attacks. In other words, this fallacy is committed when we answer a charge by a similar countercharge. For instance, it is committed when a senator defends his misuse of campaign funds by pointing out that his accusers have on occasion done the same thing. It also is committed by the South African who answers an American's arguments against apartheid by pointing to segregation in the United States. The fact that opponents act, or argue, in a certain way is irrelevant to the charge that *we* now act, or argue, incorrectly. We *both* may be acting, or arguing, incorrectly.

Argumentum ad baculum (*appeal to force*)

The fallacy of appeal to force is committed when an attempt is made to persuade someone to accept a conclusion by applying pressure of some kind or other. For instance, a lobbyist commits this fallacy when he tries to convince a senator to vote for a particular measure by reminding the senator that he (the lobbyist) speaks for a powerful industrial group.

While tradition lists the appeal to force as constituting a fallacy, it certainly is not a fallacy according to the standard definitions of that term. For instance, a senator who votes for a certain bill because of pressure applied by a lobbyist is not necessarily convinced that the bill is a good bill. Rather he is convinced of the quite different proposition that it may well be in his best interests to *vote* for the bill.

Argumentum ad misericordiam (*appeal to pity*)

This fallacy is committed when one is persuaded to accept a conclusion on the basis of pity or sympathy. For instance, it is committed by a juror who votes for acquittal out of sympathy for the accused.

Many cases generally considered to be instances of this fallacy in fact may not be. For instance, when a juror votes for acquittal out of pity, it is not at all clear that pity has persuaded him of the *innocence* of the accused. The vote for acquittal may indicate simply that the juror has been persuaded that the accused should not be punished, whether guilty or not.

The fallacy of the complex question

This fallacy is committed when a question is asked which assumes a particular answer to another question which is not asked. For example, this fallacy is committed when a lawyer persuades the jury by asking a witness *when* he joined the Communist Party without first having found out *whether* the witness ever joined. (Incidentally, while the lawyer in such a case may be guilty of trickery, *he* is not guilty of a fallacy, since *he* is not convinced by the device. But if his trickery is successful, then it is the *jurors* who commit the fallacy of the complex question.)

Argumentum ad ignorantiam (*argument from ignorance*)

This fallacy is committed when a conclusion is accepted *because* it has not been proved false. Perhaps the most famous example is the argument that God exists because no one has proved that he does not.

But we must be careful to restrict our charge of fallaciousness to arguments which purport to be *deductively* valid, for the fallacy of arguing from ignorance is a *deductive* fallacy. The status of arguments from ignorance in *inductive* reasoning is in dispute. Clearly, it *sometimes* is legitimate to argue from the failure to provide an *inductive proof* for a proposition to the conclusion that the proposition is (probably) false. For example, a scientist who spends years looking for an alleged planet between Mercury and Venus is justified in concluding from his failure to find evidence of such a planet that it does not exist.

Argumentum ad verecundiam (*appeal to authority*)

This fallacy is committed when one accepts a conclusion *because* an authority or expert, or famous person, accepts it. For instance, it is committed by anyone who is persuaded that a particular product is better than its competitors because a famous movie star uses it.

But appeal to an authority often is not fallacious. For instance, we do not reason fallaciously when we conclude that we have a particular illness primarily because an authority, a doctor, believes that we do.

Sometimes it is quite difficult to decide whether an appeal to authority constitutes a fallacy. This is especially true with respect to questions concerning topics on which even the "experts" disagree, such as religion, ethics, art, and politics. It has been argued that this disagreement among the experts places a burden on each of us to do some of our own thinking in these fields. If this is true, then an appeal to authority in these fields *in lieu of* a certain amount of study and hard thought constitutes a fallacy. (This does not mean that we ought *never* consult "experts" in these fields, but only that we must do *some* of the reasoning on these topics for ourselves.)

An interesting kind of appeal to authority occurs when an expert in a given field himself argues by appealing to some other authority. An example would be the professional philosopher who argues that the view he is defending is correct *because* St. Thomas Aquinas also held it. Appeals to authority of this kind are almost always fallacious.

Circular reasoning (*begging the question*)

It is generally said that when we assume the very thing to be proved (whether in the same or different words), or assume a more general form of the thing to be proved, we commit the fallacy of *reasoning in a circle*, or *circular reasoning*.

For example, we commit this fallacy when we argue that God exists because it says so in the Bible, where our acceptance of what is said in the Bible rests on our belief that its writing was inspired by God.

But the above characterization of circular reasoning is not correct. In particular it is defective because it makes all *deductively valid* arguments circular. For instance, the deductively valid inference from $(x)(Fx \lor Gx)$ to $Fa \lor Ga$ is circular according to the above criterion, since it assumes something (namely $(x)(Fx \lor Gx)$) which is simply a more general form of what it proves (namely $Fa \lor Ga$). Similarly, the deductively valid inference from $A \supset B$ to $\sim B \supset \sim A$ is circular according to the above criterion, since it assumes something ($A \supset B$) which is simply the thing to be proved ($\sim B \supset \sim A$) only in different words.*

Perhaps the thing to do at this point is distinguish between *mere* circularity, which is not fallacious, and *vicious* circularity, which is fallacious. We consider an argument to be *viciously circular* if it contains a premise, or employs an inference rule, which is at least as doubtful as the conclusion of the argument. Thus, when arguing with an atheist, the argument that God exists because the Bible says he does is viciously circular, since the implicit premise (that what the Bible says is true) is at least as doubtful to an atheist as the conclusion that God exists.

Notice that vicious circularity, when defined in this way, is *relative*. For instance, on this definition the above argument for God's existence is viciously circular for an *atheist*, but not for the many *believers* who do not doubt the implicit premise that what the Bible says is true.

Notice also that we can argue or reason circularly without the circularity involving a *premise*. For instance, an inductive justification of inductive reasoning, of the kind to be discussed in Section 7, Chapter Sixteen, is circular because it uses the very *rule of inference* (induction) which it is presented to justify.†

---

* Some philosophers would deny that $A \supset B$ and $\sim B \supset \sim A$ say the same thing only in different words. The dispute hinges first on the question as to whether we are dealing with *sentences*, or *propositions*, and second on the question as to whether *equivalent* sentences, or propositions, say the same thing, only in different words.

† Roughly, inductive inferences are used to infer from what is true of a given number of past cases of a given kind to what is true of all cases of that kind, past, present, or future. The circular argument to justify inductive reasoning is that in the past inductive reasoning has been moderately successful, hence in *all* cases, including future cases, it will be moderately successful.

The black-and-white fallacy

This fallacy is committed when the number of possible descriptions or alternatives in a given case is erroneously limited to just two. The man who divides all other nations in the world into those that are communist, and hence anti-U. S., and those that are anticommunist, and hence pro-U. S., commits this fallacy, because he fails to consider the possibility that some nations are *neutral*. Similarly, the man who argues for capitalism on the grounds that its alternative, socialism, is unacceptable, commits this fallacy because he overlooks the possibility of various *combinations* of socialism and capitalism as well as other kinds of economic systems.

This fallacy gets its name from the fact that human beings tend to see issues in simplified forms, in clinically pure extreme cases, overlooking the many shades of gray that lie between black and white. Black and white are *contraries*, not contradictories. (The contradictory of black is nonblack, and of white nonwhite.) Similarly, good and bad, hot and cold, etc., are *contraries*, not contradictories. When we treat pairs of contraries such as black and white as contradictories, we commit the black-and-white fallacy.

3

Inductive
Fallacies

Traditional accounts of fallacious reasoning generally include a few fallacies of an *inductive* nature. We present one or two of these traditional inductive fallacies, plus a few not generally discussed.* (Some of these fallacies do not have standard names. Consequently, newly coined names have been used in some cases.)

The fallacy of hasty generalization

This fallacy is committed when we generalize too quickly from one or a few instances. An example is the fallacious conclusion that it rains a great deal in Southern California, based on the evidence of one or two short visits. Another is the conclusion that everything sold by a particular store is of poor quality because one item bought there happened to give poor service.

These are examples of fallacious reasoning, not because they move from particular cases to generalizations, but rather because they do so *too*

---

* See Part Four on Induction and Science.

quickly, on *too little evidence*. (Two short visits to Southern California provide much less evidence than is needed to generalize about the weather anywhere. And even the best store occasionally sells a poor product.) A particularly interesting kind of fallacy of hasty generalization bears the Latin name *post hoc, ergo propter hoc* (after this, therefore because of this). This fallacy consists in concluding too hastily that an event which preceded another event is the *cause* of that event. This fallacy is committed by a sportswriter who *automatically* credits the new manager when a losing baseball team suddenly wins several games in a row. His conclusion is too hasty. There are many other possible causes of the winning streak, including poor play on the part of opposing teams, good luck, etc. Of course, the new manager *may* be responsible. The fallacy consists in assigning the credit to him on too little evidence.

However, it is difficult to know when a conclusion is made too hastily, and when not. For instance, if the baseball team continues to win most of its games, and no other explanation is brought forth, it finally becomes reasonable to conclude that the *cause* of their success is the new manager. But at what point does this conclusion cease being fallacious and become more reasonable? No answer to this difficult question has gained general acceptance.

In addition, it has been argued that *sometimes* hasty generalizations are not fallacious. For instance, if *forced* to generalize about Southern California weather on the basis of two visits when it happened to rain a great deal, the most reasonable conclusion to draw would be that the weather there is generally rainy. (But it still would be fallacious to accept the generalization as *highly probable* on such flimsy evidence. Indeed some writers have said that the fallacy of hasty generalization lies not in generalizing from too few cases, but rather in generalizing from few cases *with too high a degree of probability being assigned to the generalization*.)

The fallacy of weak analogy

This fallacy is very much like the fallacy of hasty generalization. It too involves reasoning from insufficient evidence, but consists in concluding to a *particular case* (by analogy), rather than to a generalization. For example, we commit the fallacy of weak analogy when we reason from the fact that State U. won its last football game to the conclusion that it will win its next one.

Clearly, all of the qualifying remarks concerning the fallacy of hasty generalization apply also to the fallacy of weak analogy. For example, if *forced* to bet either for or against State U. in its next game, our only evidence being that State U. won its last game, it would be reasonable to bet that State U. will win (assuming even odds). But it would be fallacious to assign a high degree of probability to the belief that State U. will win.

Statistical fallacies

The recent outpouring of statistics on all subjects, ranging from politics to sex, has resulted in a renewed interest in the almost limitless ways in which statistics are or can be misused. (The saying "figures don't lie, but liars figure", while true, represents only a small part of the story; most misuses of statistics do not involve deliberate deception.)

Unfortunately, no good categorization of statistical fallacies exists. The few discussed below barely scratch the surface:

(1) *The fallacy of the small sample.* This fallacy is the statistical analogue of the fallacy of hasty generalization. For instance, this fallacy is committed when we project the results of a poll of two or three hundred students around the nation onto the entire U. S. college student population.

An interesting variation on this fallacy concerns statistical trends involving small populations. An example is the newspaper headline stating that crimes of violence increased 25 percent in a certain locality over the previous year, where it turns out that the increase was from four crimes of this type last year to five this year.

(2) *The fallacy of using data of differing quality.* Statistical trends also can be misleading if based on information of differing quality. One of the best examples is the current claim made by many police officials around the country that crime is much more prevalent today than it was 50 or 100 years ago. These officials cite statistics on complaints, arrests, etc., per thousand population for many areas, which seem to uphold their claims that crime is increasing. The fallacy is their failure to take account of the possible variations in the *quality* of data-gathering procedures at various places and times. We have good reason to believe that the collecting of crime information is different now than it once was, having greatly improved over the years. We also have good reason to believe that even today some localities keep better records than others. Hence, we cannot

make quick comparisons based on statistics which differ so greatly in quality.

(3) *The fallacy of biased statistics.* This fallacy is committed when we use statistics drawn from a sample that we know (or should know) is not likely to be *representative* of the population being sampled. A famous example of the commission of this fallacy concerns the 1936 presidential election. The *Literary Digest* conducted a poll, obtaining the names of those polled primarily from telephone directories and lists of automobile registrations, and predicting that Alf Landon would defeat Franklin Roosevelt. The magazine's mistake consisted in failing to realize that the persons polled were very unlikely to be *representative* of the voting population as a whole. The average income of those polled was bound to be much higher than the national average, since many poor people could not afford telephones or automobiles in the 1930's; and, as is well known, *economic status* tends to influence voting preferences.

(4) *The fallacy of the unknowable statistic.* This fallacy is committed either when statistics are simply made up, or guessed at on the basis of little or no evidence, or when their approximate nature is masked in precision. A marvelous example of this fallacy is contained in the request for funds to prevent war which began

Dear Friend: In the past 5,000 years men have fought in 14,523 wars. One out of four persons living during this time have been war casualties. A nuclear war would add 1,245,000,000 men, women, and children to this tragic list.

Precise figures, such as 14,523, give the impression that historians have compiled a vast list of all wars fought in the last 5,000 years, totaling 14,523, whereas in fact no such list has been or is ever likely to be compiled. The best we can do is *estimate roughly* how many wars have occurred, based on our limited knowledge of a very small sample of known wars. (Thus, after great study, someone might be able to estimate that roughly 10,000 to 25,000 wars have occurred in the past 5,000 years, without committing the fallacy.) But we cannot even make a *rough* estimate as to the number of human beings who would be killed in a nuclear war. There is no generally accepted method for arriving at such an estimate, and even the "experts" who are willing to venture a *guess* do so hesitantly, often making estimates which differ widely from those of other "experts". For human beings today, this kind of statistic is essentially unknowable.

(5) *The fallacy of accidental or false correlation.* This fallacy consists in erroneously assuming that a correlation observed between two or more samples represents a *causal correlation.* We commit this fallacy when we reason that an observed correlation between the size of the elk population in the U. S. and the number of typewriters sold in Italy will continue to hold in the future, when we should have concluded that this correlation is accidental. If we collect large amounts of statistical data, it is bound to happen on occasion that "significant appearing" correlations will occur, such as the imaginary one concerning American elk and Italian typewriters. But we cannot *automatically* assume that such correlations really are significant. For instance, most such correlations can be dismissed as accidental, and not likely to continue in the future, on the basis of what we might call "background information". Thus, in the elk–typewriter example, we have a great deal of background information concerning typewriter sales, to say nothing of elk habits, making it extremely unlikely that there is any causal connection of the kind suggested by the statistics in question.

An interesting variety of the fallacy of accidental correlation is illustrated by the following example. Suppose it is discovered that .05 percent of all women who use a particular kind of birth control pill get a blood clot of a certain kind. If we conclude that there is a significant statistical connection between taking birth control pills and getting blood clots, then we reason fallaciously, for we must determine how many women get blood clots of this kind who do *not* use this kind of birth control pill. The statistic .05 percent indicates a causal correlation *only* if it varies significantly from the statistic concerning women who do not use the pill.

Part Four Chapter Fourteen

Induction
and Science   Induction

1

*Difference
between
Induction and
Deduction*

In Chapter One, we divided arguments into two kinds, namely *deductive* and *inductive*. We now turn to an examination of *inductive* arguments and their role in the logic or methodology of science.

However, a note of caution again is in order. While it is true that literally *nothing* in philosophy is accepted by all philosophers, the material on symbolic logic, in the first two parts of this text, comes close to being generally accepted and noncontroversial. But almost all of the material to be presented now on induction and science is highly controversial, and the viewpoint expressed is just one among many.

Recall that we defined a *valid deductive argument* as one whose premises (if true) guarantee the truth of its conclusion. Speaking metaphorically, we said that the reason such a guarantee can be provided is that the content of the conclusion of a valid deductive argument is already contained in its premises (either explicitly or implicitly). And we said that the premises of a valid deductive argument, taken together with the *negation* of its conclusion, imply a contradiction.

Now let's roughly define an **inductive argument** as an argument which has at least one contingent premise, and which has a contingent conclusion whose entire content is *not* contained in its premises. This means that we are using the phrase "inductive argument" in a very wide sense, in fact as a close synonym for "nondeductive argument".*

And let's roughly define a **valid inductive argument** as one whose premises provide *good grounds* for asserting its conclusion.

It is important to remember that the truth of the premises of a valid inductive argument does not *guarantee* the truth of its conclusion. It is always logically possible for the conclusion of a valid inductive argument to be false even though all of its premises are true. The premises of a valid inductive argument, taken together with the negation of its conclusion, do *not* imply a contradiction. For instance, a scientist could validly conclude that all things made of asbestos do not conduct electricity, on the evidence that all *tested* things made of asbestos failed to conduct electricity. The conclusion of this argument happens to be false, since (as we now know) asbestos conducts electricity at temperatures close to absolute zero. But the conclusion of the original argument, based on less evidence, *does* follow validly from its premises. We are justified in accepting the conclusion of this argument if the information contained in its premises constitutes all that we know relevant to the conductivity of asbestos.

Thus, there is a "gap" between the premises and conclusion of a valid inductive argument. This gap is the characteristic mark of all inductive arguments. It is both their *weakness* and their great *strength*. It is their weakness, because false conclusions can follow validly from true premises. It is their strength, because (for one thing) it enables us to reason from what we have observed to what we have as yet not observed. Without induction, science would be impossible, except as a *mere description* of what has been observed.

Before proceeding with our discussion of the nature of inductive argument, let's take time to refute a common misconception as to the nature of

---

* Except that we don't intend the phrase "inductive argument" to cover nondeductive reasoning about *values*. For instance, we don't intend it to cover an argument such as "Art borrowed $10 from Charles. Therefore, Art *ought* to pay $10 back to Charles as soon as he can."

the distinction between deductive and inductive inferences. According to this misconceived view, valid *deductive* reasoning involves inference from the general to the specific (particular) or from the more general to the less general, while valid *inductive* reasoning involves inference from the specific (particular) to the general, or from the less general to the more general. For example, the valid *deductive* argument

	1.	All intelligent students will get A's in Logic.
/∴	2.	If Art is an intelligent student, then Art will get A's in Logic.

proceeds from the general to the specific, and the valid *inductive* argument

	1.	So far, every intelligent student has done A work in Logic.
/∴	2.	All intelligent students (past, present, or future) do A work in Logic.

proceeds from the less general to the more general.

But only a moment's reflection is needed to see that this view of deductive and inductive reasoning is entirely erroneous. In the first place, valid *deductive* arguments do *not* always proceed from the general to the specific. For instance, they often proceed from the general to the equally general. An example is the argument

	1.	All men are mortal.
/∴	2.	All non-mortals are non-men.

In addition, they often proceed from the specific to the specific. An example is the argument

	1.	Object *a* is red.
	2.	Object *a* is a ball.
/∴	3.	Object *a* is a red ball.

And they sometimes even proceed from the specific to the general, although all cases of this kind are rather contrived. An example is the argument

1.   Art is tall.

/ ∴   2.   Given anything, if that thing is human,
then either that thing is mortal or else
Art is tall.

(In symbols, this argument reads (1) Ta; / ∴ (2) $(x)[Hx \supset (Mx \lor Ta)]$.)
And in the second place, valid *inductive* arguments do *not* always proceed from the specific to the general. For instance, they often proceed from the specific to the specific. An example is the analogical argument

1.   The class taught last year by Smith
was interesting.

/ ∴   2.   The class Smith will teach this year
will be interesting.

And they often proceed from the general to the equally general. An example is the argument

1.   All of the classes taught so far by
Smith were interesting.

/ ∴   2.   All of the Logic classes he will teach
in the future will be interesting.

Finally, they often proceed from the general to the specific. An example is the argument

1.   All of the classes taught so far by
Smith have been interesting.

/ ∴   2.   The next class taught by Smith will be
interesting.

It is clear then that there is not a shred of truth to the view that valid deductive reasoning proceeds from the general to the specific, and valid inductive reasoning from the specific to the general.

2

Kinds of Inductive Arguments

Inductive arguments can be divided into many different kinds. It is useful for our purposes to divide them into *four* basic kinds (which happen *not* to be mutually exclusive).

Inductive generalization, categorical form

When we reason or argue from a premise or premises concerning *particular instances*, or *all examined cases of a certain kind*, to a conclusion which is *universal*, or concerning *all* cases (examined or unexamined) of a certain kind, our reasoning has the form of a **categorical inductive generalization**, or **universal inductive generalization**, or simply **inductive generalization**. (These terms also apply to the *conclusions* of inductive generalizations.) An example is the argument

1. All examined copper things conduct electricity.

/ ∴   2. All copper things (examined or as yet unexamined) conduct electricity.

Categorical inductive generalizations all have the same general form, which can be put in either one of two ways. The first way is:

1. $Fa \cdot Ga$*

2. $Fb \cdot Gb$

3. $Fc \cdot Gc$
   $\vdots$

N.   No F is known not to have G.†

/ ∴   N + 1.   All F's are G's (that is, $(x)(Fx \supset Gx)$).

* We are treating F, G, and a as variables here.

† The question as to whether a premise such as N ought to be included in the general schema for inductive generalizations is in dispute. The dispute concerns whether a premise of this kind enters into the picture at the *logical level*, or at the *pragmatic level of action*. For instance, those who favor the latter would say that a premise such as N is not required in every valid inductive generalization. Instead they would want to install a *rule of action*, on the pragmatic level, stating roughly that one ought to act only on the basis of those inductive generalizations which take account of all pertinent information.

And the second (equivalent) way is:

1.   All examined F's are G's,* (that is,
$(x)[(Fx \cdot Ex) \supset Gx]$, where $Ex = $ "x
is examined for the presence or
absence of G").

/ ∴   2.   All F's are Gs (that is, $(x)(Fx \supset Gx)$).

It is generally held that the *probability*, or *degree of confirmation*, of an hypothesis, or the *evidential support* for an hypothesis, increases with each new confirming instance of it. For example, each newly examined instance of the hypothesis "All copper conducts electricity" increases the probability of that hypothesis. However, it may well be that as the number of confirming instances mount up, each new confirming instance counts slightly less than the preceding instance.†

It seems reasonable to suppose that many, perhaps most, scientific hypotheses have the form of categorical inductive generalizations. An example would be "All copper conducts electricity". But many scientists would argue that the typical and important scientific hypotheses are not categorical inductive generalizations. They would agree that inductive generalizations, as described above, *are* made by scientists. But they would claim that they are characteristic of the *early stages* of a science, giving way fairly quickly to more advanced and more sophisticated generalizations. For example, they would claim that even Galileo constructed more advanced hypotheses (inductive conclusions) than the one above, since he constructed *quantitative* hypotheses. An example would be the hypothesis (slightly simplified here) that the distance an object falls in free flight *equals* 16 times the square of the time it falls, or in symbols $S = 16t^2$. Their claim is that the *mathematical equation* is the standard, or at least most important, form of conclusion (confirmed hypothesis) drawn by scientists.

There can be no doubt that many scientific hypotheses are constructed in the form of mathematical equations. But this fact does not constitute evidence against the importance of categorical inductive generalizations in science, since mathematical equations themselves can be cast in the

---

* Or "All examined F's have the property G".

† Other things being equal, as they often are not. See Chapter Sixteen, Section 2.

form of categorical generalizations. For example, we can translate the equation $S = 16t^2$ into the categorical generalization "All freely falling bodies are such that if S is the distance they fall, and t is the time it takes them to fall that distance, then $S = 16t^2$".

Inductive generalization, statistical form

When we reason or argue from a premise or premises concerning groups of instances to a conclusion which is *statistical* in form, our reasoning has the form of a **statistical generalization**. An example is the argument

1. Half of the tosses of this coin observed so far landed heads up.

/ ∴ 2. Half of all tosses of this coin (observed or otherwise) will land heads up.

The general form of statistical generalizations can be put as follows:

1. *N* percent of all *F*'s tested for *G* have *G*.

/ ∴ 2. *N* percent of all *F*'s (tested or otherwise) have *G*.

Statistical generalizations play an important role in science. For one thing, practically all of the hypotheses in the social sciences (economics, sociology, etc.) are statistical. And for another, many of the basic hypotheses of physics itself are statistical. Two important examples would be the Second Law of Thermodynamics (the law of increasing entropy) and the gas laws. For example, the gas laws say nothing about the pressure at any given point on the surface of an enclosed container (containing a gas inside), but rather what the *average*, or *statistical*, pressure will be, calculated on the basis of the temperature and volume of the enclosed gas.

But any given statistical generalization is never so informative or useful as the corresponding universal generalization would be. Take the statistical generalization "One fifth of all adult Americans who smoke an average of one or more packs of cigarettes per day will die of lung cancer within 25 years". Obviously, if true, this constitutes very valuable information, for it warns those who fall into the stated category (adult Americans who smoke at least one pack per day) of their "chances" of getting lung cancer if they persist in smoking so heavily. But no one could conclude that *he* will get lung cancer merely by virtue of being an adult American who smokes at least a pack of cigarettes per day.

However, suppose we were to discover that heavy cigarette smoking is only one of two factors leading to lung cancer, the other factor being, say, a certain kind of abnormality in the surface tissue of the lung (let's call it "abnormality *A*"). That is, suppose we were to discover that *every investigated* case of heavy smoking in which abnormality *A* is present also is a case of lung cancer death. Then we would be able to construct the following valid inductive argument:

1. All heavy smokers who have been found to have abnormality *A* have died of lung cancer.

/ ∴ 2. All heavy smokers who have abnormality *A* die of lung cancer.

The conclusion of this argument is a categorical inductive generalization concerning the connection between smoking and death by lung cancer which would be much more informative and useful than the statistical generalization cited above. For if some person, say Art, were found on examination to have abnormality *A*, then we could present him with an argument such as

1. All heavy smokers who have abnormality *A* die of lung cancer.

2. Art has abnormality *A*.

/ ∴ 3. If Art is (or becomes) a heavy smoker, then Art will die of lung cancer.

Surely this argument is more relevant to a decision by Art as to whether to smoke or not than the previous *statistical* argument linking heavy smoking and lung cancer. A corresponding *statistical* generalization, such as "One fifth of all heavy smokers will die of lung cancer", which when combined with the information that Art is a heavy smoker, leads to the conclusion that *the chance is one in five* that Art will die of lung cancer, certainly is not so informative or useful as the conclusion that Art *definitely* will die of lung cancer if he becomes a heavy smoker.

In view of the above, the question naturally arises as to whether with sufficient knowledge we could not (at least theoretically) replace all statistical generalizations with categorical ones. It seems plausible to assume that this always can be accomplished by taking account of more and more relevant factors. For instance, in our hypothetical lung cancer example, we added a factor concerning abnormality *A* to the factor of heavy smoking to change a statistical conclusion to a categorical one. Or, to take an actual example, knowledge that a given coin is symmetrical permits the conclusion that half of all random tosses with that coin will land heads up. But it seems plausible to assume that with *better knowledge*, that is, with knowledge of more relevant factors (such as the force of each toss, its starting position, wind velocity, etc.), we could conclude that *all* tosses of a certain kind (tossed with a certain force, tossed from a certain starting position, etc.) will land heads up.

However, we cannot say *ahead of time* that all statistical generalizations are replaceable by categorical generalizations. In each case, we must *examine the world* to determine whether more relevant factors exist. (Of course, failure to find relevant factors does not *prove* that there are none. We may simply have not been sufficiently ingenious to discover them.) So the question as to whether a given statistical generalization can be replaced by a corresponding categorical generalization can be answered only by accumulating more empirical evidence, to the extent that it can be answered at all.*

On the other hand, it is clear that we can regard a categorical inductive generalization as a special kind of statistical generalization, namely the kind in which the percentage of *F*'s tested which turn out to be *G*'s happens to be 100 percent. In other words, we can take the basic pattern of categorical inductive generalizations to be

1. 100 percent of all *F*'s tested for *G* have *G*.

/ ∴ 2. 100 percent of all *F*'s (tested or otherwise) have *G*.

---

* Some philosophers claim that recent evidence discovered by physicists, in particular evidence supporting the Heisenberg Indeterminacy Principle, provides empirical reason for believing that at least some, and perhaps all, of the ultimate laws of Physics are *statistical* and not categorical.

which clearly is just a special case of the general pattern for statistical generalization.

Analogies

When we infer from a premise or premises concerning particular instances to a conclusion concerning some other particular instance, we infer **analogically**, or by **analogy**. For example, we infer *analogically* when we reason from the fact (premise) that a course given last year by a particular teacher was interesting to the conclusion that the course he is giving this year will be interesting. The general form of analogical arguments can be put as follows:

1. $a, b, \ldots$, have been observed to have properties $F, \ldots$, and G.

2. C has $F, \ldots$

/ ∴ 3. C has G.

Analogies differ in the *degree* to which they support their conclusions. For one thing, the greater the number of instances mentioned in the premises, the better the analogy. Thus, if we reason from the fact that both of *two* courses taken from a particular teacher were interesting to the conclusion that the next course we take from him will be interesting, our analogy is better than if we reason on the basis of only *one* course taken from that instructor. Analogies also are better if the instances they concern are alike in more relevant ways. Thus, if we reason from the fact that the two courses taken previously from a particular teacher both were *logic courses* (as well as interesting) to the conclusion that the next *logic course* we take from him will be interesting, our analogy is better than if the next course we take from him happens to be ethics.

But only *relevant* ways in which the instances are alike count. For instance, it would be irrelevant if the classes both happened to meet in the same room, or at the same time of day. But it is quite difficult to know in general, or even in a particular case, exactly which things are relevant and which are not. Even the room in which a course is to be taught *may* be relevant to how interesting it will be. (For example, it would be relevant if the teacher in question dislikes large, poorly lit rooms, and the next course he teaches happens to be in such a room.)

Analogical arguments can conveniently be divided into two kinds, namely **categorical analogies** and **statistical analogies**.

Valid categorical analogies have the general form

1. All F's tested or observed for G have G.

/ ∴ 2. This particular F, untested as yet for G, has G.

The argument discussed above, about taking a class from a particular teacher, is an example of a categorical analogy.

Valid statistical analogies have the general form

1. N percent (or most, or almost all, etc.) of the F's tested for G have G.

/ ∴ 2. The probability is N percent (or the probability is high) that this particular F, as yet untested for G, has G.

Most analogies made in everyday life are statistical analogies. In daily life, we rarely encounter cases in which *all* of the known cases of a certain kind have some particular relevant property. For instance, even the best teacher is likely to teach an uninteresting class at least once, thus falsifying any *categorical* analogy whose conclusion is that his next course will be interesting, but *not* falsifying the statistical analogy whose conclusion is that his next course *probably* will be interesting.

It is generally held that analogical reasoning is not *fundamental*, in that any given analogy can be shown to be an *enthymemic version* of a categorical or statistical generalization. Take the analogy whose conclusion is that the next class taught by a particular teacher probably will be interesting. In this case, the *complete* form of our reasoning would be

1. Almost all classes taught so far by the teacher in question have been interesting.

/ ∴   2.   Almost all of the classes he teaches are interesting.

       3.   This particular class will be taught by the teacher in question.

/ ∴   4.   This particular class will probably be interesting.

Inference from observed to unobservable

In the three sections above, we divided inductive inferences into three kinds, namely the categorical, statistical, and analogical. But there are many other useful ways to divide inductive inferences.

In particular, it is important to distinguish between reasoning from what is observed to what is as yet unobserved *but can be observed*, and reasoning from what is observed to what *even in principle cannot be observed.*

For instance, we reason from the observed to the *observable* when we infer from the fact that most autos of a certain kind have lasted a long time to the conclusion that a particular auto of this kind will last a long time. That an auto lasts a long time is something we can directly observe. But we reason or infer from the observed to that which even in principle *cannot be observed* when we infer from the fact that Smith's finger was pricked by a pin, followed by the rapid withdrawal of his hand, facial grimaces, exclamations of "ouch", etc., to the conclusion that Smith is in pain. In this case, we *cannot* directly observe the thing inferred to, namely Smith's pain, for it is impossible to experience or observe directly someone else's mental activity. In this case we must infer to the unobservable pain from what we take to be *causally related* to the pain, namely the withdrawal of Smith's hand, his facial expressions, his utterances, etc.*

Many of the important disputes in philosophy center around the question as to which kinds of things can be experienced or observed directly, and which kinds cannot. We can call those things which *can be* experienced or observed directly **observable entities**, and those things which even in principle *cannot be* experienced or observed directly **theoretical entities**.

---

* Actually, the reasoning is even more complex. While we cannot directly observe *anyone else's* mental experiences, we do directly observe *our own* mental experiences. So at least in part, our reasoning from a given person's behavior when stuck with a pin to his experience of pain involves an *analogy* from the fact that when *we* feel pain, we behave in similar fashion.

In addition, it is useful to divide the entities which have often been held to be theoretical into four kinds:

(1) There is a long tradition in philosophy which distinguishes properties of objects into two kinds, namely **observable**, or **manifest**, **properties**, and **dispositional**, or **power**, **properties**.* **Observable properties** are properties of objects which can be observed by means of the five senses, whereas **dispositional properties** are properties of objects which cannot be so observed. For example, we can observe that something *burns*, but not that it is *flammable*. And we can observe that something *bends*, but not that it is *flexible*. Burning and bending are *observable* properties; flammability and flexibility are *dispositional* properties. Since dispositional properties are not directly observable, we must *infer* to their existence. They constitute a kind of theoretical entity.

(2) *Physical particles* or *objects*, such as the electron, which many scientists claim cannot be directly observed even in principle, constitute another kind of theoretical entity.† But if scientists cannot directly observe electrons, then they must *infer* to their existence. And such an inference must be inductive in nature, since the conclusion of any such inference must state more than is contained in its premises.

(3) *Mental events* or *mental experiences* constitute still another kind of theoretical entity. However, this kind of theoretical entity is different from all others in that every given entity of this kind can be experienced by someone or other (namely the person who "has" the mental experience), although it cannot be observed by anyone else. For instance, a pain of mine can be (and is) experienced by me, but not by anyone else. And a pain of yours can be (and is) experienced by you, but not by anyone else. From *your* point of view, *my* pain is theoretical, while from *my* point of view, *your* pain is theoretical. This is different from the case with respect to, say, electrons, since it is claimed by some scientists that *no one* can observe electrons.

(4) Finally, many philosophers consider *physical objects* or *material objects* to be theoretical entities. They believe that it is what they call *sense*

---

* Dispositional properties are discussed in greater detail in Chapter Seventeen.

† Roughly, electrons are claimed to be unobservable because observing (in the sense of "seeing") requires the use of entities (like light rays) which cannot interact appropriately with something so small as an electron.

Induction and Science

data which we experience directly, and not the physical objects which may be causally related to them.*

If we believe in the existence of physical objects, over and above the existence of sense data, and perhaps causally related to sense data, then this belief (if rationally founded) will be based on *inductive inferences* from what we experience, namely sense data, to their cause, namely physical objects.

We characterized theoretical entities as things which we *cannot* observe. But words such as "cannot", called *modal terms*, are notoriously tricky.

In particular, the word "cannot" is ambiguous. When we say that electrons *cannot* be observed, we mean that it is *impossible* to observe them. Similarly, when we say that we *cannot* observe someone else's mental experiences, we mean that it is *impossible* for us to observe them. However, the senses of "impossible" are different in each case. In the first case, we mean that it is *physically impossible* to observe electrons directly. That is, we mean that the *laws of nature* (the way the world happens to be) precludes our observing electrons. Or, to put it another way, we mean that it is a *contingent fact* that we cannot observe electrons. But in the second case, we mean that it is *logically impossible* to observe someone else's experiences directly. For if *we* were to have someone else's experiences, they would be *our* experiences, but by hypothesis they are someone else's experiences, and not our own.

3

Cause and Effect

Inductive reasoning is used to discover the **causes** of different kinds of events. For instance, we can infer inductively from the premise that everyone observed to eat a certain kind of food gets food poisoning to the conclusion that everyone who eats that kind of food will get food poisoning.

---

* We cannot go into a detailed discussion concerning sense data at this point. But we can understand roughly what the philosopher who postulates the existence of sense data is talking about by thinking of a very vivid dream or hallucination concerning, say, seeing one's father, and comparing that experience with the experience of *really* seeing one's father. *Taken alone*, the dream or hallucination may be *identical* with the experience of really seeing one's father. Now in the case of the dream, the *experience* of seeing one's father surely is mental. So in the case of really seeing one's father, the *experience* (as opposed perhaps to its cause) must also be mental, since taken alone (out of context) it is identical with the mental dream experience of seeing one's father. The sense data philosopher merely attaches the label *sense data* to the content of our experiences, whether of the dream-hallucination kind, or the "real" vision kind. And, of course, he attaches that label to auditory experience, olfactory experience, etc., as well as to visual experience.

The same observation also provides good grounds for concluding that eating that kind of food is the *cause* of contracting food poisoning. (Contracting the food poisoning will then be considered the **effect** of the cause, that is, the effect of eating that kind of food.)

But exactly what does it *mean* to say that one thing is the cause of another, or that two things are causally related? One of the simplest of the many answers given to this question is that when we say something like "*A* causes *B*", the most we are justified in asserting is that *whenever A occurs, B occurs.** Or to be more precise, what we mean by "*A* causes *B*" is that whenever an *A*-like event occurs, a *B*-like event occurs (since events *A* and *B* are "singular", and cannot occur more than once). For instance, to say that eating food of type *F* causes food poisoning of type *P* is to say that whenever anyone eats *F* he contracts *P*, or in symbols $(x)(Fx \supset Px)$, where $Fx =$ "*x* is a person who eats food of type *F*", and $Px =$ "*x* contracts food poisoning of type *P*".

But we cannot say that *A* is the cause of *B* if *B* occurs *before* the occurrence of *A*, even if it happens to be true that whenever *A*-like events occur, *B*-like events occur. For example, suppose it is true not only that whenever someone eats food of type *F*, that person gets food poisoning of type *P*, but also true that whenever someone gets food poisoning of type *P*, that person eats food of type *F* (prior to contracting *P*). In other words, suppose it is true not only that $(x)(Fx \supset Px)$, but also true that $(x)(Px \supset Fx)$. Then, although $(x)(Px \supset Fx)$ is true, we cannot say that contracting *P* causes the eating of *F*, because the eating of *F* occurs *before* the onset of *P*. (But we *can* say that *P* and *F* are *causally connected*, or *causally related*. In general, to say that a given thing, *A*, is the cause of some other thing, *B*, is to say *more* than that *A* and *B* are causally related.)

In addition, we must note that the conception of **cause and effect**, as opposed to **causal connection**, or **causal relationship**, is one which is more frequently used in *everyday life* (including the everyday laboratory life of the scientist) than in formal scientific explanations. Hence its use is guided by practical considerations of lesser importance to formal science than those guiding the use of the concept of causal connection. In particular, *human agency* is relevant to the determination of cause.

To take a simplified example, we know inductively that any well-made match heated sufficiently in the presence of oxygen will light, in symbols $(x)\{[(Mx \cdot Hx) \cdot Px] \supset Lx\}$ (where $Mx =$ "*x* is a well-made match", $Hx =$ "*x* is heated to a sufficiently high temperature", $Px =$ "*x* is in the

---

* This answer originated with David Hume.

presence of oxygen", and $Lx = $ "x lights"). If asked why a given match lit, we can say either that it did so *because* it was scratched (heated) in the presence of oxygen, or simply that it did so *because* it was scratched (heated), omitting reference to the presence of oxygen as understood. In other words, we can furnish an instance of the antecedent of the inductive generalization $(x)\{[(Mx \cdot Hx) \cdot Px] \supset Lx\}$ as the *cause* of the analogous instance of its consequent.

However, we cannot do this in every case. For instance, the inductive generalization just referred to, namely $(x)\{[(Mx \cdot Hx) \cdot Px] \supset Lx\}$, is equivalent to the inductive generalization $(x)\{[(Mx \cdot Hx) \cdot \sim Lx] \supset \sim Px\}$. But usage does not permit us to say that in a given case oxygen was not present *because* the match didn't light when heated. That is, usage does not permit us to refer to an instance of the antecedent of the inductive generalization $(x)\{[(Mx \cdot Hx) \cdot \sim Lx] \supset \sim Px\}$ as the *cause* of the analogous instance of its consequent. This is true in spite of the fact that *if* the inductive generalization is *true*, and an instance of its antecedent is true, then the analogous instance of its consequent *must be true*.

There must be a difference between the case where we say (correctly) that the match lit *because* it was heated in the presence of oxygen, and the case where we say (incorrectly) that the match was not in the presence of oxygen *because* it was heated when it didn't light. And the difference primarily concerns *human agency*. For we can *make* a match light by scratching it (heating it) in the presence of oxygen, but we cannot *make* a match be not in the presence of oxygen by scratching it (heating it) and having it not light. (Indeed, human agency is the primary reason why we refuse to say that an event A which occurs *after* some other event B is the cause of that event. Obviously, we cannot influence the past, and hence cannot cause B to have occurred by producing A.)

4

Mill's Methods

As stated above, *inductive generalization* constitutes one way to justify conclusions about causal relationships among events or phenomena. Thus, if every observed instance in which we put sugar in unsweetened coffee is an instance in which the coffee is sweetened, we conclude that sugar will sweeten coffee. And then we are justified in saying that putting the sugar in the coffee *caused* it to be sweet.

This method of justifying causes, as well as the method involving statistical generalizations, is closely related to a set of procedures called

"Mill's Methods",* proposed as ways to *discover* causal relationships, as well as to *justify* beliefs in causal relationships. Our interest in the methods concerns their use to *justify* beliefs, since (obviously) *discovery* of beliefs is not part of the context of justification.

We present three of the five methods, omitting two as essentially similar to the others.

The method of agreement

The **method of agreement** is very much like inductive generalization. According to the method of agreement, if we find two or more instances in which a given phenomenon, P, occurs, such that only one other phenomenon, Q, is present in each of these instances, then we can conclude that P and Q are causally connected (i.e., conclude that P is the cause of Q, or Q of P).

Mill's example of a scientific use of the method of agreement concerns the fact that all observed objects having a crystalline structure have been found to have one and only one other factor in common, namely that they have solidified from a fluid state. Using the method of agreement, he concludes that having solidified from a fluid state is the *cause* of their crystalline nature. (It can't be the effect because their fluid state *precedes* their crystalline state.)

Another example is furnished by the food poisoning case previously mentioned. If eating food of type F is the only common factor among cases of food poisoning of type P, then we can conclude by the method of agreement that it is the *cause* of the food poisoning.

The main difficulty with the method of agreement is that all examined instances of a phenomenon *never* have only one other factor in common. Take the food poisoning case. In each instance in which food poisoning occurs, it may happen that the food was eaten with stainless steel utensils, or each person eating the food was over five feet tall, or some other kind of food also was eaten. If we are to assign the blame for the food poisoning to the eating of food F, then we must eliminate all of the other common factors. One way we can eliminate some of these factors is by using the second of Mill's Methods, namely the *method of difference*.

The method of difference

According to the **method of difference**, if an instance in which a certain phenomenon, P, occurs, and an instance in which the phenomenon P does

---

* After John Stuart Mill (1806–1873), who is chiefly responsible for their popularization, though not their initial formulation.

not occur, are alike in every other respect *except* one, say Q, and if Q is present only in the instance in which P is present, then P is the cause (or part of the cause) of Q, or Q is the cause (or part of the cause) of P. In other words, if there is some factor, Q, present in an instance when P is present, and absent in an instance when P is absent, where the two instances are alike in every other respect, then P is the cause of Q, or Q is the cause of P.

The food poisoning case illustrates the use of the method of difference. Suppose we have an instance of food poisoning in which food of type F is eaten, food of type G is eaten, and stainless steel utensils are used. And suppose we have an instance in which food poisoning does not occur, and in which food of type G is eaten and stainless steel utensils are used, but no food of type F is eaten. Then we are justified in concluding that eating food of type F *caused* the food poisoning.

The method of concomitant variation

According to the **method of concomitant variation**, if a given phenomenon varies in amount or degree in some regular way with the amount or degree of some other phenomenon, then the two factors are causally related.

An example of the use of the method of concomitant variation is furnished by the causal relationship between cigarette smoking and lung cancer. According to many recent surveys, the rate of death from lung cancer among American males is from 20 to 25 times higher for men who smoke about one half to one pack of cigarettes per day than among men who do not smoke at all. Hence we conclude that cigarette smoking is causally related to death by lung cancer. (Notice that we cannot say that cigarette smoking is *the* cause of death from lung cancer, since some men who do not smoke at all die of lung cancer, indicating that there must be other causes of that disease.)

Another, even better, example of the use of the method of concomitant variation is furnished by the causal relationship between air pressure and the height of a column of mercury in a barometer. In this case, there is a direct quantitative relationship between the two which is so close that we use the effect (the height of the column of mercury) to *measure* the cause (the amount of air pressure).

Mill's Methods also can be used *negatively*, to show that two factors are *not* causally related. For instance, in the food poisoning case, if we suspect that the food poisoning is caused by the use of stainless steel utensils, then if we find a case in which stainless steel utensils are used but no food poisoning occurs, we can conclude that there is no strict causal connection between the use of stainless steel utensils and food poisoning.

Many objections have been raised against the use of Mill's Methods. The most frequently encountered objection is that Mill's Methods, even when correctly applied, lead to erroneous, even absurd, consequences. One famous example concerns the drinker who drinks scotch and soda one night, bourbon and soda the next night, gin and soda the next and Irish whiskey and soda on the last night, each drinking bout being followed by a severe hangover. Using Mill's Methods, the drinker concludes that *soda*, the one common factor present on each of the four occasions, must be the cause of the hangovers.

But objections of this kind are spurious. Take the drinking example. Either the drinker in question *did* know that another factor, namely alcohol, was present in each case, or he did not. If he knew this, then he did not apply Mill's Methods correctly, since he knew that soda was not the *only* common factor. And if he did *not* know that alcohol was present in each case, then he was *justified* in applying Mill's Methods in spite of the fact that his conclusion is false, and even appears to be ridiculous. The falsity of the conclusion does not constitute evidence against Mill's Methods because these methods are *inductive*, and it is the mark of inductive methods that they sometimes, perhaps even often, yield false conclusions.

In addition, the fact that the conclusion appears ridiculous to us also is not a mark against Mill's Methods, because *we* know that bourbon, scotch, gin, etc., all contain alcohol, and *we* know that hangovers are caused by excessive intake of alcohol. But if we did not know this (and we assume the drinker does not), then the conclusion that hangovers are caused by soda consumption would appear to be quite reasonable. (Incidentally, once the drinker realizes that there is *another* common factor, alcohol, in every case in which he had a hangover, then he can use Mill's Methods to determine which of these factors causes hangovers, simply by trying a case in which soda is present, but not alcohol, and then a case in which alcohol is present, but not soda.)

It is sometimes said that Mill's Methods are fine as a way to obtain knowledge of causes, but *not* as a way to obtain *theoretical knowledge*, or knowledge of *scientific* laws: For example, we can use Mill's Methods to establish a causal connection between eating a particular kind of food and getting stomach cramps, but *not* (so it is claimed) to establish the *mechanism* in terms of which this causal connection operates. To explain how the causal connection works, we need to construct *theories*, making use of *theoretical entities*. And this (it is claimed) is an area in which Mill's Methods are of no use.

This objection to Mill's Methods is quite similar to a very general objection against induction as a whole, namely that it is irrelevant to the main task of science, namely *theory construction*. In Chapter Sixteen, it will be argued that this claim is wrong, and that induction is used just as much in theory justification as in any other kind of scientific justification. Indeed, the very distinction into the empirical and the theoretical, on which this objection rests, will be challenged. Since Mill's Methods are nothing other than standard *inductive* procedures, the defense of inductive procedures in general against this charge constitutes a defense of Mill's Methods in particular.

Finally, there is the difficulty (mentioned in the discussion of the method of agreement) that the first of Mill's Methods requires all examined instances of a given phenomenon, *P*, to have only *one* factor in common, a requirement which is never satisfied.

As stated before, *some* of the factors common to all observed *P*'s can be eliminated by means of the method of difference. But *all* such factors cannot be eliminated in this way. (For one thing, the number of common factors is simply too large to eliminate, even in wholesale batches.)

One way to get around this difficulty is to restate the method of agreement as follows: If we find two or more instances in which a given phenomenon, *P*, occurs, such that only one other *known relevant* phenomenon, *Q*, is present in each of these instances, then assume that *P* and *Q* are causally connected.

Of course, this constitutes more a rephrasing of the problem than a solution to it, for it raises the question as to *how* we are to determine that a given phenomenon is *relevant*. Unfortunately, no completely satisfactory answer to this question has been provided.*

---

* However, the answer seems to lie in the direction of so-called "background information". We know whether or not a given phenomenon is relevant because of information *other* than that the two phenomena in question have always appeared together. For instance, we know from background information that the *color* of a pair of dice is not relevant to its performance, while the *center of gravity* and precise shape are very relevant indeed. So anyone looking for the cause of the poor performance of loaded dice will ignore the fact that they all are the same color, while concentrating on their center of gravity and precise shape.

Chapter Fifteen

Probability

Probabilities, and sentences about probabilities, play an important role both in everyday life and in science, as the following examples illustrate:

1. The probability of getting a seven with an honest pair of dice is 1/6.

2. Art will probably beat Charles at squash this afternoon.

3. We'll probably have rain tomorrow.

4. The probability that a *given* American male will die of lung cancer in the next year is .0008.

5. The theory of relativity is more probable on today's evidence than on the evidence available in 1919.

6. The probability that a given birth will be a male birth equals .51.

1

Induction and Probability

In general, sentences about probabilities are not theorems of logic, and hence cannot be justified solely by *deductive* means.* Hence they must be obtained as conclusions of valid *inductive* arguments. The statistical generalizations discussed in Chapter Fourteen, Section 2, are examples of probability sentences which are obtainable as conclusions of such arguments.

2

Two Related Problems about Probabilities

In considering the various kinds of probabilities and probability sentences, we must deal with two important and related problems.

The first is the problem as to what the terms "probable", "probability", and their synonyms *mean*. In particular, we want to know whether these terms are *ambiguous* (that is, have more than one meaning) or whether they are *univocal* (that is, have only one general meaning).

The second problem concerns the question as to how we ought to *calculate* probabilities. In particular, we want to know how to obtain *initial* probability values (as opposed to probability values obtained via calculation from other probabilities).

3

Meaning of the Term "Probability"

There are a great many different views as to the meaning of the term "probability", and as to the nature of probabilities.

The classical theory

According to one of the more reasonable as well as widely accepted theories, the so-called **classical theory of probability**, a probability is a *measure of rational expectation or belief*. For instance, according to this view, the sentence "The probability is very high that it will rain tomorrow" asserts that the *rational strength of belief* in the proposition that it will rain tomorrow is very high.† And the sentence "The probability of rain tomorrow is .95" asserts that the *rational degree of belief* in the proposition that it will rain tomorrow is .95.

In assigning *numerical values* to the rational degrees of belief, it is customary to use *zero* and *one* as the limiting points. Thus, the number *one* is assigned to the strength of belief in those sentences which have the

---

* The exceptions are trivial sentences such as "Either the probability is half or it isn't".

† That is, anyone who is rational ought to believe very strongly that it will rain tomorrow. Of course, it is rational to believe strongly in a sentence of this kind *only* if there is strong *evidence* in its favor.

highest possible rational degree of belief, and the number *zero* is assigned as the strength of belief in those sentences which have the lowest possible rational degree of belief.

It is generally supposed that only *logical truths* warrant such strong belief that their probability values ought to be equal to one. And only logical falsehoods (contradictions) warrant such weak belief that their probability values ought to be equal to zero. Hence, all *contingent* (and thus all *scientific*) sentences ought to have a probability value somewhere between zero and one.

The frequency theory

According to another widely accepted and quite reasonable theory, generally called the **frequency theory of probability**, *probabilities are relative frequencies*, *and sentences about probabilities are sentences about relative frequencies*. For instance, on this view, the sentence "The probability that an American male will get lung cancer next year equals .0008" asserts that the *relative frequency* of death from lung cancer next year among American males will equal .0008 (i.e., eight American males out of 10,000 will die of lung cancer next year).

If we interpret probabilities as relative frequencies, then all of the *statistical* generalizations which are referred to above will be sentences about probabilities. For example, the statistical generalization "Half of all tosses of this coin will land heads up" will be a sentence about probabilities, which we could have expressed as "The probability of getting heads with this coin equals 1/2", or as "The relative frequency of heads (to total number of throws) with this coin equals 1/2".

4

*The Calculation
of Probabilities*

We now turn to the second problem mentioned above, as to how probability values are to be calculated. The classical theory and the frequency theory attempt to solve this problem in quite different ways.

The cornerstone of the classical theory is the so-called **principle of indifference**, according to which any two events are to be considered equally probable if there is no sufficient reason to expect one rather than the other.

Suppose we want to calculate the probability that a given die will land with an even number face up on any given throw. There are six possible results of any given throw, namely side one landing face up, side two landing face up, side three landing face up, and so on. And we have no reason to expect one of these results rather than any other. Hence, according to the principle of indifference, each of the possible results has the same probability. In addition, the probability that *one or another* of the six sides will land face up on any given throw equals one. Hence, the probability that a given side, say side one, will land face up equals 1/6. And the probability that an *even numbered* side will land face up equals 1/6 (the probability that side two will land face up), plus 1/6 (the probability that side four will land face up), plus 1/6 (the probability that side six will land face up), which equals 3/6, or 1/2. In effect then, according to the principle of indifference, the probability of an even number landing face up equals the number of possible results *favorable* to this hypothesis (namely three) divided by the total number of possible results, favorable or unfavorable (namely six).

Since the same method of calculation is to be employed in every case, we can say that in general the classical theory of probability requires that we calculate the probability of a hypothesis as equal to the number of possible results or events *favorable* to the hypothesis divided by the total number of possible results or events.

A great many textbooks, especially in mathematics, adopt the classical theory, at least to the extent that they adopt the principle of indifference. And indeed, the principle seems quite plausible. For example, it tells us that the probability of getting a non-six on a particular throw of the die equals 5/6, while the probability of getting a six only equals 1/6, and surely it is rational to believe more strongly that six will *not* show up on a given throw than that it will.

Theories, such as the classical theory, which make use of the principle of indifference often are called **a priori theories**, and the probabilities calculated by their means often are called **a priori probabilities**. This use of the term "a priori" is appropriate, because probabilities obtained by use of the principle of indifference are obtained *before*, and *without the use of*, information about the events whose probabilities are being determined.*

In contrast to the classical theory, the frequency theory makes no use of the principle of indifference, and hence no use of a priori probabilities. Instead, it calculates relative frequencies in an *empirical* manner, according to the principle that the relative frequency of a given result among as yet *unobserved* events of a given kind will be the same as the *observed*

---

* The concept of the a priori is discussed in greater detail in Part Five, Chapter Nineteen.

relative frequencies of that kind.* For instance, in calculating the probability that a given American male will die of lung cancer in a given year, we use statistical evidence as to the relative frequency of death by lung cancer in American males in previous years, and assume that the relative frequency, and hence the probability, will remain the same this year.

While we cannot give a complete exposition of the frequency theory at this point, one important feature of that theory ought to be mentioned, namely the use of *background hypotheses* or *background information*, in the correction of hypotheses about relative frequencies.

Consider, for instance, the calculation of the probability that a given birth will be male. It may happen that the relative frequency of male births to total number of births in a given nation remains relatively stable over a long period of time, at, say, .51. If we have no additional information, then the frequency theory requires that we calculate the probability that a given birth in that nation will be a male birth as .51.

But we may well have additional information. For example, we may know that a war is about to begin and have statistical evidence that in the past the relative frequency of male births has increased in wartime (because the average age of parents decreases, and younger parents tend to have a greater percentage of male offspring). Obviously, we ought not predict that the relative frequency of male births will continue to be .51. Instead, we ought to raise that value to take account of the expected increase in early marriages, with its expected increase in male births.

In like manner, many probability hypotheses can be corrected by means of background information or background hypotheses.†

5

Comparison of the Classical and Frequency Theories

Let's summarize what has just been said about the classical and frequency theories of probability.

The classical theory construes the term "probability" to *mean* "rational strength of belief". Thus, it construes the hypothesis "The

---

* This was the idea lurking behind the discussion of statistical generalizations presented in the discussion above.

† Of course, if a background hypothesis also is statistical, then the frequency theory requires that we justify it in the same way as any other statistical hypothesis. For example, the background hypothesis that wars cause an increase of .02 in the relative frequency of male births is justified if we have evidence that in the past the relative frequency of male births increased .02 during wartime.

Induction and Science

probability of getting a non-six on a given throw of this die equals 5/6"
as meaning "The rational degree of belief in the hypothesis that a non-six
will occur on any given throw of this die equals 5/6".

The classical theory calculates probability values on the basis of the
principle of indifference, according to which any two possible events are
to be considered equally probable unless there is reason to expect one
event rather than the other. Hence, in those cases in which we have no
reason to expect one result rather than another, we calculate the probability of a given event as the number of possible favorable events divided
by the total number of possible events, favorable or unfavorable.

Probability values obtained by means of the classical theory are obtained a priori in that they can be calculated before, or without the use of,
information concerning the events in question (other than information
concerning the number of events that are logically possible).

The relative frequency theory construes the term "probability" to mean
"relative frequency". Thus, it construes the hypothesis "The probability
of getting a non-six on a given throw of this die equals 5/6" to mean
"The relative frequency of non-six throws of this die compared to total
number of throws equals 5/6".

The frequency theory calculates as yet unobserved probabilities on the
basis of already observed probabilities according to the principle that the
as yet unobserved relative frequencies of a given kind will be the same as
the observed relative frequencies of that kind. (Notice that if we have no
evidence whatever about observed relative frequencies, then this theory
does not permit us to calculate any probabilities.)

Probability values calculated by means of the frequency theory are
obtained *empirically*, and never a priori, in that their calculation requires
observational evidence concerning the things the probabilities are about.

In addition to the above, there is another extremely important difference
between the two theories, which stems from the way in which they construe probabilities. On the frequency theory, probability hypotheses
generally are *predictions* about as yet unobserved relative frequencies.
Consequently, *future events* are relevant to their truth. For instance, if,
in fact, the relative frequency of male births compared to total number of
births turns out to be .51, then the hypothesis "The probability (relative
frequency) that a given birth will be male equals .51" is true. Otherwise,
it is false.

On the other hand, according to the classical theory, probabilities are rational degrees of belief. Consequently, future events are *irrelevant* to the truth values of probability sentences. For instance, if probabilities are rational degrees of belief, then the truth* of the hypothesis that the probability of getting a non-six on a given throw of a particular die equals 5/6 has nothing whatever to do with the results of future throws of the die. No matter what happens in the future, it still may be *rational to believe* quite strongly that a non-six will turn up on any given throw. The wise man sometimes is wrong in his beliefs, although right to have held them; the fool sometimes (luckily) is right in his beliefs, although wrong to have held them.

6

Objections to the Classical and Frequency Theories

Much has been written pro and con the classical and frequency theories. Indeed, the objections to the two theories have become fairly standard.

Objections to the classical theory

There are at least six major objections to the classical theory frequently encountered in the literature. Four of them concern the way in which probabilities are *calculated*. Two concern the *meaning* of the term "probability".

(1) According to the classical theory, the probability that a given event will occur equals the number of possible events favorable to the occurrence of that event divided by the total number of possible events. But if we think carefully about the number of *possible* events that may occur at any moment, we see immediately that that number is *infinite*, or at least *indefinitely large*.

Take the dice example. We said above that according to the classical theory, the probability is 1/2 that an even-numbered side will land face up on any given throw of a particular die. This is supposed to follow from the fact that exactly 1/2 of the *possible* outcomes of a throw of that die are favorable to the hypothesis that an even-numbered side will land face up on any given throw. But unfortunately, it is not true that exactly 1/2 of the *possible* outcomes are favorable. It *is* true that exactly three outcomes are *favorable* to the hypothesis. However, it is *not* true that there are

---

* Some philosophers deny that statements of rational expectations have truth values. They prefer to speak of the "correctness" or "incorrectness" of probability hypotheses.

exactly *six possible* outcomes. For one thing, the die may land on an edge. For another, it may not land at all, instead remaining suspended in mid-air. Or it may explode before hitting the table. Of course, none of these events is *likely*, or *probable*. But they are *possible*.* Of course, in artificial examples, like the dice example, we can arbitrarily rule out unlikely events of this kind. For instance, we can stipulate that only those cases in which the die lands with side one face up, or side two face up, or . . . side six face up, constitute throws. But in most cases in daily life, and most cases of interest to the scientist; we cannot do this. In life we are faced with the fact that the number of logically possible events that may occur at any given time is at least indefinitely large.

(2) The classical theory also has been objected to on the grounds that it is *grossly incomplete*, for it fails to tell us either (a) what constitutes sufficient reason to prefer or expect one possible alternative rather than another, or (b) how probability values are to be calculated in cases when we *do* have sufficient reason to prefer one alternative rather than another.

Take the coin example. Does the presence of the motto "In God we trust" on one side of a coin constitute sufficient reason to expect that side rather than the other? And suppose we assume that something, say the center of gravity of the coin, *does* constitute sufficient reason. How are we to use this information? The classical theory does not furnish a satisfactory answer to these questions.

(3) Another objection raised against the classical theory is that the method of calculation it employs yields *contradictory* probability values.

To illustrate this charge, let's make use of the formula relating the distance, D, that a thing travels with the time, T, and rate of speed, R, that it travels. Recall that if something travels a distance of exactly one mile, then $R = 1/T$, and $T = 1/R$. (This follows from the general formula that $D = R \times T$, by substituting 1 for D and transposing.)

Now let's assume that an auto travels a distance of exactly one mile, and that we know that the auto travels at a constant rate of speed somewhere between 40 and 60 miles per hour. According to the classical theory, the probability equals 1/2 that the auto travels at a rate of speed between

---

* That is, they are *logically* possible. We cannot appeal here to *physical* possibility and impossibility, because we want a theory of probability in part to help us *determine* what is physically possible, and what physically impossible. Hence, to appeal to physical possibility and impossibility at this point would constitute circular reasoning.

40 and 50 miles per hour, because the number of *possible* rates of speed between 40 and 50 miles per hour is exactly half the number of possible rates of speed between 40 and 60 miles per hour.*

Now let's calculate the probability that the *time* it takes to travel the one mile is between 1/40th and 1/50th of an hour. According to the formula that $T = 1/R$, if the auto travels at 40 miles per hour, then it takes 1/40th of an hour to travel the one mile, and if it travels at 60 miles per hour, it takes 1/60th of an hour. So it must take between 1/40th and 1/60th of an hour to travel the mile at a rate of speed between 40 and 60 miles per hour. Hence, according to the classical theory of probability, the probability is *greater* than 1/2 that the time it takes the auto to travel the mile is between 1/40th and 1/50th of an hour. This follows from the fact that the interval between 1/40 and 1/50 is greater than the interval between 1/50 and 1/60, so that more than half of the possible times between 1/40th and 1/60th of an hour are between 1/40th and 1/50th of an hour.

But now trouble arises. We first calculated that the probability is 1/2 that the rate of speed of the auto is between 40 and 50 miles per hour. We then calculated that the probability is *greater than 1/2* that the *time* it takes the auto to travel the mile is between 1/40th and 1/50th of an hour. But if the auto travels the mile at a rate of speed between 40 and 50 miles per hour, it follows that it must travel the mile in a time between 1/40th and 1/50th of an hour (because $T = 1/R$). Hence, the probability that it travels the mile in a time between 1/40th and 1/50th of an hour must *equal* the probability that it travels at a rate of speed between 40 and 50 miles per hour. In other words both probabilities must *equal* 1/2, which contradicts the previous result that the probability is *greater than* 1/2 that the auto takes between 1/40th and 1/50th of an hour to travel the mile.

Obviously, if the classical theory yields contradictory probability values, as the above example seems to indicate, then it is worthless as a theory of probability. At least one attempt has been made† to rescue the classical

---

* Actually, this isn't quite true, since the number of possible rates of speed between 40 and 50 miles per hour *exactly equals* the number of possible rates of speed between 40 and 60 miles per hour, since the number in each case is infinite. In order to make the classical theory work at all in this case, we have to assume either that only a finite number of different rates of speed are possible, or that some way can be found to distinguish between infinities of the same level. An assumption similar to one of these two assumptions must be made in every *quantitative* case. The point of the above example is that on either assumption contradictory probability values result from use of the principle of indifference, and hence from use of the classical theory.

† By Rudolf Carnap

theory from this charge, but further examination of this question is beyond the scope of this text.

(4) Another objection to the classical theory is that it calculates probability values primarily on the basis of *ignorance*, or *lack of empirical evidence*, rather than *knowledge*, or *empirical evidence*. Surely the strength of our belief in a given hypothesis ought to be based at least primarily on empirical (factual) evidence. But the principle of indifference, which the classical theory employs, tells us to assume that two events are equiprobable if we have no reason to prefer or expect one rather than the other. That is, it tells us that *if we are ignorant* or *without evidence* of a certain kind, then we can go ahead and believe in certain hypotheses. Many philosophers claim that this approach is irrational.

(5) The above objections to the classical theory are primarily objections to the *way it calculates probabilities*. They are not primarily objections to its analysis of the *meaning* of the term "probability". We now present two objections to the classical theory's claim that the term "probability" *means* roughly "rational strength of belief".

The first objection is this. If probabilities are construed as rational degrees of belief, then probability hypotheses will not be *empirically testable*. For instance, suppose that the rational strength of belief in the hypothesis that it will rain tomorrow is quite high, but that it does not in fact rain tomorow. Does this falsify the hypothesis that the probability (rational strength of belief) of the hypothesis that it will rain tomorrow is high? The answer is that it does *not*. The *mere falsity* of an hypothesis does not prove that it wasn't rational to believe it, or even to believe it quite strongly. So if we adopt the classical theory, probability sentences will be untestable by any future empirical observations.

The second objection is that there are many uses of the term "probability" which cannot be interpreted as referring to rational degrees of belief. We shall consider only one such use here.*

Suppose that the owner of a gambling casino in Las Vegas wants to calculate "fair odds" concerning a particular dice game. He might report the results of his calculations in sentences like (A): "The probability of getting a seven on given throws of the dice equals 1/6", or (B): "The probability of getting a twelve on given throws of the dice equals 1/36",

---

* Another is considered in Section 8 of this chapter.

etc. But how are we to interpret the term "probability"? For instance, can we translate the casino owner's assertion of (A) into (C): "The rational strength of belief in the hypothesis that a seven will result from some particular throw equals 1/6"? Do (A) and (C) equally state what the casino owner means by the assertion of (A)? The answer seems to be "no" for both of these questions. Instead, it seems clear that what the casino owner wants to say is better interpreted as being about *relative frequencies*. By and large, the casino owner's primary interest is not in any particular throw of the dice, but rather in *very large numbers of throws*.

In other words, he is primarily interested in what happens *in the long run*. Consequently, his assertion (A): "The probability of getting a seven on given throws of the dice equals 1/6" is best interpreted as saying something about the *relative frequency* with which sevens occur in large numbers of throws of the dice. So his hypothesis (A) is best translated into (D): "The *relative frequency* (in the long run) of sevens to total number of throws with the kind of dice to be employed equals 1/6". And, of course, this is exactly the way in which the *frequency theory of probability* treats hypotheses such as (A). Hence, it is claimed that at least in *some* of its uses the term "probability" means what the frequency theory, and not the classical theory, takes it to mean.

Objections to the frequency theory

The frequency theory also has had many objections leveled against it. We shall consider two.

(1) The first objection is that the frequency theory construes probability hypotheses to be about long run relative frequencies, whereas in fact we are usually concerned primarily with the so-called *short run*.

For instance, for reasons of mathematical simplicity, frequency theorists customarily construe the classes involved in a probability hypothesis as being *infinitely large*, and then construe probability hypotheses as stating *limits* of relative frequencies.* For instance, they construe the hypothesis

---

* The notion of a limit is a fundamental mathematical conception, but one whose precise statement is rather complex. Roughly, a series of tosses with a coin has a limit of the relative frequency of heads to total number of tosses equal to 1/2 if, as the series gets larger and larger, the relative frequency in question tends to become closer and closer to 1/2. In other words, the limit of a series of values equals some value N iff for every number M, no matter how small M happens to be, there is some point on the series such that for the remainder of the series the value in question will remain within $\pm M$ of N.

Induction and Science

"The probability that a given birth will be male equals .51" to mean "The *limit* of the relative frequency of male births to total number of births equals .51".

The standard objection to the use of limits is simply that most, perhaps even all, probability hypotheses are about *finite* classes, and finite classes cannot have limits. For instance, the class of all human births, past, present, and future, is almost certainly finite in size. Hence the hypothesis that the limit of the relative frequency of male births to total number of births equals .51 must be false, since the limit in question does not exist. But frequency theorists claim that the use of limits is justified anyway, as an *idealization* of actual cases involving finite classes. In Physics, for instance, the notion of an ideal gas is employed, even though ideal gases in fact do not exist. Similarly, we reason about actual circles and triangles *as though* they were the ideal figures studied in Geometry.

Defenders of the frequency theory also claim that it can be maintained even without the use of limits. For instance, we can always construe the above hypothesis about male births literally to mean "The relative frequency of male births to total number of births equals .51", no matter how large the class of male births and the class of all births, male or female, happen to be.

But neither the appeal to limits, nor the construal in terms of long run classes (such as the class of all human births, past, present, or future), answers the charge that probability hypotheses often are about the *short run*.

Take the hypothesis "The probability that a given birth is a male birth equals .51". A national leader who employs this hypothesis to calculate the likely size of his army 20 years hence surely does not mean to assert something about the total class of human births, past, present, or future. He is concerned with the relative frequency of male births to total number of births *in his own country during the next few years*.

Consequently, if we adopt the frequency theory, we must admit that probability hypotheses do not always state long run relative frequencies.

(In addition, we must admit that one and the same probability hypothesis may be construed differently, depending on *context*. For instance, when used by a national leader, the above probability hypothesis about male births is perhaps best construed as about a certain limited class of human births, although when considered by a geneticist, it may be best construed as about all human births, at all places and all times.)

It seems then that the frequency theory may be able to overcome the first kind of objection leveled against it, although at the expense of dealing with much smaller classes than frequency theorists generally suppose.

(2) A second, and unfortunately more serious, objection to the frequency theory is that many, perhaps even most, probability hypotheses do not seem to be about relative frequencies. For instance, probability sentences about so-called *single cases* do not seem to be about relative frequencies. Suppose someone says (A): "The probability is .4 that it will rain tomorrow". His assertion is about the single case of the weather *tomorrow*. Now it is possible that this sentence is false. But it is also possible that it is *true*. However, if we construe (A) according to the frequency theory, and thus construe it to say that the relative frequency of rain tomorrow equals .4, then (A) *must be* false. This follows from the fact that it either *will* rain tomorrow, or it *won't*, so that the relative frequency of rain tomorrow must be either *one* (if it rains) or *zero* (if it doesn't). In either case, the relative frequency cannot be .4. But surely we would not suppose that this fact *automatically falsifies* sentence (A). And yet, if we apply the frequency theory to sentences concerning single cases, such as sentence (A), then we are committed to this unwelcome conclusion.

In addition to the single case examples, there are other kinds of probability statements which do not seem to be about relative frequencies. One is the kind that states probabilities of other hypotheses or theories. For instance, it is hard to imagine what *relative frequency* the probability statement "The theory of relativity is more probable on today's evidence than on the evidence available in 1919" is about.

7

*A Joint
Classical-
Relative
Frequency
Theory*

Some theorists have tried to solve the difficulties encountered by the classical and relative frequency theories by combining the two, taking what is good in each and throwing the bad away.

Perhaps the most plausible solution of this kind is as follows:

We ought to admit that *some* probability sentences *are* about relative frequencies, and adopt roughly the frequency theory method of calculating probabilities for these cases.

And we ought to accept the idea that the classical theory is correct as to the *meanings* of at least *some* probability sentences. For example, we ought to accept the idea that a sentence such as "The theory of relativity is more probable on today's evidence than on the evidence available in 1919" *means* roughly "The *rational strength of belief* in the theory of relativity is higher on today's evidence than on the evidence available in 1919".

But we have to reject the principle of indifference as the *method* of calculating rational degrees of belief. Instead, what we need is a theory of *evidential support*, based on the idea that it is rational to believe more strongly in well confirmed hypotheses than in not so well confirmed hypotheses, where well confirmed hypotheses are those for which we have good evidential (that is, *empirical*, or *observational*), support.*

What we need then is a satisfactory theory of confirmation. But as the problems involved in the confirmation paradox (to be discussed in Chapter Seventeen) indicate, a great deal of work needs to be done on confirmation theory.

8

Is There a Third Kind of Probability?

The question naturally arises as to whether a combined theory of the kind just described, which assumes that there are exactly two distinct kinds of probabilities, one concerned with relative frequencies, the other with the rational strength of beliefs, is *complete*. Are all probabilities of either one or the other of the two kinds just mentioned? Most philosophers seem to believe that all probabilities *are* either relative frequencies or rational strengths of beliefs. But a very few do not. In particular, there is one kind of probability which a few philosophers think may be neither.

A good example of this third kind is illustrated by the sentence "The probability is .4 that the Browns will beat the Blues tomorrow", uttered by a gambler about to bet on the outcome of a particular game. In the first place, the gambler surely does not mean to assert anything about relative frequencies, since .4 is not even a *possible* relative frequency. And in the second place, he does not mean to assert that the *rational* strength of belief

---

* Of course *theoretical support* also must be considered. But theoretical support is acceptable *only* from those theories which themselves are well confirmed by means of observational support.

(or even his *own* strength of belief) in the hypothesis that the Browns will beat the Blues equals .4, since (if he is rational) *he does not believe that the Browns will beat the Blues!* (He doesn't believe that the Blues will beat the Browns either.) And it seems to make no sense to speak of the *rational strength* of belief in a sentence which *rational* men would not believe in. But if this is true, then there must be a third kind of probability, which is neither a relative frequency nor a rational strength of belief.

9

*The Probability
Calculus*

So far, we have considered the question as to how so-called *initial* probabilities are to be calculated. We now consider the question as to how, given certain probabilities (initial or otherwise), other probabilities can be calculated from them. The so-called **probability calculus** has been constructed to answer this question.

Some pairs of events are such that the occurrence of one of them has an *effect* on the occurrence of the other. For example, drawing an ace from a deck of cards (without putting it back into the deck) has an effect on the chances of getting an ace on the next draw.

But other pairs of events are such that the occurrence of one has no effect on the other. For example, drawing an ace from a deck of cards has *no* effect on the chances of getting an ace on the next draw *if* the ace has been put back into the deck before the second draw. (The cards don't "know" that an ace was picked on the first draw.) If two events are such that the occurrence of one has no effect on the occurrence of the second, they are said to be **independent events**.

In addition, some pairs of events are such that it is *logically possible* for *both* of them to occur. For example, it is logically possible for a die to land face six up on its first throw *and* also to land face six up on its second throw.

But other pairs of events are such that it is *not* logically possible for both to occur. For example, it is not logically possible for face five *and* face six to land up on a single throw of a die. If two events are such that it is not logically possible for both to occur, they are said to be **mutually exclusive events**.

Let's use the symbol *P* as an abbreviation for the term "probability". And let's use *p* and *q* as variables, ranging over events. Then we can write the basic rules of the probability calculus, as follows:

1. **Restricted Conjunction Rule**

If p and q are independent events,
then $P(p \cdot q) = P(p) \times P(q)$.

For instance, if the probability of getting a six on a given throw $(p) = 1/6$, and the probability of getting a six on some other throw (q) also $= 1/6$, then since p and q are independent of each other, the probability of getting sixes on both throws equals the probability of getting a six on the first throw *times* the probability of getting a six on the second throw. Thus, the probability of getting sixes on both throws equals $1/6 \times 1/6$, or $1/36$.

2. **General Conjunction Rule**

$P(p \cdot q) = P(p) \times P(q, \textit{if } p)$.

For instance, if the probability of picking a spade on a second draw, *given that a spade was picked on the first draw* (and not replaced) $=12/51$,* then the probability that two spades will be drawn $= 1/4 \times 12/51 = 1/17$.

Notice that if $P(q, \text{if } p) = P(q)$, then the two conjunction rules both yield the same result. In fact, this is the case in which p and q are independent of each other.

3. **Restricted Disjunction Rule**

If p and q are *mutually exclusive events*,
then $P(p \lor q) = P(p) + P(q)$.

For example, if the probability of getting a five on a given throw of a die $= 1/6$, and the probability of getting a six on a given throw of that die $= 1/6$, then the probability of getting a five *or* a six on a given throw of the die $= 1/6 + 1/6 = 2/6 = 1/3$.

4. **General Disjunction Rule**

$P(p \lor q) = P(p) + P(q) - P(p \cdot q)$.

* Because twelve spades remain out of 51 cards, where the probability is the same of picking any given card.

For instance, if the probability of getting a six on any given toss of a die $= 1/6$, then the probability of getting at least one six out of two tosses (i.e., a six on the first toss or a six on the second) $= 1/6 + 1/6 - (1/6 \times 1/6) = 2/6 - 1/36 = 11/36$.

Notice that if p and q are mutually exclusive then $P(p \cdot q) = 0$, and then the two disjunction rules yield the same result.

In addition, it is customary to assume that the probability of a *contradiction* $= 0$, and the probability of a *tautology* $= 1$. In symbols, this reads

5. $P(p \cdot \sim p) = 0$.

6. $P(p \vee \sim p) = 1$.

It follows from this that the probability of $\sim p = 1 - P(p)$. That is,

7. $P(\sim p) = 1 - P(p)$.*

The question naturally arises as to the *applicability* of these basic principles of the probability calculus. Do they apply to all types of probabilities?

It is generally held that they do. But, in fact, there is no special reason to believe that they do. In particular, it is at least questionable whether they apply to those probabilities which concern rational strength of belief.

For instance, suppose we have quite good evidence in favor of two independent scientific hypotheses, one in Physics, the other in Psychology. Suppose, in fact, that the evidence is sufficiently strong to make the rational strength of belief in the first hypothesis $= .8$ and the rational strength of belief in the second $= .7$. Then if we apply the general disjunction rule, we must conclude that the rational strength of the belief that one or the other (or both) of the hypotheses is true $= .8 + .7 - (.8 \times .7) = .94$. But why should this be the case? In fact, no good reasons have been suggested for believing either that this value is correct, or that it isn't.

Similarly, if we apply the restricted conjunction rule, then we must conclude that the rational strength of the belief that *both* of the above

---

* In addition, many other much more complicated probabilities have been worked out. For details, the reader is directed to more advanced or more specialized texts.

hypotheses are true = .56. But again, no good reasons have been suggested for believing either that this value is correct, or that it isn't.

In general, there seems to be no reason whatever to suppose that numerical values assigned to strengths of beliefs are either additive or multiplicative, and hence no reason to assume that the probability calculus applies to them.

However, as stated previously, most philosophers *do* accept the application of the probability calculus to probabilities of this kind, as well as to all other kinds.

Chapter Sixteen

Confirmation,
Explanation,
Theories

1

Empirical
Confirmation of
Categorical
Hypotheses

In Chapter Fifteen, we stated that the probability of a categorical or universal generalization is increased by each *instance* of it which we observe. Thus, the probability of the hypothesis "All copper conducts electricity" is increased by each new instance we observe of something copper which conducts electricity.

But if the *probability* (in whatever sense of that term is appropriate here) of an hypothesis is increased by its instances, so also is its **degree of confirmation**. Indeed, most philosophers *equate* the concept of degree of confirmation with one or another of the kinds of probabilities discussed in Chapter Fifteen.

To speak of the *degree of confirmation* of an hypothesis is to speak of the *degree of evidential support* for that hypothesis. That is, it is to speak of the degree to which what we have observed of the world supports a given hypothesis about the world.

Recall that one way to put the general form of categorical generalization is:

1. $Fa \cdot Ga$

2. $Fb \cdot Gb$

3. $Fc \cdot Gc$
    $\vdots$

N. No F is known not to have G.

$/ \therefore$ $N + 1$. All F's are G's (that is, $(x)(Fx \supset Gx)$).

Looked at from the point of view of *confirmation*, it is clear that each of the premises, $Fa \cdot Ga$, $Fb \cdot Gb$, etc., constitutes a **confirming instance** of $(x)(Fx \supset Gx)$. So let's introduce a slightly different pattern, in order to show more explicitly that it is those things which are *instances of*, or *follow from*, a universal generalization which *confirm* it. This basic pattern is

1. $(H \cdot A) \supset O$

2. O

_____

$/ \therefore$ 3. H

where H is the hypothesis being confirmed, A is some antecedent condition observed or confirmed to be the case, and O is the confirming observation.*

Take a very simple hypothesis, such as (H_1): "All metals, when heated, expand", in symbols $(x)[(Mx \cdot Hx) \supset Ex]$. This hypothesis, when coupled with the antecedent condition that a is a metal which is heated, implies the consequence that a expands. Hence, if we find that a does in fact expand when heated, this constitutes a confirming instance for (H_1). Putting this example into the general pattern, we get:

1. $\{(x)[(Mx \cdot Hx) \supset Ex] \cdot (Ma \cdot Ha)\} \supset Ea$

2. Ea

_____

$/ \therefore$ 3. $(x)[(Mx \cdot Hx) \supset Ex]$

* This pattern, and the succeeding patterns, are basically those of Carl Hempel.

In actual practice, we rarely encounter examples in which the observational or experimental result (on line 2) follows from a *single* categorical generalization (plus antecedent conditions). Instead, we find that the observational results follow from the hypothesis being confirmed *plus* one or more other hypotheses, generally called **auxiliary hypotheses**, where the auxiliary hypotheses already are well confirmed, and already accepted as part of the body of scientific knowledge.

In addition, in actual practice, we generally find that we cannot state the exact pattern of inference in the precise notation of predicate logic, partly because actual theories tend to contain *loose ends* or *imprecise uses of language*. But this does not mean that *in theory* they could not be put into a basic pattern of this kind.

The famous "sea of air" hypothesis,* proposed to account for the fact that suction pumps will not raise water beyond a certain height (about 34′ at sea level), is an hypothesis of this "messy" kind. According to this theory, there is a sea of air surrounding the surface of the Earth which presses down on it, just as water presses down on something at the bottom of the sea. This theory explains the ability of a pump to raise water from the ground as being due to the *pressure* of the sea of air, that is, to *air pressure*, and explains the fact that there is a limit to the height that water can be pumped as being due to the limit of the air pressure. But if this limit is 34′, and, if mercury is about 14 times heavier than water, then if the sea of air theory is correct, it follows that air pressure will hold up a column of mercury only 1/14 as high as a column of water. Hence, when we test, and discover that a column of mercury is held up about 1/14 times as high as 34′ (about 30″), this constitutes a *confirming instance* for the sea of air hypothesis.

Letting H_1 refer to the sea of air hypothesis, H_2 to the hypothesis that the sea of air can hold up a column of water about 34′ high, H_3 to the hypothesis that mercury is 14 times heavier than water, A_1 to the antecedent condition that a tube of mercury closed at one end is placed into a dish of mercury open-end down, and O_1 to the observational result that the column of mercury is held up in the tube to a height of about 30″, we can schematically illustrate this confirmation process as follows:

1. $\{[H_1 \cdot (H_2 \cdot H_3)] \cdot A_1\} \supset O_1$

---

* Proposed by Torricelli, a follower of Galileo.

2. O_1

/∴ 3. $H_1 \cdot (H_2 \cdot H_3)$*

/∴ 4. H_1†

Translating this back into English, we get roughly:

1. If the Earth is surrounded by a sea of air pressing down on it, and if this air pressure holds up a column of water 34′ high, and if mercury is 14 times heavier than water, and finally, if there is a tube of mercury closed at one end with its open end inserted into a dish of mercury, then the height of the mercury in this tube is about 30″.

2. The height of the mercury in this tube *is* about 30″.

/∴ 3. The Earth is surrounded by a sea of air pressing down on it, and this air pressure holds up a column of water 34′ high, and mercury is 14 times heavier than water.

/∴ 4. The Earth is surrounded by a sea of air pressing down on it.

Of course, even in this form, the example is greatly simplified.

Generalizing on the above example, we can say that the basic pattern of confirmation is:

1. $\{[H_1 \cdot (H_2 \cdot \ldots)] \cdot (A_1 \cdot \ldots)\} \supset O$

2. O

/∴ 3. $[H_1 \cdot (H_2 \cdot \ldots)] \cdot (A_1 \cdot \ldots)$

/∴ 4. H_1

---

* Since H_2 and H_3 are *already* well confirmed, the important confirmation is of H_1.

† H_1 follows from $H_1 \cdot (H_2 \cdot H_3)$ by *Simplification*.

The basic pattern of *disconfirmation* is similar to the one for confirmation:

1. $\{[H_1 \cdot (H_2 \cdot \ldots)] \cdot (A_1 \cdot \ldots)\} \supset O$

2. $\sim O$

/∴ 3. $\sim\{[H_1 \cdot (H_2 \cdot \ldots)] \cdot (A_1 \cdot \ldots)\}$

4. $\sim \sim (H_2 \cdot \ldots) \cdot \sim \sim (A_1 \cdot \ldots)$

/∴ 5. $\sim H_1 *$

An example is the disconfirmation of the hypothesis, H_1, that the Earth is flat, where H_2 is a theory of light which says (among other things) that light travels in straight lines, and A_1 is the antecedent condition that a particular ship comes into view over the horizon. If the hypothesis H_1 is correct (in addition to the already well confirmed hypothesis H_2), then the observational result will be that the whole ship, from top to waterline, will first be observed as a rather small object on the horizon which grows larger and larger as it approaches the shore. But in fact, when the ship comes over the horizon, the *top* is observed first. So it is *not* the case that the whole ship, from top to waterline, is observed when the ship first comes into sight. Hence, one or another of the hypotheses which yield this false observational consequence is disconfirmed. Since H_2 already is very well *confirmed*, we assign the *dis*confirmation to H_1, the hypothesis that the Earth is flat.

---

* Omitting several steps. The entire pattern is

1. $\{[H_1 \cdot (H_2 \cdot \ldots)] \cdot (A_1 \cdot \ldots)\} \supset O$

2. $\sim O$

3. $\sim\{[H_1 \cdot (H_2 \cdot \ldots)] \cdot (A_1 \cdot \ldots)\}$

4. $\sim [H_1 \cdot (H_2 \cdot \ldots)] \vee \sim (A_1 \cdot \ldots)$

5. $\sim \sim (A_1 \cdot \ldots)$

6. $\sim [H_1 \cdot (H_2 \cdot \ldots)]$

7. $\sim H_1 \vee \sim (H_2 \cdot \ldots)$

8. $\sim \sim (H_2 \cdot \ldots)$

/∴ 9. $\sim H_1$

2

Criteria for
Confirmation
Instances

There is great disagreement as to the basic *criteria* for evaluating confirmation instances of an hypothesis. The following six are frequently discussed in the literature (although there certainly is no general agreement about their validity):

It is generally held that each confirming instance *increases* the degree of confirmation of an hypothesis, and similarly each disconfirming instance decreases the degree of confirmation of an hypothesis. (Indeed, if the auxiliary hypotheses and the statements of antecedent conditions all are true, then the falsified observational consequence not only *decreases the confirmation* of any hypothesis, it also *falsifies* it.)*

Some philosophers claim that the larger the class of (physically) *possible* confirming instances, the smaller the degree of confirmation afforded by any given number of actual confirming instances. For example, they would claim that if there are only about 100 million ravens in the world, then 100,000 observations of black ravens constitute better confirmation of the hypothesis "All ravens are black" than if there are, say, ten billion ravens.

But others would claim that *at best* this criterion only applies to cases where the number of possible confirming instances is small, and it is feasible to examine all, or almost all, possible confirming cases. For instance, they might be willing to accept this criterion with respect to an hypothesis such as "All American males over seven feet tall have flat feet", since so few American males are over seven feet tall, but they would deny it with respect to hypotheses such as "All ravens are black", since there are so many ravens that it is not feasible to examine all or even most ravens for color.

Another widely accepted criterion concerns what is called **instance variety**. According to this criterion, the more that confirming instances of a given hypothesis *differ* from each other (in relevant ways†), the better the resulting confirmation. For example, having already confirmed the sea

---

* Similar remarks do *not* apply to hypotheses having other forms. For example, disconfirming instances of the hypothesis "Every substance is soluble in some solvent or other", in symbols $(x)(\exists y)Sxy$, do not falsify that hypothesis. An example would be the (slightly) disconfirming instance of a substance that is not soluble in a particular solvent.

† The vital question as to how we are to distinguish relevant from irrelevant differences has not as yet received a satisfactory answer.

of air hypothesis by a test concerning a column of mercury, we now get better confirmation by testing some *other* substance, or by performing the mercury test on a mountain top (where the air pressure ought to be lower), than by simply performing the same kind of experiment with mercury over again at roughly the same elevation.

It is easy to see *why* instance variety is so important, for each new kind of instance is a test of a different *consequence* of an hypothesis. Suppose we examine 1,000 ravens for color, but they all happen to be *male* ravens. Then, in effect, although we have 1,000 confirming cases for the hypothesis "All ravens are black", we have not tested an important consequence of that hypothesis, namely the subhypothesis "All *female* ravens are black". Since *sex* is likely to be relevant to color, we obtain far better confirmation of the hypothesis "All ravens are black" by examining, say, 500 male and 500 female ravens, than by examining 1,000 male ravens.

Some philosophers hold to a theory called the **eliminative theory of confirmation**, according to which an hypothesis is confirmed only by those of its instances which also *disconfirm competing hypotheses.*

Take the example discussed in Chapter Fourteen concerning the hypothesis (H_1): "All people who contract type P food poisoning have eaten type F food, and assume that all confirming cases up to a given time happen to be cases in which food of type G also was eaten. Then, if we find a case of food poisoning in which food of type F was eaten, but *not* food of type G, we have a case in which the hypothesis (H_2): "All people who contract type P food poisoning have eaten type G food", competitor of the hypothesis (H_1), is eliminated. Hence, an instance of this kind is confirming for (H_1).

But if we merely find another case in which P and F are present, but no competitor of the hypothesis (H_1) is eliminated, then that case does not count as a *confirming* case for (H_1), even though it is an *instance* of it.

Some philosophers require that confirming instances be observations or tests performed *after* an hypothesis has been proposed, on the grounds that we can *always* construct theories which can account for the data observed up to a given point. According to this view, the trick is to construct hypotheses which not only account for what has been observed but also predict new phenomena.

However, there are at least two major difficulties with this view. First, although it always is *theoretically* possible to construct hypotheses which account for the observed data, we often *in fact* are unable to find such an hypothesis. At least we often are unable to construct *simple* theories of this kind.

And second, upon closer inspection the criterion turns out to be not so intuitively plausible as it seemed at first glance. For example, if Brown thinks of an hypothesis *before* a confirming instance is found for it, but Jones doesn't think of it until *after* the confirming instance, it follows from the criterion in question that the hypothesis is better confirmed for Brown than for Jones, even though Brown and Jones have identical evidence for it. Surely this is unreasonable.

Finally, there are several confirmation criteria of a more technical nature. An example is the requirement that an hypothesis be *genuinely relevant* to the derivation of its confirming instances. If an instance follows from the auxiliary hypotheses plus antecedent conditions *alone*, without the need of a given hypothesis, then the hypothesis is not confirmed by that instance.

The need for this requirement stems from the fact that if a given hypothesis, P, entails some instance Q, then $P \cdot R$ (where R is any hypothesis whatever) also entails Q. But we don't want Q to confirm R, because Q is not a *genuine consequence* of R.

3

Criteria for Hypothesis Acceptance

In addition to criteria for the acceptability of *confirmation instances*, there are so-called "nonevidential" criteria for the acceptability of well confirmed hypotheses. We need such criteria because *not all* well confirmed hypotheses can be accepted into the body of scientific knowledge. In particular we need criteria in order to select between competing well confirmed hypotheses.

Perhaps the most important of the nonevidential criteria is **simplicity**. It is generally supposed, even by many scientists, that simplicity is a mere matter of convenience or elegance. But nothing could be further from the truth. Of course, in determining between *equivalent* hypotheses, we choose the simpler hypothesis for the sake of convenience. But when we choose the simpler of two *nonequivalent* hypotheses, and choose it *because* it is simpler, something much more than convenience or elegance is involved.

The most striking examples of the use of simplicity concern curve fitting. Suppose the points on the following graph represent the results of experiments relating two factors, x and y.

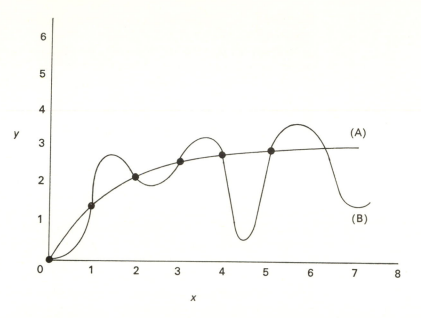

We ordinarily would draw the "smooth curve" (A) through the test points to represent our hypothesis as to how the two factors, x and y, relate to each other for values of x not yet tested for y. We surely would *not* draw the irregular curve (B) to serve this purpose. And yet *both curves*, (A) and (B), pass through all of the points representing the experimental results. Hence, the theories represented by these two curves are *equally well confirmed by the evidence.* We choose the hypothesis represented by curve (A) over the one represented by curve (B) *because it is the simpler of the two hypotheses.*

Or consider the two nonequivalent equations, (E_1): $x = y + 1$, and (E_2): $x = y^3 - 3y^2 + 3y + 1$, and suppose we observe that whenever $x = 1$, $y = 0$, whenever $x = 2$, $y = 1$, and whenever $x = 3$, $y = 2$. Since these values are exactly the ones entailed by (E_1) and (E_2), both of these hypotheses are confirmed, and indeed *equally* confirmed, by them. But surely we would reject (E_2) in favor of (E_1), because (E_1) is *simpler than* (E_2).

Notice that again our choice of the simpler hypothesis is *not* a mere matter of convenience or elegance. (E_1) and (E_2) are *different hypotheses.* They predict *different* results for values of y greater than 2. (For instance,

Induction and Science

for $y = 3$, (E_1) predicts that $x = 4$, while (E_2) predicts that $x = 10$.) Consequently, it makes a great deal of difference which one of these two hypotheses we choose. So to some extent, simplicity determines our beliefs about the world.

Statistical (Probability) Pattern of Confirmation

In Chapter Fourteen, we characterized the general form of statistical inference as

1. *N* percent of all *F*'s tested have *G*.

/∴ 2. *N* percent of all *F*'s (tested or otherwise) have *G*.

Let's now introduce a slightly different pattern, in order to illustrate more clearly how statistical hypotheses are confirmed:

1. If *N* percent of all *F*'s have *G*, then in a random sample of sufficient size,* about *N* percent of all *F*'s will probably have *G*.

2. In a particular random sample of sufficiently large size, about *N* percent of all *F*'s have *G*.

/∴ 3. *N* percent of all *F*'s have *G*.

Analogously, let's introduce a slightly different basic pattern of *disconfirmation* for statistical hypotheses:

1. If *N* percent of all *F*'s have *G*, then in a random sample of sufficiently large size, about *N* percent of all *F*'s will probably have *G*.

_____

* The question as to what constitutes a *random* sample that is *sufficiently large* is a quite difficult one.

2. Concerning a particular observed random sample of sufficiently large size it is *not* the case that about *N* percent of all *F*'s have *G*.

/∴ 3. It is not the case that *N* percent of all *F*'s have *G*.

(Notice that a disconfirming case for a statistical hypothesis in general does *not falsify* that hypothesis. This follows from the fact that *N* percent of *all F*'s still may have *G*, even though *N* percent of the *F*'s in the *sample* do not.)

In addition to the general kinds of criteria of confirmation for *categorical* hypotheses discussed above, there are special criteria for statistical hypotheses, concerned in particular with the evaluation of evidence samples. An example of this sort of criterion is *standard deviation*, based on the idea that a group of samples whose relative frequencies closely resemble each other confirm an hypothesis better than a group of samples which do not.

5

Scientific Explanation

The nature of explanation

Explanation, *confirmation*, and *prediction* all are closely related. An hypothesis is *confirmed* by what it *predicts*, and it also *explains* that which it predicts.

This close relationship often is masked by the elliptical nature of most explanations in daily life. For example, in daily life, if a child asks why a match lit, the answer "because it was scratched (heated)" constitutes an acceptable explanation. But a more *complete* explanation would be that the match lit because it was heated in the presence of oxygen, and all (well made) matches light when heated in the presence of oxygen.

This more complete explanation makes reference, first, to a *general hypothesis* (namely the hypothesis that all well made matches heated in the presence of oxygen light), and second, to **antecedent conditions** (namely the conditions that the match in question was well made, and was heated in the presence of oxygen).

In general, an explanation is satisfactory if (1) the general hypotheses appealed to are well confirmed and have satisfied the nonevidential criteria for acceptable hypotheses, such as simplicity; (2) the antecedent conditions are true, or at least well confirmed; and (3) the thing explained *follows from* the general hypotheses plus antecedent conditions.

Deductive nomological explanation

If the thing explained *deductively* follows from the general hypotheses and antecedent conditions, then the explanation is said to be a **deductive nomological explanation.*** Its basic pattern can be put as follows:

1. $H_1, H_2, \ldots$

2. $A_1, A_2, \ldots$

/∴   3. E

(where $H_1, H_2, \ldots$ are general hypotheses, $A_1, A_2, \ldots$ are antecedent conditions, and E is the event being explained).

The match explanation mentioned above is an example of a deductive nomological explanation, since the lighting of the match follows *deductively* from the general hypothesis plus antecedent conditions.

Nondeductive (probabilistic) explanation

Many explanations are not deductive. According to one standard account, **probabilistic explanations** have the general pattern:

1. The probability of E, given A, $= n$

2. a is a case of A

/∴   3. The probability of a being an event of type $E = n$.

For example, if the probability of death in any given year (E), given that one has Hodgkin's disease (A) $= .95$, and if Jones has Hodgkin's disease, then the probability that Jones will die in any given year equals .95, which explains why Jones died.† (Ordinarily, we would furnish only

---

* Using the terminology of Hans Reichenbach and Carl Hempel, whose "explanation of explanation" is being followed here.

† Perhaps it would be better to say that it *probably* explains why Jones died. Often, when more than one cause for an event is possible, we can only determine a *probable* cause for that event.

the elliptical explanation that Jones died because he had Hodgkin's disease.)

Unfortunately, nondeductive explanations are not quite that simple. For instance, we do not believe that Jones died of Hodgkin's disease *simply* because the probability = .95 that anyone with that disease won't live out the year. Our acceptance of Hodgkin's disease as the explanation of death is based *also* on our knowledge that the probability of death in any given year for those who *don't* have that disease (but otherwise are similar) is a great deal lower. So at the very least, we must amend the basic pattern of probabilistic (nondeductive) explanation to read:

1.　The probability of E, given A, $= n$.

2.　The probability of E, given $\sim A$, $= m$
　　(where n is much greater than m).

3.　a is a case of A.

$/\therefore$　4.　Probably (a is a case of E).

Explanations of hypotheses

It is often claimed that many explanations which fit one of the basic patterns described above are not *really* explanations.

Take the deductive nomological explanation that a particular match lit because all matches heated in the presence of oxygen light, and that match was heated in the presence of oxygen. It is claimed that a *real* explanation of the lighting of the match would explain it in terms of *combustion*, that is, the rapid chemical combination of oxygen with materials in the match. In other words, it is claimed that the use of mere *empirical generalizations* does not yield satisfactory explanations. The hypotheses used in genuine explanations, so it is claimed, must be *theoretical*, not *empirical*, hypotheses.*

But there is good reason to think that this claim is much too strong. In the first place, in daily life we often accept explanations that make use of empirical hypotheses, although it is true that explanations employing theoretical hypotheses (or what are *taken to be* theoretical hypotheses) are considered to be better. And in the second place, the very distinction

---

* The difference between empirical and theoretical hypotheses is explained in Section 6, below.

between empirical and theoretical hypotheses is one which many philosophers would challenge (as we shall challenge it in Section 6). At the very least, the distinction must be drawn so that many allegedly theoretical hypotheses, such as the hypothesis that food decay is caused by bacteria, turn out to be empirical. But surely the explanation that, say, a bottle of milk spoiled because of bacterial action constitutes an acceptable explanation.

Spurious explanations

Many supposedly scientific explanations fail to conform to the above model of explanation, and many acceptable scientific theories often are used in spurious explanations.

The theory of evolution constitutes a good example of a legitimate scientific theory which is sometimes used in an illegitimate way in spurious explanations.

For instance, the explanation that a given species of rabbits failed to survive because rabbits of that species were not "fit" to survive is spurious if the *only evidence* of unfitness provided is that the species in fact failed to survive. For to say that the rabbits died because they were unfit to survive comes close to saying that they failed to survive because they failed to survive, which is *logically true*, and hence has no empirical content.

Similarly, the economist who says that the price of wheat rose because *demand* was greater than *supply*, provides a spurious explanation, unless he provides further data. If his reason for believing that demand was greater than supply is simply that the price of wheat rose, then he is saying little more than that the price rose because the price rose.

Of course, many explanations in terms of supply and demand are *not* spurious. If the economist who explains that the price of certain stocks went down because supply exceeded demand then goes on to state that the increase in supply was due to the sale of large blocks of stocks by institutions and mutual funds caused by lack of confidence in the economy, then his explanation is legitimate.

The structure of an acceptable scientific explanation must be such that the event explained could have been *predicted* from the general hypotheses employed plus antecedent conditions.*

The explanation that a particular piece of metal expanded because it was

---

* At least this is true for *deductive* explanations. Whether it is true for *probabilistic* explanations is a very difficult question.

heated, and all metals expand when heated, illustrates this connection between legitimate explanations and predictions. If we had known ahead of time that the piece of metal was to be heated, then we could have *predicted* that it would expand, since metals expand when heated. Any explanation which fails this "prediction test" must be regarded as spurious.

So-called "vitalistic" explanations furnish many examples of spurious explanation. An example is the explanation that a particular organism regenerated a lost limb because of certain nonphysical teleological agencies, called "entelechies", which direct organic processes within a range left open by the principles of Physics and Chemistry.

This vitalistic explanation is spurious because it does not imply, and hence does not *predict*, exactly when or under what conditions the given organism will regenerate a limb. And it fails to predict because the general theory which it employs about entelechies, even taken in conjunction with antecedent conditions, *implies nothing specific*.

Vitalism, as a theory, suffers from the same ailment as the "Monday morning quarterback". *After* the game, the Monday morning quarterback is expert at "explaining" why the game went as it did. But *before* the game, he is unable to *predict* correctly how the game will turn out.

6

Theories and Theoretical Entities

In Section 2, Chapter Fourteen, we presented the pattern of *inductive generalization* as one of the basic patterns of nondeductive inference. Recall that one version of that pattern was

1. $Fa \cdot Ga$

2. $Fb \cdot Gb$

3. $Fc \cdot Gc$
     ⋮

N.   No F is known not to have G

───────────────────────────

/∴ $N + 1$.   All F's are G's.

This pattern dovetails nicely with the general principle behind our exposition of the notion of *confirmation*, namely that in general an hypothesis is confirmed by its *instances*. Notice that $Fa \cdot Ga$, $Fb \cdot Gb$, etc., are *instances* of the hypothesis "All *F*'s are *G*'s", and that they *confirm* that hypothesis, as well as providing evidence from which to *infer to* it. So what we have said in various places about these related matters is quite consistent.

But many philosophers would claim that this empiricist account of the matter, while adequate to explain a small *part* of scientific method, is not adequate as a complete account. In particular, they claim that what we have done is to account for the role of **empirical hypotheses** in science, while failing to account for the role of what they call **theoretical hypotheses**.

The difference between empirical and theoretical hypotheses is illustrated by the sea of air theory. When a farmer notices that his pump will raise water only to a height of about 34′, and notices that the same is true for his neighbors' pump, his conclusion that *all* pumps will raise water only to a height of about 34′ constitutes an *empirical* hypothesis. Roughly, his observation is said to be an empirical hypothesis because (1) it is a mere inductive generalization of the observational instances which constitute his evidence, and (2) his hypothesis is about the very same kinds of entities that his observational instances are about (namely pumps and water raised by pumps). In particular, his hypothesis is not theoretical because it makes no reference to **theoretical (unobservable) entities** as opposed to **empirical (observational) entities**.

But now consider the sea of air hypothesis, which explains *why* pumps raise water a maximum of about 34′. In this case, the theory is about some entities, such as *air pressure*, which are not directly observable, and which the evidence concerning pumps and water is *not* about. Hence, the sea of air hypothesis is a *theoretical hypothesis*, or simply a *theory*, whereas the pump hypothesis is merely an *empirical* hypothesis.

In general, the charge against what we have said about scientific method is (first) that *theories* have a different logic (play a different role in science) than do empirical hypotheses, and (second) that our account of inductive inference, confirmation, and explanation, applies only to empirical hypotheses.

If true, this charge is certainly of major importance, for most of the important hypotheses of science resemble the sea of air hypothesis much more than they resemble the water-pump hypothesis.

There is no denying that science does characteristically construct such hypotheses as the one about the sea of air, and indeed use them to explain lower level hypotheses such as the one about the water-pump. The question is whether there is a *significant difference* between these two kinds of hypotheses. Many philosophers would deny that there is, roughly for the following reasons:

(1) There is some question as to whether the distinction between empirical and theoretical hypotheses can be drawn even roughly in a way which supports the claim that our account of confirmation, explanation, etc., does not apply to theoretical hypotheses. In particular, it seems questionable to make the distinction between empirical and theoretical hypotheses rest on the *observability* of the entities the hypotheses are about, since many, perhaps even most, alleged theoretical hypotheses are *not* about unobservables. For instance, the hypothesis that certain kinds of food decay are caused by bacteria, which is often taken to be a theoretical hypothesis, concerns *bacteria*, which can be observed by means of a microscope.*

(2) The other criterion frequently used to distinguish empirical from theoretical hypotheses is that theoretical hypotheses say things about entities *not* mentioned in their evidence, whereas empirical hypotheses are mere generalizations of their instances, saying nothing about entities not mentioned in their evidence.

For example, the hypothesis that all ravens are black, claimed to be an empirical hypothesis, is confirmed by what constitute recognizable *instances* (such as "*a* is a raven and is black", "*b* is a raven and is black", etc.) of that hypothesis. But Newton's Law of Gravitation, claimed to be a theoretical hypothesis, does not seem to have any recognizable instances in isolation from the other universal generalizations which comprise Newtonian mechanics (such as the laws of motion). For example, the

---

* It has been claimed that entities such as bacteria are *not* observable in that they cannot be observed by the *unaided* use of one or more of the five senses. But surely the restriction of observability to what can be observed through the unaided use of the five senses is much too strong. For instance, the person who wears glasses is generally taken to perceive the observable world when he looks through his glasses. (Similar remarks apply to someone who uses a hearing aid.) There seems to be no essential difference between looking at the world through eye glasses and looking at the world through a microscope. Hence, if what is observed through eye glasses is considered to be observable, then what is observed through a microscope must be also. Bacteria, then, must be counted as observable entities. And, in general, we cannot make the distinction between empirical and theoretical hypotheses rest on the observability or nonobservability of the properties or entities they are about.

Induction and Science

motion of the Earth around the Sun at any given time does not seem to constitute an instance of Newton's gravitation law *alone*, but rather of the whole of Newtonian mechanics (given a great many antecedent conditions, such as the masses of the Earth, Sun, Moon, etc., and their velocities at a particular time).

There are two important things to be said about this claim. First, the claim that Newton's Law of Gravitation has no recognizable instances seems flatly false. For example, it seems plausible to say that the motion of the Earth around the Sun at a given time is an instance of this law, since it is a case in which two bodies (the Earth and Sun) are attracted to each other with a force which is proportional to the product of their mass and inversely proportional to the square of the distance between them, as Newton's Law of Gravitation requires. Of course, we cannot directly *observe* this attractive force, and we must use other hypotheses of Newtonian mechanics in order to infer from what we actually observed (plus antecedent conditions) to the conclusion that this *is* an instance of Newton's Law of Gravitation. But we have already argued that observability is not a pertinent criterion, and even in the case of the hypothesis that all ravens are black we must use other hypotheses in order to infer from what we actually observe (plus antecedent conditions) to the conclusion that a given case is an instance of that hypothesis. (For example, we must use a theory of light according to which *looking* black—even with a purple tinge—in certain light constitutes evidence that something *is* black.)

And second, even supposing that the first point is incorrect, that is, even supposing that empirical hypotheses *can* be distinguished from theoretical hypotheses in the way just described, it still does not follow that what we have said about science applies only to a small number of scientific hypotheses. It still may be the case that what we have said about *inductive generalization* applies to theoretical as well as empirical hypotheses. And it is in fact the case that what we have said about *confirmation* and *explanation* does in fact apply to theoretical as well as empirical hypotheses. For instance, from Newton's Law of Gravitation (H_1), plus other laws of Newtonian mechanics ($H_2 \cdot \ldots$), plus antecedent conditions ($A_1 \cdot \ldots$), we can infer to the motion of the Earth around the Sun at a particular time (O), so that the occurrence of O constitutes a *confirming instance* for H_1, and the occurrence of O is *explained* by $H_1 \cdot (H_2 \cdot \ldots)$ plus the antecedent conditions.

Hence, we are justified in concluding that what we have said constitutes a *general*, and not merely a restricted, account of the role of generalization, confirmation, and explanation in science.

7

The Justification
of Induction

No account of the philosophy of science is complete without a discussion of the problem of the justification of induction. Recall that the characteristic mark of all inductive (nondeductive) arguments is a "gap" between premises and conclusion. As soon as this gap was realized,* the question was raised as to *how any inductive argument can be valid*. That is, the question was raised as to the *rationality* of the acceptance of hypotheses on inductive grounds.

Unfortunately, a good answer to this question has been hard to come by. A great many solutions to the problem of induction have been proposed, most of which can be classified into four categories:

(1) The most obvious thought is that we are justified in using induction because it "works". All of science is based on inductive conclusions of some sort or other, and everyone knows how successful science is. Everyone knows that scientific method, which uses induction, *works*.

Unfortunately, this obvious solution to the problem is not satisfactory. It simply isn't true that we know that induction works, or is successful. At best, what we know is that it *has worked*, or *has been successful*. But will it be successful in the future? We don't know. Indeed, the problem seems to be that we haven't the *slightest reason* to think induction will be successful in the future.

It often is claimed that in fact we *do* have a very good reason for thinking that induction will be successful in the future, namely *its success in the past*. But only a little thought is needed to see that this reason will not do. For to argue that induction *will be* successful because it *has been* successful is to argue *inductively*. (The premise of such an argument is "Induction has been successful [on the whole] up to now", and its conclusion is "Induction always will be successful [on the whole]". Clearly, this argument itself is an inductive argument.) So when we argue this way, we use induction to *justify itself*, which means that we argue circularly, and hence fallaciously.

---

* The philosopher David Hume was the first person to perceive it clearly, and the first person to state and try to solve the problem of the justification of induction.

(2) Perhaps the most popular solutions to the problem of induction are those which make use of some principle concerning the *uniformity of nature*, such as the principle that *every event has a cause.*

For instance, if we assume that nature is uniform, then we can reason inductively from the fact that all *examined* pieces of copper are uniform with respect to conductivity to the conclusion that all pieces of copper *whatsoever* (examined or as yet unexamined) are uniform with respect to conductivity.

But solutions of this kind are unsatisfactory. In the first place, it is perfectly possible for nature to be uniform and yet any given case not be an example of a uniformity. Similarly, even if we are entitled to assume that every event has a cause, it doesn't follow that we are entitled to assume that a *particular* event is the cause of some other particular event. And in the second place, the assumption that every event has a cause, or that nature is uniform, itself can be challenged. *Why* assume that nature is uniform? Again, there seems to be no answer. (Remember that we cannot argue that the assumption that nature is uniform has been fruitful in the past, and hence is likely to be fruitful in the future, for such an argument would be an *inductive* argument, and we cannot use induction to justify a principle of uniformity and then use that principle to justify the use of induction.)

(3) Some philosophers have proposed justifications based on the so-called "self-corrective" nature of induction. For example, suppose we conclude that half of 10,000 tosses of a coin will land heads up, on the basis of the evidence that half of the first 100 tosses of this coin landed heads up. This conclusion may or may not be true. But suppose it is false. Then we can "correct" this conclusion simply by observing larger and larger samples of tosses of the coin, basing our conclusion as to the relative frequency of heads in the total series of 10,000 tosses on the relative frequency of heads in the largest sample we have at any given time. If we continue the process long enough, at some point we must reach the correct value. Hence, it is claimed, we are justified in using inductive reasoning in such cases, because the process is self-correcting, in that repeated applications must get us closer and closer to the truth.

But again, we must reject the proposed solution to the problem. It is true that repeated applications of the proper inductive procedure finally yield conclusions which come closer and closer to being true (in cases in which *finite* classes are involved). For instance, if one-half of 10,000 tosses of a coin *in fact* will land heads up, then repeated application of the proper inductive rules *must* yield conclusions which come closer and closer to the value 1/2.

However, there is no guarantee that inductive procedures will get closer and closer to the truth *concerning events which are still in the future*. If we get heads on exactly half of the first 5,000 tosses, then we know with deductive certainty that the relative frequency of heads compared to total tosses in the entire series of 10,000 tosses must be somewhere between 1/4 and 3/4.* Hence our prediction that half of the 10,000 tosses will be heads cannot be off by more than $\pm 1/4$.

Now suppose that after 8,000 tosses the observed relative frequency of heads is still 1/2. Then we know at this point that the relative frequency of heads in the total series of 10,000 tosses must be somewhere between 2/5 and 3/5.† Hence, at this point our prediction that half of the 10,000 tosses will be heads cannot be off by more than $\pm 1/10$.

So we are getting closer and closer to the correct value (no matter what that value happens to be), since the *largest possible error* in our predictions keeps getting smaller and smaller. But the closeness of our prediction to the correct value results from the fact that larger and larger portions of the series concern *past tosses*, and are incorporated into our *evidence*, while smaller and smaller portions of the series concern *future tosses*. At no point do we have any guarantee that we are getting any closer to the actual relative frequency of heads among *future* (unexamined) tosses of the coin. But if the self-corrective claim is to have any force, it must apply to predictions about the *future* (or the as yet unexamined past).

The situation is even worse with respect to series which are infinitely long, since the relative frequency of any given *finite portion* of an infinite series is compatible with *any* relative frequency whatsoever in the infinite series. For instance, even if every one of millions of tosses of a coin lands heads up, an infinite series of tosses (assuming an infinite series of tosses is possible) could have a limit of the relative frequency of heads to total tosses equal to zero. Hence, for infinite series, inductive practices embody no self-corrective feature whatever.

---

* If the 5,000 remaining tosses all are tails, then the relative frequency will be 1/4, and if they all are heads, then the relative frequency will be 3/4.

† If the 2,000 remaining tosses all are tails, then the relative frequency will be 2/5, and if they all are heads, then the relative frequency will be 3/5.

We must conclude, then, that we cannot justify the use of induction on the grounds that it is self-correcting.

(4) Finally, there are the so-called "dissolutions" of the problem of induction, according to which the very problem itself is a pseudoproblem. We shall consider two of the many solutions of this kind. In the first of these two solutions, it is claimed that it is not rational to doubt the principles of inductive reasoning since these principles themselves *determine* (in part) what it *means* to be rational. In other words, if you doubt the rationality (i.e., the reasonableness) of the use of induction, then you simply don't know what it *means* to be rational.

Unfortunately, this argument is defective. If we were to find ourselves in a community in which it is considered rational to believe everything said by the oldest member of the community, it would be reasonable to inquire if it *really* is rational to do so. And if the reply were that what it *means* to be rational is to believe the oldest member of the community, then it would be perfectly proper to ask *why we ought to be rational*. And put into this context the problem of induction is that we seem to have no answer to the question "why be rational", either for the peculiar concept of rationality in the imaginary community just described or for the concept of rationality in the real community.

In the second solution to be considered, it also is claimed that there is no problem of justifying the use of inductive principles because *no justification is possible*, and if none is possible, then none can be required.

Two kinds of arguments have been presented in support of this claim. First, it has been argued that a justification must be either *inductive* or *deductive*. An inductive justification would be circular, since it would use the very principles of reasoning we are trying to justify. And a deductive argument would never work, because we cannot prove deductively that nature is uniform, or that every event has a cause, or that the future will resemble the past.*

But this argument is defective. It is true that metaphysical assumptions, such as the uniformity of nature, cannot be proved deductively. But a deductive justification does not *necessarily* require that any such principle

---

* Actually, what is generally meant by such an argument is that metaphysical principles of this kind are not *theorems of logic*, or *deductively obtainable from the null set of premises*, or *knowable prior to any particular empirical observations*.

be proved. Perhaps other kinds of assumptions can be proved which will justify the use of induction.*

Second, it has been argued that just as the theorems in an axiom system cannot all be proved (without circularity or infinite regress), so also all principles of *reasoning* or *inferring* cannot be justified (without circularity or infinite regress). Hence, we should not be surprised that no justification of induction is possible.

Clearly, there is something to this argument. It is true that we cannot justify *every* principle of reasoning any more than we can prove every theorem. And it may well be that the basic inductive principle will be among those which remain forever unjustified, and hence remain forever as a kind of primitive inference rule. But the argument in question does not *prove* this. All that it proves is that *some principles or other* will remain unjustified. It does not prove that *induction* is that principle.

On the other hand, recognition of the important fact that some principles or other must remain unjustified may serve to make it more tolerable that as yet no one seems to have been able to justify the basic inductive principles which are the foundation of scientific method.

* For instance, the pragmatic justification presented by Hans Reichenbach is based on an attempt to prove deductively that if any method of predicting the future is successful, then the use of induction will be successful. Unfortunately, the justification is fallacious (for rather complicated reasons). But it has never been proved that a justification *like* it might not be successful.

Part Five Chapter Seventeen

Logic and Philosophy

Some Recent Applications of Logic in Philosophy

Logical systems of the kind developed in the first two parts of this text have been very useful tools for philosophers, logicians, scientists, and mathematicians. In particular, they have been used by some twentieth century philosophers in their attempt to get a clearer grasp on several of the central problems in philosophy.

But the application of modern symbolic logic to philosophy proper has yielded another, perhaps bitter, kind of fruit. For once the notation and proof technique of predicate logic is employed, important problems come into sharp focus, to which insufficient attention was paid previously. In this chapter we consider four of the more perplexing of these problems.

1

Dispositionals

In Chapter Fourteen, we stated that there is a long tradition in philosophy which distinguishes properties of objects into two kinds, namely *observable*, or *manifest*, properties and *dispositional*, or *power*, properties.

We stated that *observable properties* of objects can be recognized by means of one or more of the five senses, while *dispositional properties* cannot. Thus, we can observe that something *burns*, but not that it is *flammable* (although if it *is* flammable, and if we ignite it, we can observe that it burns). And we can see that something *bends*, but not that it is *flexible* (although if it *is* flexible, and we apply suitable pressure to it, then we can observe that it bends). Burning and bending are observable properties, while flammability and flexibility are dispositional properties.

Obviously, the dispositional, nonobservable, property of being flammable is *closely connected* to the observable property of burning, for to say that something is *flammable* is to say that it has the *power to burn*, or the *disposition to burn*, under certain conditions. Similarly, the dispositional property of being flexible is closely connected to the observable property of bending, for to say that something is *flexible* is to say that it has the *power to bend*, or the *disposition to bend,* under certain conditions. And so on.

It is generally recognized that most English terms ending in "-able", "-uble", and "-ible" are dispositional terms, but it is often overlooked that many other terms are dispositional also. (Perhaps it would be more accurate to say that many other terms are both dispositional *and* observational, often being used in both senses at once.) Take the term "red". Sometimes, when we say that something is red, we mean that it *looks* red, in which case we are using that term in its observational sense (as we would be using the term "bent" if we said of a stick partly immersed in water that it *looks* bent—without thereby judging whether or not it really *is* bent). And sometimes when we say that something is red, we mean that it *is* red (whatever color it may *look*), in which case we are using that term in its dispositional sense. Of course, there are times when we say that something is red meaning both that it looks red and is red.

We tend to overlook the fact that properties such as redness (*being* red) are dispositional properties, perhaps because their connections with observable properties are more complex than, say, the connections between flexibility and bending. For something can *be* red but not *look* red (for instance, under a blue light), or *look* red but not *be* red (for instance, under a red light). Nevertheless, *being* red is a dispositional property. And there is a fairly definite, although complex, relationship between being red and observable properties such as looking red, looking violet, etc.

We also tend to overlook the *dual role* played by color terms, as well as the terms referring to tastes, smells, sounds, etc. And yet there are many cases in which this duality is quite familiar. For instance, when a salesman tells a customer that a particular coat *looks* blue (under a certain light), he is using the term "blue" to refer to an observational property. But when he guarantees that a particular coat *is* blue, even though it may not *look* blue under artificial store light, he is using the term "blue" to refer to a dispositional property.

Up to this point, we have been speaking rather loosely. For instance, we said that something is flammable if it has the "disposition" or "power" to burn, under certain conditions. But what does it mean to say that something has a disposition or power?

Philosophers have only recently paid much attention to this question, perhaps because there is a simple, natural answer which seems quite satisfactory at first glance. For instance, it seems natural to suppose that if we say of a particular lump of sugar that it has the dispositional property of being soluble, we mean simply that *if* we place it in water (under suitable conditions concerning temperature, water saturation, etc.) *then* it will dissolve. Similarly, if we say that a plastic tube is flexible, we mean that *if* suitable pressure is applied to it, *then* it will bend. And so on.

Therefore, it seems initially plausible to say that given a sentence containing a dispositional term, we can replace it by an "If _____ then _____" sentence containing not the dispositional term but rather what we might call its "observational mate". For instance, we seem able to replace the dispositional sentence "Lump of sugar *s* is soluble" by the statement "If *s* is placed in water under certain conditions, then *s* will dissolve", and replace the dispositional sentence "Piece of wood *w* is flammable" by the sentence "If oxygen and heat are applied to *w* under certain conditions, then *w* will burn" (where the proper conditions are dryness, etc.).

All of this seems reasonable *until* we try to put these sentences into the symbolic notation of predicate logic, or into some other equally precise notation.

Take the dispositional sentence "Lump of sugar *s* is soluble". It seems plausible to translate that sentence into the nondispositional sentence "If *s* is placed in water, then it will dissolve", symbolized as $Ws \supset Ds$ (omitting the qualification about suitable conditions for the moment). But does the sentence $Ws \supset Ds$ really mean the same thing as the dispositional sentence "Lump of sugar *s* is soluble"? Unfortunately, it does not.

To see that it does not, consider the *false* dispositional sentence "Piece of copper *c* is soluble" and its analogous translation into "If *c* is placed in water, then *c* will dissolve", symbolized as $Wc \supset Dc$. Suppose we *never* place *c* in water, so that the antecedent Wc is false. If so, then the whole sentence $Wc \supset Dc$ will be true, because all conditional statements with false antecedents are true. But if the sentence $Wc \supset Dc$ is true, it cannot possibly be a correct translation of the *false* sentence "Piece of copper *c* is soluble", since a sentence and its correct translation cannot have different truth values.

Analogously, the translation of the sentence "Lump of sugar *s* is soluble" into $Ws \supset Ds$ also must be incorrect, even though in this case, luckily, both the sentence translated and the sentence it is translated into do have the same truth value. That this *is* a matter of luck becomes obvious when we realize that the analogous translation of the sentence "Lump of sugar *s* is *not* soluble", into "If *s* is placed in water then it will *not* dissolve", also is true if *s* is never placed in water. But surely, the two statements "*s* is soluble" and "*s* is *not* soluble" both cannot be true.

To put the difficulty another way, if we translate all dispositional sentences into nondispositional conditional sentences in the above way, then all of these conditionals with false antecedents will have to be judged to be true, even though many of the dispositional sentences they are intended to translate (for example, "Piece of copper *c* is soluble", "Lump of sugar *s* is not soluble", etc.) are false.

The conclusion we must draw is that dispositional sentences cannot be replaced by nondispositional sentences of conditional form, or at least not in this simple way. The so-called "problem of dispositionals" is to find a satisfactory way to translate sentences of this type.

2

Counterfactuals

It has been suggested that the correct analysis of dispositional sentences is not into *indicative* conditionals but rather into **subjunctive** or **contrary-to-fact conditionals**. For instance, according to this view, the correct translation of "*s* is soluble" is not into the indicative conditional "If *s* is placed in water, then it will dissolve" but rather into the subjunctive conditional "If *s* *were* placed in water, then it *would* dissolve", or into the *contrary-to-fact* conditional "If *s* *had been* placed in water, then it *would have* dissolved".

The trouble with this analysis of dispositional sentences into subjunctive or contrary-to-fact (counterfactual) conditionals is that subjunctive and counterfactual sentences themselves present a translation problem just as baffling as that presented by dispositional sentences.

Take the problems involved in translating the counterfactual "If s had been placed in water, then it would have dissolved". Suppose we try to translate that sentence into the truth functional notation of propositional or predicate logic.

The obvious starting point in such a translation procedure would seem to be to replace the "If _____ then _____" of the counter-factual by means of the $\supset$ of truth functional logic. If we do so, then the counterfactual in question translates into "(s had been placed in water) $\supset$ (s would have dissolved)". The trouble with this translation is that its antecedent and consequent are not sentences, and so the whole conditional is not a sentence. To make it a sentence, we must replace the subjunctive an-tecedent and consequent with their corresponding "mates" in the *indicative* mood. For instance, we must replace the antecedent "s had been placed in water" by the indicative sentence "s is placed in water", and replace the consequent "s would have dissolved" by the indicative sentence "s dissolves" (or "s will dissolve"). The result is the translation of the counter-factual "If s had been placed in water, then it would have dissolved" into the indicative conditional "If s is placed in water, then s will dissolve", in symbols $P \supset D$. In a similar way, we can translate all of the other counterfactuals. For instance, we can translate the counterfactual "If p had been placed under suitable pressure, then it would have bent" into "If p is placed under suitable pressure, then p bends", in symbols $P \supset B$. And so on.

But once we actually translate in this way, it becomes obvious that such translations are unsatisfactory, because the end product of this translation procedure for counterfactual sentences is exactly the same, and just as inadequate, as the end product of the translation procedure for disposi-tional sentences discussed in the last section. For example, consider the pair of counterfactual sentences "If s had been placed in water, then it would have dissolved" and its contrary "If s had been placed in water, then it would *not* have dissolved". Clearly, one or the other of these two sentences must be false. But when translated in the suggested way, they both translate into true sentences, since they both translate into sentences with the false antecedent "s is placed in water", and all conditional sentences with false antecedents are true. It follows then that the suggested method of translating counterfactual sentences cannot be correct. The

Logic and Philosophy

so-called "problem of counterfactuals" is to find a satisfactory translation for sentences which are contrary-to-fact.

3

The Raven Paradox

The discussion of the concept of confirmation in Chapter Sixteen informally presented the idea that generalizations are confirmed by their *instances*. Let's now make this idea a bit more specific, in particular with respect to one kind of generalization, by introducing a very plausible principle, often called the "confirmation principle". According to the **confirmation principle**, one way to *confirm* (increase the degree of credibility of) universal generalizations of the form "All *P*'s are *Q*'s" is to find things which are both *P*'s and *Q*'s, and one way to *disconfirm* a universal generalization of this form is to find things which are *P*'s but not *Q*'s. For example, according to this principle, evidence that there are black ravens confirms the universal generalization "All ravens are black" (the more ravens observed, the higher the *degree* of confirmation), and evidence that there are ravens which are not black disconfirms that generalization.

Equally plausible is the **equivalence principle**, which states that whatever confirms a given sentence equally confirms all logically equivalent sentences. This principle is accepted by many philosophers because they believe that there is a sense in which sentences which are equivalent say the very same thing, only in different words.* For instance, the equivalent sentences "It is not the case that it will both rain and snow" (in symbols $\sim(R \cdot S)$) and "Either it won't rain or it won't snow" (in symbols $\sim R \vee \sim S$) seem to say the very same thing, only in different words. Thus, it appears to be plausible to suppose that whatever confirms $\sim(R \cdot S)$ equally confirms $\sim R \vee \sim S$, and vice versa.

But when we put these two apparently plausible principles together, and become precise as to the correct symbolizations of universal generalizations, we immediately get into difficulty. Consider the sentence "All nonblack things are nonravens". Using the notation of predicate logic, it seems plausible to symbolize that sentence as $(x)(\sim Bx \supset \sim Rx)$, where Bx = "*x* is black", and Rx = "*x* is a raven". According to the confirmation principle, that sentence is confirmed by observations of nonblack nonravens, the more the better. The trouble is that the sentence

---

* The equivalence principle also is accepted (for other reasons) by some philosophers who reject the idea that equivalent sentences say the same thing.

$(x)(\sim Bx \supset \sim Rx)$ is *logically equivalent* to the sentence $(x)(Rx \supset Bx)$ (in English, "All ravens are black"), so that according to the equivalence principle whatever confirms the former equally confirms the latter. Thus, observations of brown shoes, green desk blotters, white chalk, blue walls, etc., all nonblack nonravens, which confirm $(x)(\sim Bx \supset \sim Rx)$ according to the confirmation principle, also equally confirm the logically equivalent sentence $(x)(Rx \supset Bx)$ according to the equivalence principle. We seem able to confirm the hypothesis that all ravens are black without ever examining ravens for color. Attractive as this sort of "indoor ornithology" may be, the natural inclination is to suspect that something must be wrong. The whole process seems paradoxical (indeed in the literature it is referred to as "the paradox of the ravens" or "the paradox of confirmation"). The problem is to remove the paradox while doing least violence to our other philosophical assumptions.

Notice that this confirmation problem is a problem in *inductive*, not deductive logic. It is not a question of going from true premises to a false conclusion by apparently valid means, because in inductive logic valid rules of inference (such as the confirmation principle—assuming that it is valid) are not supposed to *guarantee* that one cannot infer from true premises to a false conclusion by their means. Nevertheless, the paradox does pose a perplexing problem, and (hopefully) one on which light can be shed by the use of the apparatus of predicate logic.

Four general kinds of solutions to the raven paradox have been proposed. One kind attempts to solve the problem by rejecting the equivalence principle; a second by rejecting the confirmation principle; a third by rejecting the standard predicate logic symbolizations of sentences having the forms "All *P*'s and *Q*'s", "Everything is either a non-*P* or a *Q*", etc.; and a fourth by rejecting our intuitive feelings of paradoxicality at confirming a sentence such as "All ravens are black" by means of observations of brown shoes, blue walls, etc.

Strangely, it is the fourth of these possible alternatives which is most often taken. According to the most widely accepted solution to the raven paradox, it is the intuitive feeling of paradoxicality attending the confirmation of hypotheses such as "All ravens are black" by evidence such as the examination of nonblack nonravens which is mistaken. Advocates of this view claim that the more closely we examine the process in question the less paradoxical it will seem. For instance, it will appear to be less paradoxical to confirm "All ravens are black" by examination of a nonblack nonraven once we notice that *taken by itself* this evidence not only confirms that hypothesis but also the hypotheses "All ravens are nonblack", "All things are nonblack", "All things are nonravens", etc.

We tend to forget some of these other hypotheses because we know that they are false from other evidence. For instance, we know that the hypothesis "All things are nonblack" is false, because we know that there are many black things. And since any hypothesis which is disconfirmed is automatically rejected, we reject this hypothesis, thus overlooking the fact that *taken by itself* evidence concerning a nonblack nonraven confirms it. And, proponents of this view claim, prospects for indoor ornithology vanish when we notice that the hypotheses "All ravens are black" and "All ravens are nonblack" are *contraries*, so that (on the assumption that some ravens exist—whatever their color) one of these two hypotheses must be false. To decide between them, and thus to obtain any useful knowledge concerning the color of ravens, we still have to observe ravens for color.

Proponents of this view also claim that the feeling of paradoxicality arises partly from the use of information not explicitly stated as evidence. For instance, confirmation of the hypothesis "All ravens are black" by examination of, say, a brown shoe, seems paradoxical partly because we *know ahead of time* that shoes, whatever their color, are not ravens. But suppose we are not told that the thing examined is a brown shoe but only that something was observed which was nonblack, and that that thing turned out to be a nonraven. Then surely this ought to count as confirming evidence for the hypothesis "All ravens are black", because if the nonblack thing had turned out to be a *raven*, instead of a shoe, then this information would have *disconfirmed* the hypothesis in question. After all, acceptance of the hypothesis that all ravens are black leads one to expect that if something is not black then it is not a raven; the thing examined was not black, and as predicted by the hypothesis, it turned out to be not a raven.

Only a very few philosophers have proposed that we solve the raven paradox by rejecting the equivalence principle, and only a handful have suggested that we reject the confirmation principle.

Finally, there is the popular view that it is the use of predicate logic itself, in particular the use of *material implication*, which generates the problem. Advocates of this view deny that the use of a truth-functional logic sheds any light on the raven paradox, the problems of dispositionals and counterfactuals, or any problems similar to them. Rather, they claim that it is the very use of the notation of this logic in the symbolization of certain English sentences which *generates* these problems. Recall that in the discussion of material implication in Chapter Two we indicated that many uses of "if _____ then _ _ _ _ _ _" and its synonyms in English are not truth functional, so that translations of such sentences by means of " ⊃ " at best capture only *part* of their meaning. The claim is that the part of their meaning lost in the translation process is vital in certain cases, and that if more adequate translations were used, problems such as the raven paradox, dispositionals, counterfactuals, etc., would not arise.

Perhaps we ought to end our brief discussion of the raven paradox by presenting at least one reply that defenders of a truth-functional predicate logic would no doubt present against the above. Surely, they would claim, someone who asserts that "All ravens are black" at least *implies* that all nonblack things are nonravens, and someone who asserts the sentence "All nonblack things are nonravens" at least *implies* that all ravens are black. In other words, two sentences of this type (that is, two sentences that are *contrapositives*), are *equivalent*. But then, *no matter how we symbolize them*, just so long as their symbolizations are equivalent, the raven paradox will be generated. For example, the evidence that a brown shoe is nonblack and not a raven, which confirms the hypothesis "All nonblack things are nonravens", will equally confirm the equivalent hypothesis "All ravens are black". Thus the paradox is seen to arise without the express use of material implication.

4

Problems with the Identity Principle

In Chapter Nine, we introduced the inference rule called the rule of identity (**Ident**), which permits the substitution of any name or description of a thing for another name or description of that same thing. Thus, from the fact that Mark Twain (MT) wrote *Huck Finn* (HF) plus the fact that MT and Samuel Clemens (SC) are one and the same person, we can conclude by means of the rule of identity that SC wrote HF.

But certain uses of the rule of identity seem to lead to trouble. Consider its use in the following argument:

	1.	Art believes that MT wrote HF.	*p*
	2.	MT = SC	*p*
/∴	3.	Art believes that SC wrote HF.	1, 2 **Ident**

The problem is this. Suppose that Art happens to be ignorant of the fact that MT and SC are one and the same person. Then it seems possible for premises 1 and 2 of this argument both to be true when the conclusion 3 is false. If so, then it is possible to go from true premises to a false conclusion by means of the rule of identity, something no valid rule may permit.

There are many other examples in which the rule of identity seems to permit the passage from true premises to a false conclusion. Here are two more:

	1.	If you look to the East, you'll see the Morning Star (MS).	p
	2.	The Morning Star is the Evening Star (i.e., MS = ES).	p
/∴	3.	If you look to the East, you'll see the ES.	1, 2 **Ident**

Again, it seems possible for both premises to be true when the conclusion is false, making the rule of identity fail again.

Another example involves the use of a so-called "modal" context:

	1.	It is necessary that MS = MS.	p
	2.	MS = ES	p
/∴	3.	It is necessary that MS = ES.	1, 2 **Ident**

The difficulty here is this. Although it follows trivially from the premises that MS = ES, it doesn't seem to follow that it is *necessary* that MS = ES. Again we seem able to pass from true premises to a false conclusion.

Examples of this kind, in which the rule of identity seems to fail, have led some philosophers to place restrictions on that rule. Roughly, these restrictions forbid use of the rule of identity in certain contexts, sometimes referred to as "indirect" contexts, and sometimes as "intensional" contexts. But these restrictions are not completely acceptable. For one thing, many philosophers find the notion of indirect or intensional contexts far too vague. For another, it seems intuitively plausible to some that the rule of identity holds *universally*. In addition, several *other* kinds of solutions to the problems have been proposed, and those who accept any of these other solutions naturally see no reason for restricting the rule of identity. (The most widely accepted solution of this kind is the one which claims that alleged cases in which the rule of identity fails typically involve some kind of *ambiguity*, and thus do not involve genuine uses of that rule.)

Chapter Eighteen

*Logical
Paradoxes*

Modern logic also has been used in the clarification of the so-called **logical paradoxes**, some of which date back to the time of the early Greeks.

1

*Syntactic
Paradoxes*

At the end of Part Two, we very briefly discussed the predication of properties to other properties. An example is the property of *honesty*, which itself seems to have the property of being rare (in the sense that its extension is rather small). But the predication of properties to properties leads to difficulties, sometimes referred to as **syntactic paradoxes**.

If we can predicate some properties of other properties, it seems reasonable to suppose that we can predicate some properties of *themselves*. For example, it seems reasonable to suppose that the property of being *comprehensible* itself is comprehensible (in contrast to the property of being *incomprehensible*, which itself is not incomprehensible), and reasonable to suppose that the property of being *common* (as opposed to *rare*) is itself common. But *sometimes*, the predication of a property to itself yields trouble. The most famous example of this is the so-called "impredicable paradox".

Let's call any property which can be truly predicated of itself a *predicable property*, and any property which *cannot* be truly predicated of itself an *impredicable property*. Using this notation we can say that the property of being *common* is a predicable property, since it seems true that being common is a common property, and say that the property of being *rare* is an *im*predicable property, since it seems true that being rare is *not* a rare property.*

But what about the property of being *impredicable*? Can this property be truly predicated of itself? The unfortunate answer seems to be that if the property of being *impredicable is* predicated of itself, then it *is not* predicated of itself, and if it *is not* predicated of itself, then it *is* predicated of itself. Hence, the paradox.

To make this clear, let's symbolize the property of being predicable as P, and the property of being impredicable as $\bar{P}$. And let's bear in mind that to say a given property F is P is to say that FF, and to say that a given property F is $\bar{P}$ is to say that $\sim FF$.

To start with, either $\bar{P}$ is itself $\bar{P}$ or else $\bar{P}$ is P. Take the first possibility, namely that $\bar{P}$ is $\bar{P}$. If $\bar{P}$ is $\bar{P}$, then $\bar{P}$ *is* predicated of itself, and hence $\bar{P}$ is P. So if $\bar{P}$ is $\bar{P}$, then $\bar{P}$ is P.

Now suppose $\bar{P}$ is P. If $\bar{P}$ is P, then $\bar{P}$ is *not* predicated of itself, and hence $\bar{P}$ is $\bar{P}$. So if $\bar{P}$ is P, then $\bar{P}$ is $\bar{P}$.

It follows that if $\bar{P}$ is $\bar{P}$, then it is P, and if $\bar{P}$ is P, then it is $\bar{P}$. Translating this back into plain English, what we have shown is that if the property of being impredicable is *impredicable*, then it is predicated of itself, and hence is *predicable*. And if the property of being impredicable is *predicable*, then it is not predicated of itself (impredicable would have to be *im*predicable to be predicated of itself), and hence is *impredicable*.

This contradictory result can be made even more explicit by writing down the definition of $\bar{P}$, and then constructing a simple argument, as follows:

1. $\bar{P}F =_{df} \sim FF$

That is, to say that a property, F, is impredicable is to say that it is not the case that F is F. From which it follows that given any property F, F is $\bar{P}$

---

* Because there are many different kinds of rare things.

iff it is not the case that *F* is *F*. In other words,

2.　　$(F)(\bar{P}F \equiv \sim FF)$

Hence, substituting $\bar{P}$ for *F*, we get (by **UI**)

3.　　$\bar{P}\bar{P} \equiv \sim \bar{P}\bar{P}$

which is an explicit contradiction.

Several solutions to paradoxes of this kind have been proposed. One of these, the so-called "Simple Theory of Types",* has become fairly standard, and is accepted by most philosophers.

According to this theory, all entities divide into a hierarchy of types, starting with individual entities, moving to properties of individual entities, then to properties of properties of individual entities, and so on. For instance, Art is an individual entity; the property of being honest is a property Art may possess (hence honesty is a property of individuals); and the property of being rare is a property possessed by the property of being honest (hence rarity is a property of properties).

Having arranged entities in this way, the simple theory of types requires that the type of a property be higher than any property of which it can be predicated. For instance, if being old is predicated of Art, then it cannot be predicated either of itself or any other property.

It is customary to mark the distinction between properties of individuals and properties of properties by some notational device, such as the use of standard type to denote properties of individuals, and bold face type to denote properties of properties of individuals.

Using a notation of this kind, a sentence such as "Art is not old" will be symbolized as $\sim Oa$, and a sentence such as "Honesty is rare" will be symbolized as **R**H.

Notice that the sentence "Honesty is rare" is correctly symbolized as **R**H, and *not* as RH, for according to the theory of types, the property of being rare which is predicable of properties is of a type one level higher than properties which are predicable of individuals.

To summarize, the simple theory of types requires, first, that we arrange entities into a hierarchy of categories or types, starting with individuals, moving to properties of individuals, and then to properties of properties,

---

* Proposed by Bertrand Russell.

properties of properties of properties, etc.; and second, that the type of a property be one type higher than any property or entity of which it can be predicated.

An obvious consequence of the simple theory of types is that no property can be predicated of itself. And it is this consequence which solves the impredicable paradox, for if no property can be predicated of itself, then it becomes senseless to ask if the property of being impredicable is *itself* impredicable.

While most philosophers accept the simple theory of types because it solves puzzles such as the impredicable paradox, a few philosophers do not.

Perhaps their primary reason for not accepting it is that it seems not only *ad hoc*, but also *counter-intuitive*. For example, according to the simple theory of types, the rareness we can predicate of, say, a postage stamp is different from the rareness we can predicate of the property of being honest. But it seems intuitively clear that it is the very same property of rareness which is predicable of postage stamps and of honesty.

The counter-intuitive nature of the simple theory of types is further illustrated by the fact that it forbids assertion of sentences such as "Some members of every type (in the hierarchy of types) are rare", a sentence which seems not only *meaningful*, but also *true*.

Indeed, it has been argued that the *very statement* of the simple theory of types presupposes a violation of the theory itself. For instance, the simple theory of types presupposes that all individuals, properties of individuals, properties of properties, etc., have the property of being *type classifiable* (that is, have the property of belonging to exactly one category in the hierarchy of types). But the property of being type-classifiable is not permitted by the simple theory of types. Hence the theory presupposes what it will not permit.*

2

Semantic Paradoxes

While adoption of the simple theory of types has its difficulties, its adoption does have the advantage that it solves syntactic paradoxes like the impredicable paradox. But unfortunately, it fails to solve the paradoxes usually referred to as **semantic** or **epistemic paradoxes**.

* This last objection to the simple theory of types can be gotten around by use of the levels of language distinction, since the theory of types can be stated in the *meta-language* as a requirement of the *object language*, and thus in a sense not presuppose its own violation. See the next section, on semantic paradoxes, which contains a few brief critical comments on the levels of language distinction.

The most famous of the semantic paradoxes is the so-called "paradox of the liar", which goes back to the days of classical Greece. Put into more modern dress, the paradox is the following.

It seems reasonable to suppose that every declarative sentence* is either *true* or *false*. But consider the sentence

(I) Sentence (I) is false.

Is sentence (I) true, or is it false? The unfortunate answer seems to be that if sentence (I) is true, then it is false, and if it is false, then it is true.

Take the first possibility, namely that sentence (I) is true. If (I) is true, and (I) asserts that (I) is false, then it follows that (I) is false. So if (I) is true, then (I) is false.

Now suppose (I) is false. If (I) is false, and (I) asserts that (I) is false, then it follows that it is false that (I) is false, and therefore that (I) is true. So if (I) is false, then (I) is true. Either way, we have a contradiction, and hence a paradox.

An obvious thought is to solve the liar paradox by ruling out (as meaningless) any sentence which refers to itself. (Indeed the liar paradox often is conceived of [erroneously] as a paradox of self-reference.) So it appears that we can solve the paradox simply by rejecting self-referential sentences.

But unfortunately, self-reference does not cause the difficulty, and hence rejection of self-referential sentences does not solve the problem. The liar paradox can be generated without self-reference. For example, consider the following two sentences:

(II) Sentence (III) is false.

(III) Sentence (II) is true.

Sentence (II) refers to sentence (III), and sentence (III) refers to sentence (II), but neither (II) nor (III) refers to itself. So both of these sentences satisfy the requirement that sentences not be self-referential, and they seem to have the form required of legitimate declarative sentences.

But is sentence (II) true, or is it false? Again, the unfortunate answer seems to be that if it is true, then it is false, and if it is false, then it is true.

Take the first possibility, namely that sentence (II) is true. If (II) is true, and (II) asserts that (III) is false, it follows that (III) is false. But if

---

* As opposed to interrogative sentences, commands, etc., which are generally taken to be neither true nor false.

(III) is false, and (III) asserts that (II) is true, it follows that it is *false* that (II) is true and hence that (II) is false. So if (II) is true, then (II) is false.

Now suppose (II) is false. If (II) is false, and (II) asserts that (III) is false, it follows that it is false that (III) is false, and hence that (III) is true. But if (III) is true, and (III) asserts that (II) is true, it follows that (II) is true. So if (II) is false, then (II) is true. Again we have a contradiction, and hence again we have a paradox.

The most commonly accepted "solution" to semantic paradoxes, such as the liar paradox, involves the "levels of language" distinction. Those who accept this solution believe that we must distinguish between a language which is *used* and a language which is *talked about*, where the language used to talk about some other language is considered to be on a higher level than the language talked about.* They require that sentences asserting the truth or falsity of a given sentence be placed in a language at least one level higher than the given sentence. For instance, we must place the sentence "The sentence 'Art is tall' is true" in a language one level higher than the language in which the sentence "Art is tall" occurs.

It is clear that adoption of the above machinery solves the liar paradox. In the first place, all self-referential sentences, such as sentence (I), will be rejected as meaningless. And in the second place, at least one of every pair of sentences, such as sentences (II) and (III), will be rejected as meaningless. (For instance, if (II) occurs in a given language, and (III) in a language one level higher, then (II) will be rejected as meaningless—whatever the fate of (III)—because no sentence can be permitted to assert the truth or falsity of a sentence in the same, or a higher language.)

But not all philosophers accept the levels of language solution. Perhaps the main reason is that it seems to be much too strong, eliminating as meaningless not only the troublesome sentence (I), but also many apparently meaningful sentences. For instance, it eliminates the sentence "Every language (including this one) permits the expression of at least one true sentence". (This sentence may be false, but it seems to be meaningful.)

At any rate, the fact that the vast majority of philosophers accept the levels of language solution to the semantic paradoxes (as they accept the simple theory of types solution to the syntactic paradoxes) should not lead us to assume that these paradoxes have been solved, once and for all. Perhaps the future will bring better solutions.

---

* This division into higher and lower language levels is discussed in greater detail in Chapter Twenty, Section 4.

Chapter Nineteen

Logic and a Traditional Problem in Philosophy

1

Introduction

Many of the most important, as well as controversial, questions in philosophy center around the very nature of knowledge itself. In recent times* much of this controversy has been concerned with four key concepts (or terms), namely *a priori*, *a posteriori*, *analytic*, and *synthetic*.

Because of their controversial nature, no precise definition or characterization of these key concepts can be given which would be acceptable even to a majority of present-day philosophers. There is no "neutral" way to talk about them. The characterization presented here is, perhaps, as standard as any.

---

* Since the time of Immanuel Kant (1724–1804), who devised two of the key terms, *analytic* and *synthetic*.

2

The A Priori and
A Posteriori

Given that a sentence or proposition* is taken as "known", we can ask, first, *how it is known*, and second, *what kind of sentence or proposition it is that is known*. The terms *a priori* and *a posteriori* concern the first question, as to *how* things are, or can be, known.

Take the sentence "Either it will rain tomorrow (at a particular place) or it won't", in symbols $R \vee \sim R$. We can know this sentence is true *without* checking up on the weather at that particular time and place by a simple application of truth table analysis. Of course, we can also find out that the sentence in question is true by going to the particular place in question and seeing whether or not it rains there. But we need not do so. By truth table analysis we can determine that it is true *prior* to such an empirical investigation. Hence, the sentence $R \vee \sim R$ is said to be knowable *a priori*. In general, an **a priori sentence**, or **a priori proposition**, is one whose truth value can be known before, or without the need of, any experience of the things which the sentence discusses.

Most philosophers believe that at least some of our knowledge is a priori in this sense. Indeed, the belief that $R \vee \sim R$ is a true sentence would be accepted by most philosophers as a *paradigm* of a priori knowledge. But most philosophers also believe that some knowledge is *not* obtainable a priori. Take the belief that all of the books in Art's library are logic books (let's suppose that this happens to be true). Unlike the case for the belief that it either will or won't rain, we *cannot* know a priori that the sentence "All of the books in Art's library are logic books" is true. To justify our belief that it is true, we (or someone) must actually examine the contents of his library. So this sentence is said to be knowable *a posteriori*, or *after* inspection of the thing known. In general, an **a posteriori sentence**, or **a posteriori proposition**, is one whose truth value *cannot* be known before experience of the things which the sentence or proposition is about. We

---

* Again, we beg the question as to whether we should be speaking of *sentences* or of *propositions* (or even, as Kant claimed, *judgments*). We'll use all three terms in the exposition. But anyone who is partial to one or the other of these concepts can make the necessary mental substitutions without any great difficulty, and without affecting the main line of the discussion.

3

The Analytic and the Synthetic

require empirical (observational) evidence of some kind or other to determine the truth value of an a posteriori sentence or proposition.*

In addition to the question as to *how* we can know the truth values of sentences or propositions, there is the question as to *what kinds of sentences or propositions we can know.*

Obviously, sentences can be divided into kinds in many different ways. The division into analytic and synthetic sentences concerns the manner in which the *grammatical predicate* of a sentence is related to its subject.

Speaking metaphorically, we can say that the predicate of a given sentence either is "contained in" (or "part of") the concept of its subject, or not. The predicate of an **analytic sentence**, or **analytic proposition**, *is* contained in the concept of its subject. But the predicate of a **synthetic sentence**, or **synthetic proposition**, is not.

To put it another way, a sentence is *analytic* if the meaning of its predicate term is all or part of the meaning of its subject term, and *synthetic* if it is not.

Take the sentence "All bachelors are unmarried". If we assume that the term "bachelor" means "unmarried adult male", then clearly the meaning of the predicate term "unmarried" is part of the meaning of the subject term "bachelor". Hence, the sentence "All bachelors are unmarried" is analytic.

Using more traditional language, we can say that the judgment or proposition that all bachelors are unmarried is analytic because unmarriedness is part of the concept of bachelorhood.

Now consider the sentence "All bachelors weigh more than 50 pounds". Assuming again that the term "bachelor" means "unmarried adult male", it is clear that the meaning of the predicate expression "weighs more than 50 pounds" is *not* part of the meaning of the subject term "bachelor". Hence, the sentence "All bachelors weigh more than 50 pounds" is *synthetic*.

Using more traditional language, we can say that the judgment or proposition that all bachelors weigh more than 50 pounds is synthetic

---

* The distinction between the a priori and the a posteriori corresponds roughly to the distinction between *relations of ideas* and *matters of fact*, made by the philosopher David Hume (1711–1776), and to the distinction between *truths of reason* and *truths of fact*, made by the philosopher G. W. Leibnitz (1646–1716).

Logic and Philosophy

because the concept of weighing more than 50 pounds is not contained in the concept of bachelorhood.

4

Semantic and Syntactic Analyticity

It has become customary to divide analytic propositions into two kinds, namely *syntactic* and *semantic*.

A **syntactic analytic proposition** derives its analyticity from its *form* (plus the meanings of its *logical* terms), and not from the meanings of its *nonlogical terms*. (In the standard subject-predicate proposition, the nonlogical terms are the subject and predicate terms.) For example, the syntactic analytic proposition "All bachelors are bachelors" is true because *all* propositions of the form "All _____ are _____" are true, and hence is true because of its form.

On the other hand, a **semantic analytic proposition** derives its analyticity not simply from its form but also from the meanings of its *nonlogical terms*. Only *some* of the propositions having the form "All _____ are _ _ _ _ _ _" (the form of "All bachelors are unmarried") are true, or analytic, or knowable a priori. To determine the truth value of the semantic analytic truth "All bachelors are unmarried", we must know not only its form, but also the meanings of the nonlogical terms "bachelor" and "unmarried", and hence know that unmarriedness is part of the concept of bachelorhood.

5

The Synthetic A Priori

We now have divided sentences, propositions, and judgments into four kinds, a priori, a posteriori, analytic, and synthetic. But these divisions are not mutually exclusive. For instance, the sentence "All bachelors are bachelors" is not only analytic, but also a priori, since we can know that it is true without examining any bachelors. And the sentence "All bachelors weigh more than 50 pounds" is not only synthetic, but also a posteriori, since we can discover its truth value only by an actual examination of bachelors. Clearly then, there are **analytic a priori** and **synthetic a posteriori sentences**.

But are there *analytic a posteriori* or *synthetic a priori propositions*? Our first inclination is to say that there are not. In the first place, it would seem that there cannot be any analytic a posteriori propositions, because if a sentence is analytic, then mere knowledge of the *meanings* of its subject and predicate terms ought to enable us to determine its truth value, *without* any empirical observations being required. And in the second place, it would seem that there cannot be any synthetic a priori propositions, because if a proposition is synthetic then no mere *mental process*, such as comparing the meanings of its subject and predicate terms, will be sufficient to enable us to determine its truth value.

As a matter of fact, practically all philosophers agree that there are no analytic a posteriori propositions. But they disagree violently as to the existence of synthetic a priori propositions.

The most obvious reason for supposing that there are synthetic a priori propositions or judgments is that they seem to exist. For example, many philosophers consider propositions such as "If something is red (all over), then it is not green", "Seven plus five equals twelve", and "A cube has twelve edges" to be synthetic a priori.

Take the proposition "If something is red (all over), then it is not green". It is argued that this proposition is *synthetic*, because the concept of being red does not contain within it the concept of being nongreen, and also *a priori*, because we can know that it is true without actually examining red things to determine if they are green or not. So it is claimed that this proposition is **synthetic a priori**.

Similarly, it is argued that the proposition "Seven plus five equals twelve" is *synthetic*, because the concept of adding seven and five does not contain within it the concept of being twelve, and also *a priori*, because we can know that it is true without actually examining the results of adding seven things to five things to see if we obtain a collection of twelve things.

And it is argued that the proposition "A cube has twelve edges" is *synthetic*, because the concept of being a cube does not contain within it the concept of having twelve edges (for instance, we might conceive of a cube as a solid figure containing exactly six square surfaces), and also *a priori*, because we can know that it is true without actually examining cubes to determine if they have twelve edges.

6

Current Positions on the Analytic, Synthetic, A Priori, and A Posteriori

A small minority of present-day philosophers still accept Kant's view more or less as he originally formulated it. That is, they believe that some propositions are analytic a priori (for instance, the propositions "All bachelors are bachelors" and "All bachelors are unmarried"), some synthetic a posteriori (for instance, the propositions "John is tall" and "All men have hearts"), and some synthetic a priori (for instance, the propositions "If something is red (all over), then it is not green" and "A cube has twelve edges").

But many more believe that there are no synthetic a priori propositions, instead believing that all propositions can be classified as either analytic a priori or as synthetic a posteriori. This has always been the main position of the "empiricists".

Take the proposition "If something is red (all over), then it is not green", which is alleged to be synthetic a priori. An empiricist would argue that either the concept of being red *does* contain within it the idea of being nongreen, in which case this proposition is *analytic*, or else the concept of being red does *not* contain within it the concept of being nongreen, in which case the proposition in question is a posteriori. In either case, the proposition "If something is red (all over) then it is not green" is not synthetic a priori.

No doubt the empiricists are right that the proposition in question is analytic *if* the concept of being red contains within it the concept of being nongreen. But the claim that it is *a posteriori* if the concept of being red does not contain within it the concept of being nongreen needs to be argued for. Empiricists would be likely to argue for it by claiming that in general it is the very containment of one concept in another that permits us to know *a priori* that a proposition about these concepts is true. For instance, we can know a priori that the proposition "All bachelors are unmarried" is true *precisely because* unmarriedness is part of the concept of bachelorhood. In other words, empiricists would claim that it is the *analytic* nature of propositions which makes them knowable a priori.*

In the twentieth century, the controversy concerning the existence of synthetic a priori propositions has taken a back seat to the controversy as to which propositions, if any, are analytic, and which synthetic.

Some philosophers, while believing that there are *syntactic* analytic propositions, deny that there is a sharp division between *semantic* analytic propositions and synthetic propositions. (At least they deny this with respect to propositions expressed in a natural language such as English. "Artificial" or "constructed" languages are another matter.)

Their denial of a sharp division between semantic analytic and synthetic propositions stems in part from the *inherent vagueness* of the concepts denoted by most terms in natural languages.

---

* In addition, empiricists reject Kant's account (e.g., in *The Critique of Pure Reason*) as to how it is possible to know synthetic propositions a priori.

Take the term "bachelor". In some ways, that concept is quite precise. For example, it is clear that *unmarriedness* is part of the concept of bachelorhood. But in other ways, it is not precise. For instance, it is not precise with respect to the *age requirement* for bachelorhood. Clearly, anyone five years of age is too young to be called a bachelor. The same is true with respect to age ten. But what about ages 15, 20, and 25? With respect to these age brackets, we cannot answer with any degree of certainty. Bachelorhood has no minimum age requirement. It follows then, that we cannot say for certain whether a proposition such as "All bachelors are over 20 years of age" is analytic or synthetic.

This lack of a sharp division between the semantic analytic and the synthetic has resulted in at least three closely related positions on the subject:

(1) It has been argued that there is a continuous ordering of propositions from the most analytic (least synthetic), such as the propositions "All bachelors are unmarried" and "All women are human", through more and more doubtful cases, such as the propositions "All copper conducts electricity", "Grass is green", "Sugar tastes sweet", and "Mark Twain wrote *Huck Finn*", to the least analytic (most synthetic), such as the propositions "Art is tall", "Art is taller than Betsy", "All bachelors are over five feet tall", and "Over seven million people reside in New York City".

According to this view, when we say that a given proposition is a semantic analytic proposition, either what we say is false, or else it is a way of stating the relative position of the proposition on the continuous analytic-synthetic scale (just as saying that something is hot is a way of stating its relative position on the hot–cold—i.e., temperature—scale).

(2) Others argue that the vagueness of most concepts and terms in everyday use necessitates the introduction of a new category, say the "borderline case" category, placed between the semantic analytic and the synthetic categories, to take account of such propositions as "All bachelors are over 20 years of age" which are neither analytic nor synthetic.

(3) Finally, some philosophers argue that the whole idea of semantic analytic propositions is mistaken. They would be inclined to dispense with this category entirely, lumping all of its alleged members together

with the clearly synthetic propositions. In other words, they would divide all propositions into those which are *syntactic analytic* and those which are *synthetic*.

Whichever of these three views is correct,* it certainly is true that most of the words and concepts in daily use are vague, so that no sharp division between the semantic analytic and the synthetic can be made for the propositions expressed by means of the language of everyday life. However, this does not exclude the possibility of constructing *artificial* languages (so-called "logically perfect" languages) in which such a division can be made, and does not exclude the possibility of *deliberately sharpening* the key terms of a natural language so as to permit a sharp division between the semantic analytic and the synthetic to be drawn. Indeed, there is reason to suppose that the key terms of a natural language *can* be deliberately sharpened in this way, since the various sciences often do so quite successfully.

7

The Use of Logic to Clarify the Problem

In the twentieth century, many philosophers have turned to symbolic logic for aid in solving problems concerned with the analytic-synthetic distinction. This is true particularly of the philosophers called "logical positivists" or "logical empiricists".

The following account illustrates the use of symbolic logic in dealing with the analytic-synthetic distinction. (However, the view presented is one among many, and should not be taken to represent a majority view.) It also illustrates the way in which training in symbolic logic can, and does, affect the way that philosophers deal with many of the central issues in philosophy.

Recall that we stated in Section 5 above that many empiricists claim that it is the *analytic* nature of certain propositions which makes them knowable a priori. Hence it follows that they must claim that any proposition which can be known to be true a priori also is analytic. But in fact there are many propositions which can be known to be true a priori which do not

---

* There are a few philosophers who reject the analytic-synthetic distinction altogether, even denying that there is a sharp distinction between *syntactic* analytic sentences and synthetic sentences. The complexity of the arguments pro and con this view precludes their discussion here.

seem to be analytic according to the definition of analyticity furnished above. The reason for this is that the definition furnished covers only *subject-predicate type sentences*. So we need to expand the standard definition of analyticity, in order to cover a wider class of propositions.

The main idea contained in the standard definition is that the analyticity of a subject-predicate type proposition is due to its *form*, plus the meanings of its nonlogical terms. For instance, the meanings of the subject and predicate terms of a *syntactic analytic proposition* are irrelevant to the analyticity of the proposition. A *syntactic* analytic proposition *is* analytic *solely because of its form* (plus the meanings of its purely logical terms).

So the key to syntactic analyticity would seem to lie in the *form* of a proposition. Therefore, we can expand the notion of syntactic analyticity to cover all kinds of propositions, and not merely those in subject-predicate form, by stipulating that *any proposition which is true solely because of its form* (plus the meanings of its logical terms) *is a syntactic analytic proposition*.

Once we do this, all of the *tautologous sentences* of sentential logic become syntactic analytic truths. An example would be the sentence "Either Art will go to the show or he won't", in symbols $A \vee \sim A$, which is true by virtue of its form (since every sentence of the form "_____ $\vee \sim$ _____" is true).

In addition, all of the so-called "logical truths"* of predicate logic discussed in Part Two of this book become syntactic analytic truths,† because they, too, are true by virtue of their form (plus the meanings of their logical terms). An example is the logical truth, "All things are either red or not red", in symbols $(x)(Rx \vee \sim Rx)$, which is true because of its form (since every sentence of the form "All things are either _____ or not _____" is true). Another is the more complicated logical truth, "If everyone who went to the show received a door prize, then everyone who didn't get a door prize didn't go to the show," in symbols $(x)[(Px \cdot Sx) \supset Dx] \supset (x)[(Px \cdot \sim Dx) \supset \sim Sx]$, which also is true because of its form.

All of the logical truths involving *identity* also become syntactic analytic

---

* Sentences expressible in predicate logic notation which are provable from the null set of premises, i.e., all substitution instances of sentence forms which are theorems of logic.

† The expression "syntactic analytic truth" is apt here, because by extension we can speak of "syntactic analytic falsehood", meaning by that expression a sentence or proposition which is false because of its form (plus the meaning of its logical terms). Similarly, we can speak of "a priori falsehoods", meaning sentences or propositions which can be known in advance to be false.

truths by this criterion of syntactic analyticity. An example would be the sentence "Art is Art", in symbols $a = a$, since clearly every sentence of the form $x = x$ is true. Another example would be the sentence "Everything is identical with itself", in symbols $(x)(x = x)$.

Having extended the notion of syntactic analyticity, by so to speak "mapping it" onto the concept of logical truths, we must now treat the concept of *semantic* analyticity.

In the first place, we have to accept the view that we cannot make a sharp division between the propositions expressible in a natural language which are semantically analytic and those which are synthetic. Nevertheless, we must admit that some of these propositions clearly *are* semantic analytic (for example, "All bachelors are unmarried"), and some clearly synthetic (for example, "All bachelors weigh more than 50 pounds").

Next, we have to make use of the fact that we can *deliberately sharpen* a term or concept so as to enable any given proposition to be classifiable either as semantically analytic or as synthetic. For instance, by sharpening the concept of being a bachelor (or by redefining the term "bachelor") so that one must be over 20 years of age, we can make the proposition "All bachelors are over 20 years of age" a semantic analytic proposition.

Now, let's make explicit what we have done. First, we have made tacit use of a kind of "syntactic-semantic connecting principle" to the effect that *if a given sentence is such that replacement of a term or terms by their definitions results in a syntactic analytic sentence, then the given sentence is a semantic analytic sentence.* For example, we have tacitly used this principle in concluding that the sentence "All bachelors are unmarried" is semantically analytic from the fact that replacement of its subject term "bachelor" by its definition "unmarried male over 20 years of age" results in the syntactic analytic sentence "All unmarried males over 20 years of age are unmarried", in symbols $(x)\{[(Ux \cdot Mx) \cdot Ox] \supset Ux\}$.

The next step is to expand the notion of analyticity to cover the axioms and theorems of axiom systems. In particular, we are interested in axiom systems for Arithmetic, Geometry, and other empirical sciences, such as Physics.

The key with respect to the theorems of axiom systems of this kind is that *all theorems of an axiom system which deductively follow from analytic axioms are analytic.* In other words, we want all *logical consequences* of analytic sentences to be analytic.

The problem, of course, concerns the status of the *axioms* of systems for arithmetic, geometry, and other empirical sciences. Are they analytic or synthetic? The issue is much too complex to be discussed fully in an introductory text, but most philosophers (including all empiricists) today hold that at least some of the axioms of an axiom system for any given empirical science must be synthetic. They also hold that the axioms of arithmetic are analytic (indeed a great deal of the twentieth century literature on the foundations of arithmetic concerns attempts to prove this), and that the axioms of so-called *pure geometry* also are analytic, but that at least some of the axioms of *applied geometry** are synthetic.

Perhaps it would be appropriate to end our discussion of the analytic and synthetic with a word or two about the proposition "A cube has twelve edges", a theorem of geometry which Kantians claim to be synthetic a priori. If our discussion above is correct, then this proposition is analytic *if* it follows deductively from *axioms* which are analytic. And the axioms from which it follows are analytic if they are true by virtue of their form (that is, if they are logical truths) or if the axioms themselves follow from analytic propositions when terms are replaced by their definitions. But are the axioms of geometry, from which the theorem "A cube has twelve edges" follows, themselves analytic? No general agreement exists as to the answer to this important question. But empiricists are committed to the view that they are analytic, and in general to the view that there is no such thing as the synthetic a priori.

---

* The distinction between pure and applied geometry is roughly that between uninterpreted (or partially interpreted) and fully interpreted axiom systems for geometry.

It is often held that the ideal way to *systematize* a given area of knowledge is by means of what is called an **axiom system**. We shall now consider the nature of axiom systems in general and outline two slightly different axiom systems for deductive logic.

1

*The Nature of an
Axiom System*

An axiom system has three main kinds of elements: **symbols** (or words), **formulas**, and **inference rules**. Symbols divide into **defined symbols**, for which explicit definitions are presented, and **primitive** (or **undefined**) **symbols**, for which no definitions are presented. For instance, in an axiom system for anthropology we might introduce the terms "parent" and "male" as primitives, and then define the term "father" to mean "male parent". Symbols also divide into **logical symbols**, such as "and", "not", "some", etc., and **extralogical** or **nonlogical symbols**, which vary depending on the area of knowledge to be systematized. Formulas break down into **sentences** and **sentence forms** (or functions).* Formulas also divide into **axioms**, for which no justification is provided within the system, and **theorems**, which are provable, in that they can be derived from the axioms by means of the inference rules of the system. Indeed, one of the main reasons for constructing axiom systems involves the derivation of theorems from axioms. Formulas also divide into **well formed formulas**, such as $p \supset q$ and $\sim [(A \vee B) \supset \sim C]$, and those that are not, such as ($p\, q \vee$ and $AB \vee$)). (This distinction will be explained in more detail later.) And finally, inference rules divide into **primitive inference rules**, for which no justification is provided within the system, and **derived inference rules**, for which a justification *is* provided.

Of course, every system does not have to have all of these kinds of elements. For instance, we can have an axiom system without defined symbols. Similarly, we can have an axiom system without derived rules. But to be complete, an axiom system must have symbols, formulas, and inference rules.

One of the primary motives for constructing axiom systems is *rigor*. We want symbols precisely defined, and theorems rigorously proved. Consequently, it might be supposed that to include *undefined* symbols, *unproved* axioms, and *unjustified* inference rules in an axiom system is to settle for something less than the ideal. But this is an illusion. It is impossible to define *all* symbols, prove *all* sentences, or justify *all* inference rules within a given system, except either circularly or by means of an infinite (and useless) series of definitions or proofs. (For example, it would be useless to define "automobile" as "car" and then to define "car" to mean "automobile". And it would be useless to attempt to present an infinite series of definitions, because in order to understand it one would have to run through the entire series, something it is impossible to do.) So we must settle for at least some undefined symbols, unproved axioms, and unjustified inference rules.†

Of course, undefined symbols must be understood, and the axioms and inference rules must be *acceptable*. Clearly, some symbols will not do as

---

* This is not quite true for what are called *uninterpreted* systems, because it is inappropriate to speak of the formulas of such systems as sentences or sentence forms.

† It is sometimes possible to reduce the number of axioms to zero by increasing the number of primitive inference rules. But we can never reduce the number of axioms *and* primitive inference rules in a given system to zero.

primitives in a rigorous system. But the question as to *which* symbols and *which* axioms and inference rules are acceptable as primitives is in dispute. For instance, some philosophers would claim that the axioms of an axiom system for deductive logic must be *intuitively acceptable*, or *self-evidently true*, while others would say that, theoretically, any theorems of logic can serve as axioms, the choice being made to obtain the smallest possible set of axioms from which all theorems can be derived. But all philosophers would agree that (other things being equal) it is desirable to have very few axioms or primitive rules of inference, and very few undefined symbols.

So it is generally held that the best possible axiom system for a given area of knowledge is one which contains a minimum number of primitive symbols, primitive rules, and axioms, but yet is sufficiently rich to prove all of the truths of that area of knowledge.

It should be noted that the undefinability *within a system* of all terms of that system does not entail the inherent *undefinability* of any terms of that system. It may be that no terms are undefinable.

We all are familiar with at least one axiom system, namely the one for Euclidean geometry, although it is normally presented only in a semi-rigorous form. For instance, usually only a partial list of inference rules is provided. But it is clear how such defects can be remedied, and so we can take Euclidean geometry as our model of an axiom system.

2

Interpreted and Uninterpreted Systems

An **uninterpreted axiom system** is one in which the primitive symbols not only are not defined *within* the system, but are given no meaning or interpretation whatsoever. (Of course, those who construct uninterpreted axiom systems generally have particular interpretations in mind. For instance, anyone who constructs an uninterpreted axiom system for sentential logic obviously has sentential logic in mind; otherwise there would be no point in calling it an uninterpreted system *for sentential logic*.)

Uninterpreted systems are quite useful, especially when our main concern is the *structure* of a system, and not the truth of its axioms (since the axioms of uninterpreted systems are not sentences, and hence are neither true nor false). In addition, if we deal with uninterpreted systems we are less likely to make tacit use of knowledge not contained in the axioms of the system. For example, if the terms of an axiom system for Euclidean geometry are uninterpreted, it is more difficult to make tacit use of our geometric intuitions in addition to the stated axioms and inference rules of the system. In fact, Euclid himself made tacit use of information about geometry not explicitly stated in his system.

An **interpreted axiom system** is one for which all of the primitive terms are assigned a meaning or interpretation. In some axiom systems the formulas when interpreted are sentences, in others they are sentence forms.

Notice that it is one thing to define a term within a system, and another to assign a meaning to a primitive term. In this sense, a term defined within a system is defined by means of the primitive terms of the system (or other terms so defined); primitive terms are assigned meanings in other ways. For example, in applied geometry the primitive term "straight line" may be taken to mean "path of a light ray".

Although there is some dispute as to which terms are usable as primitives, other things being equal, terms whose meanings we clearly understand (however we obtained this understanding) are preferable to those which tend to be vague or figurative.

3

Properties of Axiom Systems

Consistency

The most important requirement which an acceptable axiom system must satisfy is that of *consistency*. An axiom system is **consistent** *iff* contradictory formulas cannot be derived from its axioms by means of its rules of inference. An axiom system which fails to satisfy this requirement, so that a contradiction is derivable as a theorem, is said to be **inconsistent** and is obviously worthless.

Example:

A system containing the two axioms

(A1) $p \supset \sim p$

(A2) p

plus the two inference rules

(R1)   If p and $p \supset q$, then we can
       infer q (i.e., Modus Ponens)

(R2)   If p and q, then we can infer
       $p \cdot q$ (i.e., Conjunction)

is inconsistent, since we can derive a contradiction in such a system, as follows:

1.	$p \supset {\sim}p$	**Axiom**
2.	p	**Axiom**
3.	${\sim}p$	1, 2 **MP**
4.	$p \cdot {\sim}p$	2, 3 **Conj**

The general procedure for proving that an axiom system is *inconsistent* is the same as the one for proving a set of premises inconsistent, namely the derivation of an explicit contradiction. But failure to derive a contradiction does not constitute proof that a given axiom system is consistent, for we may have failed because of lack of ingenuity. Instead, the general procedure for proving that an axiom system is *consistent* is to prove that there is a formula which is not derivable as a theorem of that system. This constitutes proof that a given axiom system is consistent because inconsistent systems permit the derivation of any and every expressible formula (since a *contradiction* logically entails any and every expressible formula). Hence, if there is some formula which cannot be derived as a theorem, then no contradiction can be derived either, and the system must be consistent.*

Expressive completeness

An axiom system is **expressively complete** *iff* its language is rich enough to express everything that the system is intended to express. For example,

---

* This criterion of consistency, known as " Post's consistency criterion", after its inventor, E. L. Post, works only for systems which also are *complete*. Incomplete systems which also are inconsistent may be such that there are formulas expressible in the system which are not provable.

Axiom Systems

the usual axiom systems for Euclidean geometry are expressively complete, because they permit every statement (true or false) concerning geometry. But an axiom system for Euclidean geometry would be expressively incomplete if, say, it contained no method for handling sentences about circles.

Completeness

There is another kind of completeness, more frequently discussed in the literature than expressive completeness, and much more difficult to state. This kind concerns the *provability* or *derivability* of formulas. Perhaps the best we can do with respect to this kind of completeness is to say that an axiom system is **complete** in this sense *iff* all of the formulas we *desire* to prove as theorems of the system in fact are provable as theorems of that system.

Although it is quite difficult to state precisely what this kind of completeness consists of *in general*, it is less difficult to characterize it with respect to four of the more important kinds of axiom systems:

(1) The axiom system for sentential logic to be outlined later in the chapter has as its axioms and theorems *tautologous sentence forms*, such as $(p \lor \sim p)$, $(\sim (p \lor p) \lor p)$, etc. Such an axiom system for sentential logic is *complete iff every* tautologous sentence form expressible in the system is provable as a theorem of the system.

(2) Some axiom systems for sentential logic have *tautologous sentences* as their axioms and theorems, rather than tautologous sentence forms. We can say that such an axiom system is complete *iff* every tautologous sentence expressible in the system is provable as a theorem of the system.

(3) The axiom system for predicate (quantifier) logic to be outlined later in this chapter has *sentence forms* as its axioms and theorems. Some of these sentence forms are tautologies, but some are not. For instance, the sentence form $(x)(Px \lor \sim Px)$, where "P" is a *predicate variable*, is a theorem of this system, but it is not a *tautologous* sentence form. However, it is *like* a tautologous sentence form in that all of its substitution instances are true sentences. For instance, the substitution instance $(x)(Ax \lor \sim Ax)$,

where "A" is a *predicate constant*, is a substitution instance of (x) $(Px \lor \sim Px)$, and is a true sentence.*

This axiom system also has tautologous theorems, such as the theorem $(Px \lor \sim Px)$. And of course all of its substitution instances are true sentences. For example, the substitution instance $(Aa \lor \sim Aa)$, where "a" is an *individual constant*, and "A", as before, is a predicate constant, is a true sentence.

In Chapter Nine, sentence forms all of whose substitution instances are true sentences were referred to as *theorems of logic*. Adopting this terminology, we can say that an axiom system for predicate logic of the above kind is *complete iff every* theorem of logic is provable as a theorem of that system. Notice that we cannot use the same criterion of completeness for predicate logic that we used for sentential logic because many theorems of predicate logic are not tautologies.

(4) An axiom system for *arithmetic* is complete *iff* every sentence expressible in the system is such that either it or its negation is a theorem of that system. To see that this criterion is adequate, consider several kinds of typical sentences of arithmetic.

First, consider *unquantified* sentences, such as $2 + 2 = 4$, $7 + 1 = 3$, etc. Clearly, every such sentence either is true, in which case it is a theorem of arithmetic, or false, in which case its negation is a theorem of arithmetic. (An example of the latter would be the sentence $\sim (7 + 1 = 3)$ which is a theorem of arithmetic.)

Next, consider *quantified* sentences, such as $(x)(y)((x + y) = (y + x))$, $\sim (x)(x = x)$, etc. Once again, it is clear that every such sentence either is true, in which case it is a theorem of arithmetic, or false, in which case its negation is a theorem of arithmetic.

Notice that the kind of completeness required of an axiom system for arithmetic is stronger than that required for sentential or predicate logic. We cannot require such a strict kind of completeness for logic, because axiom systems for logic contain either *contingent sentences* or *contingent sentence forms*, and neither they nor their negations are theorems of logic.

---

* The axiom system for predicate logic to be outlined contains no predicate constants. Hence, it is not quite correct to speak of the expression $(x)(Ax \lor \sim Ax)$ as a *substitution instance* of $(x)(Px \lor \sim Px)$ since $(x)(Ax \lor \sim Ax)$ is not a formula expressible in the system. Perhaps it would be better to speak of *interpretations* of the axioms and theorems of the system.

Axiom independence

An axiom of a given system is **independent** of the other axioms *iff* it cannot be derived from them by means of the inference rules of that system. Otherwise, an axiom is dependent. In general, once it is realized that an axiom is dependent, it is dropped as an axiom, for reasons of simplicity. Of course, it remains as a theorem of the system, since it is derivable from the remaining axioms.

Example:

We can prove that the axioms contained in the system discussed in Chapter Four, Section 3, are not independent by showing, for instance, the dependence of the axiom $(p \supset q) \equiv (\sim q \supset \sim p)$. And we can show this by deriving it as a theorem of the system, as follows:

1.	$p \supset q$	AP
2.	$\sim p \vee q$	1, **Imp**
3.	$q \vee \sim p$	2, **Comm**
4.	$\sim \sim q \vee \sim p$	3, **DN**
5.	$\sim q \supset \sim p$	4, **Impl**
6.	$(p \supset q) \supset (\sim q \supset \sim p)$	1, 5 **CP**
7.	$\sim q \supset \sim p$	AP
8.	$\sim \sim q \vee \sim p$	7, **Impl**
9.	$\sim p \vee \sim \sim q$	8, **Comm**
10.	$\sim p \vee q$	9, **DN**
11.	$p \supset q$	10, **Impl**
12.	$(\sim q \supset \sim p) \supset (p \supset q)$	7, 11 **CP**
13.	$[(p \supset q) \supset (\sim q \supset \sim p)]$ $\cdot [(\sim q \supset \sim p) \supset (p \supset q)]$	6, 12 **Conj**
14.	$(p \supset q) \equiv (\sim q \supset \sim p)$	13, **Equiv**

Naturally, the above proof does *not* make use of Contraposition, since that would make the proof viciously circular, and hence useless.

In a sense, simplicity is not a *logical* requirement, since a system which lacks simplicity is not inconsistent. But simplicity still is a requirement of good systems. A system which *completely* lacks simplicity hardly merits the label "system" at all. For instance, a "system" for arithmetic in which every term is primitive, and every true sentence an axiom (that is, a system in which there are no defined terms and no theorems), would be no system at all, but rather a mere list of arithmetic truths. The usual view that simplicity, and thus independence of axioms is "a mere matter of elegance" is incorrect, unless systematization itself is "a mere matter of elegance". A system with a great many dependent axioms, even if consistent, is not an acceptable system.

We can prove that a given axiom is *dependent* by deriving it from the other axioms of a system. But failure to find such a proof does not constitute a proof that an axiom is independent; we simply may have overlooked the proof.

To prove that an axiom is *independent* of a given set of axioms, it suffices to show that there is some characteristic or property possessed by every axiom in the given set, and also possessed by every formula derivable from that set of axioms, which is *not* possessed by the axiom in question. This proves independence because any particular axiom which does not have a property possessed by every formula derivable from a given set of axioms itself cannot be derivable from that set, and hence itself must be independent of that set.

Decision procedure

A **decision procedure** is a mechanical method for determining in a finite number of steps whether or not a given formula is a theorem of an axiom system. For example, the method of truth table analysis constitutes a decision procedure for sentential logic, since this method enables us to determine effectively in a finite number of steps whether or not a given formula is a tautology, and hence a theorem of sentential logic.

The existence of a decision procedure for a given axiom system renders all questions about the theorems of that system *routinely* answerable,

Axiom Systems

without the need for *ingenuity* in the construction of proofs. This has the advantage that all questions and disputes as to whether a particular formula is or is not a theorem of the system can be settled by the mere *mechanical manipulation* of symbols of the kind which computers can be programmed to perform.

On the other hand, axiom systems for which there is no decision procedure are generally of more interest to the logician and mathematician, since questions and disputes concerning alleged theorems of these systems, even if in principle soluble, require genius (or a good deal of luck) for their solution. Indeed many such questions may go unanswered forever.

4

Outline of an Axiom System for Sentential Logic

Object language—Meta-language

We now present the bare outline of an axiom system for sentential logic. However, to do so, we must *talk about* that system. Since there is a sense in which that axiom system itself constitutes a language, what we need is some other language to talk about that language. And since the sentential logic axiom system, "SL" for short, is the *object* of discussion, we can refer to it as the **object language**, and refer to the language used to talk about SL as the **meta-language**.

The terms "object language" and "meta-language" are relative. For instance, if we use German to talk about English, then German is the meta-language. But if we use English to talk about German, then English is the meta-language. Of course, one and the same language can be both object and meta-language. For instance, in an English grammar class conducted in English, English is used to talk about itself, and hence is both object and meta-language. (However, there appear to be limits on the use of a given language to talk about itself—and, in particular, to talk about certain of its *semantic* properties.)

Quotation marks often are used to distinguish between *talk about* (or *mention of*) a language, and *use of* a language. For instance, we can *use* English sentences to talk about, or *mention*, the state of Kansas. But we also can talk about, or mention, the *words used* to talk about the state of Kansas. In talking about the state of Kansas, we use its English name *without* quotes; in talking about the *word* which is the name of the state, we put that word, "Kansas", in quotes. Thus, we can say that "Kansas" has six letters, whereas Kansas is a state roughly in the center of the continental United States. We can also go one step further and talk about the name of the name of Kansas. Thus, we can say that "'Kansas'" contains quotation marks, whereas "Kansas" does not, and say that "Kansas" is the name of a state, whereas Kansas is not (since it *is* a state). In other words, the device of quotation marks provides a convenient and automatic way for generating names of linguistic entities.

Another device used for generating names of linguistic entity is bold-face and light-face type. For instance, we can use the term **v** in the object language SL and *v* in the meta-language when we wish to talk about "*v*".

From the point of view of logic, many other methods for naming words would do just as well as the above two. For instance, we might refer to the word "Kansas" by means of the name "Art". And then we could say (truthfully) that Art has six letters, the first one "K", the second "a", and so on. But such a notation would be inconvenient to say the least, and is never used.

We shall adopt ordinary English (suitably fortified with special terms to refer to the symbols of SL) as the meta-language both of SL and of itself. But in our informal exposition, we also shall refer to many terms and expressions of SL and its meta-language simply by placing them in quotation marks.

Syntax, semantics, pragmatics

In talking about SL, we shall discuss some of its syntactic properties and some of its semantic properties. The **syntactic properties** of a language are its *structural* properties, that is, those properties it has in abstraction from the meanings of its terms (other than the logical terms). For instance, the English sentence "John is tall" has the syntactic property of containing ten letters. And the sentence "Art is smart *and* Betsy is beautiful" has the syntactic property of being a *conjunction*.

The **semantic properties** of a language are those properties which it (or parts of it) possess by virtue of the *meanings* of its terms. For instance, English has the semantic property of containing sentences stating arithmetic truths, such as "two plus two equals four", a semantic property which SL lacks. And the sentence "Snow is white" has the semantic property of containing a color term, namely the term "white". (Notice that uninterpreted systems have no semantic properties whatever, because their symbols have no meanings.)

In addition to the syntactic and semantic properties of a language, we can speak of its *pragmatic* properties. The **pragmatic** properties of a language are those which it has in relation to its speakers (or users). For example, the English sentence "Snow is white" has the pragmatic property of *being believed* by many English-speaking people. And English itself has the pragmatic property of being spoken by most citizens of the United States.

Another way to look at the difference between syntax, semantics, and pragmatics is to say that the syntax of a language concerns the relations between the elements of the language (such as letters, words, sentences, etc.), semantics the relationships between the elements of a language and the things which the language can talk about, and pragmatics the relationships between the elements of a language, the things it talks about, *and* the users of the language.

Little will be said here about the pragmatic properties of SL. However, we should bear in mind that in considering only the syntax and semantics of a language we are *abstracting from* the total language-use situation, which by its very nature must include language users. A "language" which no one ever uses or understands is no language at all.

Similarly, we should bear in mind that in discussing the syntax of an interpreted system, we are abstracting not only from its pragmatic properties, but also from its semantic properties.*

The symbols of SL

An axiom system for sentential logic can be either interpreted or uninterpreted.† The axiom system SL, to be outlined here, is an interpreted system. This means that although the primitive terms are not defined in the system, they are to be taken to have their usual meanings.

All of the symbols of SL are primitive symbols. Among these symbols we distinguish **logical primitives** and **extra-logical primitives**. (Of course, there is no indication *within* SL as to whether a symbol is a logical or extra-logical primitive. This distinction is made in the meta-language.)

---

* However, in syntactic analyses, we often do *not* abstract from the meanings of the *logical* terms of a system. This fact is frequently overlooked.

† Some philosophers would deny that it makes sense to speak of an uninterpreted axiom system for any given area.

SL contains exactly four logical primitives, namely $\sim$, $\supset$, (, and), in bold-face type (the last two to be used as left- and right-hand parentheses respectively).

In addition, SL contains indefinitely many *sentence variables*, **p**, **q**, **r**, etc., as extra-logical primitives.

Notice that the usual logical connectives "·", $\vee$, and $\equiv$ do not occur in SL. They are omitted for reasons of simplicity, both of the number of primitive symbols and of the number of axioms. However, their counterparts will be introduced later as *defined* terms in the meta-language.

Definition of WFF

Among all of the possible finite strings of terms of SL, some are *well formed*, such as $((p \supset q) \supset p)$, $(p \supset \sim q)$, etc., and some not, such as $(pp \supset \sim)$,$)(((p$, etc. Intuitively, it is clear that all of the well-formed formulas ("WFF" for short) of SL are sentence forms. So we could define "WFF of SL" as meaning "sentence form of SL". This would be a *semantic* definition of WFF. But we cannot always provide semantic definitions of WFF. For instance, we cannot do so for uninterpreted axiom systems, since they do not have semantic properties. The definition of WFF for an uninterpreted system must therefore be a *syntactical* one. And since we want SL to serve as an example, we shall provide a purely syntactic definition of "WFF of SL".

Of course, the definition of WFF occurs in the meta-language, not in SL itself. So we need to introduce certain terms into the meta-language to *talk about* the formulas of the object language SL. For this purpose, we introduce into the meta-language the symbols P, Q, R, etc., as *formula variables*, that is, as symbols in the meta-language for which formulas in the object language can be substituted. Thus, in a given use, a formula variable denotes any formula of the object language (subject to the usual rule concerning the use of variables which requires that in a single context every occurrence of a given variable must denote the same formula).

We also introduce the symbols $\supset$, $\sim$, (, and), in light-face type, and stipulate (roughly) that these symbols denote the bold-face type symbols $\supset$, $\sim$, (, and) of the object language. (We also have available in the meta-language the light-face type symbols p, q, r, etc., that is, symbols which name particular formulas of the object language. However, these symbols are not used in the definition of WFF.)

Finally, in order to facilitate talk about the object language, we introduce the symbols $\vee$, "$\cdot$", and $\equiv$ as *defined terms* of the meta-language:

(D1):   "$(P \vee Q)$" is defined as an abbreviation for "$(\sim P \supset Q)$".

(D2):   "$(P \cdot Q)$" is defined as an abbreviation for "$\sim (\sim P \vee \sim Q)$".

(D3):   "$(P \equiv Q)$" is defined as an abbreviation for "$(P \supset Q) \cdot (Q \supset P)$".

These defined terms will be useful in talking about the WFF's of SL, but are not used in the definition of "WFF of SL" itself.

We now are ready to define the term "WFF of SL":

1.   All sentence variables of SL are WFF's of SL.

2.   If a formula P is a WFF of SL, then so is $\sim P$.

3.   If P and Q are WFF's of SL, then so is $(P \supset Q)$.

We further state that no formula is a WFF of SL unless it is according to lines 1 through 3 above.

This definition provides an effective mechanical procedure for recognizing the WFF's of SL. That is, if a formula is a WFF of SL, repeated application of the above definition will reveal this fact.* An infinite number of formulas of SL are WFF's according to this definition.

To illustrate how this definition works, we can consider the formula $(\sim(p \supset p) \supset q)$. According to line 1 of the definition, p and q both are WFF's. Therefore, according to line 3, $(p \supset p)$ is a WFF; and according to line 2, $\sim(p \supset p)$ is a WFF. Consequently, according to line 3, $(\sim(p \supset p) \supset q)$ is a WFF.

---

* However, it does *not* provide an effective mechanical procedure for determining in general *whether or not* a formula is a WFF of SL. That is, it does not provide a method for determining that a non-WFF is not a WFF of SL. But such a procedure can be provided.

The axioms and inference rules of SL

We stipulate three WFF's as the axioms of SL:

(A1): $(p \supset (q \supset p))$

(A2): $((p \supset (q \supset r)) \supset ((p \supset q) \supset (p \supset r)))$

(A3): $((\sim q \supset \sim p) \supset ((\sim q \supset p) \supset q))$

We also stipulate two rules of inference for SL. However, these two rules are formulated in the *meta-language*, not in SL itself:

(R1): If $(P \supset Q)$ and P are either axioms or theorems of SL, then Q may be inferred from them.

(R2): Any WFF may be substituted for any variable in a proof, provided the substitution is made for every occurrence of that variable.

(R1) already is familiar, since it is simply Modus Ponens. (R2) also should be familiar, since it simply states *explicitly* the rule of substitution used *implicitly* in the sentential and predicate logics presented earlier. For instance, (R2) permits inferences from $(\sim (p \supset p) \supset p)$ to $(\sim (q \supset q) \supset q)$, and to $(\sim ((p \supset q) \supset (p \supset q)) \supset (p \supset q))$, etc.

We now define a **proof of SL** as a sequence of WFF's, all of which are axioms of SL or are inferable from the axioms by repeated applications of (R1) and/or (R2).* For example, all sequences of WFF's of the object language having the forms

$(P \supset (Q \supset P))$
$(\sim P \supset (Q \supset \sim P))$

---

* A proof of P obviously will be a proof of SL in which the last line is P. For instance, a proof of $(p \supset (p \supset p))$ will be a proof of SL in which the last line is $(p \supset (p \supset p))$.

constitute proofs of SL. An example would be the sequence of formulas

$(p \supset (q \supset p))$
$(\sim p \supset (q \supset \sim p))$

which constitutes a proof of SL because the second WFF follows from the first by an application of (R2), and the first is an axiom of SL.

Another example of a proof having this form is the following sequence of formulas:

$(p \supset (q \supset p))$
$(\sim (r \supset s) \supset (q \supset \sim (r \supset s)))$

which also constitutes a proof because the second WFF follows from the first by an application of (R2).

Proofs in SL tend to be quite long and very difficult to construct, which is the price we have to pay for having so few axioms and inference rules. The following is a more complex proof in SL:

$(p \supset (q \supset p))$
$(p \supset ((q \supset p) \supset p))$
$((p \supset (q \supset r)) \supset ((p \supset q) \supset (p \supset r)))$
$((p \supset ((q \supset p) \supset p)) \supset ((p \supset (q \supset p)) \supset (p \supset p)))$
$((p \supset (q \supset p)) \supset (p \supset p))$
$(p \supset p)$

This constitutes a proof in SL because the first and third lines are axioms of SL, the second line follows from the first by (R2), the fourth line from the third by (R2), the fifth line from the second and fourth by (R1), and the sixth line from the first and fifth by (R1).

We now define a **theorem of SL** as a WFF for which a proof can be given in SL. Thus, the WFF $(\sim p \supset (q \supset \sim p))$ is a theorem of SL, since it follows from the axiom $(p \supset (q \supset p))$ by an application of (R2), and consequently a proof for it can be given in SL. (Of course, the *fact* that it is a theorem of SL, and the *fact* that the two above formulas constitute a proof in SL, cannot be stated within SL itself, but must be stated in the meta-language. Nevertheless, the proof itself is in the object language SL.)

Properties of SL

Earlier, we discussed the properties, such as completeness, consistency, expressive completeness, etc., that we want axiom systems to possess. The question arises as to which of these properties are possessed by SL, and the answer is that SL possesses *all* of them.

It has been proved that SL is complete (in the sense that every tautology is a theorem of SL), consistent, and expressively complete. In addition, it has been proved that there is a decision procedure for SL (namely truth table analysis), and that its axioms are independent.*

5

Alternative Axiom Systems for Sentential Logic

Axiom systems for sentential logic have been constructed which differ from SL in several important ways:

SL is an *interpreted* system. Many, perhaps most, axiom systems for sentential logic are *uninterpreted* systems (although, of course, it is intended that they be interpreted in the usual way).

SL has $\sim$ and $\supset$ as its primitive logical connectives. Many axiom systems for sentential logic have $\sim$ and "$\cdot$", or $\sim$ and $\vee$, as primitive symbols instead. And, of course, there are other possibilities.

SL has three axioms. Many systems contain four, or even five axioms, and a few contain less than three. Surprisingly, some axiom systems contain an *infinite number* of axioms. Of course, it is not possible actually to write down all of the axioms of such a system. So instead, *axiom patterns* (schemata) are employed in the *meta-language*, so that (roughly) all and only those formulas which are substitution instances of the axiom patterns are axioms of the system. If we had constructed SL in this way, then SL would have contained an infinite number of axioms,† and its meta-

---

* It is possible to construct a simpler axiom system for sentential logic, but the cost is even lengthier proofs.

† But only one rule of inference, namely Modus Ponens, since a rule of substitution would be unnecessary.

language would have contained exactly three axiom patterns, namely

(AP1): $(P \supset (Q \supset P))$

(AP2): $((P \supset (Q \supset R)) \supset ((P \supset Q) \supset (P \supset R)))$

(AP3): $((\sim Q \supset \sim P) \supset ((\sim Q \supset P) \supset Q))$

One might suppose that a system with an infinite number of axioms would be rejected on the ground that it lacks simplicity. But such systems have not been rejected for this reason, because their simplicity rating has been determined by the number of their meta-language axiom patterns and not the number of their axioms.

Some axiom systems for sentential logic contain axioms and theorems which are *sentences*, instead of *sentence forms*. An axiom system of this kind can be constructed by using axiom patterns in the meta-language and taking sentences rather than sentence forms as its substitution instances. Thus, instead of having $(p \supset (q \supset p))$ as an axiom, such a system might have $(A \supset (B \supset A))$, where A and B are *sentence constants*, not sentence variables. The vocabulary for this kind of system would have to be a little different than the vocabulary of SL, containing symbols which are sentence constants, but no symbols which are sentence variables.

6

Axiom Systems for Predicate Logic

Axiom systems for first order predicate (quantifier) logic are quite similar to those for sentential logic. (Indeed, to be complete a system for predicate logic must contain a system for sentential logic as a part.) Let's briefly examine a particular system of this kind, which we'll call "QL" (for Quantifier Logic).

The symbols of QL

The primitive symbols of QL will be those of SL plus a set of predicate symbols F, G, H, etc., a set of individual variables x, y, z, etc., and the symbol U, used to denote the *universal quantifier*.*

---

* We can dispense with a primitive symbol for the universal quantifier in an uninterpreted system, but for technical reasons cannot do so in an interpreted system, at least not without making the system unduly complex in other ways.

In addition, we introduce the symbol U into the meta-language to denote the symbol U of the object language, and also the symbol $\exists$, which is introduced by means of the following definition:

"$(\exists u)P$" is defined as an abbreviation for "$\sim(Uu)\sim P$".

The axioms of QL

For reasons of ease of presentation, we take infinitely many formulas as axioms of QL, and introduce five axiom patterns in the meta-language, using the letters P, Q, and R as formula variables, as before, and the letters u and w as meta-linguistic variables ranging over the object language individual variables x, y, z, etc.:

(A1): $(P \supset (Q \supset P))$

(A2): $((P \supset (Q \supset R)) \supset ((P \supset Q) \supset (P \supset R)))$

(A3): $((\sim Q \supset \sim P) \supset ((\sim Q \supset P) \supset Q))$

(A4): $(Uu)(P \supset Q) \supset (P \supset (Uu)Q)$,
where P contains no free occurrence of the variable u.

(A5): $(Uu)P \supset Q$, where Q results from P by the replacement of all free occurrences of u in P by w, and w occurs free in Q at all places at which u occurs free in P.*

The inference rules of QL

We introduce (into the meta-language) two rules of inference for QL:

(R1): If $(P \supset Q)$ and P are either axioms or theorems of QL, then Q may be inferred from them.†

---

* (A5) corresponds to the rule **UI**, introduced in Chapter Six.

† Since QL contains infinitely many axioms, we don't need a rule of inference similar to rule (R2) of SL in QL.

(R2): If *P* is an axiom or theorem of QL, then (*Uu*)*P* may be inferred from *P*.*

Properties of QL

It has been proved that QL is complete (in the sense that all sentence forms expressible in QL which are theorems of logic are provable as theorems of QL), consistent, and expressively complete. In addition, it has been proved that the axioms of QL are independent. However, not only is there no known decision procedure for QL, but it has been proved that *there cannot be a decision procedure for predicate logic*. This fact is of vital importance. For instance, the existence of a decision procedure for *sentential logic* makes possible the construction of a machine capable of solving all of the problems of sentential logic in a purely mechanical way. But there can be no machine of this kind capable of solving all of the problems of predicate logic.

7

Other Kinds of Axiom Systems

Some philosophers have held that axiom systems constitute the ideal way to systematize in the *sciences*, just as in logic or mathematics, although as a matter of fact geometry is the only science for which an axiom system has been constructed.†

Axiom systems for science differ from those for logic in several respects, the most important of which is the nature of their axioms. For instance, all of the axioms of sentential logic are *tautologies*, and are established without resort to observational (empirical) information or test. But the axioms of a system for a particular *science* cannot be established without making some observations. An example from physics is the famous formula $E = mc^2$, formulated by Einstein only after physicists had accumulated observational evidence on the nature of the universe for hundreds of years. At least some of the axioms of a system for a physical science must be *contingent* sentences (or contingent sentence forms), whereas those for sentential logic all are tautologies.

---

* (R2) corresponds to the rule **UG** introduced in Chapter Six.

† We pass over the disputes concerning the nature of geometry, remarking merely that the status of geometry *as an empirical science* has been questioned. Some philosophers would be inclined to classify geometry with logic and mathematics. Others claim that there are two kinds of geometry, one empirical, and hence scientific, the other logical.

In constructing axiom systems for science, it is more convenient to have defined terms in the object language rather than in the meta-language. But in most other respects, axiom systems for science will be very much like those for logic.

Axiom systems for arithmetic are also of great interest. In general, such systems are very much like those for deductive logic, because of the close relationship between these two fields. For instance, the axioms of a system for arithmetic can be established without resort to observational confirmation.

But axiom systems for arithmetic do differ from those for logic in several ways:

(1) As stated previously, we want an axiom system for arithmetic to be complete in a different sense than is required for logic. The difference stems from the fact that (roughly) systems for logic can express *contingent* sentences while those for arithmetic cannot. And since they cannot, all of their well-formed formulas which are sentences will be either *truths of arithmetic* or the *negations of truths of arithmetic*. Hence, to be complete, an axiom system for arithmetic must be such that every sentence expressible in the system is either a theorem of that system or else the negation of a theorem of that system.

(2) There are axiom systems for sentential and predicate logic which have been proved to be complete. Unfortunately, not only has no completeness proof been discovered for arithmetic, but it has been proved that *there cannot be a complete axiom system for all of arithmetic.**

No matter how many axioms and theorems such a system contains, we can always find some truth of arithmetic which is not a theorem of that system. Indeed, having found such a truth of arithmetic, it won't help matters to add it to the list of axioms of the system, for it has been proved that no matter how many times we do this, there will always be other truths of arithmetic discoverable which are still not axioms or theorems of the system.

The proof that we cannot have a complete axiom system for arithmetic is one of the most important proofs about axiom systems ever constructed.

---

* More precisely, what has been proved is that there cannot be a complete *and consistent* axiom system for arithmetic. Obviously, an inconsistent system could be constructed which would be complete, but such a system would be worthless.

(3) It also has been proved that *there can be no decision procedure for axiom systems for arithmetic*. Thus, just as in the case of predicate logic, we can never construct a computer which will solve all of the problems of arithmetic in a purely mechanical way.

(4) Perhaps there is some consolation in the fact that proofs of *consistency* have been constructed for certain axiom systems for arithmetic. In addition, decision procedures have been devised for *portions* of arithmetic, even if not for all of it.

8

Objections to Axiom Systems

Finally, perhaps we ought to note that some philosophers are less than enthusiastic concerning the construction of axiom systems. One reason for this lack of enthusiasm (but not the only reason) is that at least in some cases (namely axiom systems for logic) the construction of an axiom system involves a certain amount of *vicious circularity*.

Take an axiom system for predicate logic. Suppose that we want to prove that such a system is *consistent* (if in fact it is). The trouble is that a proof of consistency (in the meta-language) unavoidably employs the very "tools of reasoning" (such as Modus Ponens) which are taken as inference rules in the system itself. Now if these "tools of reasoning" themselves are consistent, then a proof that the object language system is consistent is valid. However, if they are inconsistent, then such a proof is *in*valid. So no progress is made by constructing a consistency proof, since we have to believe ahead of time in the consistency of the very rules of inference which the consistency proof establishes as consistent.*

---

* The same is true for the *axioms* of the system. Indeed, to be precise, we should speak of the consistency of the rules of inference *and* axioms, taken as a unit.

Appendix A

*Elementary
Intuitive
Logic of Sets*

1

Introduction

This appendix contains a brief account of the logic of sets. It is included because it constitutes an inherently interesting area of logic, and also because of its obvious connections both with traditional syllogistic logic and with modern symbolic logic.

2

Basic Terms

We shall use the term "set" synonymously with the terms "class", "group", "collection", etc. Thus, a **set** is any well-defined collection of distinct entities. For instance, all of the students in a particular classroom constitute a set, the natural numbers constitute a set, and even the collection of all students in a particular classroom and all children under the age of five constitute a set. *Any* collection of entities, however arbitrarily selected, constitutes a set, provided only that the collection is *well defined* (so that there is a way to determine whether a given entity is or is not a part of the collection).

The above sets were *intensionally* defined. But sets can also be extensionally defined. For instance, we can single out the set consisting solely of the numbers 3, 5, and 8, or the set consisting solely of Art and Betsy.

Let's use the capital letters F through Z as what we might call **set constants**, designating particular sets. For example, we could use the capital letter S to designate the set of scientists, and the capital letter P to designate the set of philosophers.

And let's use the capital letters A through E as what we might call **set variables**, ranging over set constants.

In addition, let's use the small letters as we did in discussing predicate logic. That is, let's use the small letters a through t as individual constants, and the letters u through z as individual variables. (For convenience sake, let's also permit the usual use of *numerals* to designate particular numbers.)

Finally, we introduce several terms of the logic of sets:

(1) We introduce the term $\in$ (the Greek letter epsilon), as an abbreviation for phrases such as "is a member of", "belongs to", "is an element of", etc. That is, we introduce the term $\in$ to signify **set membership**. Thus, the sentence "Art is a member of the set of philosophers" can be symbolized as $a \in P$, and the sentence "The number five is a member of the set of natural numbers" can be symbolized as $5 \in N$ (where $N =$ "the set of natural numbers").

(2) Often one set is *included* in, or is a **subset** of, another set. For example, the set of *women* is a subset of the set of human beings. The symbol $\subseteq$ is used to abbreviate phrases such as "is included in", "is a subset of", etc., and thus to signify set inclusion. Using this notation, we can symbolize the sentence "The set of scientists is a subset of the set of philosophers" as $S \subseteq P$, and "The set of women is a subset of the set of human beings" (in everyday English "All women are human") as $W \subseteq H$.

Obviously, set A is a subset of a set B *iff* (if and only if) every member of A also is a member of B. In symbols, this reads

$$(A \subseteq B) \equiv (x)[(x \in A) \supset (x \in B)]$$

Just as obviously, we can more precisely *define* $\subseteq$ contextually by stipulating that

$$(A \subseteq B) \;=\; df(x)[(A \in B) \supset (x \in B)]$$

(3) Often, some (or all) of the members of one set also are members of some other set. For instance, some members of the class of scientists also are members of the class of philosophers. The set of all things which are members both of the set of scientists *and* of the set of philosophers is said to be the **intersect set**, or the **intersection**, or the **product** of the set of scientists and the set of philosophers.

The symbol $\cap$ is used to designate **set intersection**. Using this symbol, we can symbolize, say, the phrase "the intersection of A and B" as $A \cap B$, and the phrase "the intersection of the set of scientists and the set of philosophers" as $S \cap P$. (Often, the symbol for set intersection is simply omitted, much as the multiplication sign is omitted in arithmetic. For instance, omitting the symbol for set intersection, $A \cap B$ can be written as AB.)

It is clear that the intersection of two sets, A and B, is the set of all things which are members of both A and B. So a given entity is a member of $A \cap B$ *iff* that entity is a member both of A and of B. In symbols, this reads

$$(x)\{[x \in (A \cap B)] \equiv [(x \in A) \cdot (x \in B)]\}.$$

So we can more precisely define $\cap$ contextually by stipulating that

$$[x \in (A \cap B)] \;=\; df\,[(x \in A) \cdot (x \in B)]$$

(4) We can also speak of the set of all those things which are members either of set A or of set B (or both). For instance, we can speak of the set of all things which are either scientists or philosophers (or both). Sets of

this kind are called the **union set**, or the **union**, or the **sum** of the two sets which they join. For example, the set of human beings is the union of the sets of male humans and female humans.

The symbol ∪ is used to designate **set union**. Using it, we can symbolize the phrase "the union of A and B" as $A \cup B$, and the phrase "the union of the set of male humans and the set of female humans" as $M \cup F$. (The term + often is used to designate set union, rather than ∪.)

Since the union of two sets, A and B, is the set of all things which are members *either* of A *or* of B (or both), it follows that a given entity is a member of $A \cup B$ *iff* that entity is a member either of A or of B (or both). In symbols, this reads

$$(x)\{[x \in (A \cup B)] \equiv [(x \in A) \vee (x \in B)]\}$$

So we can more precisely define ∪ contextually by stipulating that

$$[x \in (A \cup B)] =_{df} [(x \in A) \vee (x \in B)]$$

(5) Two allegedly different sets sometimes turn out to be *identical*, in that they have the same members. For example, the set of triangles is identical with the set of trilaterals, and the set of human beings is identical with the set of mortal humans.

The symbol = (used to symbolize identity between individuals in the discussion of predicate logic in Part Two of this text) is generally used in the logic of sets to designate **set identity**. Using this term, we can symbolize the expression "A is identical with B" as $A = B$, and the sentence "The set of animals with hearts is identical with the set of animals with kidneys" as $H = K$.

As we are using the term, two sets are *identical iff* a given thing belongs to the first set *iff* it belongs to the second. In symbols, this reads

$$(A = B) \equiv (x)[(x \in A) \equiv (x \in B)]$$

(This is often called the **principle of extensionality**, or the **principle of extensionality for sets**, and is quite important.) Obviously, we can more precisely define $=$ contextually by stipulating that

$$(A = B) = df\,(x)[(x \in A) \equiv (x \in B)]$$

(6) It is customary to use the bar symbol $^-$ to symbolize the **complement** of a set, that is, to symbolize the set of all entities (in the domain of discourse) which are *not* members of a given set. For instance, we can symbolize the phrase "the set of nonscientists" as $\bar{S}$. (In some other systems, this would be written $\sim S$, or S'.)

It also is customary to use the symbol $\neq$ to symbolize *nonidentity*. For example, we can symbolize the sentence "The set of scientists is not identical with the set of philosophers, as $S \neq P$. And it is customary to use the symbol $\notin$ to symbolize *nonmembership* in a set. For example, we can symbolize the sentence "Art is not a member of the set of students who have failed logic", as $a \notin L$.

(7) Some subsets of a given set are identical with that set, and some are not. If a subset of a given set is *not* identical with that set, then the subset is said to be a **proper subset** of the given set. For instance, the set of all humans is a proper subset of the set of all mammals.

The symbol $\subset$ is usually used as an abbreviation of the phrase "is a proper subset of". Using this symbol, we can symbolize the expression "A is a proper subset of B" as $A \subset B$, and the sentence "The set of humans is a proper subset of the set of mammals" as $H \subset M$.

Obviously, A is a proper subset of B *iff* A is a subset of B *and* A is not identical with B. In symbols, this reads

$$(A \subset B) \equiv [(A \subseteq B) \cdot (A \neq B)]$$

So we can more precisely define the term $\subset$ contextually by stipulating that

$$(A \subset B) = df\,[(A \subseteq B) \cdot (A \neq B)]$$

(8) We can also speak of the **difference** of A and B, meaning the set of all things which are members of A but not of B. For example, we might speak of the set of hydrogen compounds which are not inorganic compounds.

Nothing new is needed to symbolize sentences about the differences of sets. For instance, we can write the phrase "the difference of A and B" as $A \cap \bar{B}$, and the phrase "the difference of the set of hydrogen compounds and the set of inorganic compounds" (or the phrase "the set of organic hydrogen compounds") as $H \cap \bar{I}$.

(9) It is customary to introduce special symbols for two very important sets, namely the **universal set** and the **null set**. The **universal set** is the set containing every entity (in the domain of discourse). The symbol I is often used to designate the universal set. (The symbol V also is very common.) Clearly, the universal set is such that for every x (in the domain of discourse), x is a member of the universal set, or in symbols $(x)(x \in I)$.

The **null set** (or **empty set**) is the set containing no members whatsoever. The symbol O is often used to designate the null set. (The symbol Λ also is used.) Clearly, the null set is such that for every x, x is *not* a member of the null set, or in symbols $(x)(x \notin O)$.

It is not hard to see that there is one and only one null set. Suppose A and B are two allegedly different null sets. Then the sentences

(A): $(x)[(x \in A) \supset (x \in B)]$

(B): $(x)[(x \in B) \supset (x \in A)]$

are both true, because of their always false antecedents. But from sentences (A) and (B), plus the principle of extensionality (namely $(A = B) \equiv (x)$ $[(x \in A) \equiv (x \in B)]$), the sentence $A = B$ deductively follows. So the two allegedly different empty sets, A and B, in fact are identical. Given *any* two allegedly different empty sets, it follows that they are identical. Thus, the set of unicorns is identical with the set of centaurs, which is identical with the set of round squares, which is identical with the set of all objects which travel at a speed greater than the speed of light,* etc.

---

* Assuming present day science is correct, and nothing can travel faster than light.

(10) Finally, we introduce symbols used to indicate the specific members of certain sets. For this purpose, we use *braces*, that is, the symbols { and }. For instance, we can indicate the set whose members are the numbers 5, 8, and 9 by the expression {5, 8, 9}. And we can indicate the set of 18th century American presidents by the expression {Washington, Adams}. (Obviously, we cannot use this notation to specify the membership of most *intensionally defined* sets, such as the set of human beings, since we do not know, and cannot list, all of the members of this class.)

3

*Translating
Ordinary
Language*

Corresponding to every *property*, there is a *set* containing exactly those entities which have that property. For instance, corresponding to the property of being red, there is the set composed of exactly those things which have the property of being red, and corresponding to the property of being a philosopher, there is the set composed of exactly those entities which have the property of being philosophers.

So we can symbolize the sentence "There are red things" either in the notation of predicate logic, as $(\exists x)Rx$, or in the notation of the logic of sets, as $(\exists x)(x \in R)$, $R \neq O$, etc. Similarly, we can symbolize the sentence "Art is a philosopher", either as Pa, or as $a \in P$, and the sentence "Art is a scientist who is also a philosopher" as $Sa \cdot Pa$, or $(a \in S) \cdot (a \in P)$ or $a \in (s \cap P)$.

All of the standard categorical propositions of traditional syllogistic logic can be expressed in the notation of the logic of sets. For instance, the A proposition "All scientists are philosophers" can be interpreted to assert that the set of scientists is included in the set of philosophers", and hence symbolized as $S \subseteq P$, or as $(S \cap \bar{P}) = O$ (roughly as we symbolized it when discussing syllogistic logic). Similarly, the E proposition "No scientists are philosophers" can be symbolized as $S \subseteq \bar{P}$, or as $(S \cap P) = O$, the I proposition "Some scientists are philosophers" as $(\exists x)[(x \in S) \cdot (x \in P)]$, or as $(S \cap P) \neq O$, and the O proposition "Some scientists are not philosophers" as $(\exists x)[(x \in S) \cdot (x \notin P)]$, or as $(S \cap \bar{P}) \neq O$.

We can also use this notation to symbolize more complicated propositions. For example, the proposition "All scientists are philosophers *and* mathematicians" can be symbolized as $S \subseteq (P \cap M)$, and the proposition

"All scientists are philosophers *or* mathematicians" can be symbolized as $S \subseteq (P \cup M)$.

However, a few symbolizations are just a bit tricky. For instance, the proposition "All scientists and philosophers are mathematicians" is *not* correctly symbolized as $(S \cap P) \subseteq M$, for the proposition "All scientists and philosophers are mathematicians" does *not* assert that all things which are *both* scientists *and* philosophers are mathematicians, but rather that *scientists* are mathematicians *and philosophers* are mathematicians (or that anything which is either a scientist *or* a philosopher is a mathematician). Hence it is correctly symbolized as $(S \subseteq M) \cdot (P \subseteq M)$, or as $(S \cup P) \subseteq M$. But pitfalls of this kind ought to be familiar from the discussion on symbolization in Part Two of this text.

4

An Axiom System for the Algebra of Sets

An important part of the logic of sets (omitting, for instance, the symbol for set membership and hence omitting theorems containing that term) often is cast into axiomatic form, and referred to as the **algebra of sets**, or **algebra of classes** (as well as a **Boolean Algebra**).

One interesting feature of such a system is the *similarity* of many of its axioms and theorems with some of the better known tautologies of sentential logic, including several used in Part One in the list of 18 valid argument forms. This is illustrated by one of the standard lists of axioms for the algebra of sets, namely:

1. $(A \cup 0) = A$

2. $(A \cap 1) = A$

3. $(A \cup B) = (B \cup A)$

4. $(A \cap B) = (B \cap A)$

5. $[A \cup (B \cap C)] = [(A \cup B) \cap (A \cup C)]$

6. $[A \cap (B \cup C)] = [(A \cap B) \cup (A \cap C)]$

7. $(A \cup \bar{A}) = 1$

8. $(A \cap \bar{A}) = 0$

9. $(\exists A)(\exists B)(A \neq B)$

If we replace $\cup$ by $\vee$, $\cap$ by "$\cdot$", and $=$ by $\equiv$, in the above axioms, then 3 and 4 become the commutation laws of sentential logic, and 5 and 6 become the distribution laws. (Indeed, 3, 4, 5, and 6 are the set formulations of these laws.) The relationship between 7 and the law of the excluded middle (namely $p \vee \sim p$) is obvious, as is the relationship between 8 and the law of noncontradiction (namely $\sim(p \cdot \sim p)$).

The following are some of the interesting theorems which can be derived from these nine axioms:

10. $(A \cup A) = A$

11. $(A \cap A) = A$

12. $(A \cup 1) = 1$

13. $(A \cap 0) = 0$

14. $0 \neq 1$

15. $(A = \bar{B}) \supset (B = \bar{A})$

16. $A = \bar{\bar{A}}$

17. $[A \cup (B \cup C)] = [(A \cup B) \cup C]$

18. $[A \cap (B \cap C)] = [(A \cap B) \cap C]$

19. $(\overline{A \cup B}) = (\bar{A} \cap \bar{B})$

20. $(\overline{A \cap B}) = (\bar{A} \cup \bar{B})$

21. $0 = \bar{1}$

22. $1 = \bar{0}$

Theorem 15 is a set formulation of contraposition, 16 of *double negation*, 17 and 18 of the two *association* laws, and 19 and 20 of the two *DeMorgan* laws. (However, replacing A and B by p and q, $=$ by $\equiv$, and $^-$ by $\sim$, in

15, does not yield $(p \supset q) \equiv (\sim q \supset \sim p)$, the contraposition equivalence of sentential logic, but rather its close relative $(p \equiv \sim q) \supset (q \equiv \sim p)$.)

Finally, it should be remarked that the whole of the algebra of sets can be derived in a predicate logic system roughly like the one presented in Part Two, if we translate its basic terms into the notation of predicate logic (making use of the idea that corresponding to every property there is a set containing exactly the entities which have that property).

In general, then, the relationship between the logic of sets and the systems presented in the first three parts of this text is very close.

Appendix B

1

Introduction

The standard set of four quantifier rules (**UI**, **EI**, **UG**, **EG**) presented in Part Two very likely constitutes the most difficult material to master in the entire text. In this appendix, we present the outline of a predicate logic system containing an alternative set of quantifier rules.

These rules have the advantage that they are much simpler, and hence much easier to learn, than the standard rules. (Indeed, they may well constitute the simplest set of quantifier rules so far constructed.) But they also have two important disadvantages (which is why a more complex set of rules was presented in Part Two). First, they tend to make proofs longer and more difficult to construct (simplicity of rules generally yields complexity of proofs). And second, they forbid many legitimate proofs which mirror *informal* proofs in mathematics and logic.

The greater simplicity of the alternative rules results from the *complete elimination* of rules **UG** (Universal Generalization) and **EG** (Existential Generalization). The idea is that proofs using the standard rules in which **UG** or **EG** are employed are to be replaced by *indirect proofs* (*reductio ad absurdum proofs*).

2

Statement of the Alternative Set of Quantifier Rules

We assume a predicate logic notation of the kind presented in Part Two of this text, and take the notation and inference rules of the sentential logic presented in Part One as part of the predicate logic system to be outlined. Thus, we have at our disposal as inference rules the 18 valid argument forms, **CP**, and **IP** (reductio ad absurdum).

Now let's add two of the four **QN** rules. Where u is any individual variable,

$$(u) \sim (\ldots u \ldots) :: \sim (\exists u)(\ldots u \ldots)$$
$$(\exists u) \sim (\ldots u \ldots) :: \sim (u)(\ldots u \ldots)$$

(Addition of the other two **QN** rules, while not necessary, will simplify many proofs considerably.)

Finally, we state rules **UI** and **EI**:

1. Let u be any individual variable.

2. With respect to **UI**, let w be any individual variable or constant.

3. With respect to **EI**, let w be any individual variable which does not occur free previously in the proof.

4. In both cases, let the expression w result from the replacement of all occurrences of u free in the expression $(\ldots u \ldots)$ by occurrences of w free in the expression $(\ldots w \ldots)$. Then

   Rule UI: $(u)(\ldots u \ldots) / \therefore (\ldots w \ldots)$

   Rule EI: $(\exists u)(\ldots u \ldots) / \therefore (\ldots w \ldots)$

It should be obvious from this formulation that every inference permitted by the alternative rules also is permitted by the standard rules presented in Part Two, although the reverse is not true. So the alternative rules permit a proper subset of the inferences permitted by the standard rules. It follows that the standard rules contain features which are *logically super-fluous*, although they are certainly not superfluous in other ways (chiefly in permitting proofs which more faithfully mirror informal reasoning in mathematics and logic).

3

Proofs Using the
Alternative
Quantifier
Rules

Most proofs of any interest using the alternative rules require the use of **IP**. In many cases, the use of **IP** is straightforward and obvious. An example is the proof:

1.	$(x)(Fx \supset Gx)$	p
2.	$(x)(Gx \supset Hx)$	$/ \therefore (x)(Fx \supset Hx)$
→3.	$\sim(x)(Fx \supset Hx)$	**AP**
4.	$(\exists x) \sim (Fx \supset Hx)$	3, **QN**
5.	$\sim(Fx \supset Hx)$	4, **EI**
6.	$Fx \supset Gx$	1, **UI**
7.	$Gx \supset Hx$	2, **UI**
8.	$\sim(\sim Fx \vee Hx)$	5, **Impl**
9.	$Fx \cdot \sim Hx$	8, **DeM, DN**
10.	Fx	9, **Simp**
11.	$Fx \supset Hx$	6, 7 **HS**
12.	Hx	10, 11 **MP**
13.	$\sim Hx$	9, **Simp**
14.	$Hx \cdot \sim Hx$	12, 13 **Conj**
15.	$(x)(Fx \supset Hx)$	3, 14 **IP**

But sometimes, proofs are more difficult. An example, although certainly not an *unusually* difficult one, is the following proof that $(\exists y)(x)(Fx \supset Gy) \equiv [(\exists x)Fx \supset (\exists x)Gx]$ is a theorem of logic:

1.	$(\exists y)(x)(Fx \supset Gy)$	AP
2.	$\sim[(\exists x)Fx \supset (\exists x)Gx]$	AP
3.	$(x)(Fx \supset Gy)$	1, EI
4.	$\sim[\sim(\exists x)Fx \lor (\exists x)Gx]$	2, Impl
5.	$(\exists x)Fx \cdot \sim(\exists x)Gx$	5, DeM, DN
6.	$(\exists x)Fx$	5, Simp
7.	Fx	6, EI
8.	$Fx \supset Gy$	3, UI
9.	Gy	7, 8 MP
10.	$\sim(\exists x)Gx$	5, Simp
11.	$(x)\sim Gx$	10, QN
12.	$\sim Gy$	11, UI
13.	$Gy \cdot \sim Gy$	9, 12 Conj
14.	$[(\exists x)Fx \supset (\exists x)Gx]$	2, 13 IP
15.	$(\exists y)(x)(Fx \supset Gy)$ $\supset [(\exists x)Fx \supset (\exists x)Gx]$	1, 15 CP
16.	$\sim(\exists y)(x)(Fx \supset Gy)$	AP
17.	$(y)\sim(x)(Fx \supset Gy)$	16, QN
18.	$(y)(\exists x)\sim(Fx \supset Gy)$	17, QN
19.	$(y)(\exists x)\sim(\sim Fx \lor Gy)$	18, Impl
20.	$(y)(\exists x)(Fx \cdot \sim Gy)$	19, DeM, DN
21.	$(\exists x)(Fx \cdot \sim Gy)$	20, UI
22.	$(Fu \cdot \sim Gy)$	21, EI

23.	$\sim (\exists x)Fx$	AP
24.	$(x)\sim Fx$	23, QN
25.	$\sim Fu$	24, UI
26.	Fu	22, Simp
27.	$Fu \cdot \sim Fu$	25, 26 Conj
28.	$(\exists x)Fx$	23, 27 IP
29.	$(\exists x)Gx$	AP
30.	Gz	29, EI
31.	$(\exists x)(Fx \cdot \sim Gz)$	20, UI
32.	$Fw \cdot \sim Gz$	31, EI
33.	$\sim Gz$	32, Simp
34.	$Gz \cdot \sim Gz$	30, 33 Conj
35.	$\sim (\exists x)Gx$	29, 34 IP
36.	$(\exists x)Fx \cdot \sim (\exists x)Gx$	28, 35 Conj
37.	$\sim [\sim (\exists x)Fx \lor (\exists x)Gx]$	36, DeM, DN
38.	$\sim [(\exists x)Fx \supset (\exists x)Gx]$	37, Impl
39.	$\sim (\exists y)(x)(Fx \supset Gy)$ $\supset \sim [(\exists x)Fx \supset (\exists x)Gx]$	16, 38 CP
40.	$[(\exists x)Fx \supset (\exists x)Gx]$ $\supset (\exists y)(x)(Fx \supset Gy)$	39, Contr
41.	$\{(\exists y)(x)(Fx \supset Gy)$ $\supset [(\exists x)Fx \supset (\exists x)Gx]\}$ $\cdot \{[(\exists x)Fx \supset (\exists x)Gx]$ $\supset (\exists y)(x)(Fx \supset Gy)\}$	15, 40 Conj
42.	$(\exists y)(x)(Fx \supset Gy)$ $\equiv [(\exists x)Fx \supset (\exists x)Gx]$	41, Equiv

This proof is very long, but its basic structure is only a bit more complex than usual. To start with, the proof breaks down into three basic units. The first unit, comprising the first fifteen lines, contains a proof that the biconditional holds in *one* direction (from left to right). The second unit, lines 16 through 40 contains a proof that the biconditional holds in the *other* direction (from right to left). And the third unit, lines 41 and 42, simply combines the conclusions of the first two units, yielding the final conclusion.

The strategy *within* the first unit is only mildly complex, containing a conditional proof within which an indirect proof is constructed. It is the second unit which contains the difficult part of the proof. But even here the proof is not discouragingly complex. Its basic form consists of a conditional proof within which two subsidiary indirect proofs are constructed. The conclusions of the two indirect proofs are conjoined to form the consequent of the final step of the conditional proof.

Of course, *constructing* a long involved proof of this kind is much more difficult than merely understanding its structure once it has been constructed. In general, we hit upon a solution to a problem of this complexity only after having tried several simpler lines of attack which have failed. Sometimes, then, persistence is almost as important as insight. At any rate, it certainly is true that when insight fails we ought to follow the strategy rule to put down on paper anything valid that we can think of. As my own logic teacher, Hans Reichenbach, was fond of saying, "To some extent, we think with our fingers".

Glossary

Part One

Addition (Add): The valid implicational argument form $p \mathbin{/} \therefore p \lor q$.

And: (See **Dot**).

Antecedent: The entire expression to the left of the main $\supset$ in a conditional sentence (or sentence form).

Argument: A list of sentences (premises) offered in defense of, or justification of, another sentence (a conclusion).

Argument form: A group of sentence forms, all of whose substitution instances are arguments.

Association (Assoc): The valid equivalence argument forms

$$p \lor (q \lor r) :: (p \lor q) \lor r \quad \text{and}$$
$$p \cdot (q \cdot r) :: (p \cdot q) \cdot r$$

Atomic sentence: A sentence which contains no other sentence as a part.

Biconditional: (See **Equivalence**).

Case analysis: (See **Truth table analysis**).

Commutation (Comm): The valid equivalence argument forms

$$(p \lor q) :: (q \lor p) \quad \text{and}$$
$$(p \cdot q) :: (q \cdot p)$$

Compound sentence: A sentence which contains other sentences as parts. A non-atomic sentence.

Conclusion: A sentence in an argument for which the evidence sentences (premises) of that argument are said to offer support or justification.

Conditional: A compound sentence (or sentence form) whose main sentence connective is $\supset$. (In English, the term is ambiguous in that it often is also used when a *non*-truth functional implication is involved.) *Synonyms:* (also ambiguous in English) **Hypothetical, Implication.**

Conditional Proof, rule of (CP): The rule which permits inference from a sentence q to a sentence $p \supset q$, if the assumption of p permitted the derivation of q.

Conjunct: The entire expression to the left of, or to the right of, the main " $\cdot$ " in a conjunction.

Conjunction: (1) A compound sentence (or sentence form) whose main connective is " $\cdot$ ". (2) The valid implicational argument form

p
$q \mid \therefore p \cdot q$

Consequent: The entire expression to the right of the main $\supset$ in a conditional sentence (or sentence form).

Consistent premises: Noncontradictory premises.

Constructive Dilemma (CD): The valid implicational argument form

$p \supset q$
$r \supset s$
$p \lor r \mid \therefore q \lor s$

Contingent sentence: A sentence which is *not* a substitution instance of any tautologous or contingent sentence form.

Contingent sentence form: A sentence form which has both true and false substitution instances.

Contradiction: (1) A sentence form all of whose substitution instances are false. (2) A substitution instance of a contradictory sentence form.

Contraposition (Contra): The valid equivalence argument form

$(p \supset q) :: (\sim q \supset \sim p)$

Contrapositive (of a given sentence): The sentence obtained from the given sentence by means of contraposition.

Deductive argument: An argument whose premises are claimed to provide conclusive evidence for its conclusion. If the premises of a *valid deductive argument* are true, then its conclusion must be true, because the information contained in its conclusion is already contained in its premises.

DeMorgan's Theorem (DeM): The valid equivalence argument forms

$\sim (p \cdot q) :: (\sim p \lor \sim q)$ and
$\sim (p \lor q) :: (\sim p \cdot \sim q)$

Discovery, context of: The context concerned with the psychology of the thought processes which lead to the discovery of new conclusions. (See **Justification, context of.**)

Disjunct: The entire expression to the left of, or to the right of, the main $\lor$ in a disjunction.

Disjunction: A compound sentence (or sentence form) whose main connective is $\lor$.

Disjunctive Syllogism (DS): The valid implicational argument forms

$p \lor q$ $p \lor q$
$\sim p \mid \therefore q$ and $\sim q \mid \therefore p$

Distribution (Dist): The valid equivalence argument forms

$p \cdot (q \lor r) :: (p \cdot q) \lor (p \cdot r)$

and

$p \lor (q \cdot r) :: (p \lor q) \cdot (p \lor r)$

Dot: Symbolized as " · ". The truth functional sentence connective defined by the truth table

p	q	$p \cdot q$
T	T	T
T	F	F
F	T	F
F	F	F

Generally the best translation for the English connectives "and", "however", "but", etc. *Synonym:* **And.**

Double negation: The valid equivalence argument form

$$p :: \sim \sim p$$

Equivalence: (1) Symbolized as $\equiv$. The truth functional sentence connective defined by the truth table

p	q	$(p \equiv q)$
T	T	T
T	F	F
F	T	F
F	F	T

Roughly equivalent to the English connective "if and only if". However, many English uses of "equivalence" and "if and only if" are not truth functional. *Synonyms:* **Iff, Material equivalence, Biconditional.** (2) Abbreviation: **Equiv.** The valid argument forms

$$(p \equiv q) :: (p \supset q) \cdot (q \supset p)$$

and

$$(p \equiv q) :: (p \cdot q) \vee (\sim p \cdot \sim q)$$

Exclusive disjunction: (See **Exclusive "or".**)

Exclusive "or": The truth functional sentence connective defined by the truth table

p	q	$(p$ exclusive or $q)$
T	T	F
T	F	T
F	T	T
F	F	F

No symbol was introduced for this sentence connective in this book, but often the symbols $\dot{\vee}$ and $\wedge$ are used. The English word "or" is often used in this sense. *Synonym:* **Exclusive disjunction.**

Exportation (Exp): The valid equivalence argument form

$$[(p \cdot q) \supset r] :: [p \supset (q \supset r)].$$

Hypothetical: (See **Conditional.**)

Hypothetical Syllogism (HS): The valid implicational argument form

$$p \supset q$$
$$q \supset r \, / \therefore p \supset r.$$

Iff: (See **Equivalence.**)

Implication (Imp): (1) The valid equivalence argument form

$$(p \supset q) :: (\sim p \vee q)$$

(2) (See **Conditional.**)

Implicational argument form: One of the first eight of the eighteen valid argument forms of the sentential logic system presented in Part One. They are called *implica-*

tional forms because they are *one directional*. That is, they permit inferences from given premises to certain conclusions but do *not* permit inferences from those conclusions to the given premises.

Inclusive disjunction: (See **Vee**.)

Inclusive "or": Symbolized as $\lor$. The truth functional statement connective defined by the truth table

p	q	$p \lor q$
T	T	T
T	F	T
F	T	T
F	F	F

Corresponds roughly to the English term "or", used in its inclusive sense, and also to the English term "and/or". *Synonyms:* **Vel, Vee.**

Inconsistent premises: Contradictory premises.

Indirect Proof, rule of (IP): The rule which permits inference to the negation of a sentence from which a contradiction has been derived. *Synonym:* **Reductio ad Absurdum Proof.**

Inductive argument: An argument whose premises are intended to provide evidence, but not *conclusive* evidence, for its conclusion. It is possible for a *valid inductive argument* to have true premises and a false conclusion.

Justification, context of: The context with which formal logic is concerned, that is, the context of *rational justifications* of conclusions (See **Discovery, context of.**)

Material Implication: Symbolized as $\supset$. The truth functional sentence connective defined by the truth table

p	q	$(p \supset q)$
T	T	T
T	F	F
F	T	T
F	F	T

The truth functional connective $\supset$ captures *part* of the meaning of all (or, at least, most) English uses of connectives such as "implies", "if _____ then _ _ _ _ _ _", "provided", "assuming", etc., usually including that part of the meaning which is important for proofs of deductive arguments.

Modus Ponens (MP): The valid implicational argument form

$p \supset q$
$p \, / \therefore \, q$

Modus Tollens (MT): The valid implicational argument form

$p \supset q$
$\sim q \, / \therefore \, \sim p$

Not: Symbolized as $\sim$. The truth functional sentence connective defined by the truth table

p	$\sim p$
T	F
F	T

Corresponds roughly to the various English terms of negation. *Synonym:* **Tilde.**

Premise: A sentence in an argument presented as evidence for, or justification of, its conclusion.

Proof of an argument: A series of sentences and/or sentence forms such that each member of the series is either a premise or else follows from a previous member of the series by a valid argument form.

Proposition: The meaning or sense common to all sentences which have the same meaning; *e.g.*, the meaning common to the sentences "John took the ball", "The ball was taken by John", etc. (The question as to whether or not there are such things as propositions is in dispute.)

Propositional form: The form of a symbolized sentence (or argument) obtained by replacing each sentence constant in the symbolized sentence (or argument) by a sentence variable (taking care to replace a given capital letter by the same sentence variable throughout).

Reductio ad Absurdum Proof: (See **Indirect Proof**.)

Sentence: A linguistic expression which is either true or false.

Sentence Connective: A symbol used to combine two sentences into a larger compound sentence. (Exception : $\sim$ is considered a sentence connective but does not combine sentences.)

Sentence constant: A capital letter abbreviating an English sentence, atomic or compound.

Sentence form: An expression containing sentence variables, such that if all of its sentence variables are replaced by capital letters (abbreviations for sentences), the resulting expression is a sentence.

Sentence variable: A small letter p through z used as a place-holder in a sentence form (or other linguistic form) such that if all the sentence variables in a sentence form are replaced by capital letters (abbreviations for sentences), then the resulting expression is a sentence.

Simplification (Simp): The valid implicational argument forms

$$p \cdot q \,/\!\therefore p \quad \text{and} \quad p \cdot q \,/\!\therefore q$$

Sound argument: A valid deductive argument with true premises. All other deductive arguments are *unsound*.

Substitution instance: A sentence obtained from a sentence form by replacing all of the sentence variables in the sentence form by capital letters (abbreviations for sentences). (This term also is used in a wider sense to cover cases where variables are replaced by certain kinds of constants, or where certain kinds of variables are *quantified*.)

Tautology: (1) A sentence form all of whose substitution instances are true. (2) A substitution instance of a tautologous sentence form.

Tilde: (See **Not**.)

Truth functional: A sentence connective is truth functional if the truth values of the sentences formed by its use are determined by the truth values of the sentences it conjoins. Similarly, sentence *forms* constructed by means of truth functional sentence connectives are such that the truth values of their *substitution instances* are determined by the truth values of their component sentences.

Truth table: A table giving the truth values of all possible substitution instances of a given sentence form, in terms of the possible truth values of the component sentences of these substitution instances. (Analogously, we can also speak of the truth table of a sentence.)

Truth table analysis: A method for determining the truth value of a sentence from knowledge of the truth values of its component sentences. Similarly, a method for determining whether a sentence form is tautologous, contradictory or contingent, by considering the truth values of all possible substitution instances. *Synonym:* **Case analysis.**

Truth value: There are two truth values, namely *true* and *false*.

Valid argument: A substitution instance of a valid argument form (but not necessarily one of the eighteen valid forms listed in Part One). All other arguments are *invalid*.

Valid (deductive) argument: A substitution instance of a valid (deductive) argument form and hence such that if its premises are true its conclusion *must* be true.

Valid (deductive) argument form: A deductive argument form all of whose substitution instances are valid deductive arguments.

Valid equivalence argument form: A two-directional valid argument form. For example, Double Negation is a valid equivalence argument form.

Valid implicational argument form: A one-directional valid argument form. For example, Modus Ponens is a valid implicational argument form.

Vee: (See **Inclusive "or".**)

Vel: (See **Inclusive "or".**)

Ambiguous name: The name given to an unknown value or individual; *e.g.*, "John Doe", the *x* in $x + 7 = 3$, etc.

Asymmetry: A property of relations such that if one thing bears that relation to a second thing, then the second cannot bear it to the first. "Is the father of" is an example of an asymmetrical relation.

Bound variable: A variable within the scope of a relevant quantifier. For example, in the expression $(x)Fxy$ the variable *x*, but not the variable *y*, is bound by the (x) quantifier.

Definite description: A descriptive phrase used to select or refer to a particular individual entity; *e.g.*, "The tallest man in the world is over eight feet tall", "Mark Twain is the author of *Huck Finn*", and "The chairman of the club is late tonight".

Existential Generalization (EG): The inference rule permitting the addition of an existential quantifier to certain expressions (also permitting certain other changes in the expression). For example, in certain cases, we can infer by **EG** from $Fx \cdot Gxy$ to $(\exists x)(Fx \cdot Gxy)$, or $(\exists z)(Fz \cdot Gzy)$, or $(\exists z)(Fz \cdot Gxy)$, etc.

Existential Instantiation (EI): The rule permitting inferences from existentially quantified expressions to certain of their instances; *e.g.*, the inferences from $(\exists x)(Fx \cdot Gxy)$ to $Fx \cdot Gxy$, $Fz \cdot Gzy$, etc.

Existential quantifier: The expressions $(\exists x)$, $(\exists y)$, etc., as used in sentences such as $(\exists x)(Fx \cdot Gx)$, $(\exists x)(\exists y)Fxy$, and so on.

Expansion (of a quantified sentence): A quantified sentence "spelled out" for a particular domain of individuals; *e.g.*, the expansion of the sentence $(x)(Fx \lor Gx)$ for a domain of two individuals, *a* and *b*, is $(Fa \lor Ga) \cdot (Fb \lor Gb)$, and the expansion of the sentence $(\exists x)(Fx \cdot Gx)$ for the same domain is $(Fa \cdot Ga) \lor (Fb \cdot Gb)$.

First order predicate logic: A predicate logic which forbids sentences which ascribe properties to properties.

Free variable: An unbound variable. A variable not within the scope of a relevant quantifier. For example, in the expression $(x)Fxy \supset Gxy$, the second *x* variable and both *y* variables are free.

Functional logic: (See **Predicate logic**.)

Identity symbol: The symbol $=$, used to indicate identity between entities. For instance, we can symbolize the sentence "Mark Twain is Samuel Clemens" as $t = s$.

Indirect context: Contexts involving believing, knowing, seeking, etc., as well as those involving necessity, possibility, etc. Sentences containing indirect contexts generally contain phrases such as "believes that", "is looking for", "it is necessary that", etc., which introduce the indirect context. (Some typical sentences containing indirect contexts are "Art is looking for Betsy", "Art believes that Betsy is tall", "It is possible that it will rain tomorrow".) Standard formulations of predicate logic are not adequate to deal with most sentences containing indirect contexts.

Individual constants: The small letters *a* through *n* used to denote particular individuals, as opposed to *properties*; *e.g.*, *a* used to designate the person Art.

Individual variables: The small letters *u* through *z* used as variables replaceable by individual constants.

Intransitivity: A property of relations which are such that if one thing bears that relation to a second, and the second to a third, then the first cannot bear it to the third. "Is the father of" is an example of an intransitive relation.

Instance (of a universally quantified expression): The expression minus a quantifier which quantified the whole expression, where the variables previously quantified by the dropped quantifier are replaced either by other variables, or constants, or by themselves. For example, the expressions $Fz \supset (\exists y)Gyz$, $Fa \supset (\exists y)Gyz$, and $Fa \supset (\exists y)Gya$ are instances of $(x)[Fx \supset (\exists y)Gyx]$.

Irreflexivity: A property of relations which are such that nothing can bear it to itself. The relation "is taller than" is an example of an irreflexive relation.

Logical falsehoods: Sentences which are the negations of logical truths. Sentences which can be proved false by logic alone.

Logical truths: Theorems of logic which also are sentences, and hence true; *e.g.*, $A \vee \sim A$ and $(x)(Fx \vee \sim Fx)$. Theorems of logic which are *sentence forms* are *not* logical truths, because they have no truth values.

Nonreflexivity: A property of relations which are neither reflexive nor irreflexive. The relation "loves" is an example of a nonreflexive relation.

Nonsymmetry: A property of relations which are neither symmetrical nor asymmetrical. The relation "loves" is an example of a nonsymmetrical relation.

Nontransitivity: A property of relations which are neither transitive nor intransitive. The relation "loves" is an example of a nontransitive relation.

Predicate logic: The recently developed logic which deals with the interior structure of atomic as well as compound sentences.

Property constants: Capital letters used to denote particular *properties*, as opposed to *individuals*; *e.g.*, *F__* used to denote "__ is friendly".

Property variables: Variables (in higher order logical systems) which are replaceable by property constants. (In the higher order system discussed, the capital letters *F*, *G*, *H*, and *K* are used as property variables.)

Quantifier logic: (See **Predicate logic**.)

Quantifier Negation (QN): The rule permitting inference from a given universally (existentially) quantified expression to an equivalent existentially (universally) quantified expression. For example, we are permitted by **QN** to infer from $(x)Fx$ to $\sim(\exists x)\sim Fx$, and from $\sim(\exists x)Fx$ to $(x)\sim Fx$.

Reflexivity: A property of relations such that everything which bears that relation to anything also bears it to itself. "Belongs to the same political party as" is an example of a reflexive relation.

Relational property: A property which holds between two (or more) individual entities.

Rule of identity: The inference rule permitting the substitution of identicals. An example is the inference from *Ta* and $a = b$ to *Tb*.

Scope (of a quantifier): The extent of an expression quantified by a quantifier.

Symmetry: A property of relations such that if one thing bears that relation to a second thing, then the second must bear it to the first. "Is married to" is an example of a symmetrical relation.

Theorem of logic: A sentence or sentence form obtainable as the conclusion of a valid deductive proof in which there are no given (as opposed to assumed) premises. Some examples are $p \vee \sim p$, $A \vee \sim A$, $(x)(Fx \vee \sim Fx)$, and $(\exists x)(Fx \cdot Gx) \supset [(\exists x)Fx \cdot (\exists x)Gx]$.

Total reflexivity: A property of relations such that everything bears that relation to itself. ("Is identical with" is an example of a totally reflexive relation.)

Transitivity: A property of relations such that if one thing bears that relation to a second, and the second to a third, then the first must bear that relation to the third. "Is taller than" is an example of a transitive relation.

Truths of logic: (See **Logical truths**.)

Two-place relational property: A relational property holding between pairs of individuals. (Similarly, a *three-place relational property* holds between trios of individuals, etc.)

Universal Generalization (UG): The inference rule permitting the addition of a universal quantifier to certain expressions (also permitting certain other changes in the expression). For example, in certain cases, we can infer by **UG** from $Fx \supset Gx$ to $(x)(Fx \supset Gx)$, $(y)(Fy \supset Gy)$, etc.

Universal Instantiation (UI): The inference rule permitting inferences from universally quantified sentences (or sentence forms) to certain of their instances; *e.g.*, the inferences from $(x)(Fx \supset Gx)$ to $Fa \supset Ga$ or $Fx \supset Gx$, and from $(x)Fxy$ to Fzy.

Universal quantifier: The expressions (x), (y), etc., as used in sentences such as $(x)(Hx \supset Mx)$, $(x)Fx$, and so on.

Part Three

A **Proposition:** (See **Universal affirmative proposition**.)

Ambiguous: Having more than one meaning. For instance, the word "sock" is ambiguous, since in some contexts it means "to strike or hit", and in others it refers to an item of wearing apparel.

Appeal to authority: (See **Argumentum ad verecundiam**.)

Appeal to force: (See **Argumentum ad baculum**.)

Appeal to pity: (See **Argumentum ad misericordiam**.)

Argumentum ad baculum: The attempt to persuade by means of force or threats. *Synonym:* **Appeal to force.**

Argumentum ad hominem: The fallacy of attacking the man (who argues) rather than his argument. *Synonym:* **Genetic fallacy.**

Argumentum ad ignorantium: The fallacy of accepting a conclusion *because* it has not been proved false.

Argumentum ad misericordiam: The attempt to persuade by appeal to pity. *Synonym:* **Appeal to pity.**

Argumentum ad verecundiam: Acceptance of a conclusion solely or primarily on the word of an authority. *Synonym:* **Appeal to authority.**

Aristotelian logic: (See **Syllogistic logic**.)

Categorical proposition: A subject-predicate proposition which asserts, or denies, a relationship between two classes.

Circular reasoning: The fallacy committed by using that which one intends to infer to (or by).

Complement: The negation of a term. The *complement class* of a given class is the class of all things which are *not* members of the given class.

Contextual definition: A definition of a word or phrase in the kind of context in which it occurs. For example, the definition "x is the father of y" $= df$ "x is a parent of y, and x is male" is a contextual definition, while the definition "father" $= df$ "male parent" is not.

Contradictory propositions: Two propositions such that if one of them is true, the other must be false, and vice versa. Corresponding *A* and *O* propositions, and *E* and *I* propositions, are contradictories.

Contraposition: The inference from a given proposition to a corresponding proposition in which the subject term has been replaced by the complement of the predicate term and the predicate term has been replaced by the complement of the subject term. For example, we can infer by contraposition from SAP to $\overline{P}A\overline{S}$. Contraposition is valid only for *A* and *O* propositions.

Contraposition by limitation: The inference in which subalternation and contraposition (of the resulting proposition) are performed on an *E* proposition, resulting in a particular O proposition. For example, we can infer by contraposition by limitation from the E proposition SEP to the O proposition $\overline{P}O\overline{S}$. Contraposition by limitation is valid only on the assumption of existential import.

Contrary propositions: Two propositions such that it is not possible for both of them to be true, although it is possible for both of them to be false. Assuming existential import, corresponding A and E propositions are contraries.

Conversion: The inference rule by means of which we can infer from a given proposition to another proposition just like the first one, except that its subject and predicate terms have been reversed. For example, the proposition SEP converts to PES. Conversion is valid only for E and I propositions.

Conversion by limitation: The inference from an A proposition to the converse of a corresponding I proposition. For example, we can infer from SAP to PIS by conversion by limitation. However, conversion by limitation is valid only on the assumption of existential import.

Definition: An explanation of the meaning of a word or phrase.

Distribution (Dist): A term in a syllogism is distributed if the proposition refers to *all* members of the class designated by that term.

E Proposition: (See **Universal negative proposition**.)

Empty class: (See **Null class**.)

Enthymeme: An argument in which a premise, or premises, is omitted as understood. (Sometimes, it is the *conclusion* which is omitted as understood.)

Existential import: A categorical proposition has existential import if its subject term and predicate term, as well as their complements, do not refer to empty classes.

Extensional definition: A definition which lists all of the things to which the word or phrase being defined applies.

Fallacy: Incorrect reasoning or conclusion drawing.

Fallacy of accidental or false correlation: The fallacy of erroneously assuming that an observed correlation represents a *causal* correlation.

Fallacy of affirming the consequent: The fallacy having the general form "If p then q, q, $/\therefore p$".

Fallacy of amphiboly: A fallacy resulting from ambiguity of grammatical construction, rather than of terms.

Fallacy of biased statistics: The fallacy of reasoning from statistics or evidence known to be nonrepresentative of the population as a whole.

Fallacy of the complex question: The asking of a question which assumes a particular answer (usually damaging) to a different question which was *not* asked.

Fallacy of composition: The fallacy of reasoning from the fact that every member of a class (or every part of a whole) has a certain property to the conclusion that the class itself (or the whole itself) has that property.

Fallacy of denying the antecedent: The fallacy having the form "If p then q, $\sim p$, $/\therefore \sim q$".

Fallacy of division: The fallacy of reasoning from the fact that a certain class (or whole) has a given property to the conclusion that every member of the class (or every part of the whole) has that property.

Fallacy of equivocation: A fallacy resulting from ambiguous use of terms.

Fallacy of four terms: Fallacy committed by using one or more terms in a syllogism ambiguously. A kind of fallacy of equivocation.

Fallacy of hasty generalization: The fallacy of too quickly generalizing from one or a few instances.

Fallacy of incorrect generalization: The fallacy of generalizing on the wrong variable.

Fallacy of the small sample: The fallacy of reasoning from too small a sample. This fallacy is the statistical analogue of the fallacy of hasty generalization.

Fallacy of the undistributed middle: The fallacy of violating the requirement that the middle term of a valid syllogism be distributed at least once.

Fallacy of the unknowable statistic: The fallacy committed when statistics are made up, or guessed at, on insufficient evidence, or when the approximate nature of the statistics is masked in precision.

Fallacy of using data of differing quality: The fallacy of reasoning from data which differ in quality, without taking that fact into account.

Fallacy of weak analogy: The fallacy of reasoning analogically from insufficient evidence.

Figure: The property of a syllogism determined by the positions of its major, minor, and middle terms in its premises.

Form: The property of a syllogism determined by its mood and figure.

Formal fallacy: A fallacy which closely resembles a valid argument form of some deductive system.

Genetic fallacy: (See **Argumentum ad hominem.**)

I **Proposition:** (See **Particular affirmative proposition.**)

Informal fallacies: Fallacies of *content*, rather than structure.

Intensional definition: A definition which lists a set of properties such that the term being defined applies to all things having that set of properties, and to nothing else.

Lexical definition: A definition which attempts to report the actual usage of a word or phrase.

Major term: The predicate term of the conclusion of a syllogism.

Middle term: The term in a syllogism which occurs once in each premise, but not in the conclusion.

Minor term: The subject term of the conclusion of a syllogism.

Mood: The property of a syllogism determined by the quality of its three propositions. For example, the syllogism "(1) *HAP* (2) *PEG*, $\therefore$ *GEH*" has the mood *AEE*.

Null class: The class which has no members. *Synonym:* **Empty class.**

O **Proposition:** (See **Particular negative proposition.**)

Obversion: The inference from a given proposition to a corresponding proposition in which the quality has been changed and the predicate term replaced with its complement. For example, we can infer from *SAP* to *SE$\overline{P}$* by obversion. Obversion *always* is valid.

Ostensive definition: A definition which indicates the meaning of a word or phrase by providing a sample of the things denoted by that term.

Particular affirmative proposition: A categorical proposition having the form "Some *S* are *P*", where *S* and *P* denote classes. *Synonym: I* **Proposition.**

Particular negative proposition: A categorical proposition having the form "Some *S* are not *P*", where *S* and *P* denote classes. *Synonym: O* **Proposition.**

Quality (of a proposition): Every categorical proposition must have the *quality* either of being *affirmative* or of being *negative*.

Quantity (of a proposition): Every categorical proposition must be either *universal* or *particular*.

Reforming definition: A stipulative definition which stipulates a partly new meaning for an old term.

Singular proposition: A proposition one of whose terms refers to an individual entity rather than a class. For example, "Socrates is human" is a singular proposition.

Sorites: An enthymemic version of a chain of syllogisms.

Stipulative definition: A definition which specifies, or stipulates, the meaning of a word or phrase.

Subalternation: The inference from an *A* proposition to a corresponding *I* proposition, or from an *E* proposition to a corresponding *O* proposition. Subalternation is valid only on the assumption of existential import.

Subcontrary propositions: Two propositions such that it is not possible for both of them to be false, although it is possible for both of them to be true. Assuming existential import, corresponding *I* and *O* propositions are subcontraries.

Syllogism: An argument containing three categorical propositions, two of which are premises, and one a conclusion, such that the three propositions taken as a group contain exactly three terms, each of which occurs twice (none occurring twice in a given proposition). For example, the argument "(1) *HAM*, (2) *GAH*, /∴ (3) *GAM*" is a syllogism.

Syllogistic logic: The traditional logic centering around and developed from the syllogistic arguments of Aristotle. The term now is often used to distinguish the traditional logic from modern symbolic logic. *Synonyms:* **Aristotelian logic, traditional logic.**

Theoretical definition: A reforming definition introduced into a theoretical area of knowledge, such as a particular science, mathematics, or philosophy.

Traditional logic: (See **Syllogistic logic.**)

Tu quoque fallacy: A kind of genetic fallacy in which a charge is answered by a similar countercharge. The defense "Well, you did the same thing yourself" generally commits this fallacy.

Universal affirmative proposition: A categorical proposition having the form "All *S* are *P*", where *S* and *P* denote classes. *Synonym: A* **Proposition.**

Universal negative proposition: A categorical proposition having the form "No *S* are *P*", where *S* and *P* denote classes. *Synonym: E* **Proposition.**

Vague: Not having a precise meaning. For example, the term "tall" is vague, since there is no precise point at which something achieves the status of tallness. Most words and phrases, perhaps all words and phrases, are vague in some way or other.

Venn diagrams: Overlapping circles, used to diagram categorical propositions and categorical syllogisms.

Analogical inference: Inductive inference from particular instances to a conclusion concerning some other particular instance. An example is the inference from the evidence that three English suits purchased in the past wore well to the conclusion that the next English suit purchased will wear well.

A priori probabilities: Probabilities calculated by some a priori principle, such as the principle of indifference.

Auxiliary hypothesis: A sentence or proposition, usually a report of some observation or particular event, used with an inductive generalization to infer to a conclusion. An example is the report that Art is intelligent, used in conjunction with the inductive generalization that all intelligent students graduate to conclude that Art will graduate.

Categorical analogy: Inductive inference from the evidence that all tested F's are G's to the conclusion that some as yet untested F is a G.

Categorical inductive generalization: An inductive inference from particular instances to a universal conclusion. An example is the inference from the evidence that all *observed* ravens are black to the categorical generalization that all ravens are black.

Classical theory of probability: The theory that probabilities are measures of rational expectation or belief and are calculated according to the **Principle of indifference.**

Deductive nomological explanation: An explanation in which a description of what is explained follows *deductively* from the

general hypotheses plus antecedent conditions used to explain it.

Degree of confirmation (of a hypothesis): The degree of evidential support (for that hypothesis).

Dispositional property: An unobservable property or power. An example is the property of being flexible.

Empirical hypothesis: A hypothesis which is a mere inductive generalization from its evidence, making no reference to any kind of entity not mentioned by the evidence. An example is the empirical hypothesis that all ravens are black, based on the evidence that all observed ravens are black.

Frequency theory of probability: The theory that probabilities are relative frequencies.

General conjunction rule: The rule that

$$P(p \cdot q) = P(p) \times P(q, \text{ if } p)$$

General disjunction rule: The rule that

$$P(p \lor q) = P(p) + P(q) - P(p \cdot q)$$

Independent events: Events which are not logically or causally related. An example is the event of drawing an ace from a deck and the event of again drawing an ace from the deck when the first ace has been put back into the deck.

Inductive argument: An argument having at least one contingent premise, which has a contingent conclusion whose entire content is not contained in its premises.

Instance variety: The property of a sample or set of confirming cases which *differ* from each other in certain relevant ways. An example is a sample of ravens taken from many places and containing ravens of both sexes, of several blood types, etc.

Method of agreement: One of **Mill's Methods**, namely the method of inferring that if P is the only factor present in every observed occurrence of Q, then P and Q are causally related.

Method of concomitant variations: One of **Mill's Methods**, namely the method of inferring that if a given phenomenon varies in some regular way with some other phenomenon, then the two phenomena are causally related.

Method of difference: One of **Mill's Methods**, namely the method of inferring that whatever is present when Q is present, and absent when Q is absent, is causally related to Q.

Mill's Methods: Methods for finding causal relationships, championed by the 19th century philosopher, John Stuart Mill.

Mutually exclusive events: Events such that it is logically impossible for both to occur. An example is the event of picking an ace on a given draw and picking a deuce on the same draw.

Observable entity: That which can be experienced or observed directly. *Antonym:* **Theoretical entity.**

Principle of indifference: The principle that two events are to be considered equally probable if there is no reason to prefer one to the other.

Probabilistic explanation: An explanation in which a description of what is explained follows only *probably* from the general hypothesis plus antecedent conditions used to explain it.

Restricted conjunction rule: The rule that if p and q are independent events, then $P(p \cdot q) = P(p) \times P(q)$.

Restricted disjunction rule: The rule that if p and q are mutually exclusive events, then $P(p \vee q) = P(p) + P(q)$.

Statistical analogy: Inductive inference from the evidence that N per cent of the tested F's are G's to the conclusion that the probability is N per cent that some as yet untested F is a G.

Statistical inductive generalization: An inductive inference from particular instances to a statistical conclusion. An example is the inference from the evidence that half of all tosses with this coin *so far* landed heads up, to the statistical conclusion that half of *all* tosses with this coin will land heads up.

Theoretical entity: Postulated entity which cannot be experienced or observed directly. *Antonym:* **Observational entity.**

Theoretical hypothesis: A hypothesis which makes reference to unobservable entities of a kind not referred to in the evidence for the hypothesis. An example is the sea of air hypothesis, which makes reference to *air pressure*, which is not directly observable.

Valid inductive argument: An inductive argument whose premises provide good grounds for asserting its conclusion.

Part Five

Analytic proposition: A proposition whose predicate is "contained in" its subject.

A posteriori: That which cannot be known prior to, or without the need of, experience of the thing known. That which requires experience, or empirical evidence, of some kind.

A priori: That which can be known before, and without the need of, experience of the thing known.

Confirmation principle: The principle which states that one way to *confirm* a hypothesis of the form "All *P*'s are *Q*'s" is by finding things which are both *P*'s and *Q*'s, and one way to *disconfirm* a hypothesis of that form is to find things which are *P*'s but *not Q*'s.

Contrary-to-fact conditional (counterfactual): A subjunctive conditional whose antecedent is contrary to fact. The sentence "If Art *had* studied hard, then he *would have* become a great logician" is a contrary-to-fact conditional.

Dispositional property: An *unobservable* property or power. The property of being flexible is a dispositional property.

Equivalence principle: The principle that whatever confirms a given hypothesis equally confirms all logically equivalent hypotheses.

Impredicable paradox: The paradox concerning the predicate *impredicable*, namely that if impredicable is itself impredicable, then it is predicable, and if impredicable is not impredicable, then it is impredicable.

Levels of language theory: The theory that certain parts of the semantic apparatus of a language, in particular the truth conditions of a language, must be contained not in the language itself but in the *meta-language*, in order to get around the difficulties illustrated by paradoxes, such as the liar paradox.

Manifest property: An observable property. The property of *looking red* is an observable property.

Semantic analytic proposition: An analytic proposition whose analyticity does *not* follow from its form (plus the meaning of its logical terms), but rather also rests on the meaning of its nonlogical terms. The proposition "All bachelors are unmarried" is a semantic analytic proposition.

Semantic paradox: A paradox such that most philosophers would accept only a *semantic* solution to it. For example, the liar paradox is a semantic paradox. Most philosophers accept a semantic theory, the so-called "levels of language" theory, as a solution to this paradox.

Simple theory of types: The syntactic theory according to which all properties are categorized in a hierarchy of categories, starting with properties of things, properties of properties, properties of properties of properties, etc. The theory was proposed as a solution to syntactic paradoxes, such as the impredicable paradox.

Subjunctive conditional: A conditional sentence in the subjective mood. The sentence "If Art were to study hard, then he would be a great logician" is a subjunctive conditional.

Syntactic analytic proposition: An analytic proposition whose analyticity results from its form (plus the meanings of its logical terms). The sentence "All bachelors are bachelors" is an example.

Syntactic paradox: A paradox such that most philosophers would accept only a *syntactical* solution to it. For instance, the impredicable paradox is a syntactic paradox. Most philosophers accept a syntactic theory, the simple theory of types, as a solution to this paradox.

Synthetic a priori proposition: A proposition which is both synthetic *and* a priori. (The question as to whether any such propositions exist is one of the most important and controversial in modern philosophy.)

Synthetic proposition: A proposition whose predicate is *not* contained in its subject.

Part Six

Axiom pattern: A schema in the meta-language such that all substitution instances of it are axioms of the object language.

Axiom system: A systematized group of formulas (sentences or sentence forms), such that some of the formulas (the theorems of the system) follow from others (the axioms of the system) by specified rules of inference.

Completeness: The property of an axiom system in which all desired theorems are provable.

Consistency: The property of an axiom system which is such that no formula and its negation both are provable as theorems of the system.

Decision procedure: A mechanical method for determining in a finite number of steps whether or not a given formula is a theorem of a given system.

Defined term: A term with an explicit definition furnished in that system.

Derived inference rule (of a system): An inference rule of a system for which a justification is provided within that system.

Expressive completeness: The property of an axiom system of providing symbols which permit the expression of everything it is intended that the system be able to express.

Formula variable: A meta-language variable whose substitution instances are object language formulas.

Independence (of an axiom): The property of an axiom of not being derivable from the other axioms of a given system.

Interpreted axiom system: An axiom system such that all of its primitive symbols are assigned meanings.

Meta-language: A language used to talk about some (usually other) language.

Object language: A language which is the *object* of discussion or examination.

Post's Consistency Criterion: The criterion according to which a system is consistent *iff* there is some formula of the system not derivable as a theorem of the system.

Pragmatic Properties: The properties of a language which it has in relation to the users of the language.

Primitive inference rule (of a system): An inference rule of a system not justified within that system.

Primitive term: (See **Undefined term**.)

Semantic properties: The properties of a language which it has by virtue of the meanings of the terms (nonlogical as well as logical) in the language.

Syntactic properties: The structural properties of a language.

Undefined term (of a system): A term of the system not defined within that system. *Synonym:* **Primitive term.**

Uninterpreted axiom system: An axiom system whose primitive terms are not given a meaning. (Sometimes the term is applied to systems whose *nonlogical* terms do not have meaning, although its logical terms do have meaning.)

Use-mention: The distinction between *using* a language (to talk about other things) and *talking about* (mentioning) the language.

Well-formed formula (WFF): A formula of a system which either is a sentence or sentence form (if the system is interpreted) or else is a sentence or sentence form on an intended interpretation (if the system is uninterpreted).

Answers to Even-numbered Items

Exercise 2–1:

2. a, b, d

4. a, b, d, h, j

6. a, b, d, e, k, l

8. a, b, c, f, g, o

10. a, b, c, f, n

Exercise 3–1:

2. True

4. False

6. True

8. False

10. False

Exercise 3–2:

2. Contradiction

4. Contingent

6. Contingent

8. Contradictory

10. Tautology

Exercise 3–3:

2. $\sim H \supset J$

4. $H \supset \sim J$

6. $\sim (H \cdot J)$

8. $H \equiv J$

10. $G \cdot (J \supset H)$

12. $(J \supset G) \supset (\sim J \supset H)$

Exercise 4–1:

(B)
1. $A \supset B$ p
2. $C \supset A$ p
3. C p / $\therefore$ B
4. A 2, 3 **MP**
5. B 1, 4 **MP**

(D)
1. $A \supset B$ p
2. $\sim (B \cdot C)$ p / $\therefore A \supset \sim C$
3. $\sim B \vee \sim C$ 2, **DeM**
4. $B \supset \sim C$ 3, **Impl**
5. $A \supset \sim C$ 1, 4 *HS*

(F)
1. $F \supset G$ p
2. $\sim (H \cdot G)$ p
3. H p / $\therefore \sim F$
4. $\sim H \vee \sim G$ 2, **DeM**
5. $\sim \sim H$ 3, **DN**
6. $\sim G$ 4, 5 **DS**
7. $\sim F$ 1, 6 **MT**

(H) 1. $M \equiv N$ $p / \therefore \sim N \vee M$

    2. $(M \supset N) \cdot (N \supset M)$ 1, **Equiv**

    3. $N \supset M$ 2, **Simp**

    4. $\sim N \vee M$ 3, **Impl**

(J) 1. $D \vee \sim A$ p

    2. $\sim (A \cdot \sim B) \supset \sim C$ p

    3. $\sim D$ $p / \therefore \sim C$

    4. $\sim A$ 1, 3 **DS**

    5. $\sim A \vee \sim \sim B$ 4, **Add**

    6. $\sim (A \cdot \sim B)$ 5, **DeM**

    7. $\sim C$ 2, 6 **MP**

(L) 1. $\sim A$ p

    2. $\sim B$ p

    3. $(A \vee B) \equiv C$ $p / \therefore \sim (C \cdot D)$

    4. $[(A \vee B) \supset C] \cdot [C \supset (A \vee B)]$ 3, **Equiv**

    5. $C \supset (A \vee B)$ 4, **Simp**

    6. $\sim A \cdot \sim B$ 1, 2 **Conj**

    7. $\sim (A \vee B)$ 6, **DeM**

    8. $\sim C$ 5, 7 **MT**

    9. $\sim C \vee \sim D$ 8, **Add**

   10. $\sim (C \cdot D)$ 9, **DeM**

(N) 1. $A \supset B$ p

    2. $C \supset D$ p

    3. $(B \vee D) \supset E$ p

    4. $\sim E$ $p / \therefore \sim (A \vee C)$

5.	$\sim (B \lor D)$	3, 4 **MT**
6.	$\sim B \cdot \sim D$	5, **DeM**
7.	$\sim B$	6, **Simp**
8.	$\sim A$	1, 7 **MT**
9.	$\sim D$	6, **Simp**
10.	$\sim C$	2, 9 **MT**
11.	$\sim A \cdot \sim C$	8, 10 **Conj**
12.	$\sim (A \lor C)$	11, **DeM**

(P)

1.	$A \supset (B \supset C).$	$p \mathbin{/} \therefore (\sim C \cdot D) \supset (B \supset \sim A)$
2.	$(A \cdot B) \supset C$	1, **Exp**
3.	$(B \cdot A) \supset C$	2, **Comm**
4.	$B \supset (A \supset C)$	3, **Exp**
5.	$B \supset (\sim C \supset \sim A)$	4, **Contr**
6.	$(B \cdot \sim C) \supset \sim A$	5, **Exp**
7.	$(\sim C \cdot B) \supset \sim A$	6, **Comm**
8.	$\sim C \supset (B \supset \sim A)$	7, **Exp**
9.	$\sim \sim C \lor (B \supset \sim A)$	8, **Imp**
10.	$[\sim \sim C \lor (B \supset \sim A)] \lor \sim D$	9, **Add**
11.	$\sim \sim C \lor [(B \supset \sim A) \lor \sim D]$	10, **Assoc**
12.	$\sim \sim C \lor [\sim D \lor (B \supset \sim A)]$	11, **Comm**
13.	$(\sim \sim C \lor \sim D) \lor (B \supset \sim A)$	12, **Assoc**
14.	$\sim (\sim C \cdot D) \lor (B \supset \sim A)$	13, **DeM**
15.	$(\sim C \cdot D) \supset (B \supset \sim A)$	14, **Impl**

(R)

1.	$D \supset B$	p
2.	$D \supset (B \supset W)$	p

3.	$B \supset (W \supset S)$		$p \ / \therefore D \supset S$
4.	$(D \cdot B) \supset W$		2, **Exp**
5.	$(B \cdot D) \supset W$		4, **Comm**
6.	$B \supset (D \supset W)$		5, **Exp**
7.	$D \supset (D \supset W)$		1, 6 **HS**
8.	$(D \cdot D) \supset W$		7, **Exp**
9.	$D \supset W$		8, **Taut**
10.	$D \supset (W \supset S)$		1, 3 **HS**
11.	$(D \cdot W) \supset S$		10, **Exp**
12.	$(W \cdot D) \supset S$		11, **Comm**
13.	$W \supset (D \supset S)$		12, **Exp**
14.	$D \supset (D \supset S)$		9, 13 **HS**
15.	$(D \cdot D) \supset S$		14, **Exp**
16.	$D \supset S$		15, **Taut**

(T)	1.	$K \supset [(L \lor M) \supset R]$	p
	2.	$(R \lor S) \supset T$	$p \ / \therefore K \supset (M \supset T)$
	3.	$\sim (R \lor S) \lor T$	2, **Imp**
	4.	$(\sim R \cdot \sim S) \lor T$	3, **DeM**
	5.	$T \lor (\sim R \cdot \sim S)$	4, **Comm**
	6.	$(T \lor \sim R) \cdot (T \lor \sim S)$	5, **Dist**
	7.	$T \lor \sim R$	6, **Simp**
	8.	$\sim R \lor T$	7, **Comm**
	9.	$R \supset T$	8, **Imp**
	10.	$[K \cdot (L \lor M)] \supset R$	1, **Exp**
	11.	$[(L \lor M) \cdot K] \supset R$	10, **Comm**

12.	$(L \lor M) \supset (K \supset R)$	11, **Exp**
13.	$\sim(L \lor M) \lor (K \supset R)$	12, **Impl**
14.	$(\sim L \cdot \sim M) \lor (K \supset R)$	13, **DeM**
15.	$(K \supset R) \lor (\sim L \cdot \sim M)$	14, **Comm**
16.	$[(K \supset R) \lor \sim L] \cdot [(K \supset R) \lor \sim M]$	15, **Dist**
17.	$(K \supset R) \lor \sim M$	16, **Simp**
18.	$\sim M \lor (K \supset R)$	17, **Comm**
19.	$M \supset (K \supset R)$	18, **Impl**
20.	$(M \cdot K) \supset R$	19, **Exp**
21.	$(M \cdot K) \supset T$	9, 20 **HS**
22.	$(K \cdot M) \supset T$	21, **Comm**
23.	$K \supset (M \supset T)$	22, **Exp**

(V)	1.	$A \supset B$	p
	2.	$C \supset D$	$p \;/\; \therefore (A \lor C) \supset (B \lor D)$
	3.	$\sim A \lor B$	1, **Impl**
	4.	$(\sim A \lor B) \lor D$	3, **Add**
	5.	$\sim A \lor (B \lor D)$	4, **Assoc**
	6.	$(B \lor D) \lor \sim A$	5, **Comm**
	7.	$\sim C \lor D$	2, **Imp**
	8.	$(\sim C \lor D) \lor B$	7, **Add**
	9.	$\sim C \lor (D \lor B)$	8, **Assoc**
	10.	$\sim C \lor (B \lor D)$	9, **Comm**
	11.	$(B \lor D) \lor \sim C$	10, **Comm**
	12.	$[(B \lor D) \lor \sim A] \cdot [(B \lor D) \lor \sim C]$	6, 11 **Conj**

13.	$(B \lor D) \lor (\sim A \cdot \sim C)$	12, **Dist**
14.	$(\sim A \cdot \sim C) \lor (B \lor D)$	13, **Comm**
15.	$\sim (A \lor C) \lor (B \lor D)$	14, **DeM**
16.	$(A \lor C) \supset (B \lor D)$	15, **Imp**

(X)

1.	$\sim [D \cdot \sim (E \lor B)]$	p
2.	$\sim (E \lor F)$	p
3.	$C \supset (E \lor A)$	$p \: / \therefore \: \sim (\sim A \cdot \sim B) \lor \sim (C \lor D)$
4.	$\sim E \cdot \sim F$	2, **DeM**
5.	$\sim E$	4, **Simp**
6.	$C \supset (\sim \sim E \lor A)$	3, **DN**
7.	$C \supset (\sim E \supset A)$	6, **Impl**
8.	$(C \cdot \sim E) \supset A$	7, **Exp**
9.	$(\sim E \cdot C) \supset A$	8, **Comm**
10.	$\sim E \supset (C \supset A)$	9, **Exp**
11.	$C \supset A$	5, 10 **MP**
12.	$\sim C \lor A$	11, **Imp**
13.	$(\sim C \lor A) \lor B$	12, **Add**
14.	$\sim C \lor (A \lor B)$	13, **Assoc**
15.	$(A \lor B) \lor \sim C$	14, **Comm**
16.	$\sim D \lor \sim \sim (E \lor B)$	1, **DeM**
17.	$\sim D \lor (E \lor B)$	16, **DN**
18.	$(E \lor B) \lor \sim D$	17, **Comm**
19.	$E \lor (B \lor \sim D)$	18, **Assoc**
20.	$B \lor \sim D$	5, 19 **DS**
21.	$(B \lor \sim D) \lor A$	20, **Add**

22.	$A \lor (B \lor \sim D)$	21, **Comm**
23.	$(A \lor B) \lor \sim D$	22, **Assoc**
24.	$[(A \lor B) \lor \sim C] \cdot [(A \lor B) \lor \sim D]$	15, 23 **Conj**
25.	$(A \lor B) \lor (\sim C \cdot \sim D)$	24, **Dist**
26.	$(A \lor B) \lor \sim (C \lor D)$	25, **DeM**
27.	$\sim \sim (A \lor B) \lor \sim (C \lor D)$	26, **DN**
28.	$\sim (\sim A \cdot \sim B) \lor \sim (C \lor D)$	27, **DeM**

Exercise 5–1:

(P)	1.	$A \supset (B \supset C)$	$p \; / \therefore (\sim C \cdot D) \supset (B \supset \sim A)$
	2.	$\sim C \cdot D$	**AP**
	3.	$\sim C$	2, **Simp**
	4.	$(A \cdot B) \supset C$	1, **Exp**
	5.	$\sim (A \cdot B)$	3, 4 **MT**
	6.	$\sim A \lor \sim B$	5, **DeM**
	7.	$\sim B \lor \sim A$	6, **Comm**
	8.	$B \supset \sim A$	7, **Impl**
	9.	$(\sim C \cdot D) \supset (B \supset \sim A)$	2, 8 **CP**
(R)	1.	$D \supset B$	p
	2.	$D \supset (B \supset W)$	p
	3.	$B \supset (W \supset S)$	$p / \therefore D \supset S$

414

4.	D	**AP**
5.	$B \supset W$	2, 4 **MP**
6.	B	1, 5 **MP**
7.	$W \supset S$	3, 6 **MP**
8.	W	5, 6 **MP**
9.	S	7, 8 **MP**
10.	$D \supset S$	4, 9 **CP**

(T)

1.	$K \supset [(L \vee M) \supset R]$	p
2.	$(R \vee S) \supset T$	$p \: / \therefore K \supset (M \supset T)$
3.	K	**AP**
4.	M	**AP**
5.	$(L \vee M) \supset R$	1, 3 **MP**
6.	$M \vee L$	4, **Add**
7.	$L \vee M$	6, **Comm**
8.	R	5, 7 **MP**
9.	$R \vee S$	8, **Add**
10.	T	2, 9 **MP**
11.	$M \supset T$	4, 10 **CP**
12.	$K \supset (M \supset T)$	3, 11 **CP**

(V)

1.	$A \supset B$	p
2.	$C \supset D$	$p \: / \therefore (A \vee C) \supset (B \vee D)$
3.	$A \vee C$	**AP**
4.	$B \vee D$	1, 2, 3 **CD**
5.	$(A \vee C) \supset (B \vee D)$	3, 4 **CP**

(X)	1.	$\sim [D \cdot \sim (E \vee B)]$	p
	2.	$\sim (E \vee F)$	p
	3.	$C \supset (E \vee A)$	$p / \therefore \sim (\sim A \cdot \sim B) \vee \sim (C \vee D)$
	4.	$\sim A \cdot \sim B$	AP
	5.	$\sim E \cdot \sim F$	2, DeM
	6.	$\sim (E \vee A) \supset \sim C$	3, Contra
	7.	$(\sim E \cdot \sim A) \supset \sim C$	6, DeM
	8.	$\sim E$	5, Simp
	9.	$\sim A$	4, Simp
	10.	$\sim E \cdot \sim A$	8, 9 Conj
	11.	$\sim C$	7, 10 MP
	12.	$\sim D \vee \sim \sim (E \vee B)$	1, DeM
	13.	$\sim D \vee (E \vee B)$	12, DN
	14.	$(\sim D \vee E) \vee B$	13, Assoc
	15.	$\sim B$	4, Simp
	16.	$\sim D \vee E$	14, 15 DS
	17.	$\sim D$	8, 16 DS
	18.	$\sim C \cdot \sim D$	11, 17 Conj
	19.	$\sim (C \vee D)$	18, DeM
	20.	$(\sim A \cdot \sim B) \supset \sim (C \vee D)$	4, 19 CP
	21.	$\sim (\sim A \cdot \sim B) \vee \sim (C \vee D)$	20, Impl

Exercise 5–2:

(B) without **IP**:

1.	$H \supset (A \supset B)$	p

2.	$\sim C \supset (H \vee B)$	p
3.	$H \supset A$	$p \mathbin{/} \therefore C \vee B$
4.	$(H \cdot A) \supset B$	1, **Exp**
5.	$(A \cdot H) \supset B$	4, **Comm**
6.	$A \supset (H \supset B)$	5, **Exp**
7.	$H \supset (H \supset B)$	3, 6 **HS**
8.	$(H \cdot H) \supset B$	7, **Exp**
9.	$H \supset B$	8, **Taut**
10.	$\sim C \supset (B \vee H)$	2, **Comm**
11.	$\sim C \supset (\sim \sim B \vee H)$	10, **DN**
12.	$\sim C \supset (\sim B \supset H)$	11, **Impl**
13.	$(\sim C \cdot \sim B) \supset H$	12, **Exp**
14.	$(\sim C \cdot \sim B) \supset B$	9, 13 **HS**
15.	$\sim C \supset (\sim B \supset B)$	14, **Exp**
16.	$\sim C \supset (\sim \sim B \vee B)$	15, **Impl**
17.	$\sim C \supset (B \vee B)$	16, **DN**
18.	$\sim C \supset B$	17, **Taut**
19.	$\sim \sim C \vee B$	18, **Impl**
20.	$C \vee B$	19, **DN**

(B) with **IP**:

1.	$H \supset (A \supset B)$	p
2.	$\sim C \supset (H \vee B)$	p
3.	$H \supset A$	$p \mathbin{/} \therefore C \vee B$

4.	$\sim (C \lor B)$		AP
5.	$\sim C \cdot \sim B$		4, DeM
6.	$\sim C$		5, Simp
7.	$H \lor B$		2, 6 MP
8.	$\sim B$		5, Simp
9.	H		7, 8 DS
10.	A		3, 9 MP
11.	$A \supset B$		1, 9 MP
12.	B		10, 11 MP
13.	$B \cdot \sim B$		8, 12 Conj
14.	$C \lor B$		4, 13 IP

(D) without **IP**:

1.	$(A \lor B) \supset (C \supset \sim D)$	p
2.	$(D \lor E) \supset (A \cdot C)$	$p \; / \therefore \; \sim D$
3.	$\sim (C \supset \sim D) \supset \sim (A \lor B)$	1, **Contra**
4.	$\sim (A \cdot C) \supset \sim (D \lor E)$	2, **Contra**
5.	$\sim \sim (A \cdot C) \lor \sim (D \lor E)$	4, **Impl**
6.	$(A \cdot C) \lor \sim (D \lor E)$	5, **DN**
7.	$(A \cdot C) \lor (\sim D \cdot \sim E)$	6, **DeM**
8.	$[(A \cdot C) \lor \sim D] \cdot [(A \cdot C) \lor \sim E]$	7, **Dist**
9.	$(A \cdot C) \lor \sim D$	8, **Simp**
10.	$\sim D \lor (A \cdot C)$	9, **Comm**
11.	$(\sim D \lor A) \cdot (\sim D \lor C)$	10, **Dist**
12.	$\sim D \lor A$	11, **Simp**
13.	$(\sim D \lor A) \lor B$	12, **Add**
14.	$\sim D \lor (A \lor B)$	13, **Assoc**

15.	$D \supset (A \lor B)$	14, **Impl**
16.	$D \supset (C \supset \sim D)$	1, 15 **HS**
17.	$(D \cdot C) \supset \sim D$	16, **Exp**
18.	$(C \cdot D) \supset \sim D$	17, **Comm**
19.	$C \supset (D \supset \sim D)$	18, **Exp**
20.	$\sim D \lor C$	11, **Simp**
21.	$D \supset C$	20, **Impl**
22.	$D \supset (D \supset \sim D)$	19, 21 **HS**
23.	$(D \cdot D) \supset \sim D$	22, **Exp**
24.	$D \supset \sim D$	23, **Taut**
25.	$\sim D \lor \sim D$	24, **Impl**
26.	$\sim D$	25, **Taut**

(D) with **IP**:

1.	$(A \lor B) \supset (C \supset \sim D)$	p
2.	$(D \lor E) \supset (A \cdot C)$	$p \, / \therefore \sim D$
3.	$\sim \sim D$	**AP**
4.	D	3, **DN**
5.	$D \lor E$	4, **Add**
6.	$A \cdot C$	2, 5 **MP**
7.	A	6, **Simp**
8.	$A \lor B$	7, **Add**
9.	$C \supset \sim D$	1, 8 **MP**
10.	C	6, **Simp**
11.	$\sim D$	9, 10 **MP**
12.	$D \cdot \sim D$	4, 11 **Conj**
13.	$\sim D$	3, 12 **IP**

Exercise 5–3:

(B)   A—False
        B and C—True

(D)   A, B, C, and D—True
        E and F—False

Exercise 5–4:

(B) 1. $\sim A \vee B$ p

       2. $\sim B \vee \sim A$ p

       3. A $p \,/\, \therefore B$

       4. $\sim \sim A$ 3, **DN**

       5. B 1, 4 **DS**

       6. $\sim B$ 2, 4 **DS**

       7. $B \cdot \sim B$ 5, 6 **Conj**

(D) 1. $A \supset (C \supset B)$ p

       2. $(B \cdot C) \vee A$ p

       3. $C \vee (B \cdot A)$ p

       4. $B \supset \sim C$ p

       5. $D \vee B$ p

       6. $B \cdot \sim A$ $p \,/\, \therefore B \vee (A \supset D)$

       7. B 6, **Simp**

       8. $\sim C$ 4, 7 **MP**

       9. $B \cdot A$ 3, 8 **DS**

     10. A 9, **Simp**

11.	$\sim A$	6, **Simp**
12.	$A \cdot \sim A$	10, 11 **Conj**

Exercise 5–5:

(B) A—True
B and C—False

(D) A, B, D, and E—True
C and F—False

Exercise 7–1:

(B) Inference to line 4 violates 2nd restriction on **EI. Inference to line 6 is invalid, because the x on line 6, supposedly obtained by EG, is free.**

(D) 1. Inference to line 3 is invalid, because the y in line 3 which replaces the x in line 1 is not free.

2. Inference to line 5 is invalid, because if we substitute Fy for p in a given use of **MP**, then we cannot also substitute Fx for p in that same use.

3. Inference to line 8 violates the restriction on **EG**.

4. Inference to line 9 is invalid, because the scope of the $(\exists w)$ quantifier has been extended to cover Gy.

5. Inference to line 11 violates the 2nd restriction on **UG**.

Exercise 7–2:

(B) 1. $(x)(Kx \supset \sim Lx)$ p

2.	$(\exists x)(Mx \cdot Lx)$	$p \: / \therefore \: (\exists x)(Mx \cdot \sim Kx)$
3.	$Mx \cdot Lx$	2, **EI**
4.	$Kx \supset \sim Lx$	1, **UI**
5.	Lx	3, **Simp**
6.	$\sim \sim Lx$	5, **DN**
7.	$\sim Kx$	4, 6 **MT**
8.	Mx	3, **Simp**
9.	$Mx \cdot \sim Kx$	7, 8 **Conj**
10.	$(\exists x)(Mx \cdot \sim Kx)$	9, **EG**

(D)

1.	$(x)(Gx \supset Hx)$	p
2.	$(\exists x)(Ix \cdot \sim Hx)$	p
3.	$(x)(\sim Fx \vee Gx)$	$p \: / \therefore \: (\exists x)(Ix \cdot \sim Fx)$
4.	$Ix \cdot \sim Hx$	2, **EI**
5.	$\sim Fx \vee Gx$	3, **UI**
6.	$Gx \supset Hx$	1, **UI**
7.	$Fx \supset Gx$	5, **Impl**
8.	$Fx \supset Hx$	6, 7 **HS**
9.	$\sim Hx$	4, **Simp**
10.	$\sim Fx$	8, 9 **MT**
11.	Ix	4, **Simp**
12.	$Ix \cdot \sim Fx$	10, 11 **Conj**
13.	$(\exists x)(Ix \cdot \sim Fx)$	12, **EG**

(F)   1. $\sim (\exists x)Fx$ $p \; / \; \therefore \; Fa \supset Ga$

      2. $(x) \sim Fx$ 1, **QN**

      3. $\sim Fa$ 2, **UI**

      4. $\sim Fa \vee Ga$ 3, **Add**

      5. $Fa \supset Ga$ 4, **Impl**

(H)   1. $(x)\,[(Rx \vee Qx) \supset Sx]$ p

      2. $(\exists y)\,(\sim Qy \vee \sim Ry)$ p

      3. $(\exists z) \sim (Pz \vee \sim Qz)$ $p \; / \; \therefore \; (\exists w)Sw$

      4. $\sim (Px \vee \sim Qx)$ 3, **EI**

      5. $(Rx \vee Qx) \supset Sx$ 1, **UI**

      6. $\sim Px \cdot \sim \sim Qx$ 4, **DeM**

      7. $\sim \sim Qx$ 6, **Simp**

      8. Qx 7, **DN**

      9. $Qx \vee Rx$ 8, **Add**

     10. $Rx \vee Qx$ 9, **Comm**

     11. Sx 5, 10 **MP**

     12. $(\exists w)Sw$ 11, **EG**

(J)   1. $(x)\,[Px \supset (Ax \vee Bx)]$ p

      2. $(x)\,[(Bx \vee Cx) \supset Qx]$ $p \; / \; \therefore \; (x)\,[(Px \cdot \sim Ax) \supset Qx]$

      3. $Px \supset (Ax \vee Bx)$ 1, **UI**

      4. $(Bx \vee Cx) \supset Qx$ 2, **UI**

	5.	$Px \cdot \sim Ax$	**AP**
	6.	Px	5, **Simp**
	7.	$Ax \lor Bx$	3, 6 **MP**
	8.	$\sim Ax$	5, **Simp**
	9.	Bx	7, 8 **DS**
	10.	$Bx \lor Cx$	9, **Add**
	11.	Qx	4, 10 **MP**
	12.	$(Px \cdot \sim Ax) \supset Qx$	5, 11 **CP**
	13.	$(x)[(Px \cdot \sim Ax) \supset Qx]$	12, **UG**

(L)	1.	$(x)(Ax \supset Hx)$	p
	2.	$(\exists x)Ax \supset \sim (\exists y)Gy$	$p \ / \therefore \ (x)[(\exists y)Ay \supset \sim Gx]$
	3.	$(\exists y)Ay$	**AP**
	4.	Ay	3, **EI**
	5.	$(\exists x)Ax$	4, **EG**
	6.	$\sim (\exists y)Gy$	2, 5 **MP**
	7.	$(y) \sim Gy$	6, **QN**
	8.	$\sim Gx$	7, **UI**
	9.	$(\exists y)Ay \supset \sim Gx$	3, 8 **CP**
	10.	$(x)[(\exists y)Ay \supset \sim Gx]$	9, **UG**

(N)	1.	$(x)[Px \supset (Qx \lor Rx)]$	p
	2.	$(x)[(Sx \cdot Px) \supset \sim Qx]$	$p \ / \therefore \ (x)(Sx \supset Px) \supset (x)(Sx \supset Rx)$

3.	$(x)(Sx \supset Px)$	**AP**
4.	Sx	**AP**
5.	$Sx \supset Px$	3, **UI**
6.	Px	4, 5 **MP**
7.	$Sx \cdot Px \supset \sim Qx$	2, **UI**
8.	$Sx \cdot Px$	4, 6 **Conj**
9.	$\sim Qx$	7, 8 **MP**
10.	$Px \supset (Qx \vee Rx)$	1, **UI**
11.	$Qx \vee Rx$	6, 10 **MP**
12.	Rx	9, 11 **DS**
13.	$Sx \supset Rx$	4, 12 **CP**
14.	$(x)(Sx \supset Rx)$	13, **UG**
15.	$(x)(Sx \supset Px) \supset (x)(Sx \supset Rx)$	3, 14 **CP**

(P)			
	1.	$(x)[Ax \supset (Bx \supset \sim Cx)]$	p
	2.	$\sim (\exists x)(Cx \cdot Dx) \supset (x)(Dx \supset Ex)$	$p \ / \therefore \ \sim (\exists x)[Dx \cdot (\sim Ax \vee \sim Bx)] \supset (x)(Dx \supset Ex)$
	3.	$\sim (x)(Dx \supset Ex)$	**AP**
	4.	$\sim \sim (\exists x)(Cx \cdot Dx)$	2, 3 **MT**
	5.	$(\exists x)(Cx \cdot Dx)$	4, **DN**
	6.	$Cx \cdot Dx$	5, **EI**
	7.	$Ax \supset (Bx \supset \sim Cx)$	1, **UI**
	8.	$\sim \sim Cx$	6, **Simp, DN**

9.	$(Ax \cdot Bx) \supset \sim Cx$	7, **Exp**
10.	$\sim (Ax \cdot Bx)$	8, 9 **MT**
11.	$\sim Ax \lor \sim Bx$	10, **DeM**
12.	Dx	6, **Simp**
13.	$Dx \cdot (\sim Ax \lor \sim Bx)$	10, 12 **Conj**
14.	$(\exists x)[Dx \cdot (\sim Ax \lor \sim Bx)]$	13, **EG**
15.	$\sim \sim (\exists x)[Dx \cdot (\sim Ax \lor \sim Bx)]$	14, **DN**
16.	$\sim (x)(Dx \supset Ex) \supset$ $\sim \sim (\exists x)[Dx \cdot (\sim Ax \lor \sim Bx)]$	3, 15 **CP**
17.	$\sim (\exists x)[Dx \cdot (\sim Ax \lor \sim Bx)] \supset$ $(x)(Dx \supset Ex)$	16, **Contra**

(R)	1.	$(x)[(\exists y)(Ay \cdot Bxy) \supset Cx]$	p
	2.	$(\exists y)\{Dy \cdot (\exists x)[(Ex \cdot Fx) \cdot Byx]\}$	p
	3.	$(x)(Fx \supset Ax)$	p / $\therefore$ $(\exists x)(Cx \cdot Dx)$
	4.	$Dz \cdot (\exists x)[(Ex \cdot Fx) \cdot Bzx]$	2, **EI**
	5.	$(\exists x)[(Ex \cdot Fx) \cdot Bzx]$	4, **Simp**
	6.	$(Ew \cdot Fw) \cdot Bzw$	5, **EI**
	7.	$Ew \cdot Fw$	6, **Simp**
	8.	Fw	7, **Simp**
	9.	$Fw \supset Aw$	3, **UI**
	10.	Aw	8, 9 **MP**
	11.	$(\exists y)(Ay \cdot Bzy) \supset Cz$	1, **UI**
	12.	Bzw	6, **Simp**
	13.	$Aw \cdot Bzw$	10, 12 **Conj**
	14.	$(\exists y)(Ay \cdot Bzy)$	13, **EG**
	15.	Cz	11, 14 **MP**

16.	Dz	4, **Simp**
17.	$Cz \cdot Dz$	15, 16 **Conj**
18.	$(\exists x)(Cx \cdot Dx)$	17, **EG**

(T)	1.	$(\exists x)Fx \supset (x)[Px \supset (\exists y)Qxy]$	p
	2.	$(x)(y)(Qxy \supset Gx)$	$p\ /\therefore\ (x)[(Fx \cdot Px) \supset (\exists y)Gy]$
	3.	$\sim(\exists y)Gy$	**AP**
	4.	$(y)\sim Gy$	3, **QN**
	5.	$\sim Gx$	4, **UI**
	6.	$(y)(Qxy \supset Gx)$	2, **UI**
	7.	$Qxy \supset Gx$	6, **UI**
	8.	$\sim Qxy$	5, 7 **MT**
	9.	$(y)\sim Qxy$	8, **UG**
	10.	$\sim(\exists y)Qxy$	9, **QN**
	11.	Fx	**AP**
	12.	$(\exists x)Fx$	11, **EG**
	13.	$(x)[Px \supset (\exists y)Qxy]$	1, 12 **MP**
	14.	$Px \supset (\exists y)Qxy$	13, **UI**
	15.	$\sim Px$	10, 14 **MT**
	16.	$Fx \supset \sim Px$	11, 15 **CP**
	17.	$\sim Fx \vee \sim Px$	16, **Impl**
	18.	$\sim(Fx \cdot Px)$	17, **DeM**
	19.	$\sim(\exists y)Gy \supset \sim(Fx \cdot Px)$	3, 18 **CP**
	20.	$(Fx \cdot Px) \supset (\exists y)Gy$	19, **Contra**
	21.	$(x)[(Fx \cdot Px) \supset (\exists y)Gy]$	20, **UG**

Exercise 8–1:

(B)   Let $Fx = x > 10$
          $Gx = x > 5$
        and $Ex = x < 15$:

    T   1. $(x)[(x > 10) \supset (x > 5)]$
    T   2. $(x)[\sim(x > 10) \supset (x < 15)]$
    F / $\therefore$ $(x)[\sim(x > 5) \supset \sim(x < 15)]$

(D)   Let $Px = x$ is odd
          $Qx = x$ is even
        and $Rx = x > 10$:

    T   1. $(x)\{[(x \text{ is odd}) \cdot (x \text{ is even})] \supset (x > 10)\}$
    T   2. $(\exists x)[x \text{ is even}) \cdot \sim(x > 10)]$
    T   3. $(\exists x)[(x \text{ is odd}) \cdot \sim(x > 10)]$
    F / $\therefore$ $(\exists x)[\sim(x \text{ is odd}) \cdot \sim(x \text{ is even})]$

(F)   Let $Mx = x > 25$
          $Nx = x > 20$
          $Px = x > 15$
          $Qx = x > 10$:

    T   1. $(x)\{(x > 25) \supset [(x > 20) \supset (x > 15)]\}$
    T   2. $(x)[\sim(x > 10) \supset \sim(x > 15)]$
    F / $\therefore$ $(x)\{[\sim(x > 10) \supset [(x > 25) \vee (x > 20)]\}$

(H)   Let $Ax = x > 10$
          $Bx = x > 10$
          $Cx = x > x$:

    T   1. $(\exists x)[(x > 10) \vee \sim(x > 10)]$
    T   2. $(x)\{[(x > 10) \cdot \sim(x > 10)] \supset (x > x)\}$
    F / $\therefore$ $(\exists x)(x > x)$

(J)   Let $Fx = x = 10$
          $Gxy = x > y$:

    T   1. $(x)[(x = 10) \supset (\exists y)(x > y)]$
    T   2. $(\exists x)(x = 10)$
    T   3. $(\exists x)(\exists y)(x > y)$
    F / $\therefore$ $(x)(\exists y)(x > y)$

Exercise 8–2:

2. $(x)[(Dx \cdot Bx) \supset Nx]$

4. $\sim (x)(Wx \supset Fx)$

6. $(x)(Lx \supset \sim Dx)$

8. $(x)[(\exists y)(Fy \cdot Dxy) \supset Rx]$ or $(x)(y)[(Fy \cdot Dxy) \supset Rx]$

10. $(x)[(\exists y)(Fy \cdot Dxy) \supset Rx]$ or $(x)(y)[(Fy \cdot Dxy) \supset Rx]$

12. $(x)[(Jx \cdot Wx) \supset \sim Ex]$

14. $(x)[Dx \supset (Ix \equiv Mx)]$

16. $(x)\{[Px \cdot (\exists y)(Sy \cdot Cxy)] \supset Ex\}$

18. $(x)[Px \supset (\exists y)(\exists z)(Py \cdot Oxzy)]$

20. $(\exists x)\{Px \cdot (y)[Py \supset (\exists z)Oxzy]\}$

22. $(x)\{Px \supset (y)[Py \supset (\exists z)Oxzy]\}$

24. $(x)[(Sx \cdot Fx) \supset (\exists y)(Jy \cdot Tyx)]$

26. $(x)(Sx \supset Fx) \supset [(\exists x)(Sx \cdot Ix) \supset (\exists x)(Sx \cdot Ox)]$

28. Ambiguous: Either $(x)[(Px \cdot Hgx) \supset Hxx]$ or $(x)[Px \supset (Hgx \equiv Hxx)]$

30. $(x)\{\{Px \cdot (\exists y)(\exists z)[(Py \cdot Tz) \cdot Sxyz]\} \supset (w)(Tw \supset Sxgw)\}$

Exercise 9–1:

2.

J.	$(x)Gy$	AP
2.	Gy	1, **UI**
3.	$(x)Gy \supset Gy$	1, 2 **CP**
4.	Gy	AP
5.	$(x)Gy$	4, **UG**
6.	$Gy \supset (x)Gy$	4, 5 **CP**
7.	$3 \cdot 6$	3, 6 **Conj**
8.	$(x)Gy \equiv Gy$	7, **Equiv**

4.
1. $(\exists x)(y)Fxy$ AP

2. $(y)Fxy$ 1, **EI**

3. Fxy 2, **UI**

4. $(\exists x)Fxy$ 3, **EG**

5. $(y)(\exists x)Fxy$ 4, **UG**

6. $(\exists x)(y)Fxy \supset (y)(\exists x)Fxy$ 1, 5 **CP**

6.
1. $(x)Fx \lor (x)Gx$ AP

2. $\sim Fx$ AP

3. $(\exists x)\sim Fx$ 2, **EG**

4. $\sim (x)Fx$ 3, **QN**

5. $(x)Gx$ 1, 4 **DS**

6. Gx 5, **UI**

7. $\sim Fx \supset Gx$ 2, 7 **CP**

8. $Fx \lor Gx$ 7, **Impl, DN**

9. $(x)(Fx \lor Gx)$ 8, **UG**

10. $[(x)Fx \lor (x)Gx] \supset (x)(Fx \lor Gx)$ 1, 9 **CP**

8.
1. $(\exists x)(Fx \cdot Gx)$ AP

2. $Fx \cdot Gx$ 1, **EI**

3. Fx 2, **Simp**

4. $(\exists x)Fx$ 3, **EG**

5. Gx 2, **Simp**

6. $(\exists x)Gx$ 5, **EG**

7. $(\exists x)Fx \cdot (\exists x)Gx$ 4, 6 **Conj**

8. $(\exists x)(Fx \cdot Gx) \supset [(\exists x)Fx \cdot (\exists x)Gx]$ 1, 7 **CP**

10.

1.	$(x)Fx \cdot P$	AP
2.	$(x)Fx$	1, **Simp**
3.	Fx	2, **UI**
4.	P	1, **Simp**
5.	$Fx \cdot P$	3, 4 **Conj**
6.	$(x)(Fx \cdot P)$	5, **UG**
7.	$[(x)Fx \cdot P] \supset (x)(Fx \cdot P)$	1, 6 **CP**
8.	$(x)(Fx \cdot P)$	AP
9.	$Fx \cdot P$	8, **UI**
10.	Fx	9, **Simp**
11.	$(x)Fx$	10, **UG**
12.	P	9, **Simp**
13.	$(x)Fx \cdot P$	11, 12 **Conj**
14.	$(x)(Fx \cdot P) \supset [(x)Fx \cdot P]$	8, 13 **CP**
15.	$7 \cdot 14$	7, 14 **Conj**
16.	$[(x)Fx \cdot P] \equiv (x)(Fx \cdot P)$	15, **Equiv**

12.

1.	$(x)(P \supset Fx)$	AP
2.	P	AP
3.	$P \supset Fx$	1, **UI**
4.	Fx	2, 3 **MP**
5.	$(x)Fx$	4, **UG**
6.	$P \supset (x)Fx$	2, 5 **CP**
7.	$(x)(P \supset Fx) \supset [P \supset (x)Fx]$	1, 6 **CP**

	8.	$P \supset (x)Fx$	AP
	9.	P	AP
	10.	$(x)Fx$	8, 9 **MP**
	11.	Fx	10, **UI**
	12.	$P \supset Fx$	9, 11 **CP**
	13.	$(x)(P \supset Fx)$	12, **UG**
	14.	$[P \supset (x)Fx] \supset (x)(P \supset Fx)$	8, 13 **CP**
	15.	$7 \cdot 14$	7, 14 **Conj**
	16.	$(x)(P \supset Fx) \equiv [P \supset (x)Fx]$	15, **Equiv**

14.	1.	$(\exists x)(P \cdot Fx)$	AP
	2.	$P \cdot Fx$	1, **EI**
	3.	P	2, **Simp**
	4.	Fx	2, **Simp**
	5.	$(\exists x)Fx$	4, **EG**
	6.	$P \cdot (\exists x)Fx$	3, 5 **Conj**
	7.	$(\exists x)(P \cdot Fx) \supset [P \cdot (\exists x)Fx]$	1, 6 **CP**
	8.	$P \cdot (\exists x)Fx$	AP
	9.	P	8, **Simp**
	10.	$(\exists x)Fx$	8, **Simp**
	11.	Fx	10, **EI**
	12.	$P \cdot Fx$	9, 11 **Conj**
	13.	$(\exists x)(P \cdot Fx)$	12, **EG**
	14.	$[P \cdot (\exists x)Fx] \supset (\exists x)(P \cdot Fx)$	8, 13 **CP**
	15.	$7 \cdot 14$	7, 14 **Conj**

16.	$(\exists x)(P \cdot Fx) \equiv [P \cdot (\exists x)Fx]$	$\cdot$ 15, **Equiv**

16.
1.	$(\exists x)(Fx \supset P)$	**AP**
2.	$(x)Fx$	**AP**
3.	$Fx \supset P$	1, **EI**
4.	Fx	2, **UI**
5.	P	3, 4 **MP**
6.	$(x)Fx \supset P$	2,5 **CP**
7.	$(\exists x)(Fx \supset P) \supset [(x)Fx \supset P]$	1, 6 **CP**
8.	$\sim(\exists x)(Fx \supset P)$	**AP**
9.	$(x) \sim (Fx \supset P)$	8, **QN**
10.	$\sim(Fy \supset P)$	9, **UI**
11.	$\sim(\sim Fy \vee P)$	10, **Impl**
12.	$Fy \cdot \sim P$	11, **DeM, DN**
13.	Fy	12, **Simp**
14.	$(x)Fx$	13, **UG**
15.	$\sim P$	12, **Simp**
16.	$(x)Fx \cdot \sim P$	14, 15 **Conj**
17.	$\sim \sim (x)Fx \cdot \sim P$	16, **DN**
18.	$\sim[\sim(x)Fx \vee P]$	17, **DeM**
19.	$\sim[(x)Fx \supset P]$	18, **Impl**
20.	$\sim(\exists x)(Fx \supset P) \supset \sim[(x)Fx \supset P]$	8, 19 **CP**
21.	$[(x)Fx \supset P] \supset (\exists x)(Fx \supset P)$	20, **Contra**
22.	$7 \cdot 21$	7, 21 **Conj**
23.	$(\exists x)(Fx \supset P) \equiv [(x)Fx \supset P]$	22, **Equiv**

Exercise 9–2:

2. $(\exists x)\{Sx \cdot (y)\{[Sy \cdot (x \neq y)] \supset Ixy\}\}$

4. $Sj \cdot (x)\{[Sx \cdot (x \neq j)] \supset Ijx\}$

6. $(Ij \cdot Sj) \cdot (x)\{(Ix \cdot Sx) \supset [(x \neq j) \supset Bjx]\}$

8. $(\exists x)(\exists y)\{\{[(Cx \cdot Cy) \cdot (x \neq y)] \cdot (Rxcs \cdot Rycs)\} \cdot (z)\{Cz \supset [(z = x) \vee (z = y)]\}\}$

10. $(\exists x)\{(Sx \cdot Rxmn) \cdot (y)\{[Sy \cdot (x \neq y)] \supset Ixy\}\}$

Exercise 9–3:

(B)	1.	$(x)(Px \supset Qx)$	p
	2.	$(x)(Qx \supset Rx)$	p
	3.	$Pa \cdot {\sim}Rb \quad p \: / \therefore \; {\sim}(a = b)$	
	4.	${\sim}{\sim}(a = b)$	**AP**
	5.	$a = b$	4, **DN**
	6.	$Pa \supset Qa$	1, **UI**
	7.	$Qa \supset Ra$	2 **UI**
	8.	$Pa \supset Ra$	6, 7 **HS**
	9.	Pa	3, **Simp**
	10.	Ra	8, 9 **MP**
	11.	${\sim}Rb$	3, **Simp**
	12.	${\sim}Ra$	5, 11 **Id**
	13.	$Ra \cdot {\sim}Ra$	10, 12 **Conj**
	14.	${\sim}(a = b)$	4, 13 **IP**

(D)	1.	$(x)(y)\{[Pxy \cdot (x \neq y)] \supset Qxy\}$	p
	2.	$(\exists x)(y)[(x \neq y) \supset Pxy]$	$p \: / \therefore \; (\exists x)(y)[(x \neq y) \supset Qxy]$

3.	$(y)[(x \neq y) \supset Pxy]$	2, **EI**
4.	$x \neq y$	**AP**
5.	$(x \neq y) \supset Pxy$	3, **UI**
6.	Pxy	4, 5 **MP**
7.	$(y)\{[Pxy \cdot (x \neq y)] \supset Qxy\}$	1, **UI**
8.	$[Pxy \cdot (x \neq y)] \supset Qxy$	7, **UI**
9.	$Pxy \cdot (x \neq y)$	4, 6 **Conj**
10.	Qxy	8, 9 **MP**
11.	$(x \neq y) \supset Qxy$	4, 10 **CP**
12.	$(y)[(x \neq y) \supset Qxy]$	11, **UG**
13.	$(\exists x)(y)[x \neq y) \supset Qxy]$	12, **EG**

(F)

1.	$(\exists x)(y)\{[\sim Fxy \supset (x = y)] \cdot Gx\}$	$p \;/\; \therefore \; (x)\{\sim Gx \supset (\exists y)[\sim (y = x)$ $\cdot Fyx]\}$
2.	$\sim(\exists y)[\sim(y = z) \cdot Fyz]$	**AP**
3.	$(y) \sim [\sim(y = z) \cdot Fyz]$	2, **QN**
4.	$(y)\{[\sim Fwy \supset (w = y)] \cdot Gw\}$	1, **EI**
5.	$[\sim Fwz \supset (w = z)] \cdot Gw$	4, **UI**
6.	$\sim[\sim(w = z) \cdot Fwz]$	3, **UI**
7.	$(w = z) \vee \sim Fwz$	6, **DeM, DN**
8.	$\sim(w = z) \supset \sim Fwz$	7, **Impl, DN**
9.	$\sim Fwz \supset (w = z)$	5, **Simp**
10.	$\sim(w = z) \supset (w = z)$	8, 9 **HS**
11.	$(w = z) \vee (w = z)$	10, **Impl, DN**
12.	$w = z$	11, **Taut**
13.	Gw	5, **Simp**

14	Gz	12, 13 **Id**
15.	$\sim \sim Gz$	14, **DN**
16.	$\sim (\exists y)[\sim (y = z) \cdot Fyz] \supset \sim \sim Gz$	2, 15 **CP**
17.	$\sim Gz \supset (\exists y)[\sim (y = z) \cdot Fyz]$	16, **Contra**
18.	$(x)\{\sim Gx \supset (\exists y)[\sim (y = x) \cdot Fyx]$	17, **UG**

Exercise 9–4:

(A)   2.   Asymmetrical, intransitive, irreflexive.

      4.   Asymmetrical, transitive, irreflexive.

      6.   Symmetrical, transitive, totally reflexive.

      8.   Nonsymmetrical, nontransitive, nonreflexive.

Exercise 11–1:

(A)   2.   Indeterminate   6.   Indeterminate

      4.   True

(B)   2.   True   6.   False

      4.   Indeterminate

(C)   2.   True   6.   Indeterminate

      4.   False   8.   Indeterminate

(D) 2. Indeterminate   6. False

      4. Indeterminate   8. True

(E)

1.	$\overline{S}EP$ is true.		Hence
2.	$\overline{S}A\overline{P}$ is true.		1, Obversion
3.	PAS is true.		2, Contraposition
4.	$PE\overline{S}$ is true.		3, Obversion
5.	$\overline{S}IP$ is false.		Contradictory of 1
6.	$\overline{S}O\overline{P}$ is false.		Contradictory of 2
7.	POS is false.		Contradictory of 3
8.	PIS is false.		Contradictory of 4
9.	$\overline{S}AP$ is false.		Contrary of 1
10.	$\overline{P}AS$ is false.		9, Contraposition
11.	$\overline{P}E\overline{S}$ is false.		10, Obversion
12.	$\overline{S}E\overline{P}$ is false.		9, Obversion
13.	$\overline{S}OP$ is true.		Contradictory of 9
14.	$\overline{P}OS$ is true.		Contradictory of 10
15.	$\overline{P}I\overline{S}$ is true.		Contradictory of 11
16.	$\overline{S}I\overline{P}$ is true.		Contradictory of 12

Exercise 11–2:

2. a. PEM 6. a. $PA\overline{R}$

     b. $PM = 0$ b. $PR = 0$

4. a. MOP 8. a. LID

     b. $M\overline{P} \neq 0$ b. $LD \neq 0$

Exercise 12–1:

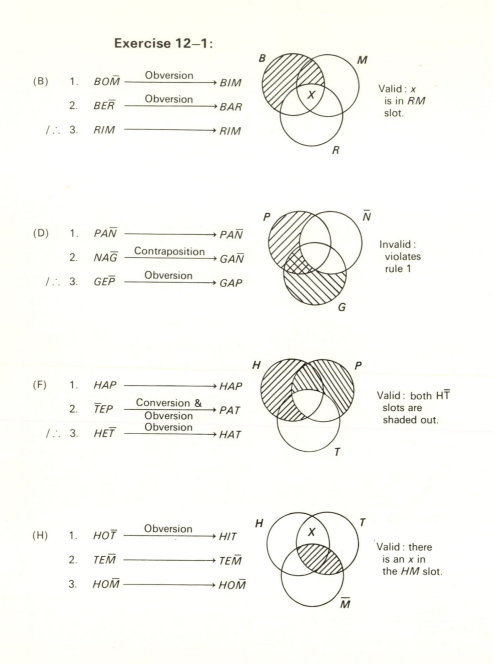

(B) 1. *BO$\overline{M}$* —— Obversion ——→ *BIM*

     2. *BE$\overline{R}$* —— Obversion ——→ *BAR*

/∴ 3. *RIM* ——————→ *RIM*

Valid : *x* is in *RM* slot.

(D) 1. *PA$\overline{N}$* ——————→ *PA$\overline{N}$*

     2. *NA$\overline{G}$* —— Contraposition ——→ *GA$\overline{N}$*

/∴ 3. *GE$\overline{P}$* —— Obversion ——→ *GAP*

Invalid : violates rule 1

(F) 1. *HAP* ——————→ *HAP*

     2. *$\overline{T}$EP* —— Conversion & Obversion ——→ *PAT*

/∴ 3. *HE$\overline{T}$* —— Obversion ——→ *HAT*

Valid : both H$\overline{T}$ slots are shaded out.

(H) 1. *HO$\overline{T}$* —— Obversion ——→ *HIT*

     2. *TE$\overline{M}$* ——————→ *TE$\overline{M}$*

     3. *HO$\overline{M}$* ——————→ *HO$\overline{M}$*

Valid : there is an *x* in the *HM* slot.

Exercise 12–2:

(B) Valid

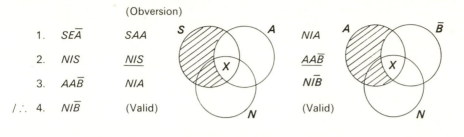

		(Obversion)
1.	$SE\overline{A}$	SAA
2.	NIS	$\underline{NIS}$
3.	$AA\overline{B}$	NIA
$/\therefore$ 4.	$NI\overline{B}$	(Valid)

NIA	
$AA\overline{B}$	
$NI\overline{B}$	
(Valid)	

(D) Valid

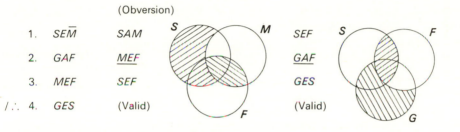

		(Obversion)
1.	$SE\overline{M}$	SAM
2.	GAF	$\underline{MEF}$
3.	MEF	SEF
$/\therefore$ 4.	GES	(Valid)

SEF	
GAF	
GES	
(Valid)	

Exercise 12–3:

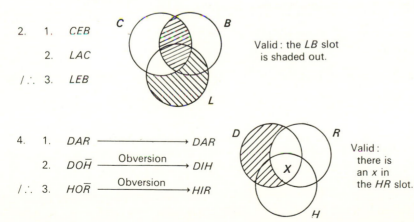

2. 1. CEB

    2. LAC

    $/\therefore$ 3. LEB

Valid: the LB slot
is shaded out.

4. 1. $DAR \longrightarrow DAR$

    2. $DO\overline{H} \xrightarrow{\text{Obversion}} DIH$

    $/\therefore$ 3. $HO\overline{R} \xrightarrow{\text{Obversion}} HIR$

Valid:
there is
an x in
the HR slot.

439

Bibliography

*Parts
One and Two*

Anderson, John M., and Henry W. Johnstone. *Natural Deduction*. Belmont, California: Wadsworth, 1962.

Barker, Stephen F. *The Elements of Logic*. New York: McGraw-Hill, 1965.

Church, Alonzo. *Introduction to Mathematical Logic*. Princeton, New Jersey: Princeton University Press, 1956.

Copi, Irving. *Symbolic Logic*, Third Edition. New York: Macmillan, 1967.

Kleene, Stephen C. *Mathematical Logic*. New York: Wiley, 1967.

Lemmon, E. J. *Beginning Logic*. London: Thomas Nelson, 1965.

Levison, Arnold B. *Study Guide for Stephen F. Barker's The Elements of Logic*. New York: McGraw-Hill, 1965.

Neidorf, Robert. *Deductive Forms*. New York: Harper, 1967.

Quine, Willard Van Orman. *Methods of Logic*. New York: Holt, 1959.

Reichenbach, Hans. *Elements of Symbolic Logic*. New York: Macmillan, 1947.

Rescher, Nicholas. *Introduction to Logic*, Second Edition. New York: St. Martin's, 1968.

Suppes, Patrick. *Introduction to Logic*. Princeton, New Jersey: Van Nostrand, 1957.

Part Three   Barker, Stephen F. *The Elements of Logic*. New York: McGraw-Hill, 1965.

Bird, Otto: *Syllogistics and Its Extentions*. Englewood Cliffs, New Jersey: Prentice-Hall, 1964.

Carrol, Lewis. *Symbolic Logic and the Game of Logic*. New York: Dover, 1958.

Cohen, Morris R., and Ernest Nagel. *An Introduction to Logic*. New York: Harcourt, 1962.

Copi, Irving. *Introduction to Logic*, Third Edition. New York: Macmillan, 1968.

Levison, Arnold B. *Study Guide for Stephen F. Barker's The Elements of Logic*. New York: McGraw-Hill, 1965.

Rescher, Nicholas. *Introduction to Logic*, Second Edition. New York: St. Martin's, 1968.

Part Four   Barker, Stephen F. *The Elements of Logic*. New York: McGraw-Hill, 1965.

Copi, Irving. *Introduction to Logic*, Third Edition. New York: Macmillan, 1968.

Hempel, Carl. *Philosophy of Natural Science*. Englewood Cliffs, New Jersey: Prentice-Hall, 1966.

Nagel, Ernest. *The Structure of Science*. New York: Harcourt, 1961.

Skyrms, Brian. *Choice and Chance*. Belmont, California: Dickenson, 1966.

Part Five   Barker, Stephen F. *The Philosophy of Mathematics*. Englewood Cliffs, New Jersey: Prentice-Hall, 1964.

Goodman, Nelson. *Fact, Fiction, and Forecast*, Second Edition. Indianapolis: Bobbs-Merrill, 1965.

Part Six   Copi, Irving. *Symbolic Logic*, Third Edition. New York: Macmillan, 1967.

Kleene, Stephen C. *Mathematical Logic*. New York: Wiley, 1967.

Mendelson, Elliot. *Introduction to Mathematical Logic*. Princeton, New Jersey: Van Nostrand, 1964.

Special Symbols

Index

All valid syllogisms must have

1. A middle term which is distributed at least once.

2. No term distributed in its conclusion which is not distributed in a premise.

3. At least one affirmative (nonnegative) premise.

4. A negative conclusion if and only if one of its premises is negative.

5. At least one particular premise if the conclusion is particular.